EVERY CHILD A LEARNER

SUCCESSFUL *Strategies for Teaching* All Children

Contents:

Every Child a Learner: Successful Strategies for Teaching All Children
SDE Sourcebook.
Published by The Society For Developmental Education, Ten Sharon Road, PO Box 577, Peterborough, New Hampshire 03458.
Phone 1-800-924-9621
FAX 1-800-337-9929

NINTH EDITION

President: Jay LaRoche
Executive Director: Jim Grant
Program Director: Irv Richardson
Editor: Aldene Fredenburg
Cover and Book Design: Susan Dunholter
Cover Photos: Tim Reeder
Publishing Manager: Lorraine Walker
Production Manager: Deborah Fredericks
Production Coordinator: Christine Landry
Type Compositor: Laura Taylor

ISBN 1-884548-09-1 (paperback)

For Discussion

"The Basic School" – Important Step for School Improvement

Enthusiasm abounds and "community" flourishes at David Cox Road School in North Carolina, one of 16 schools in a growing Basic School Network

The Oxford dictionary says that to become embroiled is to "bring affairs into a state of confusion," or to become "involved in hostility with another."

That seems to be what's happening in education circles these days. Everyone's embroiled. Discussions are often confused and sometimes almost hostile.

ART GENTILE

***In a Basic School,** children are encouraged to form relationships and apply lessons of the classroom to the world around them. Here, two fifth graders, Cherri Mason (left) and Frajovon Talley, enjoy lunch while sitting on top of the world in the David Cox School's spacious and inviting rotunda.*

As the decibel level becomes higher and higher, it's ever more difficult for combatants in this fracas to hear each other above the din of claims and counter-claims, research studies that contradict each other and minds that are made up.

Over the last 15 years, walking calmly but deliberately into the middle of this growing storm has been The Carnegie Foundation For The Advancement of Teaching, led by its president, Dr. Ernest Boyer.

And now, after years of study and mountains of research, plus on-site observations of what's working in elementary schools throughout the country, the Foundation has issued an inspiring report, *The Basic School: A Community for Learning.*

Written by Dr. Boyer in his characteristically low-key, conversational style, it is at once personal and believable, including the Preface in which he thanks those who collaborated on the report, adding, "...I'm including a special section in the appendix to recognize each by name."

But what is the Basic School, and if it's as good as it sounds, how can teachers, administrators and parents participate, or at least learn more about it?

Dr. Boyer replies: "The purpose of the Basic School is to keep the urge to learn alive in every child. We call this school 'basic,' first of all, because...

(1) It takes the push for school reform back to the beginning, to the first years of formal education.

(2) It is 'basic' because it gives priority to language and suggests a core of knowledge with coherence.

(3) It identifies key components of an effective school.

(4) Finally, it brings them all together in a single institution – the Basic School." (The staff at David Cox Road Elementary School in Charlotte, NC, which *Teaching K-8* visited last fall, has prepared a succinct, single-page answer to the question, "What is a

"In a Basic School," says Dr. John Fries (above), *principal at David Cox Road School, "the principal is the lead teacher and just as in the classroom, his or her office should make others feel welcome." In his office, shown here, the different textures on the sheetrock and concrete-block walls made wallpapering difficult. However, by sponge-painting and adding an accent border, art teacher Patty Clark, first grade teacher Vivian Vargas, and media assistant Debbie Morgan achieved a warm, yet professional image. The work was completed during the summer on the teachers' own time and cost less than $50 – a great contribution on the part of three professionals.*

A Focus On Elementary Education

In a Prologue to *The Basic School*, Dr. Boyer writes, "Clearly, the push for school renewal needs a new beginning. This time the focus must be on the early years, on elementary education. Every level of learning is important. No sector should be neglected. But school failure starts very early, and if all children do not have a good beginning, if they do not receive the support and encouragement needed during the first years of life, it will be difficult, if not impossible, to compensate fully for the failure later on."

Basic School?" To receive a free copy, send your request and a self-addressed, stamped envelope to *Teaching K-8, Basic School, 40 Richards Avenue, Norwalk, CT 06854.*)

Dr. Boyer emphasizes that the Foundation, in its report, is not simply bringing us up to date on yet another "pilot project." Rather, it has found what works in schools throughout the country, and is now incorporating all of that into what it calls the Basic School.

Last July, in preparation for this article, Patricia Broderick, *Teaching K-8's* Vice President and Editorial Director, attended a four-day Basic School Summer Institute in Chantilly, Virginia.

As a result of that meeting, early last September found *Teaching K-8* visiting The David Cox Road Elementary School for Communications and Academic Studies, one of the 16 schools that are now a part of the Basic School Network.

Our intent was to bring you, in words and photographs, the story of the Basic School. It hasn't been easy.

The excitement of the Basic School isn't so much in what one sees, because what one sees throughout a Basic School, while impressive, is replicated, in part, in isolated individual classrooms all over the country.

Rather, the excitement of the Basic School is, first of all, its collective, all-embracing sense of community (more about "community" in a moment).

There is also the collective excitement of knowing that, in the Basic School, the best practices of teachers everywhere, as we know them today, are now accessible in one place.

In addition, and this is important, there's also the collective excitement of parents who sense that something good, something special, is happening at their school. Yes, they, too, have made the connection and are now a part of this "community."

Community? Connections? As Dr. Boyer puts it: "We found, during our study, that the first and most essential ingredient of an effective school – the one idea that holds it all together – is best described by the simple word, 'connections.'

"An effective school connects people, to create community. An effective school connects the curriculum, to achieve coherence. An effective school connects classrooms and resources, to enrich the climate. And an effective school connects learning to life, to build character."

Dr. Boyer calls those four priorities – *community, coherence, climate, character* – "the building blocks for the Basic School."

Those building blocks are certainly evident at the David Cox Road Elementary School in Charlotte, North Carolina, which is in its second year as a Basic School.

Its faculty talks enthusiastically about the weekend retreat, when all of the teachers, in all grades and all disciplines, work together, as a community, to compare and ana-

Living with Purpose – one of the eight "core commonalities" – Each student's name is on a piece of the puzzle; a piece is removed if it's necessary to time out a student. This simple but effective behavior plan helps children understand how their behavior impacts the group, demonstrating "you are an important part of the whole."

Continued on page 44

In a Basic School *there's emphasis on teachers as positive role models. Here, first grade, first-year teacher Marlo Wylie joins Brooke Gladson in responding to a question asked in a guidance lesson.*

Student Services *teacher Pat Salvi, with (l. to r.) Jillian Shue and Kaylor Johnson, demonstrate that listening is a very important part of communication as they explore themes in the eight "commonalities."*

Almost everything *in the Basic School has its basis in literature. Thus, it's not surprising to enter Willette Johnson's fifth grade class and find her reading a novel to an attentive class.*

The Basic School builds on what has worked in classrooms all over the United States. Here, fifth grade teacher Jordonna Maragos introduces a literature extension activity.

Our visit to North Carolina *was in early September, and we found the Parent's Cultural Arts Committee hard at work planning programs that would be coordinated to the curriculum for the 1995-96 school year. Left to right: Joye Slade, Assistant Principal, and parents Marianne Prophet, Anilda Killes and Pat Winter (chairperson of the committee).*

Producing and Consuming – one of the eight "core commonalities" – In Joan Young's fifth grade, cooperative groups of four students, using magazines and newspapers, researched the price of clothing a student for school. Cost analysis and spreadsheets were run to discover averages, decisions were made and art was integrated into the lesson to illustrate the results.

"Measuring results," *is an important ingredient in the Basic School. First grade teacher Robin Paris (with Joshua Franks) monitors literacy progress on a regular basis.*

The School as Community: *Parent Terry Sealy (left) brings lunch to her second grade son, T.J., while Julie Glenn (right, rear) lunches with her kindergarten son, Trevor.*

The "Core Commonalities"

"Within these eight integrative themes, every traditional subject or academic discipline could, we believe, find a home." – *Dr. Ernest Boyer*

What we propose, in the Basic School, is not so much a new curriculum as a new way to think about the curriculum. There is content to be learned. But to be truly educated, students must go beyond the isolated subjects and place their learning in larger context. They must see connections.

And in the Basic School, the content of traditional subjects is integrated within a framework called the "Core Commonalities." By "core commonalities" we mean those universal experiences that are shared by all people, the essential conditions of human existence that give meaning to our lives. We've identified eight core commonalities: The Life Cycle, The Use of Symbols, Membership in Groups, A Sense of Time and Space, Response to the Aesthetics, Connections to Nature, Producing and Consuming, and Living With Purpose.

The Core Commonalities curriculum, then, addresses the fundamental learning needs of children as they grow and experience life itself. Again, all of the traditional subject matter is covered.

Students learn important content in science, history, civics, literature and the rest. But by focusing on common human experiences, children not only acquire a core of knowledge, they also discover relationships across the separate subject areas.

Basic Schools *have access to electronic tools connecting classrooms to a vast network of knowledge. Here, Linda Tinsley (fifth grade teacher) is distributing calculators to (l. to r.) Carley Harbison, Alleis Maness and Wei Jia Su.*

lyze daily, weekly and yearly curriculums.

Teachers at David Cox are experienced in using themes to integrate curriculums across the disciplines. But their enthusiasm bubbles over as they discuss ways to "spiral a theme upward from grade to grade."

"In the Basic School," Dr. Boyer explains, "teacher teams are organized not just horizontally, but vertically, with fifth-grade teachers meeting with kindergarten teachers, for example, creating a learning community capable of building a sequential course of study that spirals upward through all grade levels, with the result a seamless web of learning.

"All students have the same curriculum framework," Dr. Boyer continues, "but the content they study increases in complexity from one grade to the next. Students begin exploring commonalities in kindergarten, and they continue to learn about them through their years of schooling."

Dr. John Fries, principal of David Cox Road School, says the Basic School is "based on common sense, and I think that's one of the reasons it's very attractive to teachers. It's not just reinventing the wheel. It's saying that we should take what we know works, organize it in a fashion that makes sense, and then implement it."

When asked what the Basic School brought to his school that couldn't have been done anyway, Dr. Fries said, "I've been an educator for 28 years, I've seen reforms come and go, but the Basic School brings an organizational pattern which allows us to put our philosophies into practice.

"Yes, in the past we've done elements of everything we're now doing, but Dr. Boyer brought an organization, a systematic way of checking, by asking ourselves…

"What am I doing in my relationships with parents?

"What am I doing in my relationships with our partnerships? How am I bringing technology and new media into the classrooms?

"What areas need shoring up?"

He was asked what a reader of *Teaching K-8* could take from an article about the Basic School. Dr. Fries replied: "It could be an affirmation that what they have been doing is quality work."

Mary Ellen Bafumo, director of field work for the project who now mentors four

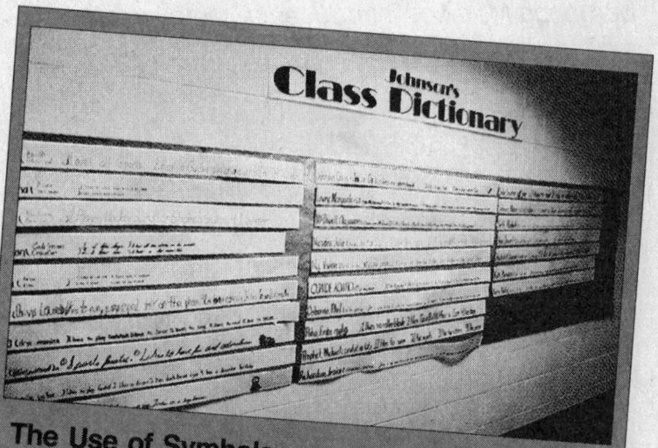

The Use of Symbols – one of the eight "core commonalities" – During the first week of school all of Willette Johnson's fifth grade students, through the use of symbols and following a dictionary format, wrote their names on a chart on the wall outside their classroom, explained how to pronounce their names and added perceptive sentences describing this "unique person."

Continued on page 46

Basic Schools, said, "No Basic School is like any other; they're all personalized. So, those teachers and principals who have a vision of what they want for their schools, might ask themselves how the Basic School can help. If they see in it something that fits their vision, they could call The Basic School Center in Princeton, at 601-921-0422."

And finally – or perhaps as a first step? – there is the Carnegie Foundation's report itself, in book form. To order *The Basic School: A Community of Learners*, call 800-777-4726 or 609-883-1759. It costs only $12, plus postage. Videos are also available.

At *Teaching K-8* we're unabashedly on the sides of kids, teachers and parents – but we suspect you knew that already.

So, what do we think about the Basic School? We think it may provide a level-headed, common-sense answer – perhaps even *the* answer – as America searches for ways to redefine what we do in our schools.

ALLEN RAYMOND

Thanks to the ingenuity *of head custodian Curtis Worthy, tennis balls silence sliding chairs and also protect the polished floors of Debbie Goforth's music room.*

Teachers at David Cox Road School Talk about the Basic School.

Janet Crossley, 1st grade:
It's a common-sense approach to educating children. It takes the long laundry list of things we do, integrates all the disciplines together in a unit – it provides relevancy, relationships, meaningful and purposeful activities for children.

Tonya Butts, 3rd grade:
When I'm teaching math and other disciplines, I find myself putting more art into it, the language of art, the language of numeracy. That's exciting to me. When I'm teaching the lesson on congruency, I'm thinking of ways I can pick up an art picture and discuss with the children, "What are the congruent shapes in this picture?" I'm starting to naturally integrate the curriculum.

Pat Hambidge, 2nd grade:
This is not just another phase in the curriculum trends that come around; this is really a neat approach, it's looking through a different lens at the basic themes and units we teach.

Melissa Dunlap, 4th grade:
The entire school has a common language, we're all thinking the same way. We have a common philosophy, common goals, a common belief about children...this is a better way, the best way to teach children. Everyone does a lot of sharing...to share your dream, your vision, with someone else.

Linda Tinsley, 5th grade:
I like to think of this school as an extended family. That's how much we care about each other – students, teachers, parents. I'm happiest at this school of anywhere I've ever been. It's the people inside who make it good, make it so special. No matter what we're talking about in class, it fits into one of the eight commonalities. The students pick up on that. I told the kids one day, "We're having social studies, math and language all right here, together."

John Fries, principal:
The eight commonalities give the teachers a language from which to join all the disciplines.

- I'm convinced the teachers find it refreshing.
- We don't live in isolation; we don't live in geography, we don't live in art, in math; there's a constant relationship going on.
- The commonalities give us an avenue to demonstrate to students that there is a relationship.
- The Basic School follows the premise that the parent is the child's first teacher, that we now have a "covenant" that says, "we jointly – we and the parents – have a responsibility for teaching your child." Don't leave them at the doorstep: come to PTA meetings, or to eat lunch, or to a conference.
- Schools across the country struggle with, "Do you trust us, do you have confidence in us?" We're re-establishing a trusting relationship.
- It's parents and staff saying, "Let's make a community, let's do it together."
- I'm convinced we're working more effectively with parents.

A Sense of Time and Space, plus Membership in Groups, two of the eight "core commonalities." Inspired by reading Paula Feder's book, "Where Does the Teacher Live?" (Dutton, 1992), Marlo Wylie's first grade students use imagination and their own drawings to speculate on where their teacher actually lives.

Why Some Parents Don't Come to School

Margaret Finders and Cynthia Lewis

Instead of assuming that absence means noncaring, educators must understand the barriers that hinder some parents from participating in their child's education.

In our roles as teachers and as parents, we have been privy to the conversations of both teachers and parents. Until recently, however, we did not acknowledge that our view of parental involvement conflicts with the views of many parents. It was not until we began talking with parents in different communities that we were forced to examine our own deeply seated assumptions about parental involvement.

From talking with Latino parents and parents in two low-income Anglo neighborhoods, we have gained insights about why they feel disenfranchised from school settings. In order to include such parents in the educational conversation, we need to understand the barriers to their involvement from their vantage point, as that of outsiders. When asked, these parents had many suggestions that may help educators re-envision family involvement in the schools.

The Institutional Perspective

The institutional perspective holds that children who do not succeed in school have parents who do not get involved in school activities or support school goals at home. Recent research emphasizes the importance of parent involvement in promoting school success (Comer 1984, Lareau 1987). At the same time, lack of participation among parents of socially and culturally diverse students is also well documented (Clark 1983, Delgado-Gaitan 1991).

The model for family involvement, despite enormous changes in the reality of family structures, is that of a two-parent, economically self-sufficient nuclear family, with a working father and homemaker mother (David 1989). As educators, we talk about "the changing family," but the language we use has changed little. The institutional view of nonparticipating parents remains based on a deficit model. "Those who *need* to come, don't come," a teacher explains, revealing an assumption that one of the main reasons for involving parents is to remediate them. It is assumed that involved parents bring a body of knowledge about the purposes of schooling to match institutional knowledge. Unless they bring such knowledge to the school, they themselves are thought to need education in becoming legitimate participants.

Administrators, too, frustrated by lack of parental involvement, express their concern in terms of a deficit model. An administrator expresses his bewilderment:

> Our parent-teacher group is the foundation of our school programs.... This group (gestures to the all-Anglo, all-women group seated in the library) is the most important organization in the school. You know, I just don't understand why *those other parents* won't even show up.

Discussions about family involvement often center on what families lack and how educators can best teach parents to support instructional agendas at home (Mansbach 1993). To revise this limited model for interaction between home and school, we must look outside of the institutional perspective.

The Voices of "Those Other Parents"

We asked some of "those other parents" what they think about building positive home/school relations. In what follows, parents whose voices are rarely heard at school

Patricia Kelly

siblings at home, these individuals' limited schooling makes it difficult for them to help their children with homework beyond the early primary level. For some, this situation is compounded by language barriers and lack of written literacy skills. One mother who attended school through 6th grade in Mexico, and whose first language is Spanish, comments about homework that "sometimes we can't help because it's too hard." Yet the norm in most schools is to send home schoolwork with little information for parents about how it should be completed.

For many parents, their own personal school experiences create obstacles to involvement. Those who have dropped out of school do not feel confident in school settings.

explain how the diverse contexts of their lives create tensions that interfere with positive home/school relations. For them, school experiences, economic and time constraints, and linguistic and cultural practices have produced a body of knowledge about school settings that frequently goes unacknowledged.

Diverse school experiences among parents. Educators often don't take into account how a parent's own school experience may influence school relationships. Listen in as one father describes his son's school progress:

> They expect me to go to school so they can tell me my kid is stupid or crazy. They've been telling me that for three years, so why should I go and hear it again? They don't do anything. They just tell me my kid is bad.
>
> See, I've been there. I know. And it scares me. They called me a boy in trouble but I was a troubled boy. Nobody helped me because they liked it when I didn't show up. If I was gone for the semester, fine with them. I dropped out nine times. They wanted me gone.

This father's experiences created mistrust and prevent him from participating more fully in his son's education. Yet, we cannot say that he doesn't care about his son. On the contrary, his message is urgent.

For many parents, their own personal school experiences create obstacles to involvement. Parents who have dropped out of school do not feel confident in school settings. Needed to help support their families or care for

Diverse economic and time constraints. Time constraints are a primary obstacle for parents whose work doesn't allow them the autonomy and flexibility characteristic of professional positions. Here, a mother expresses her frustrations:

> Teachers just don't understand that I can't come to school at just any old time. I think Judy told you that we don't have a car right now.... Andrew catches a different bus than Dawn. He gets here a half an hour before her, and then I have to make sure Judy is home because I got three kids in three different schools. And I feel like the teachers are under pressure, and they're turning it around and putting the pressure on me cause they want me to check up on Judy and I really can't.

Often, parents work at physically demanding jobs, with mothers expected to take care of child-care responsibilities as well as school-related issues. In one mother's words:

> What most people don't understand about the Hispanic community is that you come home and you take care of your husband and your family first. Then if there's time you can go out to your meetings.

In many cases, severe economic constraints prevent children from full participation in the culture of the school.

Other parents work nights, making it impossible to attend evening programs and difficult to appear at daytime meetings that interfere with family obligations and sleep.

At times, parents' financial concerns present a major obstacle to participation in their child's school activities. One mother expresses frustration that she cannot send eight dollars to school so her daughter can have a yearbook to sign like the other girls.

> I do not understand why they assume that everybody has tons of money, and every time I turn around it's more money for this and more money for that. Where do they get the idea that we've got all this money?

This mother is torn between the pressures of stretching a tight budget and wanting her daughter to belong. As is the case for others, economic constraints prevent her child from full participation in the culture of the school. This lack of a sense of belonging creates many barriers for parents.

Diverse linguistic and cultural practices. Parents who don't speak fluent English often feel inadequate in school contexts. One parent explains that "an extreme language barrier" prevented her own mother from ever going to anything at the school. Cultural mismatches can occur as often as linguistic conflicts. One Latino educator explained that asking young children to translate for their parents during conferences grates against a cultural norm. Placing children in a position of equal status with adults creates dysfunction within the family hierarchy.

One mother poignantly expresses the cultural discomfort she feels when communicating with Anglo teachers and parents:

> [In] the Hispanic culture and the Anglo culture things are done different and you really don't know—am I doing the right thing? When they call me and say, 'You bring the plates' [for class parties], do they think I can't do the cookies, too? You really don't know.

Voicing a set of values that conflicts with institutional constructions of the parent's role, a mother gives this culturally-based explanation for not attending her 12-year-old's school functions:

> It's her education, not mine. I've had to teach her to take care of herself. I work nights, so she's had to get up and get herself ready for school. I'm not going to be there all the time. She's gotta do it. She's a tough cookie.... She's almost an adult, and I get the impression that they want me to walk her through her work. And it's not that I don't care either. I really do. I think it's important, but I don't think it's my place.

This mother does not lack concern for her child. In her view, independence is essential for her daughter's success.

Whether it is for social, cultural, linguistic, or economic reasons, these parents' voices are rarely heard at school. Perhaps, as educators, we too readily categorize them as "those other parents" and fail to hear the concern that permeates such conversations. Because the experiences of these families vary greatly from our own, we operate on assumptions that interfere with our best intentions. What can be done to address the widening gap between parents who participate and those who don't?

Getting Involved: Suggestions from Parents

Parents have many suggestions for teachers and administrators about ways to promote active involvement. Their views, however, do not always match the role envisioned by educators. Possessing fewer economic resources and educational skills to participate in traditional ways (Lareau 1987), these parents operate at a disadvantage until they understand how schools are organized and how they can promote systemic change (Delgado-Gaitan 1991).

If we're truly interested in establishing a dialogue with the parents of all of our nation's students, however, we need to understand what parents think can be done. Here are some of their suggestions.

Clarify how parents can help. Parents need to know exactly how they can help. Some are active in church and other community groups, but lack information about how to become more involved in their children's schooling. One Latina mother explains that most of the parents she knows think that school involvement means attending school parties.

As Concha Delgado-Gaitan (1991) points out "... the difference between parents who participate and those who do not is that those who do have recognized that they are a critical part in their children's education." Many of the parents we spoke to don't see themselves in this capacity.

Encourage parents to be assertive. Parents who do see themselves as needed participants feel strongly that they must provide their children with a positive view of their history and culture not usually presented at school.

Some emphasize the importance of speaking up for their children. Several, for instance, have argued for or against special education placement or retention for their children; others have discussed with teachers what they saw as inappropriate disciplinary procedures. In one parent's words:

> Sometimes kids are taken advantage of because their parents don't fight for them. I say to parents, if you don't fight for your child, no one's going to fight for them.

Linda DiLorenzo

Although it may sound as if these parents are advocating adversarial positions, they are simply pleading for inclusion. Having spent much time on the teacher side of these conversations, we realize that teachers might see such talk as challenging their positions as professional decision makers. Yet, it is crucial that we expand the dialogue to include parent knowledge about school settings, even when that knowledge conflicts with our own.

Develop trust. Parents affirm the importance of establishing trust. One mother attributes a particular teacher's good turnout for parent/teacher conferences to her ability to establish a "personal relationship" with parents. Another comments on her need to be reassured that the school is open, that it's OK to drop by "anytime you can."

In the opportunities we provide for involvement, we must regularly ask ourselves what messages we convey through our dress, gestures, and talk. In one study, for example, a teacher described her school's open house in a middle-class neighborhood as "a cocktail party without cocktails" (Lareau 1987). This is the sort of "party" that many parents wouldn't feel comfortable attending.

Fear was a recurrent theme among the parents we interviewed: fear of appearing foolish or being misunderstood, fear about their children's academic standing. One mother explained:

> Parents feel like the teachers are looking at you, and I know how they feel, because I feel like that here. There are certain things and places where I still feel uncomfortable, so I won't go, and I feel bad, and I think maybe it's just me.

This mother is relaying how it feels to be culturally, linguistically, and ethnically different. Her body of knowledge does not match the institutional knowledge of the school and she is therefore excluded from home/school conversations.

Build on home experiences. Our assumptions about the home environments of our students can either build or sever links between home and school. An assumption that "these kids don't live in good environments" can destroy the very network we are trying to create. Too often we tell parents what we want them to do at home with no understanding of the rich social interaction that already occurs there (Keenan et al. 1993). One mother expresses her frustrations:

> Whenever I go to school, they want to tell me what to do at home. They want to tell me how to raise my kid. They never ask me what I think. They never ask me anything.

When we asked parents general questions about their home activities and how these activities might build on what happens at school, most thought there was no connection. They claimed not to engage in much reading and writing at home, although their specific answers to questions contradicted this belief. One mother talks about her time at home with her teenage daughter:

> My husband works nights and sometimes she sleeps with me.... We would lay down in bed and discuss the books she reads.

Many of the parents we spoke to mentioned Bible reading as a regular family event, yet they did not see this reading in relation to schoolwork. In one mother's words:

> I read the Bible to the children in Spanish, but when I see they're not understanding me, I stop (laughing). Then they go and look in the English Bible to find out what I said.

Although the Bible is not a text read at public schools, we can build on the literacy practices and social interactions that surround it. For instance, we can draw upon a student's ability to compare multiple versions of a text. We also can include among the texts we read legends, folktales, and mythology—literature that, like the Bible, is meant to teach us about our strengths and weaknesses as we strive to make our lives meaningful.

As teachers, of course, we marvel at the way in which such home interactions do, indeed, support our goals for learning at school; but we won't know about these practices unless we begin to form relationships with parents that allow them to share such knowledge.

Use parent expertise. Moll (1992) underscores the importance of empowering parents to contribute "*intellectually* to the development of lessons." He recommends assessing the "funds of knowledge" in the community, citing a teacher who discovered that many parents in the Latino community where she taught had expertise in the field of construction. Consequently, the class developed a unit on construction, which included reading, writing, speaking, and building, all with the help of responsive community experts—the children's parents.

Parents made similar suggestions—for example, cooking ethnic foods with students, sharing information about multicultural heritage, and bringing in role models from the community. Latino parents repeatedly emphasized that the presence of more teachers from their culture would benefit their children as role models and would help them in home/school interactions.

Parents also suggested extending literacy by writing pen pal letters with students or involving their older children in tutoring and letter writing with younger students. To help break down the barriers that language differences create, one parent suggested that bilingual and monolingual parents form partnerships to participate in school functions together.

An Invitation for Involvement

Too often, the social, economic, linguistic, and cultural practices of parents are represented as serious problems rather than valued knowledge. When we reexamine our assumptions about parental absence, we may find that our interpretations of parents who care may simply be parents who are like us, parents who feel comfortable in the teacher's domain.

Instead of operating on the assumption that absence translates into noncaring, we need to focus on ways to draw parents into the schools. If we make explicit the multiple ways we value the language, culture, and knowledge of the parents in our communities, parents may more readily accept our invitations. ■

References

Clark, R. M. (1983). *Family Life and School Achievement: Why Poor Black Children Succeed or Fail.* Chicago: University of Chicago Press.

Comer, J. P. (1984). "Homeschool Relationships as They Affect the Academic Success of Children." *Education and Urban Society* 16: 323-337.

David, M. E. (1989). "Schooling and the Family." In *Critical Pedagogy, the State, and Cultural Struggle*, edited by H. Giroux and P. McLaren. Albany, N.Y.: State University of New York Press.

Delgado-Gaitan, C. (1991). "Involving Parents in the Schools: A Process of Empowerment." *American Journal of Education* 100: 20-46.

Keenan, J. W., J. Willett, and J. Solsken. (1993). "Constructing an Urban Village: School/Home Collaboration in a Multicultural Classroom." *Language Arts* 70: 204-214.

Lareau, A. (1987). "Social Class Differences in Family-School Relationships: The Importance of Cultural Capital." *Sociology of Education* 60: 73-85.

Mansbach, S. C. (February/March 1993). "We Must Put Family Literacy on the National Agenda." *Reading Today*: 37.

Moll, L. (1992). "Bilingual Classroom Studies and Community Analysis: Some Recent Trends." *Educational Researcher* 21: 20-24.

Margaret Finders is completing a doctoral program in English Education at The University of Iowa and will be an Assistant Professor at Purdue University as of August 1994. **Cynthia Lewis** is completing a doctoral program in Reading at The University of Iowa and will be on the faculty at Grinnell College as of August 1994. They can be reached at N259 Lindquist Center, The University of Iowa, Iowa City, IA 52242.

Carolyn Colvin assisted with this article.

VOICES VOICES VOICES

VOICES VOICES VOICES

"That young children are question-asking, answer seeking characters is among the obvious features of human development. And that is true regardless of family, race, ethnicity, economic background, or where on this earth children are found. When children start school a message is conveyed to them that is as influential as it is subtle and unverbalized: "Forget or set aside your world of questions and interests. Your job, our responsibility is to get you to learn rules, facts and skills without which you are nothing. School is not for play or for dreaming. It is work, serious work. And if you pay attention, work hard, someday when you are big, you will understand . . . School does not extinguish in children the interests and probings of that "other world." That is impossible. What school does is erect a barrier between two worlds, a kind of Berlin Wall that seems in no danger of being torn down."

— *Seymour Sarason*
The Predictable Failure of Educational Reform:
Can We Change Course Before It's Too Late?
Jossey-Bass, 350 Sansome Street, San Francisco, CA 94101
(415) 433-1740

Conversing with Parents Through Dialogue Journals

What to do when parents can't find time to meet with you? One solution is to hold a conversation on paper

BY JANE BASKWILL

Dialogue journals have become increasingly popular with teachers of middle, junior and senior high schools. By their very nature, dialogue journals provide a place for students to think out loud and share that thinking with the teacher.

They also provide a means for teachers and students to carry on a conversation, over time, about topics related to literature, science, history and other curriculum areas. When done well, the interaction is natural, individual and thought-provoking for both parties.

Several years ago, I decided to try using dialogue journals with the parents of my primary grade children. I had been looking for a way to establish a more effective means of communication with parents than I already had in place.

I was constantly being disappointed at the lack of turn-out for Home and School meetings, although I realized that many parents were unable to make these meetings for very legitimate reasons.

An idea is born. I racked my brain to come up with an alternate way to have a conversation with a parent without necessarily having a meeting. I did not want to spend all my evenings on the telephone.

It occurred to me that parents might be willing to try having a conversation on paper. Thus the idea of dialogue journals with my parents was born.

I knew that most adults have very little confidence in their own writing. However, I also knew that most wrote letters or notes to family and friends. Therefore, if I could establish that family tone from the beginning, I might have greater participation.

...ON WORKING WITH PARENTS

Through past experience, I was aware that the parents in my community felt they had little knowledge or expertise to share with the school. They thought they were no longer able to keep up with the changes in the educational system. I therefore wanted to begin our conversations on common ground, with topics of their choice which inspired confidence.

While sitting around the swimming pool during the summer months waiting for my own children, I had shared many conversations with parents about child development, growth spurts, nightmares, behavior and a

Continued on page 50

***The author** meets with parents to answer questions about dialogue journals.*

Jane Baskwill is principal of Kingston and District School, a K-7 school in Kingston, Nova Scotia.

Conversations on paper *continued from page 49*

host of other topics pertaining to children.

These conversations were sharings, with no member seeming to be an expert on anything, but where individual strengths seemed to surface as a particular topic arose. Parents were keen observers of their children's behavior. It was this strength that would be our common ground.

And so I found some modestly-sized notebooks and waited for the opportunity to give them out. It happened to coincide with the time for report card conferences. These meetings usually had the highest attendance, so I decided to give the journals out individually after each conference. In this way, I could explain what they were all about. By the end of the week, I had distributed all of the journals and was waiting anxiously for my first "conversation" to begin. I wondered what to expect.

Jane made *a point of answering each journal entry within a few days of receiving it. That way, she was able to avoid a backlog.*

Dear Mrs. Baskwill:
This afternoon we baked the chocolate chip Rocky Road pie out of Maria's birthday present recipe cards. The family liked it a lot so I told Maria "You can bring your recipe over to your teacher and she can put it in your recipe book." Maria was very upset. "No, Mommy, you can't do that. Then you can never make this pie again, and I just love it so much." I explained that I was going to copy the recipe, but she still didn't want to take it to school!...

Dear Mrs. Allen:
It's amazing what goes on inside a child's mind! I could picture Maria worrying over that recipe. Perhaps after you make it a few times and it isn't so new to her any more, she might be ready to let you copy it for school. The children certainly were impressed with the cake! I enjoyed my piece!...

A father *signs his dialogue journal before sending it to school.*

Once our conversation had started, it was easy to keep it going. Mrs. Allen, like the other parents who wrote to me, began with something that had happened at home, an event or a conversation that related to an occurrence or topic at school.

Sometimes I would relate something similar that I had experienced with my own children, offer a suggestion I had read about, or draw on what I had observed over the course of my teaching career.

Dear Mrs. Rand:
The other day when I was reading a story to my children, I noticed that Amanda got a little impatient when I had to interrupt the story to answer questions Nicholas was asking. I had to ask Amanda to be patient while Nicholas asked his questions and promise to read the story again without interruption the next time.

I even mentioned to her that if she was bothered by the interruptions she might want to do something else and I would call her when the story started again. She chose to stay and didn't seem bothered any longer by Nicholas' questions.

With three little ones in the family, you must see some of this when you read to them. At school, Kristie certainly enjoys hearing stories read. She often mentions favorites you have read at home. I'd be interested to hear what happens at story time in your home...

A few days later, I received this reply:

Dear Mrs. Baskwill:
I know what you mean about reading to more than one child at a time., Kristie is the oldest and gets upset when the little ones act "stupid," as she puts it.

I finally couldn't take the bickering so I made a deal. I read each child a story they choose alone, without the others, and read at least one to all of them together. They all seem to like that plan. It gives them each some special time alone and they look forward to it.

I found that I enjoyed writing in the journals. They did not come in all at once. Parents would send the journal to school with their child whenever they felt they had written something they wanted to share. In this way, control of the journal ultimately rested in the hands of the parent.

Some wrote right away; others took a few weeks to get started. I tried to answer each journal entry within a few days after receiving it. This, too, ensured that I didn't get a backlog. Occasionally, a parent wanted to ask a particular question or wanted specific information. For example:

Dear Mrs. Baskwill:
...Lately, I have noticed Maria is picking up lots of stories and wanting to "read" them. She can read the ones she has me read. I think they are just in her memory. I think this is okay, but I am not sure. Will she still learn to read if she memorizes the stories?...

Dear Mrs. Allen:
Reconstructing a story from memory is a very important stage for Maria to be at. Maria already knows how the language of that story is supposed to work and can use that knowledge to

help her read the story on her own. This builds her confidence in herself as a reader and gives her the satisfaction that she is able to enjoy a favorite story independently – just as the other members of the family would. At school I have noticed Maria trying to keep her finger under the words as she reads. She often will go back over a line of the story when she has not put in enough words to match the print.

As I gained practice writing in the journals, I found it was important to try to answer the questions the parents asked, no matter how hard or how easy. I tried not to make judgments about what was being asked, but to take each question as it came. Sometimes my responses provided some insight into what a child was doing, while at other times I simply reassured the parent that their child was okay.

As parents notice changes in their child's literacy development, they begin to draw on a mental picture of the way they think *they* learned in school. If this picture is different than the actual philosophy in operation in the school or classroom, the parent will have difficulty understanding or accepting the changes that have taken place

Dear Mrs. Baskwill:
Thank you for the magazine you sent home. I think I understand now what you're trying to do to teach reading. I know school has changed since I was there, but I didn't realize how much! You were right, the picture I have in my mind is not the same as your classroom ...

The dialogue journal also provides parents with a place to do some thinking on paper. Parents often look at a problem differently when they try to express themselves in their journal.

Dear Mrs. Baskwill:
... I finally decided I had the courage to write and ask you about this. Max and I have discussed it over and over and I think now we need to ask you. We are very worried about Aaron. His printing is very sloppy and some of this letters are backwards. He is always writing in big letters. He never brings home any papers like Kal used to – with the letters on it. Maybe this is why his printing isn't very neat.

Now mind you, the boy loves to write! He always has a paper and pencil – even in the car! He leaves me notes on my pillow and even makes notes on paper airplanes and flies them downstairs when he is supposed to be asleep. Kal never wrote anything like that when he was Aaron's age. He just brought home his printing – never any "published" books. The books are a good idea – all the grandparents want them!

As I am writing this, it occurs to me that Aaron has learned a lot about writing. I hadn't realized it before. I guess I was so used to sheets of letters coming home that the things Aaron brings didn't seem like "real" school work. Now I'm not sure what my question really is! Silly, right? Would you mind if Max and I helped Aaron a bit with his printing? ...

On the surface, this may seem like a very minor concern, but it, like other seemingly insignificant issues, can become a source of conflict between parents and teachers. Because parents may be unsure of what they want to ask, they may not be able to immediately form a question during a face-to-face meeting.

On paper, something happens. Parents seem to examine an issue from more than one point of view. They take time to think things through as they try to collect their thoughts and express them clearly. It often seems as if parents begin talking to themselves as they relate what they've observed and begin asking themselves new questions.

Through dialogue journals, parents draw on the strength of observation, which they have so naturally cultivated over the years, and apply it to their understanding of their child's literacy development.

Dear Mrs. Baskwill:
So far Ben has been enjoying school. We read a story every night before he goes to bed. Sometimes it is the same story over again. He enjoys reading "Clifford's Halloween"! I think the scary parts are the ones he likes best. The suspense in the stories are his favorite parts. When Ben draws he likes to draw monsters. I find Ben will keep things inside, but will tell me later when he is ready. I guess that is a normal thing for them to do....

I have continued to use dialogue journals with the parents of the children I teach, and I have found another benefit, one I had not considered at the outset. Through dialogue journals, I have come to know these families better than any I have ever known before.

In addition, my families have come to know me better. Not simply as a name on a door, or a face across a meeting table, but as a person who shares an interest in the development of their children. These parents and I feel a responsibility to each other to share our children's growth.

"Dear Mrs. Baskwill:
...Looking back over this scribbler and what I've written, it amazes me. I never realized how much Maria and I have learned! I am really glad that I decided to try writing. The funny thing was, once I started I didn't want to stop. It was easier than I thought it would be – like writing letters ..."

Allowing Parents to Request a Teacher

THOMAS E. BRACKBILL

I'm certain that most, if not all, principals have had to deal with students and parents who, for a variety of reasons, request a certain teacher for the upcoming year. Although we consider such criteria as teacher and parent input, heterogeneous grouping, class size, boy/girl ratios, special-needs students, and the personalities of teachers and students in establishing class lists, I've always been bothered by requests for particular teachers by some parents, particularly those connected to the school as staff members, volunteers, or PTO officers.

In the past, I've felt obligated to accommodate their requests even though I felt that I was giving preferential treatment to a select few. If we were going to be fair, we had to provide equal access for all parents who wanted to request a certain teacher. I decided that accommodating parent requests actually could work to our advantage—if we established reasonable boundaries to protect the integrity of class assignments, and if the faculty was supportive of the policy.

Our rural K–5 school in southeastern Pennsylvania has an enrollment of 500 students. All grade levels have at least three classes, and one has four. For practical purposes, we've always allowed parents of incoming kindergarten students to request either the half-day morning or afternoon session—but not the teacher. Since our fifth graders were moving on to middle school, we would accept placement requests only for students entering grades 1–5.

Securing faculty support was not as difficult as I had imagined. We agreed that only I would handle the requests, that teachers would not be told who made requests, and that every grade level would have classes balanced in both size and heterogeneity, regardless of the number of requests. Although they were apprehensive about the outcome, the teachers agreed to try the new arrangement for the 1994–95 school year.

In March 1994, I informed all parents by letter that they would be allowed to make a written request for a specific teacher for the next year. I told them the office would accept written requests only during the month of April, and that these would be honored on a first-come, first-served basis wherever possible. I felt that only around 20 percent of parents would make requests, and if we could honor 60 percent of the requests, the policy would be a success.

A Flood of Requests

Was I wrong! On the first day we accepted requests, we received 128. By the end of the month, I had received 218—a full 52 percent of the eligible school population! As the requests came in, I separated them by each teacher's name and identified each child as a high, average, or low achiever, based on information supplied by the child's current teacher.

In May, I started to compile and balance the new class lists. Two factors gave me needed flexibility in accommodating placement requests. First, we had encouraged parents to make two choices, and half of those making requests did so. Second, because 48 percent of the parents did not make a request, I could freely assign a large number of children.

Here are the results of our placement policy:

- We were able to honor all requests, accommodating 200 first choices and 18 second choices.
- All teachers were named in placement requests, but only two received more requests than their classes could hold.
- Sixty percent of the parents of high-achieving students made requests, compared to 50 percent of parents of average students and 40 percent of the parents of low-achieving students.
- We received a much higher percentage of requests for grades 4 and 5.
- Parental support for the new request policy was overwhelmingly positive. We did not receive a single complaint about class placement!

Examining the Results

The results of our new policy have made all of us examine our beliefs about the way schools operate. We have come to the following conclusions:

- Teachers have an obligation to establish and maintain trusting relationships with parents.
- Parental choice and responsibility are linked. Parents must be careful of what they choose for their children.
- When the best interests of a child are at stake, a parent's input is at least as important and valuable as that of the school.
- Having parents provide input on a child's placement gives them another good reason to be involved with their children's education.
- Parents and teachers who already have established a good working relationship should be permitted to capitalize on it.

All in all, the request process went smoothly at our school, and we were able to maintain the integrity of balanced classes. At no cost to anyone, we have given all of our parents a degree of choice in their children's class assignments, as well as an opportunity to exercise more control over their children's education. □

Thomas E. Brackbill is principal of Providence Elementary School in New Providence, Pennsylvania.

Year-Round School

The Best Thing Since Sliced Bread

Elaine Warrick-Harris

Elaine Warrick-Harris is Assistant Principal/Year-Round Coordinator, Balfour Elementary School, Asheboro, North Carolina.

Teachers, I ask you two questions. How many of your students helped to harvest crops last year? And how many mothers of students in your classroom stayed at home? It is true that some communities still depend heavily on agriculture, but modern farming's sophistication is such that children no longer carry the responsibilities that they once did. Fewer family situations today include a stay-at-home mother. Most teachers would probably answer the above questions by saying "none" or "very few." Therefore, a reasonable follow-up question would be, "Why do we continue to organize learning schedules for students based on the agricultural practices of 100 years ago?"

The outdated and agriculturally sensitive school calendar has other disadvantages. For example, vandalism to empty school buildings, especially over the summer months, is a growing problem. Students who have nothing to do during summer too often turn to mischief, or worse. On the other hand, Brekke (1984) and Ballinger (1987) indicate that schools operating on a year-round schedule have been able to reduce the incidence of vandalism and burglary.

Year-Round Education (YRE) is an excellent solution to the problems of vandalism, loss of productive learning time and unsupervised children. The term "year-round" is actually misleading. Other more descriptive terms might be "continuous learning," "all-seasons learning" or even "four-seasons school." "Year-round school" is the term most frequently associated with the organizational system that uses the school facility during every season. The year-round school is *not*, however, an alternative curriculum for learning. Quinlan, George and Emmett (1987) define YRE as a reorganization of the school calendar into instructional blocks and vacations distributed across the calendar year to ensure continuous learning. The single-track schedule, for example, offers nine weeks of instruction followed by a three-week break.

Traditional curriculum content continues to be used within the year-round schedule. Students' learning in a year-round school, however, can progress with less of an interruption during the summer months. Students retain more information during four short breaks than they would after the normal ten-week summer vacation. This continuity of instruction, along with remedial reviews offered during the breaks, helps reduce the number of students who must be retained in grade.

In addition, the year-round schedule leads to less teacher stress and burnout. Rather than the feast-or-famine break schedule practiced by most schools, teachers benefit from a cycle of evenly spaced vacations.

Parents, too, gain from YRE. Families have more options for arranging vacations and can enjoy off-season rates and less-crowded vacation sites. In addition, many working parents favor a YRE schedule because it provides them with an opportunity for child care most of the year.

With so many benefits associated with YRE, it is logical to ask, "Why doesn't everyone have year-round school?"

One School's Story

Tradition is one reason why more schools have not adopted a year-round schedule. It is not easy to replace a practice that has been in place for decades with an alternative that could disrupt teachers' and parents' social and familial patterns. Usually, a change this drastic is associated with broader and potentially problematic circumstances. The initiation of YRE at Balfour Elementary School, in Asheboro, North Carolina, fits this description.

Five years ago, Balfour Elementary School, built in 1926, was representative of the small community school of long ago. The majority of the 312 students walked to school and only one bus was needed. By 1989, however, the school's enrollment and costs were both spiraling out of control. Essentially, the building was too old and too small.

A successful school bond referendum enabled the Board of Education to fund construction of a spacious new school within a mile

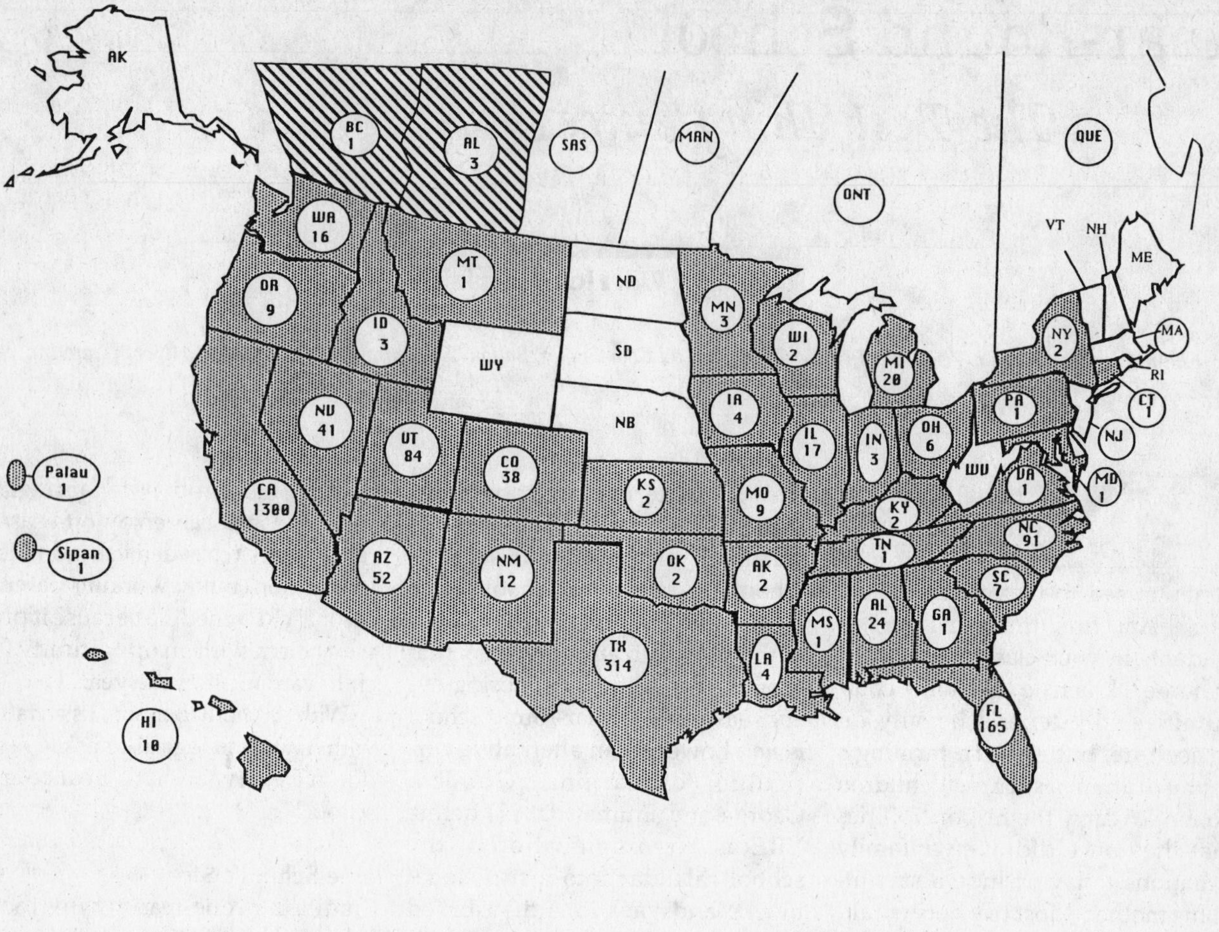

Number of Public/Private Schools with Year-Round Programs by State, Territory and Province 1994-95.
Source for all figures: National Association for Year-Round Education.

of the old structure. During the planning stage for the new school, the system superintendent challenged Balfour's principal and staff to explore the concept of year-round education. They visited other year-round schools in North Carolina and read published research on YRE. One report in particular (Ballinger, Kirschembaum & Poimbeauf, 1987), had great impact as it indicated that the continued flow of learning engendered by YRE was beneficial to students at all levels. These researchers found that no year-round school had reported a drop in academic achievement; in fact, all showed a higher gain in academic scores when compared to schools following the August-June structure. It seemed apparent that this new schedule would benefit Balfour's students. The faculty voted to accept the year-round plan.

After much exploration, discussion and debate, the Board of Education unanimously voted to offer the plan as an option. Part of the school would continue on the traditional August-June schedule, and an alternate path would be established for year-round school. Parents could choose from either option.

Staffing

After developing a clear concept of how the school would function, the next major task was to devise a staffing schedule for the year-round plan. Since faculty representatives had already visited year-round schools, read extensively on the topic and helped develop the reorganization plan, they were well aware of the new schedule's demands. They were asked to declare their scheduling preference—traditional or year-round. Some readily agreed to the 12-month schedule, some had conflicting family obligations and others were willing to teach under either pattern. Eventually, slots for each grade level were filled.

Allowing the staff to study the organizational plan and choose whether they wanted to participate ensured successful implementation of the plan. The competitiveness that can occur when new practices and old systems operate simultaneously was kept at a minimum, helping everyone to feel some investment in the project.

Community Support

A committee of faculty members

developed a plan for distributing information to help parents make informed choices. First, they wrote a series of articles for the local newspaper in which they explained the YRE plan. In addition, they printed and distributed flyers inviting parents to an informational meeting. At this well-attended session, the principal and central office staff gave an overview, and teachers and school board members supplied information gathered from their research and school visits. Advantages and disadvantages of the two systems were discussed, and parents were walked through a typical year-round calendar.

After the presentations, the parents were divided into small discussion groups. A teacher, principal, school board member or superintendent monitored each group discussion and answered questions. At the close of the session, parents were asked to respond to a survey about the new plan to show if they were interested, uncertain or preferred the traditional plan. The year-round plan would be implemented if at least 100 students could be enrolled. The initial level of interest fell short, but after releasing additional information and holding a second meeting we eventually received 175 applications. Asheboro's first year-round school was set.

Several factors led to the successful recruitment effort. First, the teachers played a central role. Parents trusted the teachers because they, too, would be affected by the new schedule, and would have to make as many adjustments as the students and parents. The teachers' endorsement gave the plan credence. Second, the involvement of the Board of Education and the Superintendent of Schools communicated high-level support for the project. Their participation helped alleviate parents' and teachers' concerns that the reorganization might fail due to the lack of administrative support. Third, by giving parents a choice, those who opted for the new plan had an investment in ensuring its success.

Growth of Public Year-Round Education in the United States over a Ten-Year Period

School Year	States	Districts	Schools	Students
1985-86	16	63	410	354,087
1986-87	14	69	408	362,669
1987-88	Data Not Collected			
1988-89	16	95	494	428,961
1989-90	19	115	618	520,323
1990-91	22	152	859	733,660
1991-92	23	204	1,646	1,345,921
1992-93	26	301	2,017	1,567,920
1993-94	33	366	1,941	1,407,377
1994-95	35	414	2,214	1,640,929

The New School

When the new Balfour Elementary School opened on July 13, 1992, 154 students and eight classroom teachers followed the year-round schedule. Class sizes ranged from 19-26, and enrollment stayed constant throughout the year. New students were placed in a traditional classroom unless they had previously attended another year-round school. This practice allowed them to meet the state's 180-day school attendance law.

As with any new program, challenges arose, especially the first time we had to accommodate students from both programs in the same building. Blending 398 students on two different schedules was a *real* challenge. Suddenly, we had to be mindful of the two schools in all areas. For example, class pictures could not be taken before the traditional students arrived. The Southern Association Accreditation team could not visit when the year-round faculty was on their three-week break. Faculty from both systems learned to be very flexible. When the year-round students were away, for example, lunch schedules had to be changed.

Another area of concern was teacher morale. The new year-round schedule often attracted media attention. To avoid unnecessary rivalry, the administration took extra steps to show *all* the teachers that their efforts were appreciated.

Unique Qualities of the Plan

The success of the year-round concept depended on the united effort of teachers, administrators and parents. But no matter how hard a group works, the effort will fail if the plan is not positive. Balfour's year-round concept succeeds because of the opportunities it offers to students and families. Some of the components of the year-round schedule that help make it successful follow:

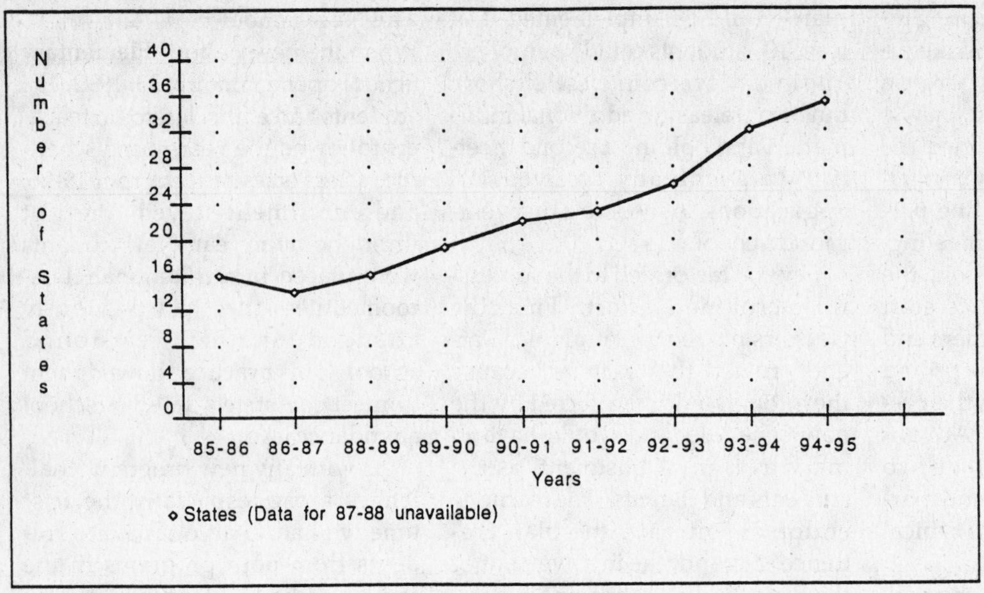

States with YRE Schools (Public and Private)

The Single-Track Calendar. School begins in mid-July and ends in early June. Throughout the year, students go to school for nine weeks and then have a three-week break. This is known as the 45-15 single track. Students still attend school for 180 days, but their vacations are paced more evenly than in the August-June system. This allows students to be monitored more closely throughout the entire year and keeps in place necessary support services. In addition, students have less time to forget concepts and skills.

Child Care—Before and After School. Many of the school's students have two working parents. The school offers child care before and after school hours. A child care coordinator is available beginning at 6:30 a.m. and she oversees activities until the bell rings at 8:00 a.m. The cost is $2.00 per morning.

The child care coordinator leaves the campus during the day, returns at 2:30 p.m. and continues until 6:00 p.m. After-school care includes a snack and the cost is $3.00 per child, per afternoon. Parents can choose the days they need the service and budget costs are minimized.

Intersession—The Three-Week Break. After the nine weeks of academic classes, the year-round students have a three-week break called "intersession." They either spend the time with their families or take advantage of a structured program provided by the school. During the first week of intersession, child care is available from 6:30 a.m. until 6:00 p.m. (preregistration ensures adequate staff allocation). Lunch is available, as usual, at the regular price; children on free or reduced lunch programs continue to receive this benefit.

During the second week of intersession, called Discovery Plus, children can participate in enrichment activities. Discovery Plus is available from 8:00 a.m. until noon. Early morning child care continues. Parents pay a $25.00 fee for five mornings of field trips, crafts and learning projects. At the end of the morning session, students are picked up by parents or remain in the school's child care program.

Learning Plus is offered in the third week of intersession. Students who need help can receive academic remediation. Free bus transportation is provided and the

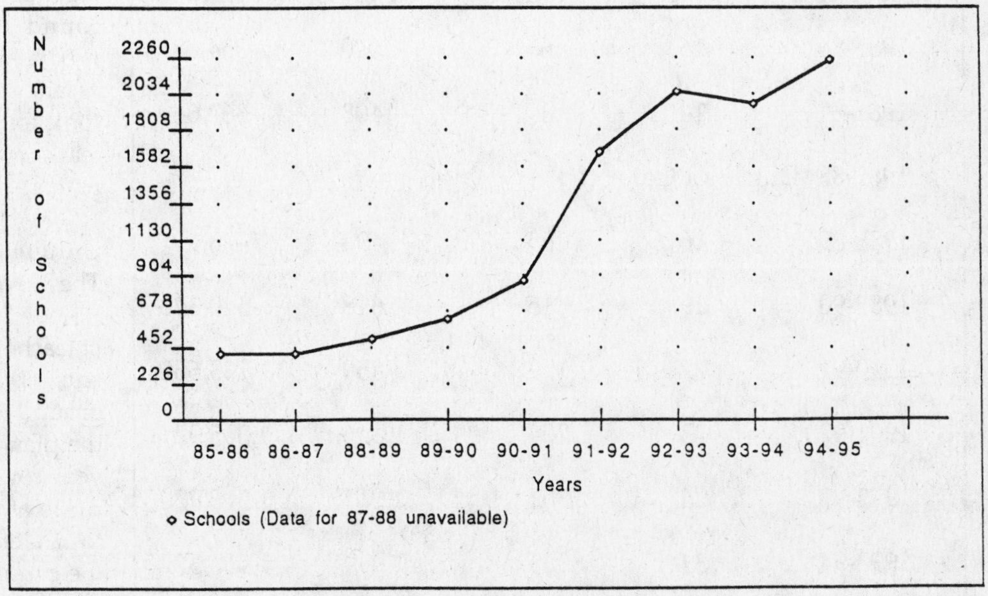

Schools with YRE Schools (Public and Private)

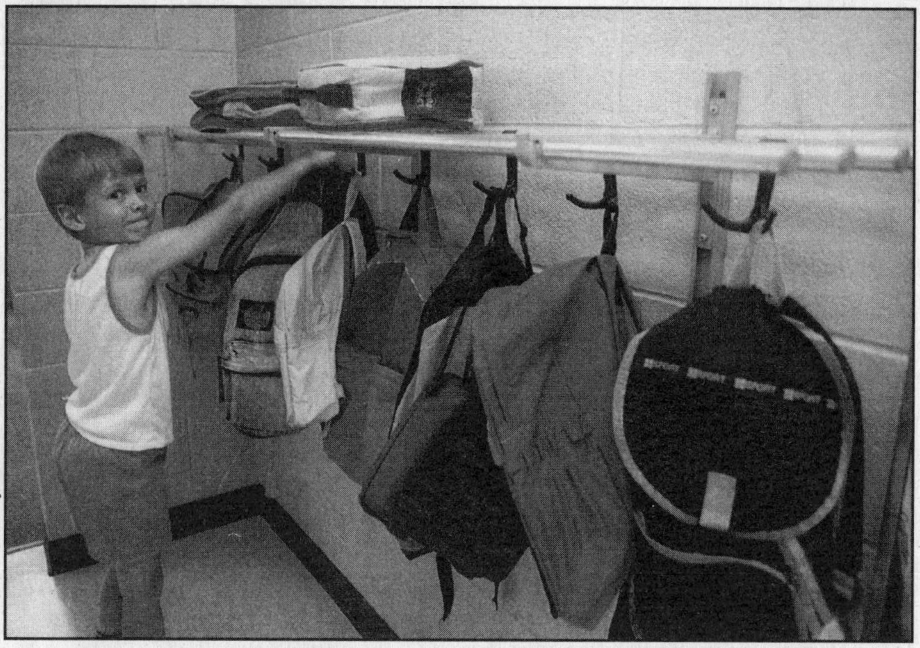

Photos courtesy of author

William Luck, 7, puts his book bag on the coat/bag rack in Mrs. Hardin's room on the first day of school at Balfour.

program runs on a half-day schedule. The year-round teachers are offered the opportunity to teach in the Learning Plus program and receive additional pay for their participation. Other certified teachers are added as necessary. The Learning Plus program is financed with summer school funds appropriated by the state. Those who need remediation receive it every nine weeks, and thereby show improvement throughout the year. Even better, they do not have to wait for summer school to receive help. Consequently, they return to class better prepared than if they had been on vacation for ten weeks. The students appear to retain information better and take less time to readjust to the school routine. Charles Ballinger (1987) of the National Association for Year-Round Education explains, "Remediation can occur throughout the year by using more frequent vacation periods, rather than limiting it to summer school after nine months of failure and frustration."

The three-week intersession can be credited for much of the program's wide acceptance. Everyone benefits! Children enjoy the positive social opportunities and the change of pace from the normal school routine. In addition, their confidence levels rise as they experience greater academic success when they return to school. Parents appreciate the high-quality activities and the availability of child care services during the three-week intersession vacation period. Teachers, too, benefit from the intersession. If they choose to teach during the Learning Plus week they earn extra income. But most of all, whether they teach in the intersession or not, they recognize the advantages of extra help for the children. Teachers taking advantage of the intersession break frequently use this time to develop course materials or relieve stress by taking a trip or relaxing at home.

Possible Disadvantages of Year-Round Education

We are creatures of habit and tradition. A great majority of parents, students and teachers have never known a school schedule other than the August-June agricultural one. Anything different represents a

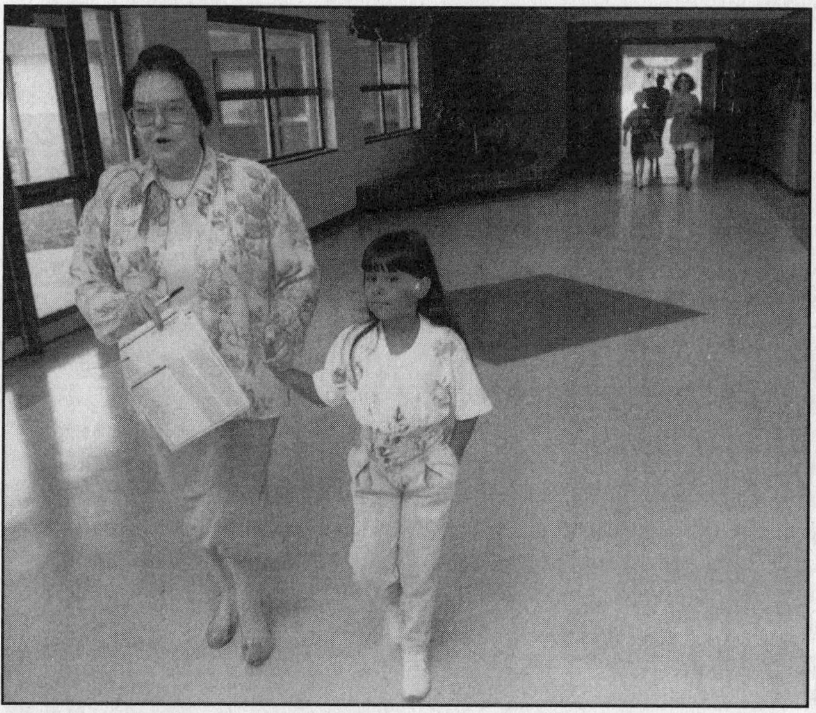

First day of the new year at Balfour School. School secretary Margaret Womick shows 2nd-grader Lucia Mata (7) to her classroom.

break in tradition and a disruption. Parents with older children who are not on the year-round schedule may have to deal with separate calendars for the school year. Most camps, and other organized recreational activities, are planned only for the summertime. Teachers who want to earn an advanced degree may be unable to attend college classes during the summer.

Program Adjustments

Charles Ballinger (1987) says that "Schools need to allow at least a year or two for people to get accustomed to the idea." After the program's initial year, Balfour did make adjustments in several areas, mostly by responding to the increased demand for enrollment. Parents from other schools within the system also began requesting a year-round schedule. In response, two additional elementary schools and one middle school began offering the plan. Now children from kindergarten through 8th grade are on a year-round schedule. All four schools participate in the three-week intersession of Child Care, Discovery Plus and Learning Plus at one site.

Growth. More states are offering year-round education. The figures on pages 283-285 indicate the growth of this education innovation.

Conclusion

I was reared on a farm in eastern North Carolina, one of five children who helped plant, cultivate and harvest corn, tobacco, cotton and watermelons. These crops were our livelihood and each member of the family worked long hours. School never began before Labor Day and was finished by late May. In the spring, my father instructed my brothers to leave school at noon and walk the dusty roads home to help with the planting. My mother worked in our home; her never-ending duties included planting, growing, harvesting and preserving vegetables and fruits to last our family the whole year. Our mother was always waiting for us when we came home at the end of the school day.

These are warm memories of a family working together. But times have changed. Many children come home to an empty house and spend the summer days trying to find something to do. Social and academic pressures, too, are higher for today's children. One way for schools to respond to today's shift in societal structures and academic expectations is to implement Year-Round Education.

Worthen and Zsiray (1994) summarize the important educational implications of the year-round program. They state that a year-round schedule has much to offer students. Nevertheless, they advise educators to advance "carefully, competently, and compassionately." Based on my research and three years' experience with the year-round school, I heartily agree with both points.

All in favor of year-round education, say "Aye."

References

Ballinger, C. E., Kirschembaum, N., & Poimbeauf, R. P. (1987). The various year-round plans. In *The year-round school: Where learning never stops* (pp. 16-24) (Fastback 259). Bloomington, IN: Phi Delta Kappa.

Ballinger, C. (1987). Unleashing the school calendar. *Thrust for Educational Leadership, 16*(4), 16-18.

Ballinger, C. (1988). Rethinking the school calendar. *Educational Leadership, 45*(5), 57-61.

Brekke, N. R. (1984). Year-round education: Cost saving and educationally effective. *ERS Spectrum, 2*(3), 25-30.

Quinlan, C., George, C., & Emmett, T. (1987). *Year-round education: Year-round opportunities: A study of year-round education in California.* Sacramento, CA: California State Department of Education.

Thomas, J. B. (1991). Year-round schools: How a new calendar would change life for your kids. *Better Homes and Gardens, 69*(12), 36.

Worthen, B. R., & Zsiray, S. W. (1994). *What twenty years of educational studies reveal about year-round education.* Chapel Hill, NC: NC Education Policy Research Center, The University of North Carolina.

Additional Readings on Year-Round Education

Archibald, R. S. (1992). The president's message. *The Year-Rounder,* p. 1. (Available from National Association for Year-Round Education, P.O. Box 11386, San Diego CA 92171-1386)

Forte, L. (1994). Going year-round. *The Education Digest, 59*(9), 7-9.

Glines, D. (1992). Year-round education: What lies ahead? *Thrust for Educational Leadership, 21*(6), 19-21.

Gregory, S. S. (1994). Everyone into the school. *Time, 144*(5), 48-49.

Grotjohn, D. K., & Banks, K. (1993, April). *An evaluation synthesis: Year-round schools and achievement.* Paper presented at the 1993 annual meeting of the American Educational Research Association, Atlanta, GA.

National Association for Year-Round Education. (1992). *Nineteenth reference directory of year-round education programs for the 1992-93 school year.* San Diego, CA: Author.

Shuster, T., & Rodger, P. L. (1992). *Concerning year-round education: A final report of an evaluative survey.* Logan, UT: Department of Psychology, Utah State University.

White, W. D. (1993, February). *Year-round education from start to finish.* Paper presented at the annual conference of the National Association for Year-Round Education, Las Vegas, NV.

For more information, write: National Association for Year-Round Education, P.O. Box 711386, San Diego CA 92171-1386, or call 619-276-5296.

Elaine Warrick-Harris presents at educational conferences, speaks to school board members, college classes and parent groups. She may be contacted at Balfour School at 910-672-0322 in Asheboro, NC. She is also a member of the ACEI Executive Board.

Approaching Kindergarten: A Look at Preschoolers in the United States

Nicholas Zill, Mary Collins, Jerry West, and Elvie Germino Hausken

Kindergarten is now a nearly universal experience for children in the United States, with 98% of all children attending kindergarten prior to entering first grade. However, the population of children that comes to kindergarten is increasingly diverse. Growing numbers of children in the United States come from different racial–ethnic and cultural backgrounds, family types, parent education levels, income strata, and language backgrounds. The majority of children come to kindergarten with some experience in center-based programs (such as child care centers or preschools), but the percentage of children with such experience and the quality of these experiences vary across many of these same characteristics of children and families.

Schools in the United States are expected to respond to this diversity in children's backgrounds and educational needs by providing all children with appropriate activities and instruction to ensure that each child begins his or her schooling with a good start. Knowing the range of developmental accomplishments and difficulties that children bring with them when they arrive at kindergarten can help us understand the demands being placed on schools to meet the needs of the entering children. Indeed, some of the difficulties discussed here are only experienced as difficulties when children enter school.

Parents of a national sample of 4,423 children from 3 to 5 years of age who had not yet started kindergarten were asked about specific accomplishments and difficulties of their children (see chart on right). Parents, usually the mother, were asked to rate how well their child demonstrated behaviors indicating emerging literacy and numeracy skills, such as pretending to read stories or counting to 20, and small-motor skills, such as buttoning clothes and holding

Nicholas Zill, *Ph.D., is a vice president and director of child and family studies at Westat, Inc., in Rockville, Maryland. He has been involved in several national studies of child well-being and family functioning in the United States and is a member of the Resource Group on School Readiness of the National Education Goals Panel.*

Mary Collins, *Ph.D., is a senior study director at Westat, Inc., and project director of the National Household Education Survey.*

Jerry West, *Ph.D., is a statistician with the U.S. Department of Education National Center for Education Statistics. He has been involved in the development of several national surveys of preprimary children and their families and is the project officer for a longitudinal study of kindergartners.*

Elvie Germino Hausken, *Ed.D., is a statistician with the U.S. Department of Education National Center for Education Statistics and a former elementary school teacher. She is currently involved in the development of national surveys of children, their families, and schools.*

This report is an excerpt from N. Zill, M. Collins, J. West, and E.G. Hausken, Approaching Kindergarten: A Look at Preschoolers in the United States, *NCES 95-280 (Washington, DC: U.S. Department of Education, 1995). For ordering information, call The National Library of Education at 1-800-424-1616.*

Developmental Accomplishments and Difficulties Included in the 1993 National Household Education Survey

Emerging literacy and numeracy

- Identifies all, some, or none of the primary colors by name
- Recognizes all, most, some, or none of the letters of the alphabet
- Counts not at all; to 5, 10, 20, 50; or to 100 or more
- Pretends to read, telling connected stories
- Writes own name, even if some of the letters are backwards

Small-motor development

- Can button clothes
- Holds pencil properly
- Writes/draws, rather than scribbles

Gross-motor functioning

- Trips, stumbles, or falls easily

General health

- Health excellent, very good, good, fair, or poor

Social and emotional development

- Very restless, fidgets a lot
- Has short attention span
- Often has temper tantrums
- Can be left with caregiver without a big fuss

Speech development

- Speech understandable to strangers
- Started speaking late
- Stutters or stammers

Figure 1. Percentage of Preschoolers with Developmental Accomplishments As Reported by Parents

Characteristic	All preschoolers	3-year-olds	4-year-olds	5-year-olds
Estimated number of children (thousands)	8,579	3,889	3,713	976
Literacy–numeracy indicators				
Identifies primary colors	78%	69%	84%	89%
Recognizes most or all letters	44%	27%	57%	66%
Counts to 20	52%	37%	62%	78%
Pretends to read or reads stories*	70%	65%	73%	79%
Writes own name, even if some letters are backwards	50%	22%	70%	84%
Small-motor indicators				
Can button his/her clothes	89%	83%	93%	94%
Holds pencil properly	91%	87%	94%	94%
Writes/draws, rather than scribbles	66%	50%	78%	84%
Health status				
Excellent, very good	88%	88%	88%	87%
Good, fair, or poor	12%	12%	12%	13%

*Includes telling connected stories when pretending to read and reading actual words.
Note: Preschoolers are 3- to 5-year-olds who have not yet entered kindergarten or primary school.
Source: U.S. Department of Education, National Center for Education Statistics, National Household Education Survey, 1993.

a pencil properly. Parents were also asked to rate the extent to which their child showed signs of physical activity-attention difficulties, such as restlessness and inattention, speech difficulties, and less than optimal health. These data were collected in January through April 1993 as part of the National Household Education Survey (NHES). The NHES is sponsored by the National Center for Education Statistics (NCES) of the U.S. Department of Education. Westat, Inc., conducted the survey for NCES.

Accomplishments and difficulties

Three- to five-year-olds. The percentage of children displaying signs of emerging literacy and small-motor skills increases with age within the 3- to 5-year-old population (see Figure 1) and within months of age among 4-year-olds. For example, the percentage of preschoolers reported to write their own name more than triples between ages 3 and 4, while the percentage recognizing most letters of the alphabet more than doubles. Other accomplishments show more moderate age differences. Developmental difficulties show much smaller changes across ages (see Figure 2), and some show no change.

More girls than boys demonstrate each of the literacy and small-motor skills covered in the survey, and more boys than girls exhibit signs of physical activity-attention difficulties or speech difficulties. Though differences between boys and girls are widespread, they are not large.

Hispanic preschoolers are reported to show fewer signs of emerging literacy and more indication of physical activity-attention difficulties, and to be in less than good general health than White non-Hispanic or Black non-Hispanic children. Controlling for related risk factors, such as a mother with limited education and a minority language status, reduces these ethnic differences but does not eliminate them. Black non-Hispanic preschoolers show fewer signs of emerging literacy and are more likely to be reported as in less than good health than White non-Hispanic preschoolers. However, racial differences are wholly accounted for by related risk factors, such as low maternal education, poverty, and single parenthood.

Four-year-olds. This part of the study focused on 2,000 children who had turned 4 by the end of the previous calendar year and were about 6 months away from starting kindergarten at the time of the survey. A majority of these 4-year-olds displays each of the small-motor skills and signs of emerging literacy asked about in the survey (Figure 3). The proportion of children displaying each of these behaviors varies greatly across specific accomplishments, however. More than 9 out of 10 can button their own clothes and hold a pencil properly, and more than 8 out of 10 can identify the primary colors by name. Fewer, about 6 in 10, can count to 20 or recognize most letters of the alphabet.

Much smaller proportions of preschoolers exhibit any of the developmental difficulties, although a substantial minority displays signs of physical activity-attention difficulties. At age 4, nearly 3 in 10 are said to be very restless and fidgety and nearly 1 in 4 to have short attention spans.

Figure 2. Percentage of Preschoolers with Developmental Difficulties As Reported by Parents

Characteristic	All preschoolers	3-year-olds	4-year-olds	5-year-olds
Estimated number of children (thousands)	8,579	3,889	3,713	976
Physical activity-attention indicators				
Is restless, fidgets a lot	27%	27%	29%	22%
Has short attention span	24%	25%	23%	21%
Has temper tantrums	25%	29%	23%	17%
Trips or falls easily	13%	13%	13%	12%
Speech development indicators				
Started speaking late	16%	18%	15%	15%
Not understandable to a stranger	9%	11%	8%	9%
Stutters or stammers	8%	9%	7%	9%

Note: Preschoolers are 3- to 5-year-olds who have not yet entered kindergarten or primary school.
Source: U.S. Department of Education, National Center for Education Statistics, National Household Education Survey, 1993.

Nearly 1 in 8 is reported by their parents to be in less than very good health. About 1 in 13 stutters or stammers or speaks in a way that is not understandable to a stranger.

Figure 3. Percentage of 4-Year-Olds with Accomplishments and Difficulties As Reported by Parents

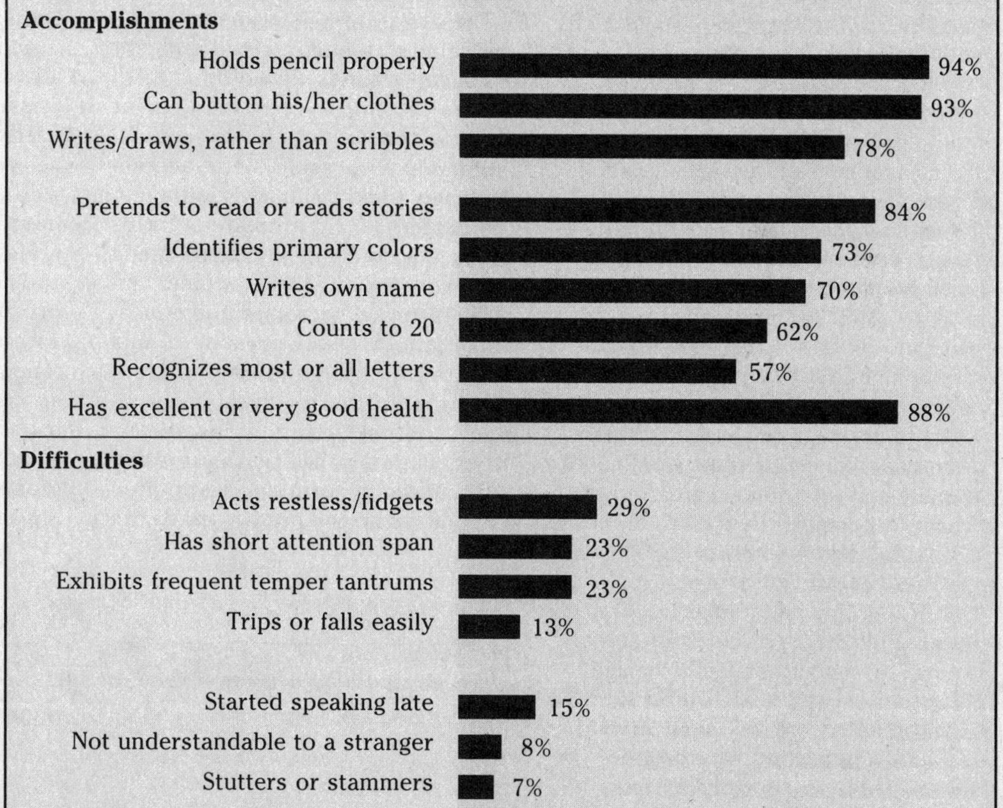

Source: U.S. Department of Education, National Center for Education Statistics, National Household Education Survey, 1993.

Family risk factors and 4-year-olds

Sociodemographic risk factors that have been found to be associated with problems in learning after children start school are also correlated with the accomplishments and difficulties children bring with them when they arrive at kindergarten. Five family risk factors are examined:

- mother has less than a high school education;
- family is below the official poverty line;
- mother speaks a language other than English as her primary language;
- mother was unmarried at the time of the child's birth; and
- only one parent is present in the home.

Half of today's preschoolers are affected by at least one of these risk factors, and 15% are affected by three or more of them.

The risk factors are found to be associated with fewer accomplishments and more difficulties in children, even after other child and family characteristics are taken into account. Of the developmental domains, only small-motor development is not found to be related to any of the risk factors. In general, the more risk factors the child is subject to, the lower the number of accomplishments and the higher the number of difficulties he or she is likely to have exhibited. Compared with children from families with no risk factors, twice as many 4-year-olds from families with three or more risk factors have short attention spans (37% versus 17%), and nearly double the number are said to be very restless (41% versus 22%). Three times as many speak in a way that is not understandable to strangers (14% versus 5%) or stutter or stammer (16% versus 5%). Almost five times as many are in less than very good health (23% versus 5%). Four-year-olds from families with three or more risk factors have nearly one-and-a-half times *fewer* literacy accomplishments (an average of 2.5 out of 5) than those from families with no risk factors (who have an average of 3.9 accomplishments out of 5).

The relative importance of individual risk factors varies across developmental domains. Nevertheless, low maternal education and minority language status are most consistently associated with fewer signs of emerging literacy and a greater number of difficulties in preschoolers.

Attending Head Start, prekindergarten, or other center-based preschool programs is linked to higher emerging literacy scores in 4-year-olds, and remains statistically significant when other child and family characteristics are taken into account. This benefit of preschool attendance accrues to children from both high-risk and low-risk family backgrounds. On the other hand, preschool attendance is found not to be associated with fewer behavioral or speech difficulties or with better health status in preschoolers. It is possible that further research taking into account measures of program quality (for example, child–staff ratio) would show some effect in these other domains.

Summary

The results of the study point to a need for innovative approaches in providing early education services for children from low-socioeconomic circumstances. As previous studies have shown, existing preschool programs have beneficial effects in the area of emerging literacy and numeracy. But they do not appear to be ameliorating the behavioral, speech, and health difficulties of preschoolers. The need for earlier and more effective interventions for young children with special educational needs has been recognized in federal legislation (e.g., Individuals with Disabilities Education Act, Chapter 1; and the Elementary and Secondary Education Act).

The survey results also emphasize the value of a multifaceted concept of educational risk. Five different risk factors are employed in the present study. All are found to have some relationship to preschoolers' accomplishments and difficulties, although the pattern of relationships varies across developmental domains. Many observers believe that low family income is *the* key factor behind educational failure, but the results of this research do not support this view. When compared to low family income, the risk factors of low maternal education, minority language status, and family structure were often as good or better predictors of the child's developmental accomplishments and difficulties.

By showing the considerable variation that exists in the accomplishments and difficulties of children about to start school, the study highlights the challenges that kindergarten teachers face in meeting the needs of children who are not only demographically but also developmentally diverse. Teachers must maintain the interest and promote the growth of children who have already demonstrated signs of early literacy and numeracy while simultaneously encouraging the development of these behaviors in children who have not yet acquired them. Similarly, they must meet the needs of children with difficulties while reserving sufficient attention and effort for those with few or no difficulties. Although there has always been variation in children entering kindergarten, the commitment to meeting the educational and developmental needs of *all* children in an increasingly diverse society presents greater challenges to teachers, schools, and communities.

Achieving this goal requires that all early childhood programs and classrooms be organized to meet the needs of children at all levels of development, that teachers be selected who have the energy, warmth, and imagination to respond to young children with varying capabilities and needs, that these teachers be appropriately trained and provided with sufficient resources and assistance so they do not have to neglect some children in order to nurture others. There is still much to learn about how well kindergarten programs around the country are meeting these requirements.

VOICES VOICES VOICES VOICES

Childhood is the most basic human right of children.

— David Elkind

"Approaching Kindergarten: A Look at Preschoolers in the United States," by Nicholas Zill, Mary Collins, Jerry West, and Elvie Germino Hausken, from the November 1995 issue of *Young Children* magazine, is reprinted with the permission of the National Association for the Education of Young Children.

TRANSITIONAL *Classrooms*

BY ANTHONY COLETTA

Transitional classrooms are designed for normal children who need more time to acquire the maturity, learning habits, motivation, and attention span needed to succeed in school. For such children, the extra year of time and stimulation promotes success and supports positive self-esteem. These children, according to language consultant Katrina deHirsch, develop slowly despite excellent intelligence, and fare better if their school entrance is deferred, "since one more year would make the difference between success and failure."

Participants are placed either in a readiness class prior to kindergarten, or a transitional first between kindergarten and first grade. After completing the readiness class, students enter kindergarten. The transitional first grade is for students who have finished kindergarten but who have been identified as needing extra time before entering first grade.

The additional year is provided within a child-centered environment. In many schools, transitional classrooms provide a model for primary-grade teachers interested in creating a "developmentally appropriate curriculum." Susan Sweitzer, Director of Education and Training for the Gesell Institute in New Haven, Connecticut, recommends the use of traditional classrooms as a "transition" to developmentally appropriate practice. She states: "Until we get to the point where these practices are extended up to the early grades, there have to be some options."

Clearly, children do not languish or "mark time" in these programs. A well-planned transition class is intellectually stimulating. Moreover, the curriculum does not repeat what the students have experienced the year before. Instead, the concepts are extended and elaborated upon.

Clearly, children do not languish or "mark time" in these programs. A well-planned transition class is intellectually stimulating. Moreover, the curriculum does not repeat what the students have experienced the year before. Instead, the concepts are extended and elaborated upon. The additional year allows the children to mature in all areas of development while they are exposed to stimulating learning experiences. As Harvard University Professor Jerome Bruner, author of ***Towards a Theory of Instruction***, says about readiness, the teacher "provides opportunities for its nurture."

As early as 1958, Gordon Liddle and Dale Long reported in the ***Elementary School Journal*** that transitional classrooms were valuable in improving academic performance. During the 1970s and 1980s, students in New Hampshire's public schools consistently achieved the highest scores on the Scholastic Aptitude Test (SAT), even though New

Hampshire ranks 50th in state aid to public schools. In ***All Grown Up & No Place to Go***, David Elkind writes that "In New Hampshire children are not hurried. It is one of the few states in the nation that provides 'readiness' classes for children who have completed kindergarten but who are not yet ready for first grade."

Research on Transitional Classrooms

The extent to which extra-year programs yield academic gains is subject to controversy, but their beneficial effect on social growth and self-esteem seems clear. As Robert Lichtenstein states in a paper entitled, "Reanalysis of Research on Early Retention and Extra Year Programs," transitional classrooms "offer significant advantages in non-academic areas (e.g., self-concept, adjustment, attitude toward school)."

Jonathan Sandoval, Professor of Education at the University of California, published research in which he studied high school students who years ago had completed the transitional (junior) first grade. The results showed beneficial outcomes: The children placed in the transitional class were superior to the control group on three out of four indicators of academic progress. The students also had favorable attitudes about the transitional program, indicating that the experiences helped them do better socially and emotionally, as well as academically. Sandoval speculated that without the transitional program, they might not have done as well.

A much publicized 1985 study, conducted by Professors Lorrie Shepard and Mary Lee Smith, concluded that transitional classrooms, though not harmful, do not boost academic performance in schools as had been expected. They conducted a study of 80 children in Boulder, Colorado, which led them to state there were no clear advantages to having an extra year of school prior to first grade. However, even they found a slight difference in achievement test scores in favor of the extra-year students. And, Shepard and Smith's published conclusions omitted the positive social-emotional effects of giving children more time to grow. Their original study includes figures showing that in every area of "Teacher Ratings" (reading, math, social maturity, learner self-concept, and attention), the group receiving the extra year (the "retained" group) scored higher. Most important, the figures were especially higher in the areas of social maturity and learner self-concept. The Shepard and Smith study also does not separate those children who repeated kindergarten from those who were placed in transition programs. All were part of the "retained" group.

Shepard and Smith contend in their book, ***Flunking Grades***, that the study of extra-year programs is "limited by the lack of systematic investigation of long-term effects." However, they do not mention Betty McCarty's eight-year study of the effect of kindergarten non-promotion on developmentally immature children. McCarty's results indicated that non-promotion of developmentally young kindergarten children had a positive effect on subsequent levels of peer acceptance, academic attitude, classroom adjustment, and academic achievement.

In general, studies which have reported negative effects of transitional classrooms, such as those described in Gilbert Gredler's article, "Transitional Classes," studied children who were academically at risk. It must, however, be remembered that a transitional program is not intended for remediation. It is developmental, and therefore is based on the premise that children have not yet acquired academic skills.

More than 25 studies of transitional classroom programs are summarized in Dr. James K. Uphoff's ***School Readiness and Transition Programs: Real Facts From Real Schools.*** According to Uphoff, these studies show that students in transitional classes have at least done as well as fellow students in regard to academic achievement in later years, and in many cases they have surpassed the national averages. The classes have also produced very positive benefits in regard to student self-concept, and emotional and social maturity. Further, there has been overwhelmingly strong satisfaction and support for transitional classes among parents whose children participated in such classes.

The Transitional Class Debate

Transitional classrooms have become a controversial issue. Supporters view them favorably because they help children who might do poorly in a rigid, academic curriculum, by providing instead the opportunity to be successful in a more relaxed, developmentally appropriate environment. Extra-year programs are therefore seen as a clear alternative to grade retention.

Critics, however, argue that such classrooms often become a "dumping ground" for children with low abilities and emotional problems. There may be merit to this argument if schools use transitional classrooms for children who have handicaps or learning problems, or if they inaccurately identify children using techniques and instruments which are insensitive to maturational factors.

Critics also argue that transitional classrooms are a form of retention in which children are stigmatized because they do not progress directly to the next grade. However, as Dr. James Uphoff writes in the article "Proving Your Program Works," "Clearly there is a tremendous difference between a child whose school experience has been one of failure, and a child in a success-oriented program providing time to grow.

The National Association for the Education of Young Children (NAEYC) opposes transitional classrooms because it believes lack of school readiness is most often due to rigid, inappropriate curriculums. NAEYC argues the schools should change so children do not need extra time in order to succeed. They have proposed a shift toward more developmentally appropriate practices in kindergarten and in the primary grades as a way of reducing the large number of children deemed to be unready for school. In an NAEYC publication titled, ***Kindergarten Policies: What Is Best for Children,*** co-author Johanne Peck states that instead of increasing the age of school entry, "resources and energy should instead be redirected to offering a good program." Many supporters of this position feel that transitional programs impede progress toward the goal of creating appropriate curriculums for all students.

There may be some truth to this, but I am not aware of any hard data which supports this position. And, eliminating readiness and transition classes does not mean that a school will quickly or even eventually implement a developmental curriculum. Many schools will have great difficulty changing to a system that requires additional teacher training and smaller class sizes.

Robert Wood, director of the Northeast Foundation for Children and co-author of ***A Notebook for Teachers***, believes that kindergarten teachers are hard-pressed to create a curriculum that meets the individual needs of children, when the developmental age range in a typical class may vary as much as three years. In an average kindergarten, where some children behave like 4 year-olds and others like 5 or 6 year-olds, responding to individual student needs requires high levels of diagnostic teaching skills and more specialized preparation than teachers normally receive.

School personnel interested in providing a developmentally appropriate curriculum for all students realize it is a worthwhile goal that may take time to achieve. In the meantime, many of these schools have established, or are considering, transitional classrooms. To be effective, such programs must be carefully implemented. A series of guidelines that can help parents and educators prepare for success are included in my book, ***What's Best for Kids.***

PROPER PLACEMENT *in the beginning* Assures Success AT THE END

BY JIM GRANT

When I graduated from Keene State College in 1967, I found a job teaching 5th grade in a small, rural community in New Hampshire. My first year as a teacher was a tremendous experience, and I felt I had achieved a lot of success. When I went back for my second year, the Assistant Superintendent of Schools came to see me. He said, "Jim, we're pleased with you, and we want to give you a chance to experience upward mobility. We're going to make you Principal of the Temple Elementary School."

"Well," I said, "I may not look very bright, but I am gifted in math, and I know that would make me Temple's fifth principal in twenty-four months. I'm not sure I can stand that kind of upward mobility." In spite of my reservations, when I woke up the following Monday, I was the principal of an elementary school.

The teacher of the first/second multiage classroom presented me with my first challenge. "I don't know what I'm going to do with my twenty-five children," she said. "They're all over the place. I have trouble getting them to slow down long enough for me to teach them."

I went to her classroom, opened the door, and quickly closed it. Nothing in my teacher education classes or one year of actual teaching experience had prepared me to deal with what I saw.

It was then that I brought in my former teacher, Nancy Richard, as an early childhood consultant who could advise me on the children's development. She observed the class and said, "You have second graders doing third grade work, second graders doing second grade work, second graders doing first grade work, first graders doing second grade work, first graders doing first grade work, first graders doing no work at all, and then there are two boys in the corner who aren't toilet trained after lunch."

"Some of these children," she continued, "aren't yet ready to do first grade work. Chronologically, they are 6, but developmentally they are still too young to succeed in that class." She then suggested I take a course on "developmental readiness."

In that course, I was surprised to learn that up to twenty-five percent of the children in American schools repeat a grade, and as many as another twenty-five percent are often struggling and not succeeding in their current grade. I checked the registers covering a six-year period at my school and proved those statistics were flawed. In my school, thirty-three percent of the kids had repeated! This informal sur-

"A child who is eager and ready for kindergarten and first grade is likely to become a lifelong learner. A child who is pushed to do too much too soon will never really like school and is likely to have problems all the way through. These are your child's formative years, and starting school should be a positive, rewarding experience."

— Judy Keshner, *Starting School*

vey also showed that most of the children who repeated were boys, and the grade most children repeated was first grade.

Being a bright, young, "overplaced" principal, I immediately made two brilliant deductions: boys are stupid, and first grade teachers are incompetent. Further reflection, observation, and discussion led me to some different conclusions, however. I began to consider the possibility that girls tended to develop more rapidly in certain respects than boys, and that these differences reached the crisis point in first grade, when all the children were expected to learn how to read and write.

One September in the late 1960's, we began to screen children to help determine their developmental readiness for a first grade experience. We discovered that many of the children eligible for first grade on the basis of their age that year were at risk for a traditional first grade program. When I shared that news with their parents and recommended that the developmentally young children remain in kindergarten for another year, the parents were very unhappy. They decided to send all of those late-blooming children into first grade together, thinking that the children being together would somehow make a difference in their developmental readiness for the demands of first grade.

Of course, it did not. By the middle of October, several of the children had been withdrawn from first grade at their parents' request and moved back to kindergarten. The problems that were surfacing at home and at school made the parents realize that these children really did need more time to grow and prepare for first grade. The rest of the developmentally young children ended up taking two years to complete first grade.

The next year, when we assessed the entering children's developmental levels, we did more to inform the parents — at PTA meetings, in one-on-one meetings, through literature. That year, many children who were developmentally young stayed in kindergarten for an extra year, and then entered first grade when most were 7-years-old. That first group of children, who had the advantage of an extra year to grow, graduated from high school in 1982, and many went on to graduate from college in 1986. We've been using this developmental approach in schools across New Hampshire for well over two decades — with success.

Nationwide, thousands of schools also began providing developmentally young children with extra-time options during the 1960's, helping tens of thousands of students master the curriculum and achieve success in school. This concept, which was formulated in 1911 and formalized as a Title III government program in New Hampshire in 1966, spread rapidly as teachers and parents recognized firsthand how much some children benefited from having an extra year to develop, which then gave them a much greater chance to succeed in school.

Now, when many parents and politicians are demanding stricter standards and measurements of progress, at the same time that many young children are feeling the effects of the disintegration of families and communities, there is a greater need than ever to provide extra-time options for children who are developmentally too young to succeed in a particular grade or program.

Time-flexibility Options

Programs that provide children with an extra year of growing time have many different names, but they share a number of common features. A good time-flexibility program offers reasonable class sizes, an environment rich in materials, and a room with space for movement. Here children can develop their physical and motor capabilities, learn social skills, work with hands-on math and science materials, practice listening and speaking, gain experience with different types of literature, explore the creative arts, and develop problem-solving abilities. As a result, children in these programs can develop the habits of success and a positive attitude toward school.

These programs emphasize an interest-based approach to learning rather than a curriculum based on text books and "time-on-task," access to a wide variety of literature instead of just basal readers and workbooks, and the use of authentic assessments rather than standardized achievement tests. All of these characteristics should be found in any of the time-flexibility options described below:

Readiness Classes for "Young 5's"

Many schools continue to find that a large number of entering students are developmentally too young to learn and succeed in kindergarten. This may be due to a child's innate but still normal rate of development, or environmental factors which have left a child unprepared to work well in a kindergarten class. Readiness classes provide the time needed to grow and make the transition to the school environment in a supportive setting, which then makes kindergarten a much more positive and educational experience. This is particularly important because, as kindergarten teacher Judy Keshner explains in her booklet, *Starting School*, kindergarten "is not a preview of what is to come — it is the foundation on which the following years will grow. Each grade builds on the one that came before, and kindergarten sets the pattern and the tone."

Developmental "Two-tier" Kindergarten

In this type of program, all 5-year-olds enter kindergarten at the same time, based on the legal entrance age, but some stay for one year and some stay for two. After enrollment, each child is developmentally assessed and continues to be observed throughout the year, so that detailed information about children's rate and stage of development is available. At the end of the school year, those children who are developmentally ready move on to first grade. Children who need more time to develop in order to enhance their experience in first grade can remain in kindergarten for a second year, or move into the sort of pre-first or transition class described below.

Pre-first Grade, Transition Grade, Bridge Classes

Call it what you will, this sort of extra-year option has been adopted by concerned parents, teachers, and administrators across America. It provides developmentally young 6-year-olds with a continuous-progress, full-day program in which they have extra time to grow and learn. This helps them make the very difficult and important transition from the play-oriented learning of kindergarten to the more formal "academic tasks" which become increasingly important in first grade. Developmentally young children who have had this extra-year experience are then much better prepared to enter first grade with confidence and a reasonable expectation of success.

Readiness/First Grade (R/1) Configuration

This approach acknowledges the reality that continues to exist in most first grade classes: children who need extra time to grow are blended with those who are developmentally ready for first grade. What makes the R/1 configuration different is that the parents of children who need extra time know from the very beginning that their children can have two years to complete this blended first grade, if needed. This takes the pressure off everyone — students, teachers, and mom and dad. There are no high-stakes campaigns to pass "or else," and no end-of-the-year trauma for children who just need more time to grow and develop.

Some schools chose the R/1 configuration to save money — by not having a separate readiness class, they save on classroom space, staffing, and materials. Other schools choose this option because it is the one the educators prefer and the community accepts. It also provides many benefits of the multi-age classes described below, such as allowing developmentally young students to work closely with and learn from more experienced students during their first year, and then to become the models for new students during their second year.

Multi-age Primary Classes

An increasing number of schools now offer multi-age primary classrooms, in which children of different ages work and learn together, staying together with the teacher for a multi-year placement. These classrooms eliminate the artificial time constraints created by having separate grades from kindergarten through third grade.

One important result is that more time is available for teaching and learning, especially at the start of the year, as teachers and students don't have to spend time getting to know one another and learning to work well together. This approach also eliminates worries about "running out of time" to complete the curriculum by the end of each year, and it eliminates many high-stakes decisions which otherwise have to be made each year. In addition, if a child needs extra time to develop and complete the curriculum before moving on, a multi-age class works particularly well because it already contains a wide range of age levels and a flexible timetable, rather than a rigid, lock-step grade structure.

Multi-age classrooms decrease the risk of failure for all children, because these classes allow students to develop and learn at their own rate in a much less hurried environment. Staying in the same class with the same teacher and classmates for more than one year also provides a sense of consistency and belonging, which can be particularly helpful for the many children who now grow up in fast-changing families and communities. And, the developmental diversity that naturally occurs in a multi-age classroom makes it easier for transfer and special-needs students to be included in them.

An Extra Year of Preschool

Unfortunately, too many parents have to cope with schools which do not offer viable extra-time options for children who are developmentally too young to succeed in kindergarten. Under these circumstances, allowing developmentally young children to spend an extra year in preschool can be a very positive alternative to sending them off to kindergarten and waiting to find out if they "sink or swim." Having an extra year to grow and learn in a supportive preschool environment greatly decreases the odds that such children will flounder and need rescuing in the primary grades.

High-quality preschools provide children with a range of developmentally appropriate activities that foster continued growth and learning. And, the mixed age levels found in most preschools makes it easy for developmentally young children to fit in, just as in a multi-age class. This sort of environment also tends to make preschool teachers aware of the importance of readiness and adept at working with children who are at various developmental levels. Unfortunately, in most cases this option is only available to financially advantaged parents.

An Extra Year at Home

Some parents may prefer to provide their late bloomer with day care and learning experiences at home for an extra year. In situations where there is a parent at home every day who has the time, inclination, and understanding to work with a child in this way, it can be a viable alternative, especially now that more materials and support networks have been developed for the small but growing number of parents who opt to provide their children's entire education at home.

In many cases, parents can simply notify the local school of their intent and send children to kindergarten when they are 6-years-old. However, young children need opportunities to grow and learn with their peers, which contribute in many ways to a child's overall development. And, well-trained preschool and elementary school teachers can often provide a wider range of supportive and educational learning experiences for a developmentally young child than a parent.

Dropping Out and "Stopping Out"

When developmentally young children do not take extra time early in their educational career, they tend to take the time later on. They may repeat a grade in middle school or high school, or flunk out or drop out altogether. They may also obtain their high school diploma but feel the need to take time off before going to college. Some "stop out" — a phrase used to describe students who take a leave of absence while at college. Statistics show that a large number of students do take time off during college, and interestingly enough, the percentage is about the same as the percentage of children found to need extra time when they start school!

Some young people may be ready to put the extra time to better use when they are older, but too many end up with negative attitudes, low self-esteem, and poor skills that interfere with their ability to create productive and fulfilling lives. Early intervention in a positive and supportive way can be far more effective than a wait-and-see approach.

Editor's note: Do you feel on the defensive when parents challenge you to answer the question, "Why are you wasting so much time on free play? Our children are here to learn, *not to play!"*

Do you feel ill-equipped not only to answer the challenge but to explain the values of play with such persuasiveness that your critic becomes an ally, an advocate instead of an adversary? Read on!

Wanted: Advocates for Play in the Primary Grades

Sandra J. Stone

In our national pursuit of academic excellence, young children in the primary grades have too long endured the absence of play in the classroom. Even in our kindergartens we see an erosion of quality playtime. If we are to be true advocates for children, then we must be outspoken advocates for play. In the present restructuring movement in our nation's schools, educators of young children must let their voices be heard. We must not succumb to the narrow definition of *learning* that undervalues or eliminates play as a curricular tool in the classroom (Bergen 1988).

Play is deemed by many experts as vitally important to the growth of the whole child (Piaget 1962; Vygotsky 1976; Elkind 1981; Bruner 1983; Fein 1986; Bergen 1988). The National Association for the Education of Young Children (NAEYC) supports children's play as "a primary vehicle for and indicator of their mental growth. Play enables children to progress along the developmental sequence from the sensorimotor intelligence of infancy to preoperational thought in the preschool years to the concrete operational thinking exhibited by primary children. . . . In addition to its role in cognitive development, play serves important functions in children's physical, emotional, and social development. . . . Therefore, child-initiated, child-directed, teacher-supported play is an essential component of developmentally appropriate practice" (Bredekamp 1987, 54).

The Association for Childhood Education International (ACEI) also takes a strong position on play. ACEI "recognizes the need for children of all ages to play and affirms the essential role of play in children's healthy development. . . . ACEI supports those adults who respect and understand the power of play in children's lives and who use their knowledge about how children play at different ages to guide their practices with children" (Isenberg & Quisenberry 1988, 138). Frost calls play an "indispensable element in child development. It is the child's natural process of learning and development and, consequently, a critical ingredient in the educative process" (1992, 19).

With such strong proponents of play as a curricular choice, one would think that play would enjoy a place of honor in our primary classrooms, where children participate in play as a cherished component of appropriate practice. However, what we find across our nation are educators who have or are unwittingly sacrificing play in their endeavor to reach prescribed academic goals. Even teachers who know the importance of play to a child's development find themselves on the defensive when questioned

***Sandra J. Stone,** Ed.D., is an assistant professor in literacy and early childhood education at Northern Arizona University in Flagstaff and conducts research in the area of play and literacy. She is the author of* Playing: A Kid's Curriculum *(GoodYear Books).*

about play in their classrooms. We have become too embarrassed to give playtime a place because of "more important" curricular priorities. Hence, play is reduced to recess time, hidden in the curriculum, or tagged as miscellaneous "free time." Children who *need* to play (a need for all children) go undercover, hoping their play in the classroom will not be discovered; or even worse, children deny themselves the play they need in order to please those they love and respect.

To those who value play and understand its critical importance to the growth and development of young children, the question is how do we empower ourselves to become true advocates of play?

We must not succumb to the narrow definition of learning that undervalues or eliminates play as a curricular tool in the kindergarten and primary classroom.

Recognizing what play is

First, we must be able to recognize play in order to promote and nurture it in our classrooms. Play is defined as intrinsically motivated, freely chosen, process-oriented over product-oriented, nonliteral, and enjoyable (Johnson, Christie, & Yawkey 1987). Although play is hands-on learning, hands-on learning is not always play. Teachers must not assume that active learning constitutes play. Good teachers of young children should know the difference and provide for both. Because play is nonliteral, internal reality takes precedence over external reality. "This 'as if' stance allows children to escape the constraints of here and now and experiment with new possibilities" (Johnson, Christie, & Yawkey 1987, 12).

In order to recognize play, looking at play types is helpful. Smilansky's (1968) adaptations of Piaget's (1962) cognitive play categories are standard for play observers. There are four categories: functional, constructive, dramatic, and games with rules.

Functional play. Functional play is when the child runs, jumps, splashes in water, or repetitively manipulates objects or materials. In this type of play, the child repeats muscle movements with or without objects just for the sake of movement. In a primary classroom, teachers can see many forms of functional play. Examples include all of these actions: the child who pulls on her shoe while sitting at circle time, re-

© The Growth Program

© The Growth Program

Research substantiates a strong relationship between play and cognitive development. Play affords young children the opportunity to use divergent thinking. Children figure out solutions to problems as they play. Children discover scientific concepts, such as force, gravity, and balance, as they play with blocks.

peatedly taps her pencil, hoards a small piece of playdough and rolls it over and over again in her hand, or plays with the tiniest grain of sand on the carpet. Children gain great pleasure in playing in and with the environment, not for a product but for the sheer enjoyment of movement. Unfortunately, teachers of young children who are not knowledgeable of this form of play may reprimand the child for not paying attention or redirect the child to more "educational" involvement.

Constructive play. Constructive play is when children use objects or materials to make things. They create, construct, and solve problems. In constructive play, children build with Legos and blocks. They make things with playdough, paint, paper, and sand. Constructive play is probably the most frequently allowed play in the primary classroom. However, art, music, and project creation can only be play as long as they meet the criteria for play. As previously stated, play is intrinsically motivated, freely chosen, process-oriented over product-oriented, nonliteral, and enjoyable (Johnson, Christie, & Yawkey 1987). If these criteria are not met, then the activities may be active learning or even work, but they are not play. Too often, well-defined teacher-initiated activities become work projects rather than creative play construction by the children (Stone 1993). Again, the knowledgeable teacher must know the difference and adequately provide for both.

Dramatic play. Dramatic play is when children role-play or make make-believe transformations. Dramatic play becomes *socio*dramatic play when children role-play together. In dramatic play, one child may pretend she is a mother or superhero. Another child may transform a block into a car, a banana into a phone, playdough into pizza, or himself into a monster. Dramatic play is the most highly developed form of symbolic play, in which the child begins the incredible process of using objects as symbols for objects and events in the real world. Symbolic play is a critical foundation for literacy development and the key to representational thought (Piaget 1962). In sociodramatic play, the child is given multiple opportunities to be social as well as to play out his emotions. Thus, dramatic play's importance for the developing child in the primary grades should not be underestimated and should be given high priority in the primary classroom.

Games with rules. This is the type of play in which children make or use rules to play games. These may be simple or complex rules that are preestablished by the players. Examples of games with rules are tag, hide-and-seek, dodge ball, and card or board games. But do not overlook games of play in which children establish simple rules, such as "I'll hop first and then you are next" or "You can only race your car between these lines." Children develop or use rules to establish how the play is supposed to go. Games with rules support a child's development as she orders her world for consistency, fairness, stability, and predictability (Stone 1993).

Primary teachers will provide beginning games with rules while understanding the limitations of the children's thought processes as well as the need to increase the complexity of rules as the children's understanding increases. Close observation of children's abilities and choices will help the teacher in selecting appropriate games with rules, keeping in mind that children will choose those games they understand and enjoy.

Although primary children will engage in constructive, dramatic, and games with rules more frequently than functional play, all four types of play are important for the development of young children in the primary grades. Knowing the types of children's play will help teachers not only recognize forms of play when they see them but will help teachers facilitate, honor, and plan for play's place in the primary classroom.

Verbalizing our knowledge of the benefits/values of play

To be a true advocate of children's play, a teacher must be able to verbalize her knowledge about the values of play. Stone notes that the "research on the values of play is formidable. In fact, there is so much evidence of play's overall benefits that to provide an 'education' without play seems ludicrous" (1993, 7). Knowledge of the values of play can empower a teacher to promote play in the classroom as well as guide her in effectively using play as a curricular tool.

First, play creates a natural learning environment. Wasserman describes five benefits of play: children are able to generate (create) something new, take

To be a true advocate of children's play, a teacher must be able to verbalize her knowledge about the values of play.

risks, avoid the fear of failure, be autonomous, and actively engage their minds and bodies (1992, 135). Then, play provides the natural and experiential learning that supports the child's construction of his own knowledge of the world and his place in it. It significantly affects the development of the whole child. Within play's natural learning environment, children develop cognitively, socially, emotionally, and physically.

Cognitive development. Research substantiates a strong relationship between play and cognitive development. The appearance of symbolic play is considered one of the most significant cognitive developments of the young child. Symbolic play has a crucial role in developing abstract thought (Vygotsky 1976). Symbolic play signals the development of representational thought (Piaget 1962). The key importance of representational thought is that the child is now able to represent objects and events symbolically. When children begin to pretend (dramatic) play, they are using objects to symbolize other objects and events. This is a necessary step in representing the objects mentally. Even though this process begins at about 1½ years old, it does not peak until about age 6. Because children use dramatic play to practice representing objects symbolically, many opportunities to engage in symbolic play in the early primary grades should be provided to continue this foundation in the child's development of abstract thought as well as to further literacy development.

Play also affords young children the opportunity to use divergent thinking. Children research solutions to problems as they play. If a child is building a tower, she explores many ways to keep the tower from falling over. Each problem she encounters in constructive play gives her opportunity to think divergently and find solutions.

Play is the natural place for children to express creativity. Children create, invent, and design as they draw, build, and dramatize. In constructive play, the child sculpts with clay, designs with paint, and constructs with blocks, all expressions of the child's creativity. In dramatic play, the "child is able to take a multitude of experiences and lace them together into new ones, which represents a monument to her creativity" (Stone 1993, 120).

Play encourages problem-solving. Problems encountered in play represent real, thus meaningful, problems to young children (Tegano, Sawyers, & Moran 1989). Real problems provide the motivation to engage in the problem-solving process. Providing a play context for young children is an effective way to help young children develop problem-solving skills across all dimensions naturally. Instead of talking through problems, children play through problems for solutions. Tegano, Sawyers, and Moran note that "children who are encouraged to find and 'play' with their problems (trying out various solutions) are more apt to learn generalizable skills and be better equipped to cope with real-life problems" (1989, 97).

Play also provides an avenue for concept development by which children test out and revise their concepts of the world. In mud play, the child develops concepts of mass, volume, and the nature of change. The child develops mathematical concepts of number, matching, classifying, and measurement when he plays with cars, cards, paints, and puzzles. Children discover scientific concepts such as force, gravity, and balance as they experiment with blocks.

© The Growth Program

Play is the primary mode for children's social development. Play encourages social interaction. Children learn how to negotiate, resolve conflicts, solve problems, get along with each other, take turns, be patient, cooperate, and share. Play also helps children understand concepts of fairness and competition.

Perspective taking is a cognitive process that often takes place during sociodramatic play. The child learns how to see the world from another's point of view as she takes on the roles of different characters. The social interaction also allows her to see things from her playmate's point of view. Being able to see something from someone's else's view is a developmental milestone for the egocentric child and is a process facilitated by play.

Play provides a rich environment for language development. As the young child interacts with others, he must communicate meaning and also develop narrative language, as demonstrated in sociodramatic play. His vocabulary undergoes incredible growth during play. Especially valuable to his language development is that in play the new words are tied to meaning and experiences enacted or engaged in by the child.

Values of Play

Emotional
- acts as a medium for expressing thoughts/feelings
- softens the realities of the world
- serves as a risk-free environment
- releases children's stress
- decreases children's anxiety
- builds well-being/self-concept

Physical
- motor development
- balancing of systems
- body command
- distance judgment
- hand–eye coordination
- testing of bodies
- self-assurance

Cognitive
- abstract thought
- divergent thinking
- creativity
- problem solving
- concept development
- perspective taking
- language development

Social
- decentering
- practicing of social patterns
- encouraging social interaction
- learning to get along

Social development. Play is the primary mode for children's social development. Play encourages social interaction. Children learn how to negotiate, resolve conflicts, solve problems, get along with each other, take turns, be patient, cooperate, and share. Play also helps children understand concepts of fairness and competition.

Even though perspective taking is a cognitive skill, it is also vital to a child's social development. Play supports children in their self-decentering process. This is especially important as children learn to deal with their friends' feelings and attitudes.

Play contributes to children's social competence by giving them the opportunity to be social. It also provides children with an arena in which to practice social conventions, with the freedom to accept or reject those conventions. Play is the perfect opportunity for children to develop friendships and to see that someone else values them.

Emotional development. Play is a medium through which children can express their feelings as well as learn to cope with them. They can express feelings of happiness, sadness, anger, or worry in a world separate from the real world. In this world of play, these feelings are freely explored and expressed because they are not in the "real world." In pretend play, the feelings can be understood and worked out. Play provides this safe context for emotional development. A child scolded by a parent or teacher can scold a doll in the play context, and this is acceptable. A child can replay, over and over again, an unsettling incident, such as seeing someone hurt on the playground. He plays the scene until he is able to cope with his feelings of fear. In this sense, play softens the realities of the world. Play is a risk-free environment in which unpleasant experiences can be worked out.

Elkind (1981) suggests that play is also a release from the stresses children face. Physiological evidence links play with anxiety reduction (Barnett & Storm 1981). In our hurried society, play gives children a place of solitude where they can escape and be in control of their world, their thoughts, their feelings.

Physical development. Play is the primary way children develop physically. Play provides opportunities for both fine- and gross-motor development. Children can test out their balancing systems as they do acrobatics, develop a command of their bodies as they skip and hop, and judge distances as they jump and throw. Play also gives children opportunities to develop hand–eye coordination as they build, paint, cut, and paste. As children play, they test out their bodies to see how they best function. And, as children develop a command of their bodies, play helps them "feel physically confident, secure, and self-

assured" (Isenberg & Quisenberry 1988, 139).

Knowing the cognitive, social, emotional, and physical benefits of play to the development of young children is essential for us to be advocates for children's play. We need to be able to verbalize our knowledge of the value of play to parents, teachers, and administrators.

Being "open" advocates for play

Knowing what play is, the types of play, and the benefits of play empowers us as "open" advocates for play. No longer do we have to hide play in our curriculums, give only cursory "free time" for children to play, or be embarrassed when someone sees our children playing. Equipped with the knowledge of the value of play, teachers can not only allow play in their classrooms but vigorously plan for it.

Posting the values of play in a prominent place in the classroom (see box on p. 47) and displaying the play cartoon (above) let parents and colleagues and, most of all, the children know that "Play is valued here!"

Play centers can be labeled with the benefits children gain through the play experience at each specific center. For example, at the home center, a chart may be posted that reads, "Children are learning to use more elaborate language, get along, share, negotiate, plan, use social skills, and make friends." At the art center, the chart could indicate that "Children are learning to create, invent, share, socialize, and plan."

In addition to posting the values of play, it is equally important to demonstrate that learning is taking place. We can display evidence of things children have invented or solved, show examples of language or stories created, and use anecdotal records to substantiate times of negotiation, planning, and sharing. Teachers may take photo-

Posting the values of play in a prominent place in the classroom lets parents and colleagues know that "Play is valued here!"

graphs of castles and spaceships constructed from Legos or videotape children's dramatizations.

Vivid examples of the benefits of play further support the position that play is important, but even more importantly, this information helps guide our teaching decisions as we become astute observers of what is happening during play.

Another way to become an open advocate of play is to inform others. We can share timely articles with colleagues, schedule discussion groups with interested teachers and parents, and exchange valuable play experiences with each other.

Involving parents

Parents can be valued partners in creating and supporting quality play experiences for their children. A class newsletter informing parents and periodically highlighting the importance of children's play can be a useful educational tool. At informative parent meetings planned throughout the year, when we may normally discuss literacy development and math strategies, we can also share how play supports children's learning, growth, and development.

Teachers upgrade the importance of play by bringing it into the context of parent conferences. Letting parents see how play is integrated into our curriculum and how we use play to help each child in his development is valuable. This can include sharing each child's play experiences that document growth, for example, in imagination, problem solving, negotiation, and language development.

Parents can extend play at home. Teachers can help them see the importance of play in their children's learning and can make play kits for children to take home. These kits might be

Involving Parents in Creating Prop Boxes

Dear Parents,

One of my goals for this school year is to increase the opportunities and materials for sociodramatic play of stories in literature. Research supports sociodramatic play as one of the most important forms of play because it involves the use of such skills as symbolic representation, perspective taking, precise use of language, cooperation, and sharing. Research has also shown that acting out stories helps children improve their comprehension abilities as well as story-element understanding.

I have begun a collection of "prop boxes" that will be placed in the play stage in our classroom. Each box contains some clothing, accessories, and props for a specific story we will be reading this year. For example, the "Henny Penny" prop box contains an acorn, umbrella, hat, stool, and a few clothing items for each character.

I need your help in completing the remaining prop boxes. Please review the story list below and return the bottom portion of this letter, indicating which story you and your child would be willing to work on and find props for to bring to our classroom. Items are often found at home, from a neighbor, or at a secondhand store. I would appreciate it if you could work with your child to complete a single story; however, if you have an item that would fit another story, please send it in.

Thank you for your support of this project that will benefit your children. I'm looking forward to a wonderful year.

Story list

"Stone Soup"
"The Gingerbread Boy"
"Jack and the Beanstalk"
"The Little Red Hen"
"The Elves and the Shoemaker"
"The Hare and the Tortoise"
"Little Red Riding Hood"
"The City Mouse and the Country Mouse"
"The Lion and the Mouse"
"Cinderella"
Where the Wild Things Are
Sylvester and the Magic Pebble
There's a Nightmare in My Closet
"Henny Penny"
"The Three Bears"
"The Three Little Pigs"

Please decide on which story you would like to work. Write down your first and second choices on the bottom portion of this page, tear it off, and return it as soon as possible. I will send a list of possible items that you may want to include in your prop box as well as a bag for putting everything into. Thanks so much for your help!

Sincerely,

- -

Child's name ______________________________

Parent's name ______________________________

___ I would like to put together the following prop box:

First choice ______________ Second choice ______________

___ I would like to put together a prop box that is not on this list.

Title ______________________________

___ I cannot help at this time. Ask me again another time.

Courtesy of Kim Huff and Kim Rimbey, Washington School District, Phoenix, Arizona.

Inviting Help from Parents for Dramatic Play

Dear Parents,

One of my goals for this school year is to increase the opportunities and materials for sociodramatic play. Research supports sociodramatic play as one of the most important forms of play because it involves the use of such skills as symbolic representation, perspective taking, precise use of language, cooperation, and sharing.

I have begun a collection of "character boxes" for the children's use in our housekeeping center. Each box contains some clothing, accessories, and props for creating an individual character. For example, the farmer box includes overalls, a flannel shirt, a straw hat, and a bandanna.

I need your help in completing the remaining characters. Please review the character list and return the bottom portion, indicating what character you and your child would be willing to work on and donate to our classroom. You can find items at home (clean those closets!) or ask a neighbor or look at a secondhand store. I would appreciate it if you could work with your child to complete a single character; however, if you discover an item that would fit another character, please also send it in.

Thank you for your support of this project that will benefit your children. I'm looking forward to a wonderful year.

Character list

artist	doctor	painter
bride/groom	firefighter	pilot
business person	grocery clerk	police officer
cheerleader	hairdresser	postal worker
chef	judge/lawyer	prince/princess
circus performer	mechanic	teacher
construction worker	mountain climber	waitress/waiter
cowboy/cowgirl	musician	zookeeper

Or, name any other character you can think of!

Sincerely,

- -

Child's name ______________________________

Parent's name ______________________________

Character we will be willing to complete for a character box:

____

____

Specific items we can donate for another character: ________

____

____

____

Courtesy of Kim Huff and Kim Rimbey, Washington School District, Phoenix, Arizona.

simple props for dramatic play, felt flannelboard figures to play out a favorite story, or puppets, Popsicle sticks, even playdough. Children can bring the kits back and tell about or demonstrate what they did at home. This type of homework for young children is extremely valuable.

We want to involve parents in planning play environments in the classroom or playground. One easy way is to send home requests for props for sociodramatic play, puppets, and art and building materials (see boxes on p. 49 and this page). Inviting parents to observe or participate in the children's play and having them as partners strengthen our advocacy role.

Investigating ways to integrate play into the curriculum

Play's integration into the curriculum can be done by creating a variety of play centers, not overlooking a home center for one. The home center is an acceptable play center in kindergarten, but it is not usually used in the primary grades. However, it has continued value for 6- to 8-year-olds. Children are still developing language and narrative story. They continue to plan and make friends. They still need the support that play gives to a good self-concept. Unfortunately, just when young children are becoming "good players," the home center is removed from the classroom.

Besides providing a natural environment for language development, the home center welcomes literacy's integration. Note pads, pencils, recipe book and cards, phone, telephone book, magazines and books are supplies to be added. The home center creates a meaningful environment for functional use of literacy elements (Neuman & Roskos 1990).

Math may also be integrated into the home center by adding measuring cups and spoons. Introducing a toy "pet" and a pet care book incorporates social studies. The possibilities are endless.

Sociodramatic play centers in the primary grades are an excellent medium for children to act out favorite storybooks or curricular themes. Acting out stories using simple props supports wholistic retelling and demonstrates children's story sense. Thematic play centers are another wonderful educational tool for primary teachers. For example, a thematic unit on oceans lends itself to a play area complete with a submarine made from a box and underwater creatures painted by the children. In play centers like this that provide a meaningful setting, children use more elaborate vocabulary, such as words like submerge, periscope, depth, fathom, and sonar.

Children may also create their own play centers based on their interests. During this process, the children will invent, design, problem solve, and plan—all higher-order thinking skills.

Primary school children can play with flannelboard story figures from favorite storybooks. This enhances story sense, story sequence, and language use. They can make their own flannel-board story figures and create their own stories. Flannel-board story play is excellent rehearsal for a creative writing activity. Flannel-board pieces can also be used by children to play with numbers, create sets, and visualize mathematical operations such as multiplication.

There's no need to limit the types of centers in our classrooms just because we are teaching primary children. In an art or music center, children create, design, and invent. Even primary children continue to enjoy building at a blocks center. Their skills are becoming more refined and their projects more complex. How sad it is to deny them this creative time when their minds are envisioning magnificent structures, spaceships, and gadgets. We want to document the children's ingenuity and insights by photographing their creations or recording their ideas in anecdotal records.

Play may be infused into all of the content areas of an integrated curriculum: setting up a store when studying economics, creating a rain-forest play center when studying the environment, and providing simple props for recreating history through sociodramatic play. With a few props, children become pioneers, archaeologists, and astronauts. As we evaluate our class environments (indoor and outdoor play), let's look at them with "playful" eyes. We can ask ourselves, "Where can play be added to support my children's cognitive, social, emotional, and physical growth?"

© Elisabeth Nichols

Play's integration into the curriculum can be done by creating a variety of play centers, not overlooking a home center for one. A home center has continued value for 6- to 8-year-olds. Children are still developing language and narrative story. They continue to plan and make friends. They still need the support that play gives to a good self-concept. Unfortunately, just when young children are becoming "good players," the home center is removed from the classroom.

Creating quality time for play

When planning for play, it is crucial to provide enough time for play to evolve. Children cannot be herded from one center to another at the ringing of a bell every 15 minutes. Children should have at least 30 minutes or more for play to evolve. However we choose to provide for play in our classrooms, whether it is integrated into the curriculum through centers or is given a block of time, we want to make sure the time is sufficient for quality play to take place.

Honoring children's play

To be an advocate for play also means to honor children's play. This is done by providing time for play, also by planning for and encouraging play.

A teacher who plans for play is most likely to encourage continued play. We can encourage play by expressing pleasure in the children's play, such as tasting newly made playdough pizza or admiring an intricately constructed Lego spaceship or agreeing to be Daddy at the home center. Honoring children's play involves respect for the process. Teachers who do not understand the value of play will communicate their nonvaluing feelings by retreating from or ignoring the play. A teacher who does not honor play may say to herself, "The children are just playing. While they are 'busy,' I will do more important things." A teacher who honors play encourages children to play. She will involve herself in the play as an observer, supporter, or participant.

Creating "play" support groups

While play is acceptable for preschool and kindergarten children, advocating play in the primary grades is, indeed, a challenge. We need to find colleagues in our schools, school districts, or the wider educational community who also value play for young children. A support group will strengthen our roles as advocates. Many voices are better than one isolated voice. Support groups share information, exchange ideas, and confirm beliefs. A support group does not have to be large. It can be as small as two people or as many as one hundred. The important thing is to have someone who supports our position of advocacy for play.

Becoming an advocate for play in the primary grades is not an easy role. Critics lie in wait to spear such frivolous use of time in public schools. To keep play in classrooms where it exists and to return play to classrooms void of play are efforts demanding courageous people.

References

Barnett, L.A., & B. Storm. 1981. Play, pleasure, and pain: The reduction of anxiety through play. *Leisure Sciences* 4: 161–75.

Bergen, D., ed. 1988. *Play as a medium for learning and development.* Portsmouth, NH: Heinemann.

Bredekamp, S., ed. 1987. *Developmentally appropriate practice in early childhood programs serving children from birth through age 8.* Exp. ed. Washington, DC: NAEYC.

Bruner, J. 1983. Play, thought, and language. *Peabody Journal of Education* 60 (3): 60–69.

Elkind, D. 1981. *The hurried child: Growing up too fast too soon.* Menlo Park: CA: Addison-Wesley.

Fein, G. 1986. The play of children. In *The young child at play: Reviews of research,* eds. G. Fein & M. Rivkin, *Vol. 4,* vii–ix. Washington, DC: NAEYC.

Frost, J.L. 1992. *Play and playscapes.* Albany, NY: Delmar.

Isenberg, J., & N.L. Quisenberry. 1988. Play: A necessity for all children. *Childhood Education* 64: 138–45.

Johnson, J.E., J.F. Christie, & T.D. Yawkey. 1987. *Play and early childhood development.* Glenview, IL: Scott, Foresman.

Neuman, S.B., & K. Roskos. 1990. Play, print, and purpose: Enriching play environments for literacy development. *The Reading Teacher* 44 (3): 214–21.

Piaget, J. 1962. *Play, dreams, and imitation in childhood.* New York: Norton.

Smilansky, S. 1968. *The effects of sociodramatic play on disadvantaged preschool children.* New York: Wiley.

Stone, S.J. 1993. *Playing: A kid's curriculum.* Glenview, IL: GoodYear Books.

Tegano, D.W., J.K. Sawyers, & J.D. Moran III. 1989. Problem-finding and solving in play: The teacher's role. *Childhood Education* 66 (2): 92–97.

Vygotsky, L.S. 1976. Play and its role in the mental development of the child. In *Play: Its role in development and evolution,* eds. J.S. Bruner, A. Jolly, & K. Sylva, 537–44. New York: Basic Books.

Wasserman, S. 1992. Serious play in the classroom. *Childhood Education* 68 (3): 133–39.

For further reading

Almy, M. 1984. A child's right to play. *Childhood Education* 60: 350.

Athey, I. 1984. Contributions of play to development. In *Child's play: Developmental and applied,* eds. T.D. Yawkey & A.D. Pellegrini, 9–27. Hillsdale, NJ: Erlbaum.

Bogdanoff, R.F., & E.T. Dolch. 1979. Old games for young children: A link to our heritage. *Young Children* 34 (2): 37–45.

Christie, J.F. 1987. Play and story comprehension: A critique of recent training research. *Journal of Research and Development* 21 (1): 36–42.

Elkind, D. 1990. Academic pressure—too much, too soon: The demise of play. In *Children's play and learning: Perspectives and policy implications,* eds. E. Klugman & S. Smilansky, 3–17. New York: Teachers College Press.

Flavell, J.H. 1963. *The developmental psychology of Jean Piaget.* Princeton, NJ: Van Nostrand.

Frost, J.L., ed. 1986. *Early childhood education rediscovered.* New York: Holt, Rinehart, and Winston.

Henniger, M.L. 1993. Enriching the outdoor play experiences. *Childhood Education* 70 (2): 87–90.

Isenberg, J.P., & M.R. Jalongo. 1993. *Creative expression and play in the early childhood curriculum.* New York: Merrill.

Pepler, D.J. 1982. Play and divergent thinking. In *The play of children: Current theory and research,* eds. D.J. Pepler & H. Rubin, 64–78. Contributions to Human Development, vol. 6. Basel, Switzerland: Karger.

Rubin, K.H. 1980. Fantasy play: Its role in the development of social skills and social cognition. In *Children's play,* ed. K.H. Rubin, 69–84. San Francisco: Jossey-Bass.

Rubin, K.H., G.G. Fein, & B. Vandenberg. 1983. Play. In *Handbook of child psychology,* vol. 4, ed. P.H. Mussen. New York: Wiley.

Rubin, K.H., K.S. Watson, & T.W. Jambor. 1978. Free-play behaviors in preschool and kindergarten children. *Child Development* 49: 534–36.

Strom, R.D., ed. 1981. *Growing through play.* Monterey, CA: Brooks/Cole.

Sutton-Smith, B. 1986. The spirit of play. In *The young child at play. Reviews of research, vol. 4,* eds. G. Fein & M. Rivkin, 3–16. Washington, DC: NAEYC.

Van Hoorn, J., P. Nourot, B. Scales, & K. Alward. 1993. *Play at the center of the curriculum.* New York: Merrill.

Fourth-Grade Slump: The Cause and Cure

A new study reveals the impact of children's early childhood experience on their later achievement.

REBECCA A. MARCON

Parents, teachers, and administrators are often perplexed by what is often referred to as "fourth-grade slump." Why do so many bright, achieving children in the primary grades have difficulty making the transition to the upper elementary grades?

Although a number of ideas have been put forward, recent research suggests that the root of the difficulty lies in children's early childhood experiences, which influence how young children approach learning tasks. The impact is especially noticeable during the transition to fourth grade, which for many children is cognitively difficult because of increased expectations for independent thought, applications of previously learned concepts to new problems, and mastery of more complex skills and ideas. The transition can also be socially difficult because of increased expectations of maturity.

The latest results of an ongoing study in the District of Columbia Public Schools address this crucial transition period by comparing the outcomes of different models of early childhood education.

In the initial study, prompted by an unacceptably high first-grade retention rate, we set out in 1986–87 to examine the impact of different preschool models on the school success of inner-city, public school children. We studied the progress of four-year-olds enrolled in the District's prekindergarten or Head Start programs. The children were predominantly minority students (97 percent African American) and poor (76 percent qualified for subsidized lunch). More than two-thirds lived in single-parent families.

Three Early Childhood Models

A preliminary survey, based on classroom observations and teacher responses, identified three different preschool models operating in the D.C. school system:

- The *child-initiated* classrooms, called Model CI, had child-development-oriented teachers who allowed children to select the focus of their learning.
- The *academically directed* classrooms, or Model AD, had academically oriented teachers who preferred more teacher-directed instruction.
- The *middle-of-the-road* classrooms, called Model M, represented teaching beliefs and practices which fell between.

> **"Pushing children too soon into 'formalized academics' can actually backfire when children move into the later childhood grades where they are required to think more independently."**

Our initial findings showed that children enrolled in the more child-development-oriented Model CI actually mastered more basic skills than those in Model AD or Model M classrooms. Furthermore, the Model M compromise approach did not work for any of the four-year-olds. By the end of the preschool year, Model M children were significantly behind the others in language, social, and motor development, as well as overall adaptive functioning and mastery of basic skills.

In the second and third years of the study, Model M children remained behind their peers as they moved into kindergarten and first grade, where Model CI children continued to excel while Model AD children's social development declined, along with their mastery of first-grade reading and math objectives.

As a result of the initial three-year study, we now knew that previous, inappropriate early learning experiences in many of the District's early childhood programs clearly hindered children's progress in the preprimary and pri-

Rebecca A. Marcon is a developmental psychologist and associate professor of psychology at the University of North Florida in Jacksonville.

Chad J. Walker

mary years, and we had a clearer notion of the type of early childhood program that was needed.

Examining Fourth-Grade Transition

We continued to study the impact of early childhood experiences even as the District of Columbia system responded to the initial findings by instituting reforms in its early childhood programs. Having discovered ways to increase children's chances of making a successful transition from preschool to first grade, we now focused on the progress of the original study groups as they advanced through the primary grades.

The negative impact of overly academic early childhood programs on achievement and social development was clearly apparent by the fourth grade. Children who had attended Model AD prekindergarten programs were scoring noticeably lower in the fourth grade despite their adequate performance on third-grade standardized achievement tests. The Model AD children were also developmentally behind their peers and displayed notably higher levels of maladaptive behavior (*i.e.*, defiant behavior, anxiety, and distractibility).

As shown in *Figure 1*, children whose preschool experience was academically focused showed the greatest decline in school grades between third and fourth grades. At the same time, the long-term positive effects of a more active, child-initiated preschool experience showed up most clearly during this transition. Patterns of developmental change were more difficult to identify, although children with overly academic preschool experiences had not advanced as rapidly in social development by the fourth grade.

Figure 1

Changes in Scores from 3rd to 4th Grade

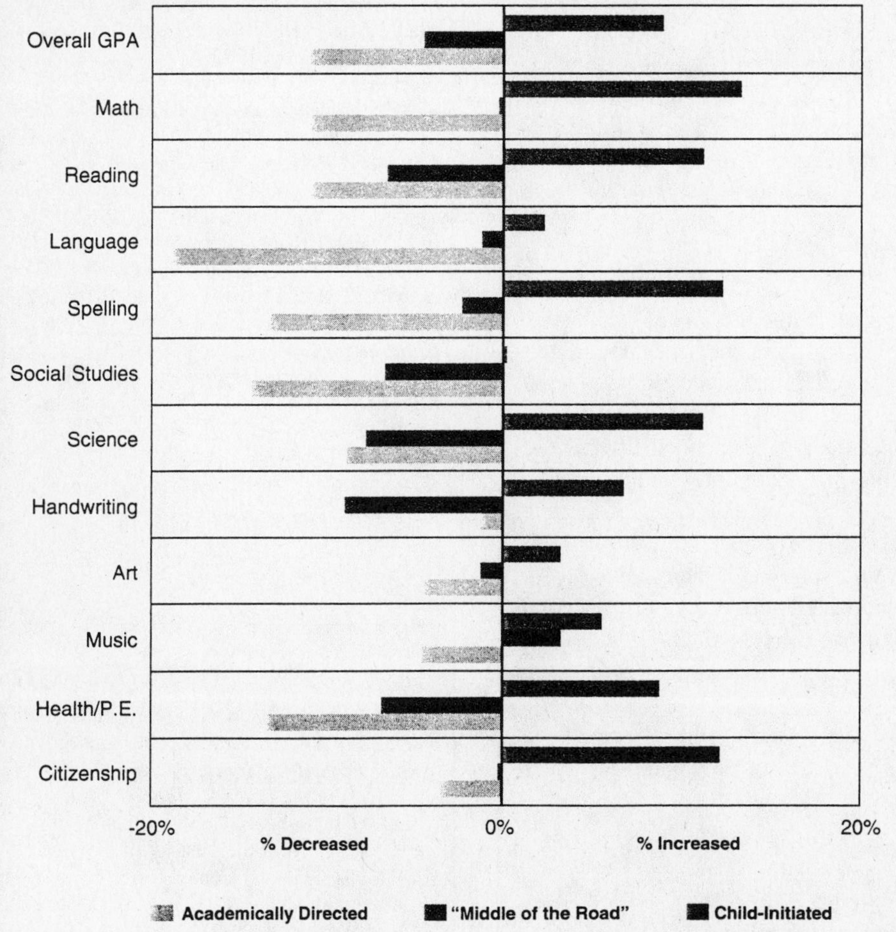

SOURCE: District of Columbia Public Schools

In comparing children's academic progress since first grade, the study found that while all children's grades were typically lower by fourth grade, the three-year drop in performance was especially disconcerting for Model AD children. Their overall grade-point average dropped 22 percent from first to fourth grades, compared to only 5 and 6 percent for Model CI and M children. More specifically, Model AD grades decreased by 36 percent in math, 32 percent in reading and language, 30 percent in spelling and social studies, 23 percent in science, and 16 percent in health and physical education.

Ending Fourth-Grade Slump

Our findings show that fourth-grade slump can be traced back to inappropriate early childhood learning experiences for many children. The findings indicate that preschool programs are most successful when they correspond to children's level of development and natural approach to learning, and that children's academic and developmental progress through the elementary grades is enhanced by active, child-initiated early learning experiences.

The study also shows that later progress is slowed for most children when formal learning experiences are introduced too early. Pushing children too soon into "formalized academics" can actually backfire when children move into the later childhood grades where they are required to think more independently. This is because teacher-directed early childhood approaches that tell young children what to do, when to do it, and how to do it curtail development of autonomy.

According to developmental authority Constance Kamii, such teacher-directed approaches produce passive students who wait to be told what to think and do next. Therefore, it is not surprising that children who lack the early foundations of autonomy—the root of critical thinking and effective choice making—find the transition to fourth grade difficult.

While the benefits of developmentally appropriate early childhood experiences may take a while to unfold, they become especially prominent by fourth grade, if not sooner. As we work to assure that all our children start school *ready to learn* by 2000, it is equally important that our schools be *ready to receive* these eager young learners. If we wish children to be independent and self-reliant, to choose wisely between options, and to think critically, our teaching styles and curricular focus must better reflect those desired outcomes. The early childhood years can either foster children's sense of autonomy or curtail it. As educators, the choice is ours. □

A Blueprint for Change

During the school year 1986–87, the District of Columbia Public Schools responded to a high first-grade retention rate by initiating a three-year study to evaluate and determine the impact of early learning programs on children's long-term school success. The resulting 1990 report concluded that children enrolled in child-centered classrooms, where developmentally appropriate practices were implemented, had a higher passing rate in first grade than their peers in academically-oriented programs.

The district also authorized a three-year follow-up study that compared the previously studied children as they progressed from the primary to the upper elementary grades. This study indicated that by the age of 9 students from academically-oriented programs were clearly behind.

Because the evidence showed that child-initiated early childhood programs were effective, our next step was to develop a pilot project based on continuous progress and performance assessment. We began by allowing seven schools to replace skill-oriented academic programs with child-initiated, integrated, thematic learning programs from prekindergarten to third grade. The program has been expanded to include about half of our elementary schools and will eventually include all pre-K through third grades.

The program is success-oriented, capitalizing on the interests and capabilities of students while considering individual learning rates and styles. Our decision to emphasize social, emotional, and cognitive development in the early learning years is based on a growing body of evidence supporting such practices for young children, as well as increasing awareness that early retention is detrimental to a child's academic success.

Early on, we realized the need for authentic assessment instruments that would accurately reflect actual learning experiences while providing information about a child's overall development—social, emotional, physical, aesthetic, and cognitive. Research led us to the Work Sampling System developed by Samuel Meisels and others at the University of Michigan. The system's three-pronged performance assessment approach, which we've adapted, uses developmental checklists, portfolios, and summary reports. Because it provides a comprehensive overview of children's developmental progress, the system is not only highly effective, but popular with many teachers, students, and parents.

Overall, we have been pleased with our new approach to early childhood education. Based on the findings of our studies, we feel our youngest students will now be better prepared for the academic challenges ahead.

Franklin L. Smith
Superintendent
District of Columbia Public Schools

References

Elkind, D. "In Defense of Early Childhood Education." *Principal* 65:5 (May 1986): 6–9.

Kamii, C. "One Intelligence Indivisible." *Phi Delta Kappan* 65 (January 1984): 410–415.

Marcon, R. "Differential Effects of Three Preschool Models on Inner-city 4-year-olds." *Early Childhood Research Quarterly* 7:4 (1992): 517–530.

Marcon, R. "Socio-emotional Versus Academic Emphasis: Impact on Kindergartners' Development and Achievement." *Early Child Development and Care* 96 (December 1993): 81–91.

Marcon, R. "Doing the Right Thing for Children: Linking Research and Policy Reform in the District of Columbia Public Schools." *Young Children* 50:1 (November 1994): 8–20.

Schweinhart, L. J.; Barnes, H. V.; Weikart, D. P. *Significant Benefits: The High/Scope Perry Preschool Study through Age 27*. Ypsilanti, Mich.: High/Scope Educational Research Foundation, 1993.

Schweinhart, L. J.; Weikart, D. P.; Larner, M. B. "Consequences of Three Preschool Curriculum Models through Age 15." *Early Childhood Research Quarterly* 1:1 (1986): 15–45.

Sykes, M. R. "Creating a Climate for Change in a Major Urban School System." *Young Children* 50:1 (November 1994): 4–7.

Woods, C. "Responsive Teaching: Creating Partnerships for Systemic Change." *Young Children* 50:1 (November 1994): 21–28.

Zigler, E. "Should Four-year-olds Be in School?" *Principal* 65:5 (May 1986): 10–14.

For Further Information

The full report on which this article is based, *Early Learning and Early Identification Follow-Up Study: Transition from the Early to the Later Childhood Grades 1990-93*, by Rebecca A. Marcon, is available for $14 from the District of Columbia Public Schools, Center for Systemic Educational Change, 415 12th Street, N.W., Washington, D.C. 20004; (202) 724-4099.

The American Lock-Step Graded School Organization

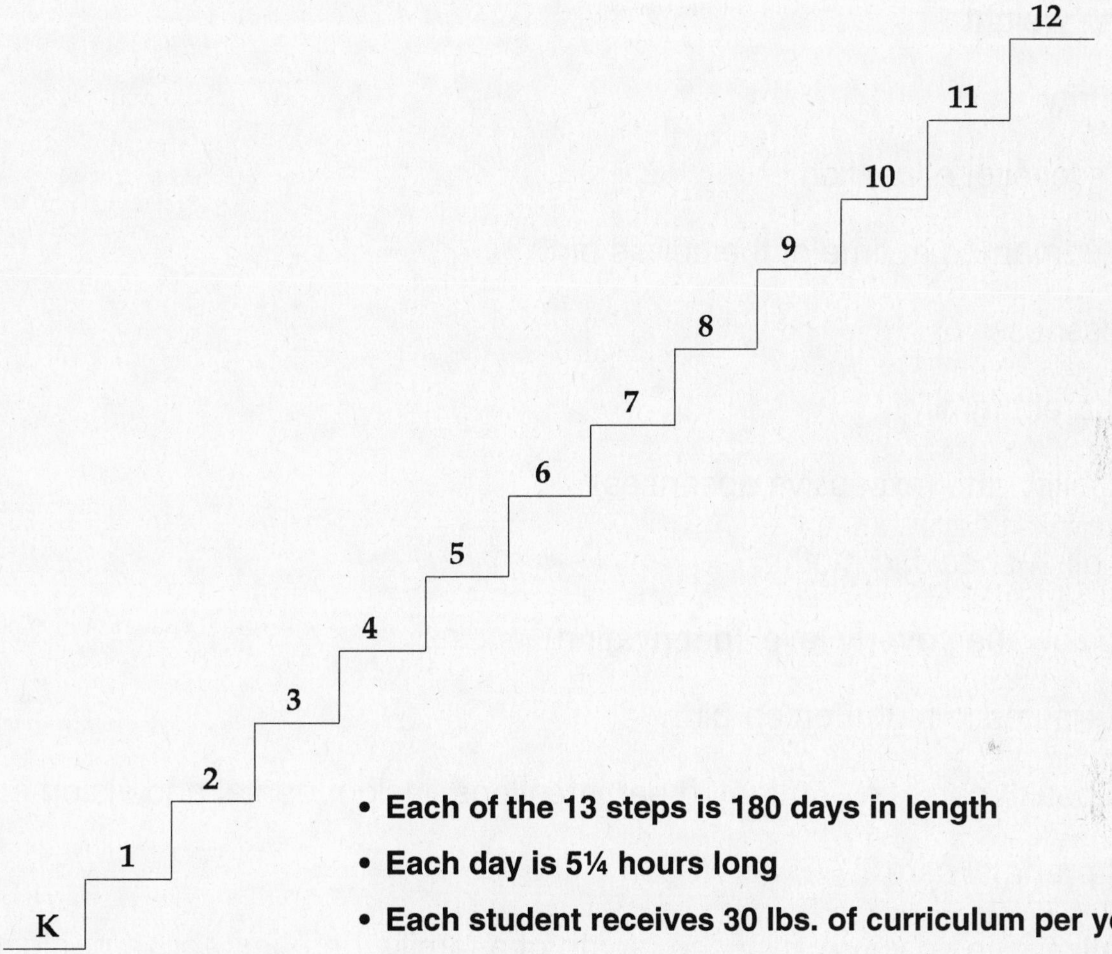

- **Each of the 13 steps is 180 days in length**
- **Each day is 5¼ hours long**
- **Each student receives 30 lbs. of curriculum per year**

Factors and circumstances that may influence developmental readiness

1. Chronological age at entrance
2. Gender
3. Low birth weight
4. Prematurity
5. Mother's level of education
6. Mother unmarried at time of the child's birth
7. Homelessness
8. Single parent family
9. High mobility rate (excessive absenses)
10. Non-English speaking mother
11. Living below the poverty level (deprivation)
12. Difficult/traumatic birth/Forcep birth
13. Lack of health care, i.e., untreated ear infections, lack of dental and vision care
14. Lack of prenatal care
15. Traumatized, i.e., divorce, violence, death of a family member, abuse/neglect
16. Smoking/alcohol/drugs prenatally
17. Lack of pre-school experience
18. Family in crisis
19. Malnutrition
20. Chemically injured, i.e., lead, pesticides, etc.

Note: Some factors are not considered to be a root cause of unreadiness in children, however they may exacerbate the condition

Top Five Family Risk Factors

1. Mother has less than a high school education

2. The mother speaks a language other than English as her main language

3. The family lives below the official poverty line

4. The mother was unmarried at the time of the child's birth

5. Only one parent is present in the home

NOTE:

- One half of today's preschoolers are affected by at least one of these risk factors and fifteen percent are affected by three or more of them

- Children with one or more of these characteristics may be educationally disadvantaged or "at-risk" of school failure

— *National Center for Education Statistics*

Readiness Factors Associated with Poverty

<u>Children living below the poverty threshold:</u>

1. Experience a higher family stress level
2. Lack health care
3. Live in unhealthy living conditions
4. Live in an unsafe neighborhood
5. Often are exposed to pollution
6. Have poor nutrition
7. Have few available resources for learning
8. Are four times as likely to be abused or neglected
9. Have inadequate clothing
10. Are more likely to be exposed to secondhand smoke
11. Are more likely to be exposed to an alcohol / drug environment
12. Are more likely to be placed in a poor quality day care situation
13. Are twice as likely to drop out of school
14. Have a higher rated juvenile delinquency
15. Are five to seven times more likely to be a pregnant teenager
16. Often have excessive absences
17. Have a higher incidence of giving birth to a low birth weight and/or premature baby
18. Have a family who is more likely to be highly transient
19. Are more likely to have excessive absences.

When Compared to Boys . . .

<u>Girls entering kindergarten are more likely to:</u>

- Hold a pencil correctly
- Button their clothes
- Write or draw rather than scribble
- Be able to identify more primary colors
- Count to 20 or beyond
- Write their own name
- Recognize more letters of the alphabet
- Have a longer attention span
- Fidget less
- Show an interest in reading
- Have speech understandable to a stranger
- Not stutter or stammer

AND

- Take the teacher's red pencil and go over and correct Skippy's work!

On-Time Bloomers Have More Assets

They:

seem to cope better emotionally

often are older and more mature

seem better able to focus and attend

seem to have the physical stamina to sustain a demanding school experience

often have a greater general knowledge base

seem better able to complete tasks

seem to have higher social abilities

have more school related accomplishments

Tend to have fewer school related difficulties

As decisions about preschool, kindergarten and first grade arise, the following reasons to give children extra time should be considered:

Family patterns of slow development — "late bloomers"

Prematurity or physical problems in early life

Immature motor development — awkwardness, poor motor skills, such as in catching or throwing a ball, drawing or cutting

Easy distractibility and short attention span

Difficulty with right-left hand or eye-hand coordination, such as in copying a circle or diamond

Lagging social development — difficulty taking turns, sharing, or playing. If the child is shunned by children her own age, take it seriously.

Each of these might be a reason to allow a child to mature another year before starting preschool, or to stay in preschool or kindergarten a year longer."

— T. Berry Brazelton, M.D., *Touchpoints*

Children who attend
preschool are more likely to:

Identify more primary colors
Recognize more letters
Recognize more numbers
Be able to count higher
Write his/her own name
Write or draw rather than scribble
Transition into kindergarten more easily
Be able to follow directions
Understand school routine
Have higher socialization skills

AND

Be overall more ready to
participate successfully in school

Factors That Influence Developmental Diversity

by James K. Uphoff, Ed.D.
College of Education and Human Services Wright State University
Dayton, OH 45435 • (513) 873-3231

The school bells ring in late summer and thousands of children march through the school house doors without anyone having given any thought as to whether or not these children are ready — physically, socially, emotionally, academically — for the curriculum awaiting them. This document aims to provide you, the parent, with a number of major elements which should be considered as you make this vital decision. These same considerations are also relevant when parents are thinking about giving their child the *gift of time,* another year in the current grade in order to grow and mature, or a year in a readiness, K or a transition K-1 program. Too often parents and school officials alike confuse verbal brightness with readiness for school. *Being bright and being ready for school are not the same thing!* An inappropriate start in school too often "tarnishes" that brightness.

Today's K-3 curriculum has been pushed down by our American "faster is better" culture to the point that what is often found in today's kindergarten was found in late first or early second grade just three decades ago! Many schools are trying to change from the "sit-still, paper-pencil" approach of the present to a more active, involved, manipulative curriculum which enables young children to learn best. However, until this latter learning environment is available for your child, you must consider whether or not the child is ready. The material which follows is presented to help you make this very tough decision!

Each of the following factors indicates a potential for problems. The more of these factors which apply to an individual child, the more likely he/she is to encounter difficulty — academically, socially, emotionally, and/or physically — and each of these areas is crucial to a well-rounded human being. No one factor should be the only basis for making a decision. Look at all of the factors, then decide.

Readiness Factors

Chronological Age at School Entrance: My own research and that of many others indicates that children who are less than five and one-half years of age at the time of school entrance into kindergarten are much more likely to encounter problems. This would put the date at about March 25th for many schools. The younger the child is, the more likely the current academic paper/pencil kindergarten curriculum is inappropriate.

Problems at Birth: When labor lasts a long time or is less than four hours; or when labor is unusually difficult, the child is more likely to experience problems. Long labor too often results in reduced oxygen and/or nourishment for the child just before birth. Some studies have found birth trauma to be associated with later emotional problems including, in the extreme, suicidal tendencies.

Early General Health & Nutrition: Poor nutrition in the pre-school years puts the child at greater risk in terms of school success. The child who experiences many serious ear infections during these years has been found to have more difficulty in learning to read. Allergies, asthma, and other similar problems can also inhibit such learning. Any type of illness or problem which results in a passive child — in bed or just "being very quiet" day after day — is more likely to result in a physically delayed development. Lack of body and muscle control can be a major problem for learners.

Family Status: Any act which lessens the stability of the child's family security is a problem and the closer such acts/events occur to the start of school, the more likely that start is to be a negative one. Such destabilizers as the following should be considered.

1. **Death** of anyone close to the child. This includes family, friends, neighbors, pets, etc.
2. **Moves** from one house/apartment to another even though the adults may see it as a positive relocation—more space, own bedroom for child, etc. The child may miss friends, neighbors, the dog next door, etc.
3. **Separation** from parents or close family members whether by jobs, military duty, divorce, prison, remarriage, moves, etc., can create problems for child in early school experiences.
4. **Birth of a Sibling** or the addition of new step-family members can be very upsetting.

Birth Order: If the gap between child #1 and #2 is less than three years, then #2 is more likely to have problems in school. When there are more than 3 children in a family, the baby of the family (last born) often experiences less independence and initiative. There are exceptions to these factors as with the others, but they remain as predictors, never-the-less.

Low Birth Weight: A premature child with low weight often experiences significant delays in many aspects of his/her development.

Sex: Boys are about one month behind girls in physiological development at birth; about 6 months behind at age 5; and about 24 months behind girls at age 11-12. (Some contend that we males never catch up!) Boys need extra time more than girls, but research shows that girls actually benefit from it more. Their eyes, motor skills, etc., etc., are ahead by nature, and when given time become even "aheader"! Boys fail far more often than do girls and have many more school problems than do girls.

Vision: Being able to see clearly does *not* mean that a child's vision is ready for school work. It is not until age 8 that 90% of children have sufficient eye-muscle development to do *with ease* what reading demands of the eyes. The younger the child is, the more likely he/she does *not* have all of the vision development required. For example, many children have problems with focusing. Their eyes work like a zoom lens on a projector zooming in and out until a sharp focus is obtained. Much time can be spent in this process and much is missed while focusing is taking place. Other eye problems include the muscle ability to maintain focus and smooth movement from left to right, lazy eye, and midline problems.

Memory Level: If a child has difficulty remembering such common items as prayers, commercials, home address/telephone number, etc., then the child may well experience problems with the typical primary grade curriculum. Many times memory success is associated with one's ability to concentrate—attention span, thus this factor is related to the next one.

Attention Span: Research has clearly shown a strong connection between the amount of time a child spends working on skill content (three Rs) and the achievement level reached. The child who is easily distracted and finds it difficult to focus attention for 10-15 minutes at a time on a single activity is also a child who is probably going to experience much frustration in school. Discipline problems are likely, as are academic ones. Sitting still is very difficult for the typical 5½- to 6½-year-old child and this normal physiological condition is at great odds with the typical sit still/paper-pencil curriculum imposed after Sputnik went up over 30 years ago!

Social Skills: The child with delayed social development is often reluctant to leave the security of a known situation (home/sitter/preschool/etc.). This child is very hesitant about mixing with other children, is passive, and slow to become involved. Noninvolvement is often associated with lower learning levels. Tears, urinary "accidents," morning tummy aches, a return to thumb sucking, etc., are all signals of such a delay. Some research has found correlations between short labor deliveries and problems such as these.

Speaking Skills: The ability of a child to communicate clearly is closely related to maturation. In order to pronounce sounds distinctly and correctly, muscle control is essential. Hearing must also be of good quality and this has often been reduced by early ear infections, allergies, etc. Inappropriate speech patterns (baby talk) and/or incorrect articulation (an "r" sounds like a "w") are major concern signals.

Reading Interest: If a child does not like to be read to, has little desire to watch a TV story all the way through, or rarely picks up a book to read to him/herself, then the odds are high that this child is not ready for the curriculum of the typical kindergarten. Few of us do well those things in which we are not yet interested and our children are no different!

Small Motor Skills: The ability to cut, draw, paste, and manipulate pencils, colors, etc., are very important in today's pushed-down kindergarten. The child who has some difficulty with these, uses an awkward grip on the pencil (ice-pick, one or no fingertips on the pencil, etc.), and/or has trouble holding small cards in the hand during a game is a candidate for frustrations. Eye/hand coordination is vital for a high degree of success.

Large Motor Skills: It is typical for a 5- to 6-year-old child to "trip over a piece of string," yet the typical curriculum assumes major control over one's body movements. Ability to skip, jump on one foot at a time, walk a balance beam, hop, jump from a standing position, etc., is an ability which research has found to be related to overall success with some particular skills tested just before starting school predicting reading success levels in 5th and 8th grades!

Summary

"Is my child ready for school?" is a major question for parents to answer. This small document merely highlights some of the key factors one should consider when making such a decision. I urge all schools to adopt a thorough assessment procedure which checks all of these factors so as to provide parents with more information upon which to base their decisions.

A child's self-concept needs to be positive. He/she should see school as a good place to be, a place where he/she finds success and support. Giving the child the best start in school demands that the parent and school work together to be sure that the curriculum available will enable this child to find success and positive experiences. Parents can also provide support for the school in its efforts to reduce the amount of paper work in the early grades. Working together, the home and the school can help each child establish a firm foundation for a lifetime of learning.

For more information on transition and readiness programs, see Dr. Uphoff's book Real Facts from Real Schools, *published by Programs for Education, 1994.*

The book provides a historical perspective on the development of readiness and transition programs, presents an in-depth look at the major issues raised by attacks on such programs, and summarizes more than three dozen research studies.

The chronologically younger children in any grade are far more likely than the older children in that grade to:

- have failed a grade
- become dropouts
- be referred for testing for special services and special education
- be diagnosed as Learning Disabled
- be sent to the principal's office for discipline problems even when in high school
- be receiving various types of counseling services
- be receiving lower grades than their ability scores would indicate as reasonable
- be behind their grade peers in athletic skill level
- be chosen less frequently for leadership roles by peers or adults
- be in special service programs such as Title I
- be in speech therapy programs
- be slower in social development
- rank lower in their graduating class
- be a suicide victim
- be more of a follower than a leader
- be less attentive in class
- earn lower grades
- score lower on achievement tests

School Readiness and Transition Programs
Real Facts From Real Schools
by James K. Uphoff, Ed.D.

Ways to Protect All Children from Developmentally Inappropriate School Practices

- Eliminate board copying
- Teach skills in context
- Beware of time-on-task practices
- Eliminate the following bell curve practices:
  - Long term-tracking by ability
  - Unfair competition
  - Comparative reporting
  - Promotion/social promotion/grade skipping/academic retention; replace with continuous progress practices
- Avoid ditto sheets and workbooks as a classroom management tool
- Eliminate the "seating chart" mentality
- Eliminate discipline programs that are punitive in nature
- Eliminate group standardized testing before grade four
- Postpone teaching those concepts that are presented too early in the curriculum, i.e., greater than/less than, the missing addend, etc.

How Teachers Can Help Parents Help Their Children Succeed in School

- Form a parent/teacher partnership
- Involve parents in setting goals for their children
- Inform parents as to what most children should know and be able to do at each grade/level/program
- Teach parents strategies to teach their own child
- Sponsor traveling back packs that provide parents with instructional resource materials
- Encourage parents to seek outside private tutoring services (Caution: This advice may be against school board policy in some school systems)
- Homework requirements should be mutually agreed on between each individual home and school
- Make home visits!

Classroom-Tested Ideas, Strategies and Advice to Help Late Bloomers

- Become familiar with the ages and stages of child development. Use this knowledge as a base line for matching curriculum and instruction to the child
- Utilize cooperative learning groups as much as possible
- Keep late bloomers in close proximity to the teacher
- Provide carrels for those children who are visually distracted
- Provide noise-suppressing headsets for those children who are auditorily distracted
- Try different colored overlays as a way to help bring clarity to printed material
- Teach to a child's strength first and then teach to his/her weakness
- Utilize book recordings
- Use learning centers to support thematic instruction
- Utilize computers to engage and motivate all children
- Try contract teaching as a strategy to assure task completion
- Provide pencil grips and fat pencils to children who have difficulty with fine motor skills
- Revise grade-level expectations to where the child is vs. where he ought to be
- Utilize flexible and creative grouping practices, i.e. ability grouping, grouping by developmental level, skills attainment, hobby, interest area, etc.
- Create an "unofficial I.E.P." for the "tweeners"
- Use calculators!
- Make provisions for children to have extended visits to the previous year's teacher
- Try speaking phones

Suggested Ways School Systems Can Accommodate the Wide Range of Differently-Ready Children

- Reduce and maintain small class size
- Provide an additional recess when appropriate
- Encourage community volunteers in the classroom
- Make counseling services available
- Grant students "Honorary membership status" in special-needs tutoring situations
- Make children "special friends of Title I" and allow them to be included unofficially in Title I programs
- Implement multiage and looping classrooms with a staggered classroom configuration
- Initiate a summer school program
- Provide all day kindergarten programs
- Create a pod system where children stay with a team of teachers in a family setting for several years
- Make instructional materials available to parents along with appropriate teaching strategies
- Provide half steps or transition grades/programs
- Sponsor workshops on parenting and child development

Jim Grant / Bob Johnson

Children Progress Through School on a Broken Front

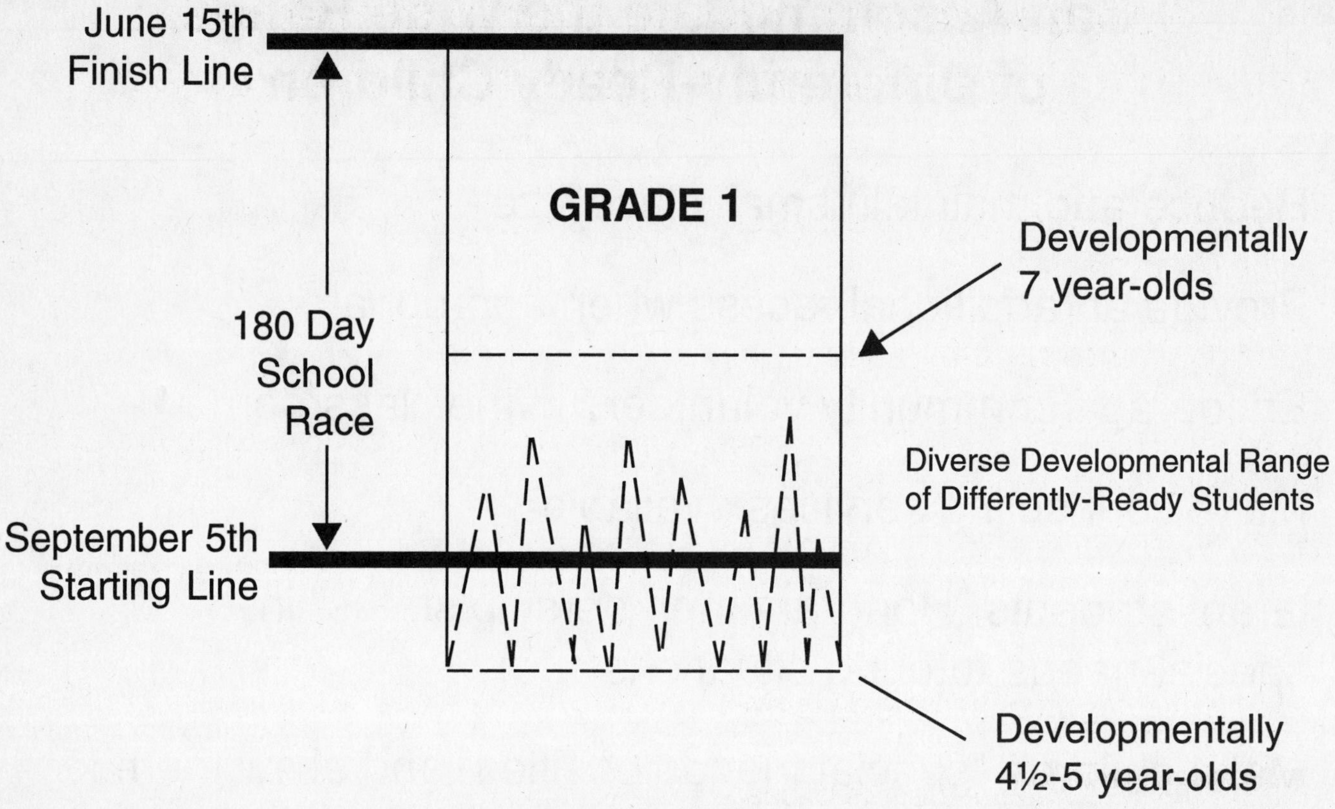

Children Enter School on a Broken Front

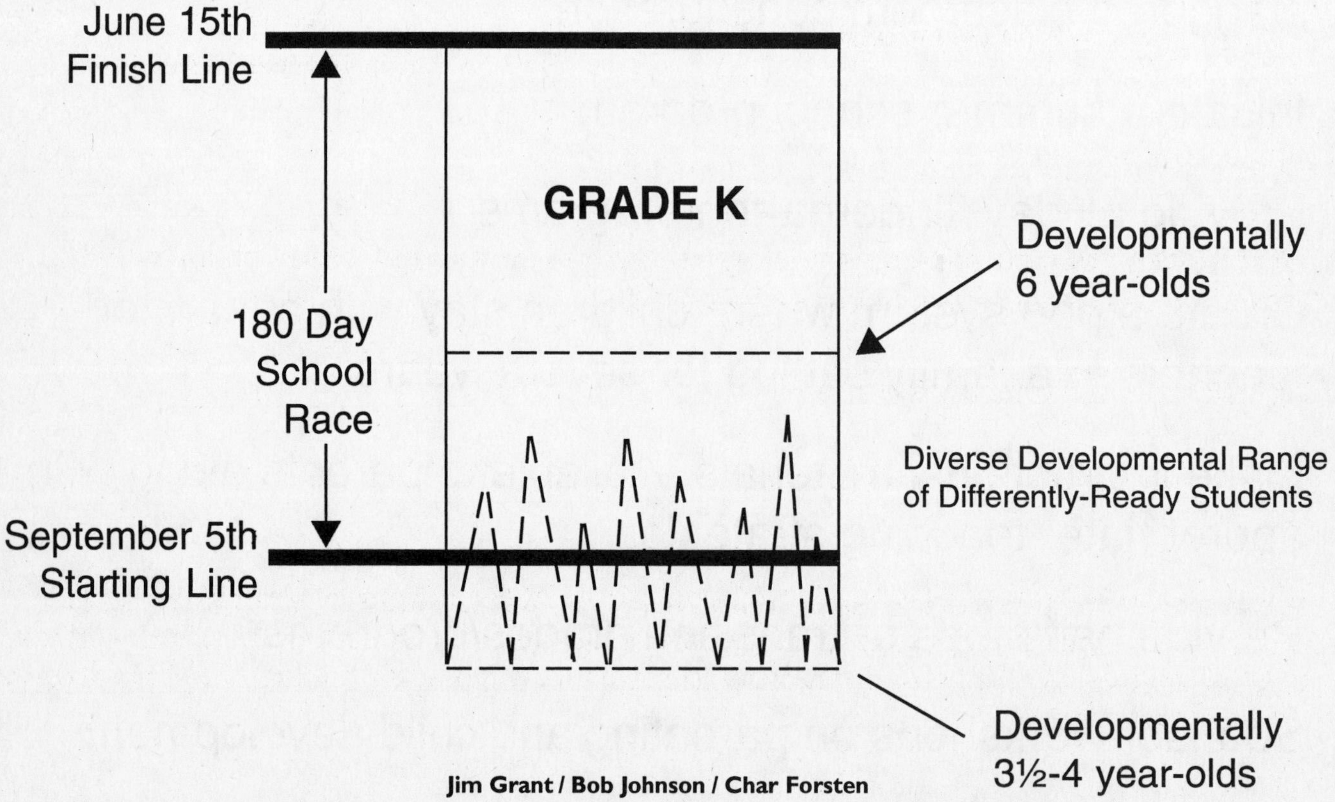

LOOK BEFORE YOU LEAP!

Some students may be placed at-risk when remaining in the same grade for a second year

1. A student whose parent(s) are opposed to an additional year of time through grade level retention

2. An unmotivated student

3. An emotionally disturbed student (Note: Some students exhibit emotional problems from being in over their heads.)

4. A student with a behavior disorder (Note: Some students exhibit behavior problems as a result of being in over their heads)

5. Some children who are raised in poverty

6. A student who has a history of excessive absenteeism

7. A student who is below average in ability (slower learners)

8. A student who is already one year older than his/her peers

9. A student who is considered too "street wise" for his/her age

10. A student who has a multitude of complex problems

11. A child with very low self-esteem (Note: In many, if not in most, cases students in the wrong grade exhibit signs of low self-esteem)

12. A child from a highly transient family

13. Some linguistically different students

Notes: Some of these students may show some level of improvement when retained as a result of the stress of being in the wrong grade being removed. These are cautions and not a rigid list of students to eliminate from consideration for an extra year of learning time through grade level retention.

Students Who Most Likely Will Benefit From Grade Level Expansion

1. A child whose parent(s) strongly support having their child remain in the same grade or program another year

2. A student who is chronologically too young for his/her present grade level placement

3. A developmentally young child who has been inadvertently assigned to the wrong grade or program

4. A student who is in the average or above average ability range

5. A student who has indicated he/she wants to remain in the same grade or program another year

6. A student who has never had an extra year of time in any form and is <u>not</u> already one year older than his/her classmates

7. A child who doesn't appear to have learning problems or other extenuating circumstances other than being a late bloomer

8. A student with good school attendance

9. A student who is not highly transient

10. A child who is physically small for his/her age

Common Sense Tips to Make an Informed Grade Level Retention Decision for Individual Students

1. Always present parents with multiple options and strategies from which to choose. Children with very different beginnings need very different beginnings!

2. Always explore alternatives to grade level retention first. Think of grade level retention as the intervention strategy of last resort

3. Parent(s) should never be pressured to retain a child against their wishes. Forced retentions simply do not work.

4. Don't cause students to be two years older than their classmates. Students two or more years overage are most likely to drop out of school.

5. Always make high stakes decisions with an ad hoc child study team, i.e., parents, teacher, principal, counselor, etc.

6. Don't substitute grade level retention in place of special education intervention. They are two very different interventions.

7. Do not make a grade level retention decision based on a single factor, i.e., standardized tests, chronological age, reading level, etc.

8. If a student needs more time in a grade, do it during the early childhood years

9. Don't hesitate to change a child's placement mid-year (Grade re-placement)

10. Only retain an upper grade student if you have his/her unconditional support

11. Provide retained students remedial and support services when needed. Many developmentally young students also have learning problems

12. When possible, allow the child to stay with the same teacher a second year. Take the child's feelings into account when making this decision

13. Parents must be allowed the right to cast the deciding vote to retain or not to retain their child

14. Create and adopt flexible grade level retention guidelines versus a rigid grade level retention policy. A <u>no retention policy</u> is an extremist position leaving no room to make case by case individual decisions. Such an absolute position denies the existence of students placed in the wrong grade

15. Remember, grade level retention research is reported as an average of a group. An individual retention is a very personal one child, one family at a time decision, and is NOT a group activity

16. Bear in mind that keeping students in a grade or program another year without changing the curriculum and instruction will most likely produce dismal results

17. Don't overstate the benefits of retention. Be modest in your claims.

18. Remember, <u>people stigmatize people</u> (A stigma is an adult "gift" to children!)

19. The social promotion fad of recent years is not without consequences, and generally creates a host of other problems.

20. Taking an extra year of learning time in a transition class is <u>not</u> the same experience as grade level retention. This is <u>not</u> "another form of retention!"

21. Remaining an extra year in a multiage continuous progress classroom is <u>not</u> considered grade level retention. This also is <u>not</u> "another form of retention!"

22. <u>All students will come to school ready to learn by the year 2000</u>. A noble goal that is very unlikely to happen. Until this goal is met it is likely that different students will need different amounts of learning time to participate successfully in school.

Range of Learners

Learning Disabled	Title I	"Gray-Area" Children	Non-labeled Learners	Gifted & Talented
		Children with "Invisible" Disabilities		

Promotion/Retention

Promotion and retention policies are stated in writing, disseminated to all concerned, and followed

These policies take into account such factors as age, achievement, school adjustment, parental support, alternative programs, and teacher recommendations.

The procedures for retention are clearly specified.

Preventive or remedial programs are provided as soon as their need becomes evident.

Standards for Quality Elementary and Middle Schools

4-Year-Olds

Signs and Signals of Preschool Stress

Child's Name ______________________________ Birthdate ______________

***At Home* – A 4-year-old suffering from preschool-related stress may:**

		Often	Never	Rare
1.	not want to leave Mom/Dad			
2.	hide shoes so as not to have to go to preschool			
3.	complain about stomachaches or headaches			
4.	have bathroom "accidents"			
5.	come home exhausted			
6.	have nightmares			

***At Preschool* – A 4-year-old experiencing the stress of being in the wrong group or program may:**

1.	have difficulty separating from Mom/Dad			
2.	cling to the teacher, showing a high degree of dependency			
3.	not participate in "cooperative" play — instead, his or her play is "isolated" (child plays alone) or "parallel" (playing next to other children but not with them)			
4.	not like the other children			
5.	show "young" fine-motor coordination while cutting, gluing, drawing, etc.			
6.	demonstrate a lack of awareness of appropriate behavior in the "classroom"			
7.	not catch on to "classroom" routines, which more mature classmates adapt to easily			
8.	find it difficult to select activities and stick with them			
9.	become "outspoken" and/or want to leave when asked to perform a task that is too difficult			

***In General* – A 4-year-old who is under excessive amount of stress at preschool may:**

1.	cry easily			
2.	lack self-control or self-discipline (biting, hitting and kicking)			
3.	appear to be "shy"			
4.	revert to thumbsucking, nail biting or "baby talk"			
5.	become aggressive during games and other activities involving the taking of turns or sharing			

Note: All children display some stress signs at times. Severe stress is indicated when a child consistently displays several stress signs over an extended period of time.

5-Year-Olds

Signs and Signals of School Stress

Child's Name ______________________________ Birthdate ______________

At Home – **How often does this 5-year-old child:**

		Often	Never	Rarely
1.	not want to leave Mom/Dad			
2.	not want to go to school			
3.	suffer from stomach aches or headaches, particularly in the morning before school			
4.	dislike school or complain that school is "dumb"			
5.	complain that the teacher does not allow enough time to finish his or her school work			
6.	need to rest, but resist taking a nap			
7.	revert to bedwetting			

At School – **How often does this 5-year-old child:**

1.	show little interest in kindergarten "academics"			
2.	ask if it's time to go home			
3.	seem unable to hold scissors as directed by the teacher			
4.	worry that Mom/Dad will forget to pick him or her up after school			
5.	have a difficult time following the daily routine			
6.	talk incessantly			
7.	complain that school work is "too hard" ("I can't do it,") or "too easy" ("It's so easy I'm not going to do it," or "too boring")			
8.	interrupt the teacher constantly			
9.	seem unable to shift easily from one task to the next			
10.	seem overly restless during class and frequently in motion when supposed to be working at a task			

In General – **How often does this 5-year-old child:**

1.	become withdrawn			
2.	revert to thumbsucking or infantile speech			
3.	compare herself negatively to other children ("They can do it, but I can't")			
4.	complain that she has no friends			
5.	cry easily and frequently			
6.	make up stories			
7.	bite his or her nails			
8.	seem depressed			

Note: All children display some stress signs at times. Severe stress is indicated when a child consistently displays several stress signs over an extended period of time.

6-Year-Olds

Signs and Signals of School Stress

Child's Name______________________________ Birthdate______________

At Home – **How often does this 6-year-old child:**

		Never	Rarely	Ofte
1.	complain of before-school stomach aches			
2.	revert to bed-wetting			
3.	behave in a manner that seems out of character to the parent			
4.	ask to stay at home			

At School – **How often does this 6-year-old child:**

		Never	Rarely	Ofte
1.	want to play with 5-year-olds			
2.	want to play with toys during class time			
3.	choose recess, gym and music as favorite subjects			
4.	feel overwhelmed by the size and activity level in the lunchroom			
5.	have a high rate of absenteeism			
6.	try to take frequent "in-house field trips" to the pencil sharpener, bathroom, school nurse, custodian, etc.			
7.	mark papers randomly			
8.	"act out" on the playground			
9.	reverse, invert, substitute, or omit letters and numbers when reading and/or writing (this is also not unusual for properly placed students either			
10.	complain about being bored with school work, when in reality he or she cannot do the work			
11.	have a short attention span — unable to stay focused on a twenty minute reading lesson			
12.	have difficulty understanding the teacher's instructions			

In General – **How often does this 6-year-old child:**

		Never	Rarely	Ofte
1.	cry easily or frequently			
2.	tire quickly			
3.	need constant reassurance and praise			
4.	become withdrawn and shy			
5.	develop a nervous tic — a twitching eye, a nervous cough, frequent clearing of the throat or twirling of hair			
6.	return to thumbsucking			
7.	lie or "adjust the truth" about school			
8.	revert to soiling his or her pants			
9.	make restless body movements, such as rocking in a chair, jiggling legs, etc.			
10.	dawdle			
11.	seem depressed			
12.	feel harried / hurried			

7-Year-Olds

Signs and Signals of School Stress

Child's Name____ Birthdate________________

***At Home* – A 7-year-old suffering from school-related stress may:**

		Never	Rarely	Often
1.	develop a psychosomatic illness such as a stomach ache, a headache, a sore leg, a limp, "a temp", etc.			
2.	wet the bed or soil his/her pants			
3.	develop a well-founded fear of going on to third grade			
4.	frequently ask to stay at home			

***At School* – A 7-year-old experiencing the stress of being in the wrong grade or program may:**

		Never	Rarely	Often
1.	prefer to play with younger children			
2.	constantly erase his or her work (many 7-year-olds do a great deal of erasing)			
3.	try to create diversions from the work at hand			
4.	frequently be absent			
5.	act agressively on the playground			
6.	develop poor work habits, such as ripping up papers, losing papers, keeping a messy desk			
7.	have difficulty staying on task or lesson			
8.	revert, invert, substitute or omit letters and numbers when reading and/or writing			
9.	feel badgered about reading			
10.	be "consistently inconsistent" about work			
11.	focus exclusively on one subject, such as math and have no interest in other subjects			

***In General* – A 7-year-old who is under an excessive amount of stress at school may:**

		Never	Rarely	Often
1.	cry easily			
2.	"stretch" the truth			
3.	withdraw			
4.	develop a nervous tic — a twitching eye, a nervous cough, frequent clearing of the throat or twirling of hair, etc.			
5.	pull out his or her hair			
6.	seem depressed			
7.	complain about "everything"			

Note: All children display some stress signs at times. Severe stress is indicated when a child consistently displays several stress signs over an extended period of time.

Excerpted from "I Hate School! Revised and Updated for the 1990's Some Common Sense Answers for Educators & Parents Who Want To Know Why & What To Do About It" by Jim Grant. © 1994 Modern Learning Press, Rosemont, NJ 08556

8-Year-Olds

Signs and Signals of School Stress

Child's Name______________________________________ Birthdate__________

***At Home* – An 8-year-old suffering from school-related stress may:**

	Never	Rarely	Of
1. complain about "too much" school work			
2. pick on siblings			
3. develop a psychosomatic illness such as a stomach ache, a headache, a sore leg, a limp, "a temp", etc.			
4. be difficult to direct			

***At School* – An 8-year-old experiencing the stress of being in the wrong grade or program may:**

1. prefer to play with younger children			
2. dislike certain subjects (which means she may know she's behind and doesn't know how to do the work)			
3. write laboriously and find cursive writing extremely difficult			
4. feel overwhelmed by the volume of work			
5. seem incapable of working independently			
6. ask for permission to visit previous grade			
7. frequently say, "My old teacher did it this way"			
8. find that even a reasonable amount of copying from the chalkboard is extremely difficult			
9. be unable to memorize the multiplication tables			
10. habitually lose or destroy papers			
11. find shifting to hardcover textbooks extremely difficult			

***In General* – An 8-year-old who is under an excessive amount of stress at school may:**

1. cherish toys and make them more important during class time than is appropriate for his or her age			
2. develop a nervous tic — a twitching eye, a nervous cough, frequent clearing of the throat or twirling of hair, etc.			
3. not seem to fit into his or her own peer group			
4. take out frustrations on other children during play			
5. be picked on or rejected by peers, and called names such as "dumb," "stupid," "airhead," etc.			
6. have difficulty learning to tell time and prefer to wear a digital watch			
7. chew on pencils, buttons, collars, or whatever is handy			
8. find change threatening and have difficulty handling new situations			

Note: All children display some stress signs at times. Severe stress is indicated when a child consistently displays several stress signs over an extended period of time.

9-Year-Olds

Signs and Signals of School Stress

Child's Name____ Birthdate_______________

***At Home* – A 9-year-old suffering from school-related stress may:**

	Never	Rarely	Often
1. demand excessive assistance with homework, thus causing family tension			
2. express fear about going on to the next grade			

***At School* – A 9-year-old experiencing the stress of being in the wrong grade or program may:**

1. prefer to play with younger children			
2. often mix manuscript and cursive writing (some mixing is normal)			
3. observe what is happening elsewhere in the classroom, rather than focusing on the work at hand			
4. complete only parts of assignments			
5. look for excuses to leave the classroom ("May I go to the lunch room and find out what's on the menu?")			
6. be the last one chosen for team games and sports			
7. need to be taught the same concepts again and again — for example, he or she may need the rules of division, capitalization, and punctuation repeated frequently, and then will forget them again over the weekend or during a vacation period			
8. be unable to memorize the multiplication and/or division tables, and so need to keep sneaking peeks at the charts			
9. constantly break pencils, necessitating extra trips to the pencil sharpener			
10. be unable to locate pencils, pens, papers and book in his/her own desk			
11. forget how to "set up" a paper with name, date, subject and margins			
12. copy another child's work when under extreme pressure			
13. "trail" the teacher around the classroom			

***In General* – A 9-year-old who is under an excessive amount of stress at school may:**

1. need an abundance of supervision and reassurance			
2. not work well independently			
3. develop a preoccupation with "being right"			
4. procrastinate and avoid work			
5. daydream frequently			
6. develop a nervous tic — a twitching eye, a nervous cough, frequent clearing of the throat or twirling of hair			
7. seem depressed			

Note: All children display some stress signs at times. Severe stress is indicated when a child consistently displays several stress signs over an extended period of time.

Excerpted from "I Hate School! Revised and Updated for the 1990's Some Common Sense Answers for Educators & Parents Who Want To Know Why & What To Do About It" by Jim Grant. © 1994 Modern Learning Press, Rosemont, NJ 08556

BUILDING towards Multiage

BY DEBBY LAWSON AND ANNA WILLIAMS

I had been searching for better educational practices to help children develop life-long learning skills. After listening to principals discuss their desire to restructure their schools using multiage classrooms, and after reading about multiage groupings, I decided to attend the "First Impressions" Conference in Austin, Texas, in the winter of 1994.

Participants at the conference received a copy of *First Impressions: Report of the Task Force on Early Childhood and Elementary Education in Texas.* This report described developmentally appropriate practices and recommended mixed-age, heterogeneous classes as one of the best ways to develop each student's potential. My school's contingency attended on Saturday; I was so intrigued by the presentations that I returned on Sunday.

The presenters at the conference were from schools that had reorganized into multiage classes. They had read, researched and prepared themselves to structure their schools to present the best possible education for all children.

I knew I wanted to improve my educational practices, and now I had a direction. After re-reading material from the conference, I shared the ideas with Anna, my teaching partner, knowing she would share my interest and excitement. Together we had already implemented theme-based integrated teaching, and had founds ways to combine our classes for cooperative groups and centers.

Throughout the spring, we re-searched and visited schools I had heard about during the conference. We soon knew multiage was the way we wanted to teach.

At this time, the administration decided our primary school was too crowded and made the decision to move all eight second grades to the elementary school. This move put our idea of organizing a multiage classroom on hold.

However, the new elementary school was also short of room, so when we proposed a team-teaching situation in a 1½ classroom space, our principal agreed, feeling that this team-teaching experience would help prepare us for multiage teaching in the future.

—Debby Lawson

The mission of early childhood and elementary education is to nurture the intellectual, emotional, social, and physical growth of all children. Our responsibility, as parents and educators, community members and citizens, is to create developmentally appropriate educational settings that prepare all children for success in school and active participation in the civic, economic, and cultural lives of their communities.

— *First Impressions: Report of the Task Force on Early Childhood and Elementary Education;* Texas Education Agency

Now, the work and excitement began in preparation for our new team-taught second-grade classroom. We read, planned, and visited schools. We structured our classroom around twelve centers and collected theme-based, developmentally appropriate activities for each. In order to make the students responsible for their own learning at the centers, folders for each student included a sheet listing centers for that theme, a space to show dates of completion and a place to write short notes about their work. Teachers would check the center folders periodically, giving rubric grades, writing notes of encouragement and holding conferences as needed.

During the year of team teaching, we constantly evaluated what was and was not working with our class, and made changes accordingly. We began to present choices within centers, and found that our learners inevitably chose the most challenging tasks that they were capable of completing. We observed significant improvement in reading, research skills, and cooperative group work, as well as a reduction in discipline problems. The class, named Wil-son Village by the students (by combining our last names) developed a strong sense of community.

Throughout the year, we read constantly about multiage classrooms. In the winter, we attended a two-day multiage conference in Austin. Not only were the workshops invaluable, but the workbook *Staying Focused on the Children* has remained an inestimable resource. All multiage strategies we tried had good results when used with our double class of second graders.

About the middle of May, administrators decided that we could teach a multiage classroom in the fall of '95. This would enable the primary school to create a 1-2 classroom and return two second grade classes to that campus. We welcomed the chance, but realized we still had a lot of work and learning to do. We knew our team teaching experience and our past experience of teaching both first and second grade were going to be invaluable.

Unfortunately, the end of May is not the time to recruit parents of first graders to enter an experimental situation. The few who visited our classroom during the last two days of school, however, did sign their children up to participate.

During the summer, we continued reading and planning. Our ultimate visit to the ACT Academy, a year-round multiage K-12 school in McKinney, Texas, gave us outstanding ideas. Their extensive time for inservice and planning, as well as a wealth of resources, set an example impossible for us to fully implement. But observing their use of Reading and Writing Workshop, rubrics, poem-of-the-week lessons, and room space were valuable tools for our planning.

To prepare ourselves for first graders, we traded district-adopted supplies and began to modify centers and learning expectations to fit a broader range of students. We also looked at the Texas Essential Elements for both grade levels and began to work on themes that would enable us to meet both grade levels' expectations.

We chose a linking theme for the year of "Round as a ..." We began our theme with a second-grade science unit on bubbles. We expanded the theme by pulling in all the round cookie and pancake stories in the first-grade reading anthology.

Being the only multiage classroom in the school, and having the only first graders in the school, was a true challenge. We had to choose themes that would work for first graders, but would allow us to participate in schoolwide second-grade activities, such as "Christmas Around the World," where the students trade classrooms. For example, we decided to teach "Australia" this year and "Canada" the next. Careful planning was needed, but we felt less pressure to "get it all in," since we would spend two years with the same group of students.

In planning how to meet needs of both first and second graders, we knew there needed to some separate teaching time. For instance, we knew first graders would need to begin the year with direct reading instruction. To accomplish this, we scheduled direct teaching of reading by one teacher during center time, which was facilitated by the other teacher. Also, our school uses Saxon Math, which dictates that the different grade levels be separated during Math. All other instruction and student work was planned to be done with the grade levels combined.

Despite all our preparations, the year got off to a very rocky start. Some of the students were placed in our class without their parents being introduced to and understanding the multiage concept. A few immediately requested their child's removal. Another problem was that, even though we had fewer first grade students, too many of them were students with "special needs." Many parents had chosen our situation with the attitude that "maybe this will work." As problems developed, we met with both schools' administrators and decided a few students would benefit from a more traditional setting. Conferences were held with the parents, and those students returned to the primary campus. It was heartbreaking, but it was good to at last have our class set, although we now had a more uneven number of first and second graders.

Our central organization was theme-based; the learning was student-generated. Our primary concern was "learning to learn." We gathered thematic literature, pictures, references, and related science, math, geography and other "real world" materials. We filled centers with ideas and problems to solve, but our students determined how long a theme lasted and the direction in which it progressed. Students helped construct rubrics to evaluate their writing and projects. Having problems with a number of possible right answers rather than simply right or wrong answers encouraged higher-order thinking skills. Even spelling, which was directly taught, was evaluated by students' webs of worlds. Although our family ranged from first grade "identified" children with learning problems to "gifted" second graders, it seemed easy to meet all their learning needs. A variety of means were used to measure each student's success.

One second grade girl came to us [from another teacher] with a portfolio filled with incomplete work and a folder of comments to her parents stating that she was unmotivated and never finished anything. When we made learning her responsibility, especially in cooperative groups and centers, she slowly blossomed into the able learner she was capable of being. Her confidence grew throughout the year. Her mother, who began the year with serious doubts about our setting, even volunteered to speak with parents who inquired about our multiage program for the fall.

STRATEGIES WE FOUND SUCCESSFUL

GROUPINGS (FLEXIBLE)
Cooperative
Mini lessons
Whole/small
Reading (traditional and book study)
Free choices
Tutorials
Interest

AUTHENTIC ASSESSMENT
Checklist
Portfolios
Portfolios conferences
Rubrics
Peer and Individual Evaluations

TEAM TEACHING
Modeling
Building on teachers' strengths
Conferences
Flexible groupings
Greater accountability
Closely observing students

TEACHING TOOLS
Weekly letter to the class for editing
Centers
(Writing, Reading, Science, Health, Geography, Math, Computers, Listening, Blocks, Crafts, Puzzles, and Games
DEAR (Drop Everything and Read)
Accelerated Reader
Author Study
Authentic Writing and Reading
Graphic Organizers
Print-rich environment (surrounded with literature, weekly poems, written direction in centers)
Room Design (movable/flexible areas, rugs, bean bags, lap boards, tables and a couple of desks)
Choices
Integrated Skills
Celebrations
Active learning
Singing
Meaningful Content

READINGS WE FOUND USEFUL

Arredondo, Blackburn, Brandt, Marzano, Moffet, Peckeriz; *Teachers' Manual: Dimensions of Learning*, 1992.

Bredekamp, Sue, ed. *Developmentally Appropriate Practice in Early Childhood Programs Serving Children From Birth Through Age 8*, National Association for the Education of Young Children, 1986.

Brooks, Brooks. *In Search of Understanding: The Case for the Constructivist Classroom*, Association for Supervision and Curriculum Development, 1993.

Fox, Mem. *Radical Reflections, 1993.*

Gardner, Howard, *Frames of Mind: The Theory of Multiple Intelligences*, 1993.

Kovalik, *ITI: The Model, Integrated Thematic Instruction*, Books for Educators, 1994.

Routman, Regie, *Invitations: Changing as Teachers and Learners, K-12;* Heinemann, 1991.

SDE Sourcebook, *Staying Focused on the Children*, The Society for Developmental Education, 1994.

Texas Education Agency, *First Impressions: Report of the Task Force on Early Childhood and Elementary Education*, 1994.

Wayman, Breaking *Language Barriers*, 1985.

Another child, a very small, immature first grader with little confidence, grew from a child who read only three or four words and required constant help with spelling, to an avid reader and writer, who filled his journal's pages with his thoughts. The most wonderful example of his growth was in May, when as the facilitator of a cooperative group of nine first and second graders, he quickly and confidently organized his group to enable everyone to accomplish the task at hand.

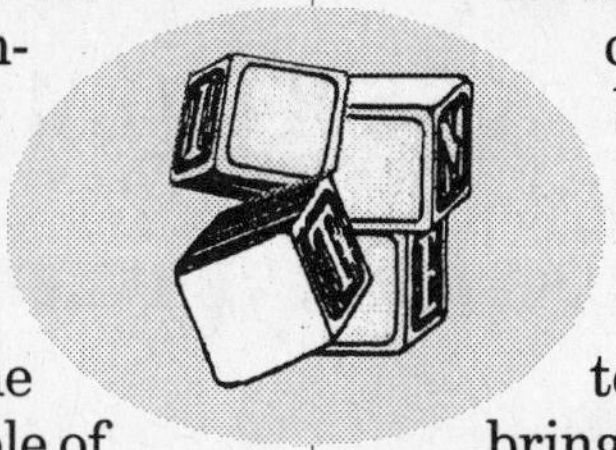

Watching students learning to learn and achieving told us we were successful. A checklist backed by each student's portfolio reflected progress. We pre-tested and post-tested all students in word recognition, and the majority of students showed at least two years' growth. All students' journals displayed considerable growth in writing skills. The Accelerated Reader Program, in use at our school, showed each student's significant progress in reading and comprehension, as well as the increasing number of books our students were reading. The class even exceeded our goal of reading and passing tests on two thousand books between October and May!

Changing from "traditional" teaching to team teaching, and bringing that teaming to a multiage class, takes a lot of research and planning, and constant evaluation. However, this time and commitment was clearly worth our efforts. Not only did we observe and collect data showing growth in curriculum areas for our individual students, but we also saw incredible growth in learning, thinking, working skills and cooperative skills. Everyone worked to help everyone learn. We cheered as we met and exceeded individual and class goals.

Parents' attitudes also changed. Even those with serious doubts about this strange "megaclass" recognized their children's progress. Most wrote or spoke strongly in favor of multiage classrooms. One parent who had moved to San Antonio looked until she found a similar setting for her daughter. We began the year with about fifteen parents requesting our 1-2 multiage classroom, and ended with requests from forty-five parents for a multiage 2-3.

Unfortunately, next year our classroom will not be multiage. The administration decided that, because of the addition of sixth grade to our campus, the resulting overcrowding eliminated the possibility of having space for a larger multiage classroom. We've reconciled ourselves to utilizing as much of our new learning as possible with individual classes. However, we will never lose our commitment to team teaching in a multiage setting as the best possible method of creating a true community of learners.

During the 1995-96 school year, Debby Lawson and Anna Williams team-taught a first/second grade multiage class in the Comal School District in New Braunfels, Texas. This year, because of district space considerations, Lawson will be teaching second grade, and Williams third grade. They hope to be able to teach another multiage class in the future.

VOICES VOICES VOICES

VOICES VOICES VOICES

A Position Statement of the National Association for the Education of Young Children

"The primary grades hold the potential for starting children on a course of lifelong learning. Whether schools achieve this potential for children is largely dependent on the degree to which teachers adopt principles of developmentally appropriate practice."

— "Appropriate Education in the Primary Grades", from *Developmentally Appropriate Practice in Early Childhood Programs Serving Children From Birth Through Age 8,* National Association for the Education of Young Children, 1986.

Designing Literacy Learning Experiences in a Multiage Classroom

MARILYN L. CHAPMAN

Multiage environments illustrate the need for an approach to effective organization that is appropriate to any classroom: flexible grouping.

Mixed-age or multiage classes are becoming more popular in both the United States and Canada as we move toward more child-centered and developmental approaches to education (Lodish, 1992). In "The Case for Mixed-Age Grouping in Early Education," Katz, Evangelou, and Hartman (1990) recommend mixed-age grouping on the grounds that it promotes social and cognitive benefits for both younger and older students. Their argument is based on a review of the literature on mixed-age groupings in preschool programs, cooperative learning and cross-age tutoring at the elementary school level, and on developmental theories such as Vygotsky's (1978) zone of proximal development. Yet, as Katz et al. (1990) admit, "Empirical data on the educational principles that guide instruction in mixed-age environments are not yet available" (p. 32) and that "although mixed-age grouping is a straightforward concept, the practical details of implementation are not well researched" (p. 47).

One of the major focuses in the primary school curriculum—indeed, often the central aim—is literacy learning. From a Vygotskian perspective, children are socialized into literacy through interaction with literate others. This suggests an apprenticeship approach to literacy, which can occur in two ways. First, adults can provide support for children's literacy acquisition through "scaffolding" (Wood, Bruner, & Ross, 1976), encouraging children to do what they can and providing input or assistance when needed. Likewise, collaborative partners in the classroom can assist each other in aspects of literacy over which they do not yet have control (Wells & Chang-Wells, 1992). Advocates of multiage classes suggest that teachers can apply Vygotsky's theory by capitalizing on a wider age and ability range than we would normally find in single-grade classrooms, so that older or more able students can act as mentors of younger or less able children. But what might a literacy program in a multiage classroom look like? How do we organize activities to incorporate both teacher- and peer-guided literacy learning? These are important questions, yet there has been little research examining language and literacy learning in multiage classrooms.

In this article, I describe some of the findings of a 2-year study of literacy learning in a primary multiage classroom. While the research project was multifaceted, I focus here on the ways in which the teacher organized her classroom not only to address the literacy learning needs of different-aged children but also to capitalize on this diversity. I begin by providing the context of the study, relating how the project began, and describing the focal classroom. Next, I discuss different kinds of groupings and show how the teacher grouped and regrouped the children on a typical school day. Finally, I present a way of thinking about organization for literacy learning and teaching in relation to Vygotsky's (1978) theory of the zone of proximal development, which is central to multiage grouping but applicable to every classroom.

Context of the Study

Several years ago, my friend Colleen Politano and I worked on the team that developed the ungraded Primary Program in British Columbia, Canada

This research was funded by a UBC-HSS Research Grant, #S92-0139.

(British Columbia Ministry of Education, 1990). When our writing task was completed, we went on to implement the program in different ways: Colleen became a teacher of a multiage primary class, and I became a teacher educator and researcher at the university. A collaborative research project developed as a natural outgrowth of our mutual interests, our desire to continue our friendship, and our concern for the need to document literacy learning in a multiage classroom setting.

Colleen taught in a public school in a small suburban community on the outskirts of a large city. The children came from working-class homes, and in about two-thirds of the families, both parents worked outside the home. The parents had a variety of occupations that included natural resource (logging and fishing) and service industries (e.g., clerks in retail stores, hair dressers) and the civil service. Colleen had taught in the same school for many years prior to working on the Primary Program and was well known and respected as a teacher by the community. Furthermore, Colleen had taught many of the children's older siblings or neighbors' children. Thus, while the idea of multiage classrooms was new to the parents, they were generally supportive of whatever approach Colleen wanted to implement. Also, Colleen held some parent evenings to explain the Primary Program in general and multiage grouping specifically. She provided information and addressed concerns at other occasions, such as parent-teacher interviews, and had many informal discussion with parents as well.

Most of the children in Colleen's class were Caucasian, English-only speakers; a few were Asian. One of the children in the class during both years (enrolled in kindergarten in the first year) was Alexis, a "special needs" child who had cerebral palsy. While Alexis could not produce speech to communicate, she was learning to sign. Alexis spent the majority of the school day in the classroom and was accompanied by Rhonda, a special education teaching assistant. On some days, Alexis was away from the class for an hour or so to receive therapy of one form or another.

Colleen had had experience teaching kindergarten through Grade 3 in separate grades and in combinations ("split grades"), and she was eager to teach a multiage class. During the 1991–92 school year, she enrolled 12 kindergartners, 6 first graders, and 6 second graders. First- and second-grade children attended school for full days, while the kindergarten children attended school for 4 afternoons a week and for a full day each Wednesday. The following year, the second graders "graduated" to another class; Colleen kept 16 of the children and received 9 new students, resulting in a class of 12 first graders and 13 second graders. Although Colleen had wanted a 3-year age spread both years, like most teachers her class composition resulted from the numbers of children enrolled in each grade, class size constraints, and the budget for staffing.

Colleen's classroom reflected her whole language philosophy of language and literacy learning. She believes that children learn literacy best when immersed in a literate community (e.g., being read to frequently, provided with a multitude of books); when they have opportunities for demonstrations of literacy by literate others (e.g., when they see adults and older children reading and writing); when meaning is emphasized rather than correctness (e.g., encouraging children to write with invented spellings [Chomsky, 1971]); and when instruction is provided in the context of functional and personal use (e.g., the daily agenda, sign-up charts, journals). She also has a strong conviction that literacy acquisition is fostered when children have opportunities to interact with each other in collaborative literacy experiences, especially when children of different ages and abilities work together. Throughout the school year, Colleen strove to establish a collaborative learning climate, encouraging the children to read and write together and to help each other. During reading and writing periods, she sometimes allowed the children to self-select partners or group members; at other times she structured the groups so that there was at least one second grader working with younger children.

> *Literacy acquisition is fostered when children have opportunities to interact with each other in collaborative literacy experiences, especially when children of different ages and abilities work together.*

For 2 years I visited Colleen's classroom on a regular basis to observe and videotape the classroom literacy events, to talk with the children about their learning, and to collect "artifacts" such as samples of the children's writing. In addition, the continuing conversation between Colleen and me helped provide both of us with insights into the "what," "how," and "why" of her children's literacy learning experiences. My role was one of participant-observer (Bogdan & Biklen, 1982). The research was truly collaborative in that our personal understandings were mutually constructed through our dialogue surrounding theory, research, and classroom reality.

When Colleen first introduced me to the class, I explained to the children that I was a university teacher and that I wanted to learn more about how kids learn so I could help my students become good teachers. The first two visits were primarily to get to know the children and to accustom them to my presence. On the third visit, I introduced the video camera and let the children "play" with it; on the fourth visit, I began video recording. After a while, the children became used to my being there and observing and videotaping them. I kept extensive field notes and collected photocopies of children's work and printed material in the classroom throughout the project.

Organizing for Teaching and Learning in a Multiage Classroom

During the development of the British Columbia Primary Program (1990), we had many discussions about grouping practices. We were aware that traditional ability groups were found to be unhelpful to, and indeed harmful for, many learners (Allington, 1983; Eder, 1981; Kulik & Kulik, 1982). Ability groups actually widen the gap between less able and more able learners (Shannon, 1985). However, we did not believe that whole language equates with whole-class instruction. We were excited about elements of individualized instruction, cooperative learning, peer writing, and literature response groups. One of the major problems we had to address was how to balance the need for creating a classroom community with the children's different levels of ability. It had been our experience that "grade levels" were artificial constructs when we taught "straight grades" and that any single grade consisted of a range of abilities, even though the curriculum guide indicated otherwise. Teaching a multiage class allowed us to "come out of the closet" regarding the normal variations in ability among children of the same age. On the other hand, we did not want to group by ability or substitute age for grade as a means of grouping. Clearly, there was no one approach to organization; rather, there needed to be different groupings for different purposes. I will begin by describing the ways in which Colleen used whole-class, small-group, partner, and individual groupings in her language arts program. Then I will use an example of one school day to show how one type of grouping flowed from another.

Whole-Class Experiences

Whole-class experiences occurred every day, and many were part of the daily or weekly routine. Colleen interacted with the children as a whole class for a variety of purposes, including:

- Community building—To establish a feeling of belonging, of being a class, Colleen held morning meetings in which the class went over the agenda together. In the second year, she added weekly class meetings in which they talked about, and reflected on, their experiences together at school.
- Sharing experiences—Just as "the family that does things together stays together," the class that has a set of shared experiences develops emotional bonds. Colleen's class had many shared experiences built into the daily classroom routines—morning news, storytime, singing, and so on. Other shared experiences took the form of special events, such as field trips or watching performances. Whole-class shared experiences were followed up by small-group collaborative activities and/or individual responses, which will be described later.
- Planning—When activities were going to involve the whole class, planning included everyone. For example, all the children participated in planning the food and activities for a party. Whole-class planning was also used for academic situations; for example, at the introduction of a unit Colleen engaged the whole class in making a K-W-L (Know, Wonder, Learned) web (Brownlie, Close, & Wingren, 1988).
- Decision making—Although decisions have been traditionally considered the teacher's domain, Colleen believed it was important to involve the children in decisions that affected their lives. For example, special class meetings were called to discuss problems arising on the playground and how to resolve them.

- Introducing new concepts, skills, or forms of representation—Although we used to think that learning is always hierarchical in nature, it is clear that this is not always the case. We believe that just because a student has difficulty learning one aspect of writing, for example, it does not mean that he or she will always encounter difficulty. Thus, Colleen usually introduced new concepts, skills, or forms of representation (e.g., writing scripts, Venn diagrams) to the class as a whole.
- Reading/writing/thinking strategies—Colleen used whole-class experiences for strategies such as the daily "mystery message" (a morning message, written as a cloze activity) and "C.O.P.S" (a morning message, written with errors, which the class edited for Capital letters, Omissions, Punctuation, and Spelling [Politano & Davies, 1994]). Her reasons for using such strategies were to provide models for problem solving; to have students share ideas in a nonjudgmental fashion; and, most importantly, to provide opportunities for the children to reflect on and talk about their thinking, reading, and writing processes. Engaging in such strategies with the whole class provided the children with insights into different ways of thinking and enabled them to take risks in a supportive context.
- Processing and reflecting—Whether following a whole-class reading/writing/thinking strategy lesson, small-group work, or independent work, Colleen encouraged the children to talk about their learning experiences. Following the work of Vygotsky (1978), Colleen understood that talk is essential in the development of thought—students learn to be reflective by participating in discussions with the guidance of more able others, especially adults; later on, they will internalize such talk as "inner speech." Colleen initiated these sessions with an open-ended question, often, "What did you learn today?" She would then move toward process-oriented questions such as, "What did you notice about your thinking?" "What worked well for you?" "What did you struggle with?" "How did you figure things out?" Colleen also wanted the children to make connections with prior knowledge, asking, "How did what you did today connect with something you learned before?" She also promoted setting new learning goals, using prompts such as: "Where do you think you might want to go with this?" "How else might you want to work on this?" "How might you want to do things differently another time?"
- Focusing and closure—At or near the beginning of the day or period, Colleen had the children come together as a group before they went off to work individually or in small groups. In this way, she could ensure that the children had a clear understanding of what was expected and could clarify any misunderstandings. Likewise, she had them come together, after they had been working independently or in groups, to review their learning and to establish closure.
- Celebrating—Like many primary teachers, Colleen's class had celebrations for holidays and special days, such as Valentine's Day. They also had celebrations for academic reasons. For example, they concluded a unit or theme with a whole-class celebration (Davies, Politano, & Cameron, 1993). These celebrations provided the children with opportunities to share the results of individual or small-group projects or inquiries and also to evaluate their learning, thus providing closure to units of study (as, for example, by adding the "L" to a Know-Wonder-Learned web).

Teacher-Led Small Groups

Although whole-class teaching and learning activities are useful in many situations, they are not always appropriate. Some teachers have overgeneralized the research findings on ability grouping to conclude that any form of grouping is poor practice. For example, Lapp and Flood (1992) found that some teachers believe that "whole language" implies whole-class instruction. Colleen sometimes felt the need to interact with a smaller number of students so that she could give them more attention and assistance. She avoided the drawbacks of ability grouping when she grouped students in different ways for different purposes (not always by ability). She focused on the needs of learners in specific learning contexts rather than grouping them by age or grade or by categorizing them generically into high, middle, and low. There are many different bases for grouping students: skill, interest, work habits, content, strategies, task/activity, random selection, student choice, and social reasons (Flood, Lapp, Flood, & Nagel, 1992). The following are ways that Colleen used teacher-led small groups:

- Common need—Colleen formed temporary groups based on common needs. For example, sometimes she worked with a group of emergent writers whom she felt would benefit from some specific help in using invented spelling.

> *Some teachers have overgeneralized the research findings on ability grouping to conclude that any form of grouping is poor practice.*

- Guided practice—Colleen encouraged those students who were ready to work together in collaborative groups or to work independently to do so, while continuing to work with a group of students that needed more of her assistance. This occurred, for example, when she introduced Venn diagrams. Some of the children caught on quite quickly and were eager to try them on their own or with a partner. Other children, not all of whom were the younger ones in the class, stayed at the teaching area with her for an extended period.
- Task-focused help—Many instances of this kind of grouping occur in classrooms at all levels. In a manner similar to teacher-guided practice, Colleen provided students with help in completing tasks if they were not able to do so independently.
- Sharing reading and writing assessment—Traditional reading groups were designed to provide students with opportunities for oral reading practice and to allow the teacher to evaluate the children's reading. Colleen achieved these aims (without the accompanying drawbacks) through group reading and writing conferences, or "reading and writing clubs" (Anderson & Chapman, 1994). In "reading clubs," children read orally from self-selected texts (i.e., each child has a different book); in "writing clubs," the children read their own writing. As well as eliminating the problems associated with traditional reading groups, reading and writing clubs allowed more purposeful oral reading practice, a more authentic audience situation, modeling by more able readers and writers, and opportunities for the children to interact and respond to each other. (A detailed explanation of reading and writing clubs is provided in Appendix A.)

Small Student Groups

Research has provided us with tremendous insights into the value of students working in groups without the teacher; currently the most popular method is "cooperative learning" (Johnson & Johnson, 1991; Kagan, 1992). Although Colleen did not follow a particular cooperative learning program, many of the small-group situations in her class shared some or all of the criteria for cooperative learning: a cooperative goal structure (rather than competitive or individualistic); face-to-face interaction; interdependence (to be successful, all had to work together on a common goal—sometimes resources were shared); and individual accountability (everyone had to contribute). At other times children worked on their own projects or writing with the assistance of others, when needed. Colleen strove to balance support with independence—older children learned not to "take over" and do younger children's writing, for example, but to provide help when it was requested or to ask if a younger child wanted help (Chapman, 1994). Colleen used student groups for:

- Supported practice—Colleen's students helped each other learn and extend their reading and writing abilities. She often used a teaching-learning sequence flowing from: whole-class, teacher-led, or guided activity → small groups of students working together → students working independently. Thus, the children provided support for each other on their way to independence.
- Shared tasks—Colleen's students sometimes worked together in small groups on a single project, such as making a book. Colleen believed that children become better readers and writers by reading and writing; thus, it was critical that all members of the group participated actively rather than relying on one or a few students to do all of the work. After viewing some of the videotapes during the early period of the project, she became aware that one boy avoided writing by

always choosing to work in a group or with a partner. Therefore, she became even more diligent about "kidwatching" (Goodman, 1985) when children worked in small groups.

- Collaborative responses—A form of shared task, a collaborative response sometimes followed whole-class experiences—for example, after hearing a story about a rabbit, 2 girls chose to work together to write a script for a play, and 3 boys collaborated on a rabbit story of their own.
- Common interest—When children had a common interest, they often chose to work together. For example, one group of students was fascinated by pirates, and they shared enthusiasm as well as their knowledge and resources. Sometimes the children worked collaboratively on a single project; at other times, they worked on individual creations. For some children, the opportunity to work with others who had a common interest provided the motivation to challenge themselves and to sustain their attention over a period of time.
- Sharing reading, writing, and "creations"—Often the children independently reenacted group activities they learned with their teacher. One example of this was the reading club undertaken by a group of 4 girls (a second grader, a first grader, and two kindergartners). Of particular interest was the writing that 2 of the kindergarten children did during this activity. They had observed Colleen writing notes during reading club (her anecdotal records), so they made their own by stapling papers together to make notebooks. One child copied the titles of the books they were reading, while the other produced letter strings. Another frequent activity was the sharing in groups of 4 or 5 those things they had produced during a particular period, as in "authors' circles" (Harste, Short, & Burke, 1988).

Partners or "Buddies"

Partner learning activities were a subset of peer group learning activities. In some instances, Colleen preferred to have students work as partners rather than in larger groups, for example, to maximize participation or to manage behavior. Partner learning activities involved same-age students; older and younger "buddies" in the class, or "big and little buddies," such as the pairing of one of Colleen's students and a fifth grader. Colleen used partnerships for:

- Supported practice—"Buddy reading," a practice common in primary classrooms provides support to emergent and developing readers. As such, it can provide purposeful practice that complements (but does not replace) sustained silent reading. Colleen developed an activity she called "Six Ps Reading": Pick a partner (sometimes Colleen picked for them); Pick a book; Practice; Polish (select a bit of text, reread, and improve); Present (read aloud to the class); and Praise. Sometimes the children read aloud a whole book, if it was short. More often, they selected a page or two. Each partner selected one class member who would make a positive comment on their reading. ("Six Ps" later evolved into "Nine Ps," details of which are provided in Politano & Davies, 1994.)
- Mentoring—Mentoring occurred informally and was usually initiated by a younger child (Chapman, 1994). It became apparent that some of the kindergarten children idolized particular second graders and often chose to sit next to them. In these instances, a younger child often observed and emulated the older one, and the older child provided one-on-one guidance and assistance.
- Tutoring—Tutoring was more often facilitated or organized by Colleen. Colleen wanted to convey to the children that 1 teacher + 24 children = 25 teachers + 25 learners. She encouraged the children to ask for help from another student before coming to her, as a general problem-solving strategy. Also, she often paired a more able student with a less able one.
- Shared task or response, common interest—These partnerships were similar to those described previously. Although Colleen wanted the children to develop friendships, she encouraged them to choose a variety of partners and, at other times, paired up children herself. Some children preferred working with a partner to working independently, for example in coauthoring stories or reports. This

was particularly helpful in providing support for younger or less able students.

Individual Experiences

We believe that a program of school experiences relying entirely on individualized learning is neither practical in terms of teacher time nor desirable in terms of student learning. Like many teachers, Colleen found that well-timed individualized assistance or assessment was very effective. The first two of the following descriptions involved Colleen with an individual student: the last two consisted of students working independently.

- One-on-one instruction—This often occurred informally as Colleen circulated around the classroom while children were at work. "On-the-spot mini-lessons" complemented whole-class and group instruction. A combination of whole-class, small group, and individualized instruction provided less able students with more teacher time than any one approach could have.

> *We believe that a program of school experiences relying entirely on individualized learning is neither practical in terms of teacher time nor desirable in terms of student learning.*

- Individual assessment—Colleen used individualized assessment in two ways. First, she did it as needed with particular children when she felt the need for in-depth information. It was apparent from her ongoing interactions with students in whole-class and small-group situations (e.g., reading club) that most students were progressing well in reading. In some instances, however, she wanted more information about particular students, so she conducted individual reading conferences to get richer and more specific information about these children. Second, Colleen used individualized conferences with the whole class several times a year, over a period of a week or so, in preparation for reporting. Reporting in Colleen's classroom was a very collaborative process, and these conferences were central to it (Davies, Politano, Cameron, & Gregory, 1992).
- Independent practice—We believe that once students are able to do something independently, independent practice, such as sustained silent reading, is one of the best ways to improve. We also feel that independent practice, be it at school or at home, is only appropriate when students can be successful. When students are expected to practice something independently that is beyond their level of competence, they can become frustrated and, as a result, may either "give up" or "act out." Therefore, Colleen used independent reading and writing as an integral part of her language arts program, but to a lesser degree than in many traditional classrooms because so much of the children's reading and writing was collaborative.
- Individual response—Traditionally, all students have been expected to do the same follow-up activity to a lesson. However, to address the diversity in the children's learning needs, to engage them in their learning, and to utilize both social and personal dimensions of learning, we developed the notion of shared experience/individual responses. In other words, Colleen engaged the children in a shared experience, such as reading a story to them, and either provided an open-ended activity so that they could respond individually within a particular framework or invited them to choose the form of their responses. For example, after hearing a story, children might want to write a poem, create a poster, dramatize the story, create a Venn diagram, and so on. To do this, the children needed a repertoire of representations learned through whole-class experiences and developed through small-group and partner-supported practice.

One Day's Agenda: Grouping and Regrouping

I selected this particular day, from spring of the first year, because it was a Wednesday and the kindergarten children attended all day. The school had a nonstandard timetable. The children went home an hour earlier on Wednesdays, and the time was made up by starting earlier than usual each day. Because Wednesdays were short days and there were gym periods, Colleen scheduled no formal math. (I point this out because it could appear that there was no math in this classroom, which was not the case.) Colleen had written the following agenda on the board. Next to each item I have added [in brackets] the groups she used:

Exploration [independent, same-age/mixed-age partner and small group]

Group Meeting [whole group → same-age/mixed-age partner → whole-group]

Gym

Recess

Reading and Writing Workshop [independent, same-age/mixed-age partner, and small group]

Reading Club [teacher-led, mixed-age small group]

Music [whole class]

Lunch

Storytime [whole class]

Theme Time [independent, same-age/mixed-age partner and small group]

Reflection [same-age/mixed-age partner and small group → whole-class]

Hop on Home

Exploration was the way that Colleen liked to start the day so that the children could have an opportunity to choose from a variety of activities. On this particular day, the children came into the classroom and put their coats and lunch kits away and then moved to a variety of independent and collaborative activities. Some children were observed returning books to the classroom library, discussing books informally with each other, and sometimes selecting or trading books to take home later that day. A group of boys clustered at the "creative center" to work on building pirate ships from styrofoam trays, cardboard boxes, and other recyclables. Two girls and a boy were in the house corner; a boy and a girl were writing on the class computer. Other children were observed in the puppet centre, building constructions with wooden blocks, working with math manipulatives, playing games, and so on. Two of the kindergarten children hauled a Big Book onto the floor to read, and another kindergartner walked around the room with Colleen's pointer, pointing to and attempting to read words on charts and signs around the classroom. During this time, Patrick, a first grader who was the helper of the day, went around with a class list to take attendance. At various times he confirmed names with Naoto, who was in second grade. Meanwhile, Colleen spoke to one of the mothers briefly at the door, and then circulated around the room, chatting with the children and recording her observations.

Group Meeting followed Exploration. Colleen had put the "clean up" music on and the children hummed and sang as they tidied up and gathered at the carpet. The meeting began with a shared reading of the agenda written on the board. Next, Colleen asked if anyone had any news to share with the class. Gemma gave a detailed account of the latest *Emergency 911* television show. Next, Shane told of an accident he had seen, which prompted a flurry of hand waving by children wanting to tell about an accident they had seen or been in. Seeing this, Colleen asked the children to turn to someone sitting nearby, sit "face-to-face and knee-to-knee," and to talk in partners about accidents. This was followed by a whole-class discussion of safety.

Next came solving the "mystery message" collaboratively, which Colleen had written on a chart:

_. J.'s m_ _ i_ _ _ ing _ _ g t_ _ r_bb_ _ _ _ d _ _.

[D. J.'s mom is bringing the rabbit today.]

This was followed by "C.O.P.S.," a collaborative edit of the next part of the morning message, where children checked for capitals, omissions, punctuation, and spelling:

we wll nd to thnk ov sum rulz four raBit safe

which resulted in two alternative versions, "We will need to think of some rules for rabbit safety" and, "We will need to think of some rules for our rabbit to be safe." When conducting the mystery message and C.O.P.S. activities, she had different expectations for different children. For example, she asked kindergarten children to volunteer beginning letters of words and asked older children to contribute the correct spelling for "four." After these activities, D. J. spoke a little about handling bunnies; and the class developed a list of rules, which Colleen recorded on a chart. By this time, Gym was fast approaching, so Colleen wrapped up the Group Meeting, organized the children for Gym, and took them to the gym door.

Gym was taught by another teacher, providing Colleen with her "prep time." At the end of the gym period, the children came trooping back in, got their snacks and coats, and went out for recess.

During *Reading and Writing Workshop*, the children were allowed to read and/or write what they wanted. Some children read in small same-age groups (3 kindergarten girls reread a familiar Big Book together); mixed-age groups (1 second grader, 2 first graders, and a kindergartner held their own "reading club"); with partners (some same-age, others older/younger combinations), and individually. The same kinds of groupings were seen with children writing.

Reading Club ran concurrently with *Reading and Writing Workshop*. On Monday, Colleen had put up a sign-up sheet. Shaun and Evelyn (first grade); Bradley and Karl (kindergarten); and Chelsea (second grade) had signed up for today's Reading Club. Colleen notified the children that Reading Club would begin in 5 minutes, so these children got their books ready, Colleen got her notebook, and they met at a round table. During Reading Club, the children read aloud and responded to each other's reading. Colleen kept notes. All of the other children were working on a variety of reading and writing activities and, for the most part, were very focused. At one point, Colleen excused herself from Reading Club and asked Chelsea to take over briefly. Colleen went to talk to a couple of children who were not behaving appropriately and then returned to the table. At the close of Reading Club, the group of children went to reading and writing activities like the others while Colleen collected her thoughts and finished recording her observations. Next, she circulated around the classroom, observing and interacting with the children.

Music was held next, at the carpet, after the children had put their reading and writing things away. Just as the children started to sing an old favorite, D. J.'s mother came in with Midnight, the rabbit, who was going to be the new class pet. D. J. was in his glory as he told about the rabbit, and the children were eager to hold him and pet him. There was a whole-class discussion about how to treat rabbits and a rereading of the rules chart they had developed earlier. Just before noon, the discussion was interrupted by the principal's voice on the public address system with announcements. The children got ready for lunch and tried to get to know Midnight at the same time.

Storytime was held immediately after lunch, so the children gathered at the carpet. Today's story was *Miffy in the Snow* (Bruna, 1963), which Colleen chose because she had decided to do a rabbit theme to capitalize on the children's excitement surrounding Midnight's arrival. After reading and discussing the story, Colleen told the children that she wanted them to do some writing in response to the story. "How can you represent your thinking in writing about this story about Miffy or about other rabbits?" she asked. The children volunteered the following ideas, which Colleen recorded on the chalkboard:

story—Miffy
—Once upon a time

list of facts

web

picture with labels

clay pictures with titles

Venn diagram

script

rebus

Since Colleen had asked specifically for writing, when 2 children volunteered "picture" and "clay pictures," she asked the class how they could add writing. Two other children suggested adding labels and titles, and Colleen recorded their ideas. When she asked for clarification about "clay pictures," Philomena reminded her that they had recently read *The New Baby Calf* (Chase, 1984). Quickly, Shane pulled the book off the shelf nearby, and the class discussed the illustrations. This sparked the suggestion by Patrick that they could make a Venn diagram comparing rabbits and calves. When Alison contributed the idea of "script," Colleen quickly showed how this could be done.

Theme Time flowed naturally from the story reading. During Theme Time, the children worked on a variety of representations, including those on the list they had generated. As observed in Reading and Writing Workshop time, the children chose to work individually, with same-age and older/younger partners and small groups. They also took time to visit with Midnight, with D. J. "supervising" them so that the rabbit could become adjusted to his new home. During Theme Time, Colleen circulated around the classroom, interacting with and helping children, and recording her observations. Fifteen minutes before Home Time, Colleen asked the children to put their things away, but to bring what they had been working on to the meeting area.

Reflection was a time for sharing and talking about their learning and what they had been working on during the day. We believe that collaborative talk about experiences scaffolded by the teacher leads to reflection. First, Colleen asked the children to find one or two other people to whom they could tell one important thing they had learned that day. Next, she asked the children who would like to share their ideas with the whole class. (Sometimes, but not on this particular day, Colleen had them record their reflections in writing.) Finally, Colleen read from a notice that was to be taken home, and 2 children handed them out. Now it was time to say goodbye, get their coats, pack sacks and lunch kits, and *Hop on Home*.

Conclusions

We often search for the "one best way" in teaching. Clearly, when it comes to grouping for instruction, whether we have a straight-grade or a mixed-age class, there is no one best way. We need to use groups of different sizes, of different compositions, for different purposes; we need to group and regroup. One way to think about grouping is by applying Vygotsky's (1978) notion of the zone of proximal development, defined as "the distance between the [student's] actual developmental level as determined by independent problem solving and the level of potential development as determined through problem solving under adult guidance or in collaboration with more capable peers" (p. 86). To Vygotsky, each student has two developmental levels: his or her actual or attained developmental level, which is his or her "can do" or competency zone; just beyond this is the student's "learning zone," within reach and attainable with assistance (and farther out is the learner's "frustration zone" [see Figure 1]). When working at their actual or attained developmental levels, students experience feelings of confidence and success; when working at their zones of proximal development, they experience feelings of challenge and uncertainty. One of our main tasks as teachers is to create a balance so that students have opportunities to work both "at their developmental levels" and "in their learning zones."

> Learning Zone (zone of proximal development)—By definition, when students are learning, they are working with the new, the unknown. To take risks in their thinking and learning, they benefit from a "safety net" or support (Holdaway, 1984).
>
> —Maximum support is provided with new learning; thus, we begin with whole-class experiences or small-group, teacher-led instruction. Sometimes small-group cooperative learning activities are appropriate as well.
>
> —Moderate support as we extend students' learning or provide guided practice by using small student groups and partner activities. Some students may need continued teacher support—for example, through teacher-led small group or individual instruction as well. In multiage classes, we have the built-in opportunity to create partnerships or small groups with a mix of ages so that older children can provide mentoring or tutoring. Teachers of straight grades can achieve this intent by ensuring that an advanced or capable student is in each group or by enlisting older buddies from another class.
>
> "Can Do" or Competency Zone (attained developmental level)
>
> —Minimal support is provided when students are assured of success on their own. During this stage, independent practice and individual responses are appropriate. However, some children may want to work collaboratively, and the teacher may need to continue to monitor students' progress and provide feedback.

As Flood et al. (1992) suggest, flexible grouping holds great promise. Rather than looking for the one best way to organize, we need to group flexibly to meet our instructional purposes and to support students' learning.

In reality, every classroom is a multiage classroom, with a range of abilities, background knowledge, and levels of development. Graded organizations of classrooms and curriculums have created barriers that are not reflective of the diversity within groups of children of the same age, nor do they match the reality of life outside school. The methods described here—flexible grouping, collaboration, open-ended activities, choice, a variety of representations, shared experiences/individual responses—are not unique to multiage classes. But if we approach teaching in a multiage classroom with a graded mindset—expecting the same thing of each child of the same age and grouping children by age, grade, or ability within it—then nothing much has changed except for increasing the demands on the teacher. Hopefully, however, multiage grouping may enable us to transform the way we think about learning and teaching by compelling us to acknowledge diversity and to utilize it in supporting the learning of all our children.

Flexible grouping holds great promise. Rather than looking for the one best way to organize, we need to group flexibly to meet our instructional purposes and to support students' learning.

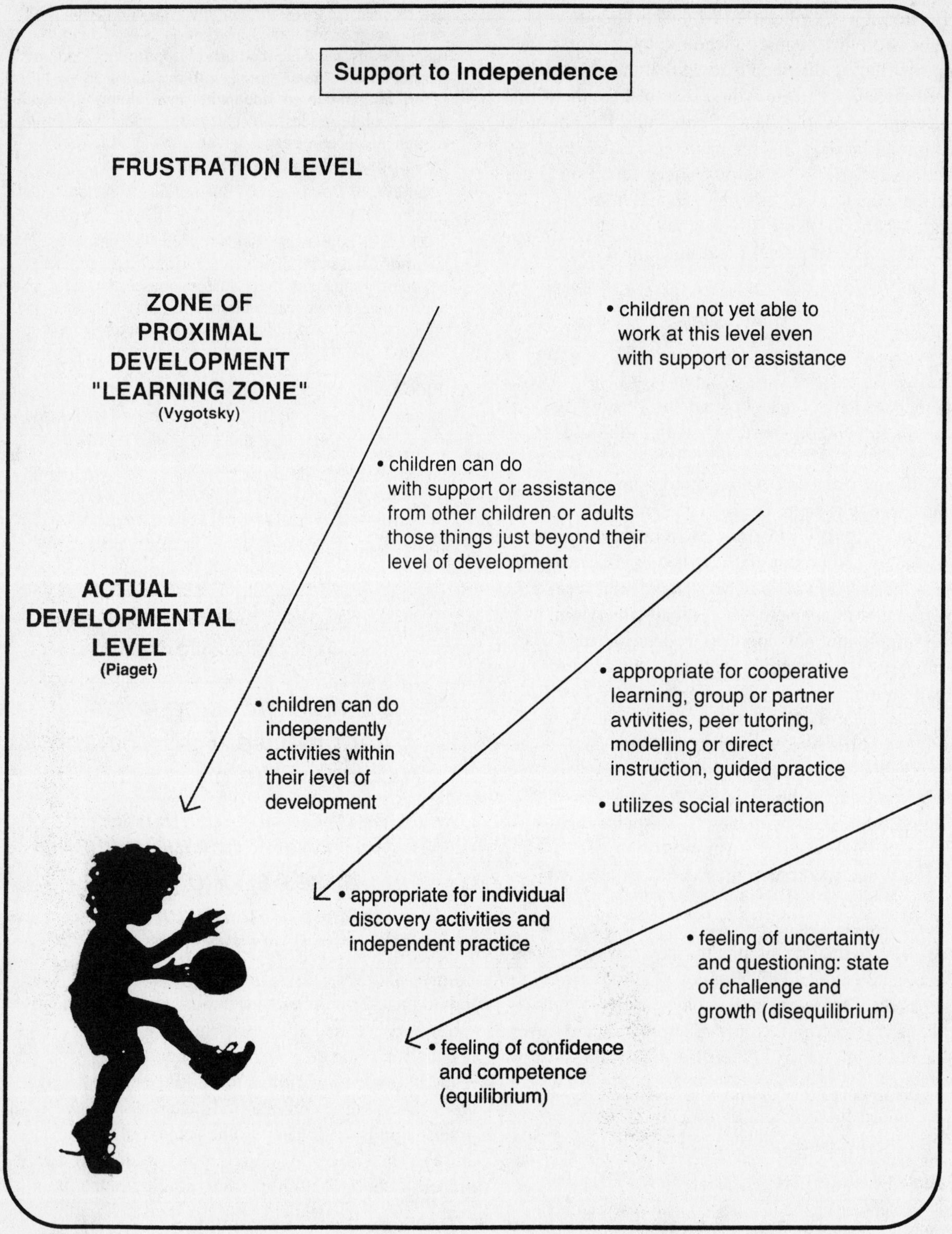
Support to Independence
FRUSTRATION LEVEL
ZONE OF PROXIMAL DEVELOPMENT "LEARNING ZONE" (Vygotsky)
• children not yet able to work at this level even with support or assistance
• children can do with support or assistance from other children or adults those things just beyond their level of development
ACTUAL DEVELOPMENTAL LEVEL (Piaget)
• appropriate for cooperative learning, group or partner avtivities, peer tutoring, modelling or direct instruction, guided practice
• utilizes social interaction
• children can do independently activities within their level of development
• appropriate for individual discovery activities and independent practice
• feeling of uncertainty and questioning: state of challenge and growth (disequilibrium)
• feeling of confidence and competence (equilibrium)

Figure 1. Support to Independence

References

Allington, R. (1983). The reading instruction provided readers of differing ability. *The Elementary School Journal, 83,* 255–265.

Anderson, J., & Chapman, M. (1994). A day in two whole-language classrooms. *Whole-language: Practice and theory* (2nd ed.) (pp. 23–65). Scarborough, Ontario, Canada: Allyn & Bacon, Canada.

Bogdan, R., & Biklen, S. (1982). *Qualitative research for education: An introduction to theory and methods.* Boston: Allyn & Bacon.

British Columbia Ministry of Education. (1990). *Primary program: Foundation document.* Victoria, British Columbia, Canada: Author.

Brownlie, F., Close, S., & Wingren, L. (1988). *Reaching for higher thought: Reading, writing, thinking strategies.* Edmonton, Alberta, Canada: Arnold Publishing.

Bruna, R. (1963). *Miffy in the snow.* New York: Methuen.

Chapman, M. L. (1994). Literacy learning in a primary multi-age classroom: Some findings from an investigation of peer writing events. In C. Kinzer & D. Leu (Eds.), *Multidimensional aspects of literacy research, theory, and practice: Forty-third yearbook of the National Reading Conference* (pp. 550–559). Chicago: National Reading Conference.

Chase, E. (1984). *The new baby calf.* Richmond Hill, Ontario, Canada: Scholastic.

Chomsky, C. (1971). Invented spelling in the open classroom. *Word, 27,* 499–518.

Davies, A., Politano, C., & Cameron, C. (1993). *Making themes work.* Winnipeg, Canada: Peguis.

Davies, A., Politano, C., Cameron, C., & Gregory, K. (1992). *Together is better: Collaborative assessment, evaluation and reporting.* Winnipeg, Canada: Peguis.

Eder, D. (1981). Ability grouping as a self-fulfilling prophecy: A micro-analysis of teacher-student interaction. *Sociology of Education, 54,* 151–162.

Flood, J., Lapp, D., Flood, S., & Nagel, G. (1992). Am I allowed to group? Using flexible patterns for effective instruction. *The Reading Teacher, 45,* 608–616.

Goodman, Y. (1985). Kidwatching: Observing children in the classroom. In A. Jaggar & M. T. Smith-Burke (Eds.), *Observing the language learner* (pp. 9–18). Newark, DE: International Reading Association, and Urbana, IL: National Council of Teachers of English.

Harste, J., Short, K., & Burke, C. (1988). *Creating classrooms for authors: The reading-writing connection.* Portsmouth, NH: Heinemann.

Holdaway, D. (1984). *Stability and change in literacy learning.* London, Ontario, Canada: The University of Western Ontario.

Johnson, D., & Johnson, R. (1991). *Learning together and alone: Cooperation, competition and individualization* (3rd ed.). Englewood Cliffs, NJ: Prentice-Hall.

Kagan, S. (1992). *Cooperative learning.* San Juan Capistrano, CA: Resources for Teachers.

Katz, L., Evangelou, D., & Hartman, J. (1990). *The case for mixed-age grouping in early education.* Washington, DC: National Association for the Education of Young Children.

Kulik, C., & Kulik, J. (1982). Effects of ability grouping on secondary school students: A meta-analysis of evaluation findings. *American Educational Research Journal, 19,* 415–428.

Lapp, D., & Flood, J. (1992). *Teaching reading to every child* (3rd ed.). New York: Macmillan.

Lodish, R. (1992). The pros and cons of mixed-age grouping. *Principal, 71,* 20–22.

Politano, C., & Davies, A. (1994). *Multiage and more.* Winnipeg, Canada: Peguis.

Shannon, P. (1985). Reading instruction and social class. *Language Arts, 62,* 604–613.

Vygotsky, L. S. (1978). *Mind in society: The development of higher psychological processes.* Cambridge, MA: MIT Press.

Wells, G., & Chang-Wells, G. L. (1992). *Constructing knowledge together: Classrooms as centers of inquiry and literacy.* Portsmouth, NH: Heinemann.

Wood, D., Bruner, J., & Ross, G. (1976). The role of tutoring in problem-solving. *Journal of Child Psychology and Psychiatry, 17,* 89–100.

Marilyn Chapman is an assistant professor in the Department of Language Education at the University of British Columbia, Vancouver, Canada, where she coordinates and teaches an Integrated Primary Teacher Education Program.

Appendix A
Reading & Writing Clubs: Group Reading and Writing Conferences

Purpose

Reading and Writing Clubs provide students with opportunities to share their reading (different texts, self-selected by students) and writing with each other and to learn from each other. They enable a teacher to interact with the students about their reading and writing and to collect assessment evidence effectively and efficiently (minus the drawbacks of individual conferences).

Scheduling

Reading Clubs or Writing Clubs are conducted over a week and can be alternated, that is, reading one week, writing the next. You meet with each student once a week in a small group. To determine group size, divide the number of students by 5. If the numbers do not divide evenly, put the smaller number on Friday so that if a student were absent on the day of his or her club meeting, she or he can join Friday's group. Put up a sign-up sheet on Monday. Allow about 5 minutes per student for the meeting (e.g., 25 minutes for a group of 5) and an additional 5 minutes for yourself afterwards for personal reflection and to finish recording your observations.

Preparing the Students

In order to save time, teach students your routines. You may want students to have personal reading records (e.g., reading logs) and writing folders (drafts or pieces in progress and recently completed work) which they bring to the appropriate meetings.

Reading: Each student brings his or her reading log and one thing she or he has read during the past week (or two, if you alternate reading and writing), with a section marked for reading aloud and sharing. Students are asked to read their selections aloud to the group (1–2 minutes each). For young children, it may be a whole book; for older students, it may only be a page or so.

—The other students respond to the reading (comments and questions).

—Optional: Begin by having students take about 1 minute each to tell about some of the things they have been reading.

Writing: Each student brings his or her writing folder with a selection ready for reading aloud and sharing (which may be a draft or just published). Students are asked to read their selected pieces, or portions of them, aloud to the group (1–2 minutes each).

—The other students respond to the reading (with positive comments, questions, and suggestions).

—Optional: Each student has about 1 minute to tell about some of the things she or he has been writing.

Teacher Preparation

Bring individual reading writing-record sheets, file cards, or a notebook with a page for each student. These will be used for recording your observations as each student shares his or her reading or writing. (Remember to record date, title, etc.) Also, you may want to bring a class "weekly at-a-glance" recording sheet or post-it notes on which to note students' behaviors in the "audience role," for example, listening and speaking skills and showing respect for ideas of others.

Analysis and Interpretation

The information from Reading and Writing Clubs may need to be combined with in-depth individual conferences for some students (e.g., an individual reading assessment or a conference to review a writing file). The records provide information about a student's performance and progress in reading and writing, attitude towards reading and writing, and reading and writing strategies used. It also provides information about students' social-emotional development, communication and interpersonal skills, and social responsibility.

VOICES VOICES VOICES VOICES VOICES VOICES

When she should have been applying herself to her lessons, she was listening to the recitations of the older children. "Much of the training and inspiration of my early days consisted, not in the things which I was supposed to be studying, but in hearing, while seated unnoticed at my desk, the conversation of Mr. Brace and the older classes." As she listened from "hour to hour" with "eager ears" she absorbed precocious intellectual frameworks, a love of ideas and expression, and a desire to excel in the handling of them.

— Joan D. Hedrick, *Harriet Beecher Stowe*. New York: Oxford University Press, 1993.

CHAPTER 1

The Multiyear Classroom
A Stable Force in Children's Lives

Our experience indicates that the most important variable in a positive elementary school program is the constant attention of a single teacher/caregiver with whom the child can develop a predictable and meaningful relationship. As children reach the ages of eleven and twelve, peers become more important and teachers less important to children.

But especially in these first stages of independence, children need one teacher there as an anchor, as well as an object for rebellion.

— Chip Wood, *Yardsticks*

What is Looping?

Looping is a pretty simple concept. A teacher decides that, instead of spending one year with a class of children, she wants to spend two, or sometimes three, so she talks the teacher in the next grade into dropping back to her present grade level, and moves to the next grade along with her kids. It's a relatively inexpensive, easy reform.

But why does it work so well? According to Dr. Joseph Rappa, superintendent of the Attleboro, Massachusetts, school district (which provides multiyear assignments to all of its first- through eighth-grade students with all of its 400 teachers),

> Student attendance in grades 2 through 8 has been increased from 92 percent average daily attendance (ADA) to 97.2 percent ADA. Retention rates have decreased by over 43 percent in those same grades. Discipline and suspensions, especially at the middle schools (grades 5 through 8), have declined significantly. Special education referrals have decreased by over 55 percent, and staff attendance has improved markedly from an average of seven days absent per staff member per year, to less than three. (Rappa 1993)

Most teachers, when talking about looping, mention time as a factor: a month of learning time built into the second and sometimes third year at the beginning of school, another month built into the end of the first year, as students end the year on a high note. But time is a tool, to be used with other child-friendly strategies, to promote what is at the core of looping — relationship.

On Michael Combs — and the Looping Model

Michael entered first grade having multiple disabilities with a full-time aide. We worked closely with the resource teacher and aide in developing a daily contract for appropriate behavior. Our goal was to provide a secure and stable environment in which Michael would require the services of an aide only half a day at the end of first grade. Michael adapted gradually to the routines, and by the beginning of second grade met our goal of a half day with the aide. Since the first grade class looped to second grade with the same teacher and classmates, Michael adjusted well to second grade. By the end of second grade an aide was no longer needed. He began third grade with a new teacher, no aide, and new classmates. Presently, he is functioning well and with no special education services and is looking forward to fourth grade. We believe the looping model enabled Michael to function academically and socially during a difficult adjustment period in his life.

Pam Clem, Teacher
First and Second Grades

Ashby Lee Elementary School
Quicksburg, Virginia

Relationship — that of teacher to student, to the parents, to other teachers, and to the curriculum — is what gives looping its power. Given time, a teacher can:

- develop a deeper understanding of students' learning styles and needs, both academic and emotional.
- better understand students' family dynamics and the parents' needs and expectations regarding their children's education.
- approach the curriculum in more depth, knowing that there is more time to help students make connections in their learning.
- understand the requirements of the teachers coming before and after, and develop a more all-encompassing view of the educational process through which her students will pass.

Looping has gotten a lot of press coverage lately, and within the past year there's been a groundswell of interest in it; but it's not a new concept. Rudolf Steiner, an Austrian educator and philosopher, founded the Waldorf Schools in the early 1900s in order to educate the children of domestics who worked for the Waldorf Astoria cigarette factory in Stuttgart, Germany. Waldorf schools still follow his precepts to this day; a Waldorf teacher stays with a group of students from first through eighth grade.

In Germany, children are grouped heterogeneously and stay with the same teacher from grades one through four; Japan and Israel also have multiyear "family groupings" in the lower grades, and multiyear teacher-student relationships by content area in their secondary schools. For instance, a secondary math teacher will teach the same students algebra, geometry and other content areas, while the science teacher will teach life sciences, chemistry and physics.

In the United States, although multiyear education hasn't been the norm for over 150 years, teachers have been quietly practicing "teacher rotation" for years. (see page 17).

Easy to Implement

Although some schools approach looping very formally, setting up committees, visiting other schools, and seeking parent and school board approval before adopting a multiyear configuration, it's actually about the easiest school reform to implement. Since most school principals have the authority to reassign teachers within their schools by simply notifying the school board and the superintendent, all it really takes to begin looping is two teachers willing to try the concept and an understanding principal willing to give them the nod.

The cost of implementing looping is minimal, usually limited to some new instructional materials and supplies for the teachers and perhaps some staff development funds to help them get up to speed on their new curriculums. Extensive training is not necessary; any experienced teacher will already have most of the skills necessary to succeed in a looping classroom.

TEACHER ROTATION

"Shall teachers in city graded schools be advanced from grade to grade with their pupils through a series of two, three, four or more years, so that they may come to know the children they teach and be able to build the work of the latter years on that of the earlier years, or shall teachers be required to remain year after year in the same grade while the children, promoted from grade to grade, are taught by a different teacher each year? This I believe to be one of the most important questions of city school administration."

"To this plan two objections are frequently raised: (1) that the teacher may be inefficient, and that no group of children should be condemned to the care and instruction of an inefficient teacher through a series of years; (2) that the full influence of the personality of any one teacher has been exhausted by the end of a year, and children should therefore come in contact with a new personality each year. The answer to both objections is easy and evident. The inefficient teacher should be eliminated. The man or woman who is unable to teach a group of children through more than one year should not be permitted to waste their money, time and opportunity through a single year."

"A personality which a child between the ages of 6 and 12 may exhaust in a year must be very shallow. What the child needs is not an everchanging personality, but a guide along the pathway of knowledge to the high road of life."

Looking at some advantages:

- There is a savings of time at the end of the first year of the cycle because with the exception of a few pupils who may be assigned elsewhere, the grouping process has taken care of itself.
- There is a savings of time at the beginning of the second year in which the teacher and pupils have worked together. The teacher understands the placement of each pupil in the curriculum and each pupil knows his classmates and the "ground rules" which operate within the class.
- Teacher Rotation emphasizes the importance of the teacher being a specialist in teaching children instead of being a specialist in a given subject area.
- Parents are better able to understand the school program because they know the teacher and understand her methods of working with children.

— Officer of Education
Department of Education, 1913

In contrast to other major reforms like year-round education and multiage education, looping doesn't require a long lead time, extensive planning, or substantial research. And because looping can be implemented quietly, in a low-key fashion, it won't as readily become a target of pressure groups opposed to school reform.

Parental support is an essential ingredient of any school reform. Luckily, looping is a concept embraced enthusiastically by most parents once they understand its benefits. (Parents have actually initiated some looping arrangements by saying to a favorite teacher, "You've given my child the best year he's ever had. I wish you could have him for another year!")

Few Potential Problems

Any education reform has problems, and looping has its share. Fortunately, the problems associated with looping are few, and most are avoided with a little planning (see "Look Before You Loop," page 105).

In brief, my son Brandon had a wonderful year in kindergarten. However, the transition from kindergarten to first grade was not so wonderful. Weeks before first grade, questions and concerns about his teacher, classmates, room location, etc., began to come from Brandon. The first two weeks of first grade were a real struggle for both Brandon and me, but thanks to a great teacher we survived.

Brandon was to be with the same teacher and class in the second grade. Knowing this through the summer, we had absolutely no anxiety when we began second grade. In fact, he was anxious to go back to school to see his teacher and friends. It was a very pleasant experience. To quote Brandon when he came home from school on the first day of second grade, "It was just like a family reunion." I just hope the rest of our school years can be as nice as this one has been.

Sheila Green, Parent
Brandon Green, Student
Ashby Lee Elementary School
Quicksburg, Virginia

Looping Versus Multiage

Many educators who have taught both multiage classes and single-grade, multiyear or "looping" classes say they prefer the latter. Char Forsten, former elementary school teacher and principal of Dublin Consolidated School of Dublin, New Hampshire, says,

> I've done multiage and looping; I prefer multiage to single-grade, single-year teaching, but I must admit looping is easier.
>
> With multiage there's always movement in and out of the class as a group of older students leaves and is replaced by a group of younger students. With looping in a single-grade class, the ability range and age range are less, and the class population stays the same except for occasional new kids moving in, and you can really get momentum.

Multiage education does have some advantages over looping; with the wider age range, there's more of an opportunity for children to "eavesdrop" on each other's learning, and older children get to act as positive role models and mentors for younger children. This role as the older, more knowledgeable student is perceived as very important, and children in a multiage class look forward to the time when they can be the veterans in the class.

Also, with the seamless, continuous progress curriculum possible in a multiage class, children can truly learn at their own rates, and may have the option of spending an additional year of learning time in a multiage class without the trauma of grade-level retention.

On the other hand, multiage programs take a lot more work and planning and a lot more energy than single-grade looping classes. A teacher thinking about multiage may want to try looping first, and either stay with the looping configuration or use it as a good solid first step to multiage education.

Not a lot has been written on looping, but a few good articles exist on the topic. We've included two here, and have referenced others in the bibliography.

"Twice the Learning and Twice the Love," by teacher Deborah Jacoby (see next page), is a narrative of her experiences with her first multiyear class. It is reprinted here with the permission of *Teaching K-8* Magazine. It provides a good personal look at many of the benefits of looping.

"Multi-Year Teacher/Student Relationships Are a Long-Overdue Arrangement," by Daniel L. Burke, a superintendent of an Antioch, Illinois school district, gives an overview of some of the multiyear programs in existence around the country (see page 21). The article is reprinted from the magazine, *Phi Delta Kappan*.

Fixing the Design Flaw

Adjusting our most important instructional resource . . . TIME

- All-Day Kindergarten
- Pre-Kindergarten program (transitional program for young fives)
- Transitional first grade (for young sixes)
- Grade level retention (extra time in a grade)
- Private tutoring outside of school
- Lengthened school day
- Extended school year
- Year-round school calendar
- Schedule nonacademic subjects after academic time
- Conduct some school programs on Saturdays and during intercessions
- Homework
- Schedule some sports and extra-curricular programs during intercessions
- Out of school learning
- Postgraduate year after high school
- Block schedule
- Team teaching
- Summer school
- Technology
- Flexible scheduling
- Subtractive education
- Multiage / Multiyear classrooms

Kindergarten/First Grade Configuration Options

Caution: The special needs population tends to be overrepresented in transition classes.

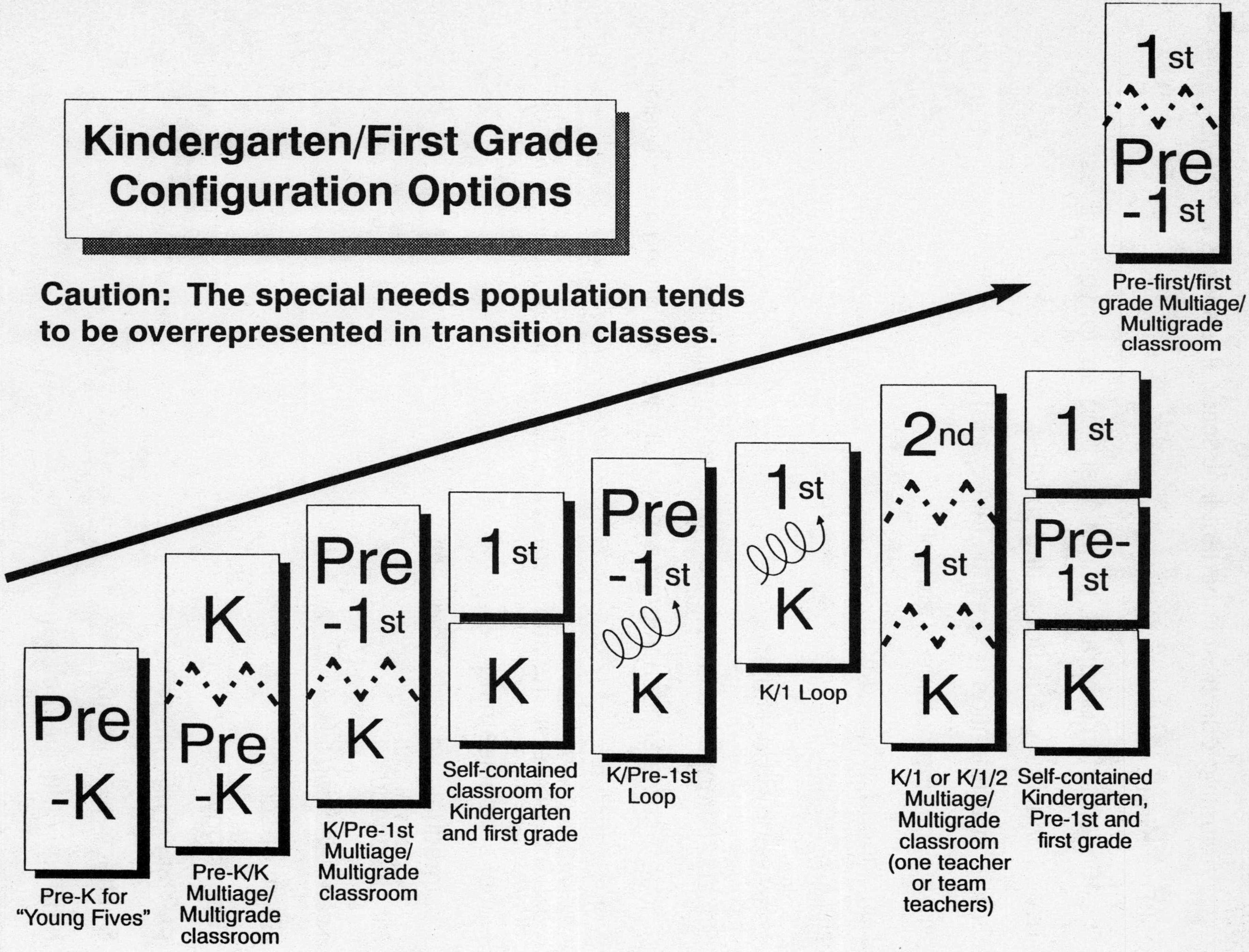

Looping Requires a Two-Teacher Partnership

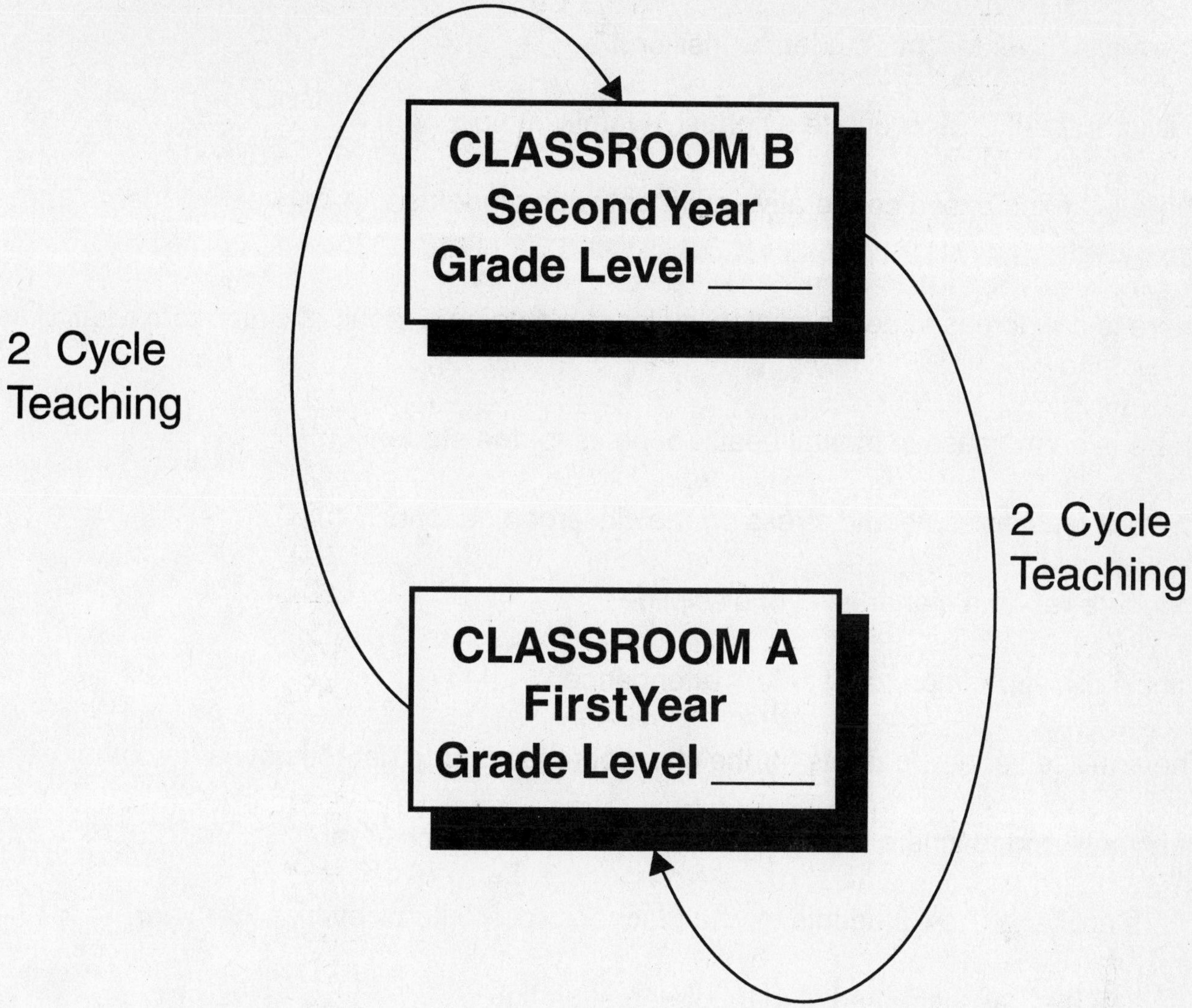

The classroom A teacher is "promoted" to classroom B with the class and keeps students for a second year. The classroom B teacher returns to classroom A to pick up a new class and begins another two-year cycle.

Note: This is a multiyear continuous progress configuration and is **<u>not</u>** a true multiage classroom

Looping Facts

- Student attendance in grades 2 through 8 has been increased from 92% average daily attendance (ADA) to 97.2% ADA
- Retention rates have decreased by over 43% in those same grades
- Discipline and suspensions, especially at the middle schools (grades 5 through 8), have declined significantly
- Special education referrals have decreased by over 55%
- Staff attendance has improved markedly from an average of seven days absent per staff member per year, to less than three

Joseph B. Rappa, ED.D
Provided by the Attleboro, Massachusetts School System

Multiple Year Classroom Benefits

1. There are fewer teacher/student transitions
2. Multiyear relationships create a cohesive family atmosphere
3. There is an increased cooperative spirit between students and between students and teacher(s)
4. There is an increased sense of stability for students as a result of classroom routine and consistency
5. There is an increase in mental health benefits for the students
6. There is less pressure and stress on the classroom teacher
7. Teachers report a higher level of discipline
8. Principals report improved student attendance
9. There are fewer new parents for the classroom teacher to get to know every other year
10. Principals and teachers report an increase in parent involvement
11. There are fewer new students for the teacher to get to know every other year
12. The teacher has increased student observation time
13. Teachers are not pressured to make high stakes decisions and may postpone these important decisions until they have more instructional time with the students
14. There tends to be a decrease in special needs referrals
15. Educators report fewer grade level retentions
16. A multiple year configuration allows for semi-seamless curriculum
17. Multiple year classrooms are more time efficient instructionally

Note: Most of the benefits of a multiage classroom accrue to students and teacher(s) being in a close relationship for multiple years.

Jim Grant / Bob Johnson / Char Forsten

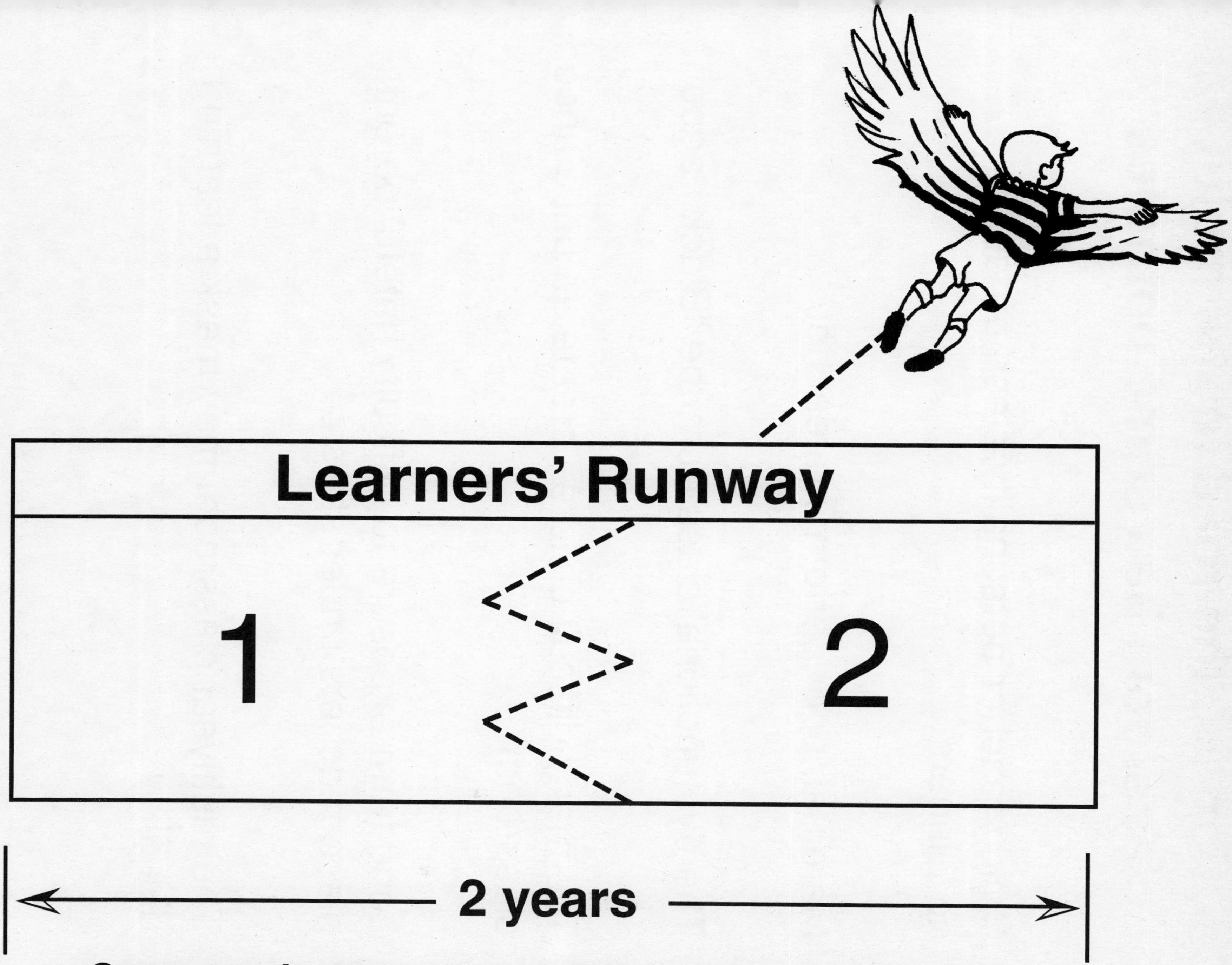

Some students need extra time, not an extra year

Caution . . . the road to the multiyear classroom has some potholes

1. Child / teacher personality clash produces no winners

2. Marginal, poor performing teacher

3. The dysfunctional class from the "Black Lagoon"

4. Too many difficult children create an unbalanced classroom

5. Long term exposure to difficult / hateful parents place teachers under stress

6. The multiyear classroom may mask a learning disability

Looping With Kindergarten (½ day) and First Grade

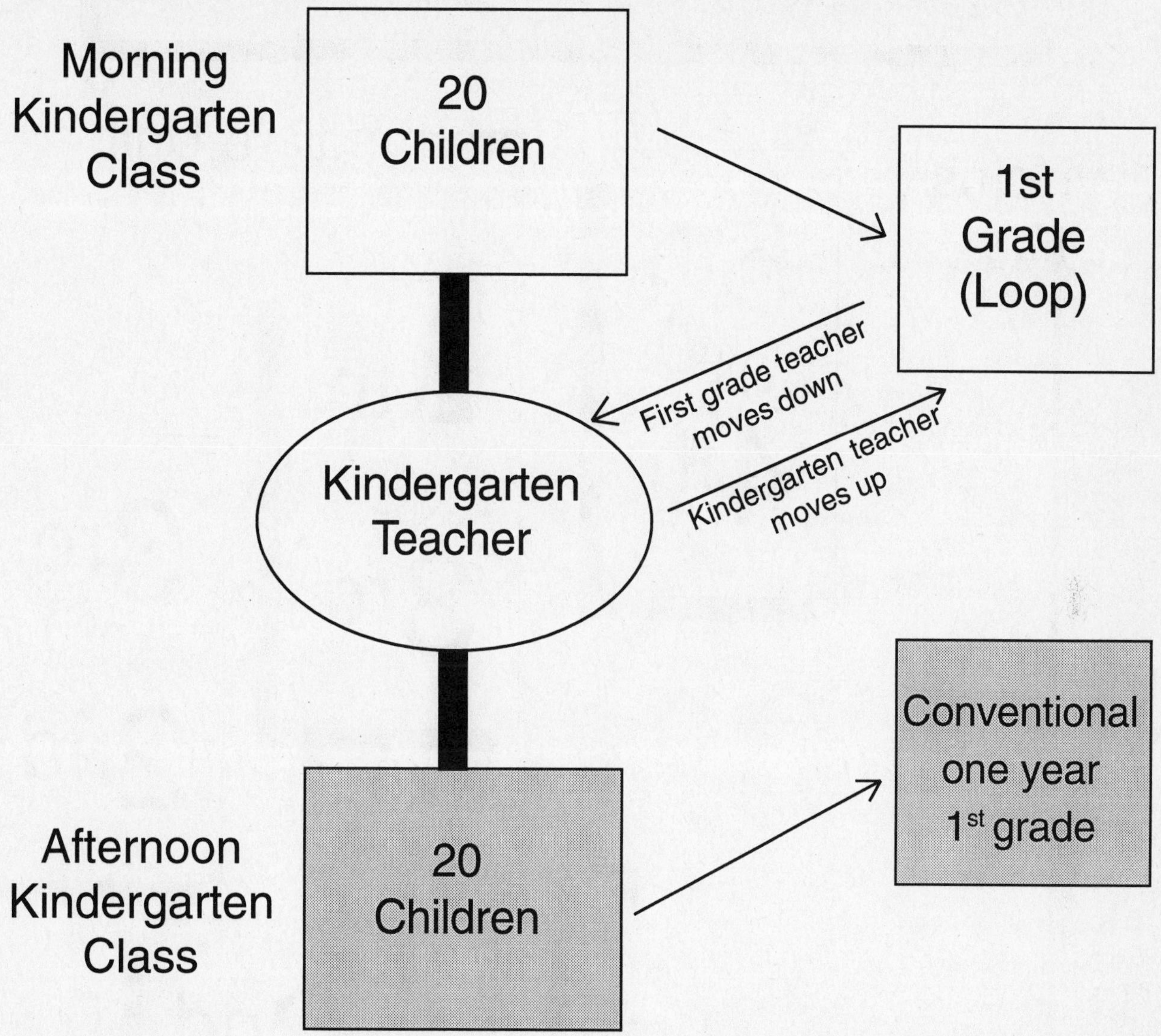

Note: Looping with a two session ½ day kindergarten program requires two first grades.

Student Selection:

- The AM class can loop
- 10 students from the AM plus 10 students from the PM can loop
- The PM class can loop
- Select 20 out of 40 AM/PM student to loop (Random selection)

Multiyear Configuration

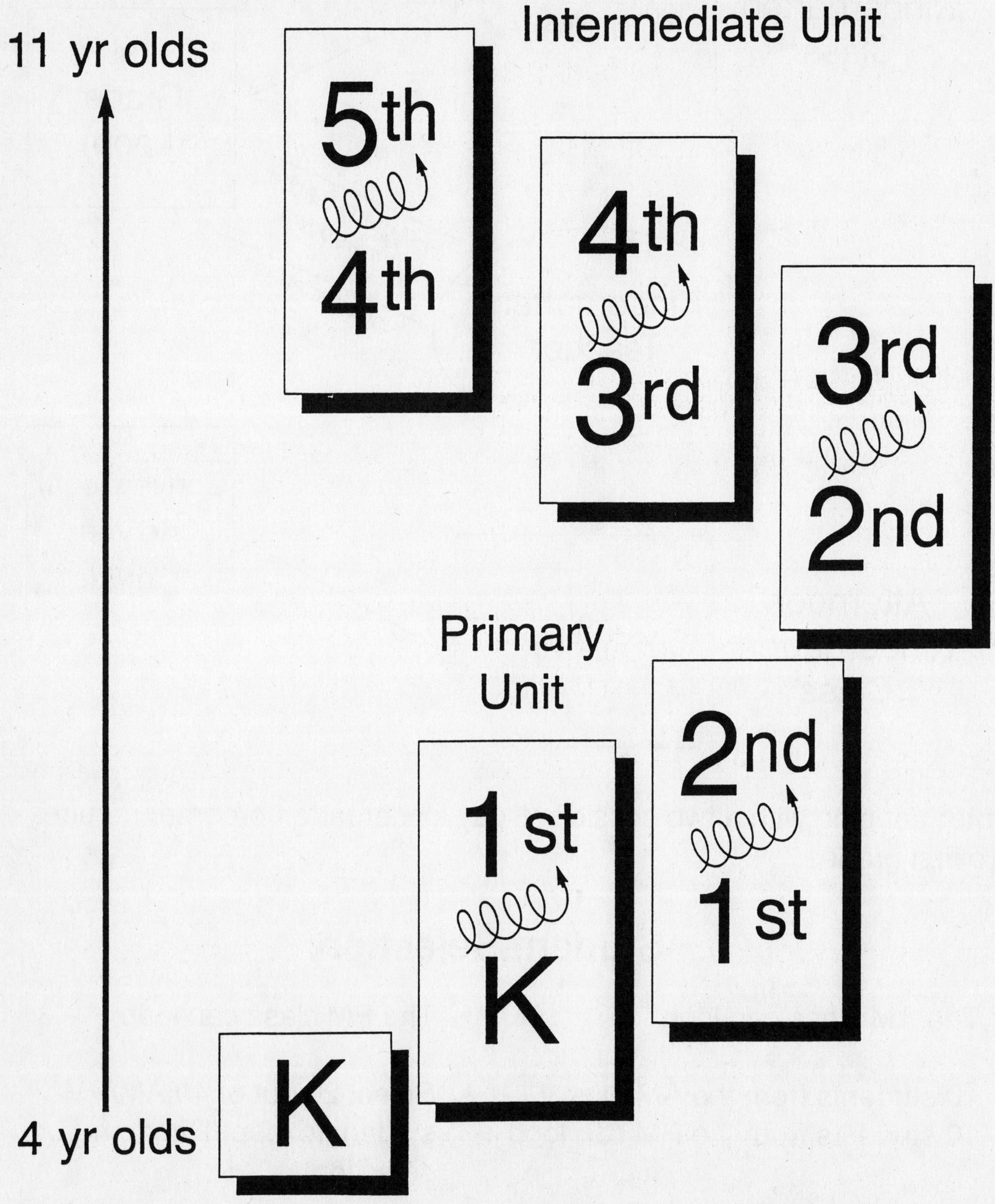

The Positive Aspects of Implementing Looping

1. The looping reform does not place your career at risk
2. A short lead time is required for implementation
3. No extensive training is necessary
4. The multiyear classroom builds a teacher's confidence
5. There is a low stress level for teachers
6. Curriculum changes are minimal
7. Additional physical space is not required
8. Midyear decision allows the teacher to "road test" the class
9. Looping is a 100% obstacle-free reform
10. All the down sides of looping are totally correctable
11. Program termination is possible without being "noticed"
12. Looping can be the prerequisite ground work for a future multiage configuration
13. There are minimal things to go wrong with this reform
14. Looping with a partial class is permissible (the class must remain heterogeneous)
15. Minimal financial resources are required
16. The only permission necessary to secure is from the parents of the future second year students

Things teachers should be aware of when looping:

Teachers:

- who change grade levels may lose their teaching assistant

- must learn the curriculum of a new grade

- may need special training for: Health, DARE, etc.

- must learn the ages and stages of the students at the new grade level

- may move to a grade with mandated:
    1. Testing
    2. Curriculum content
    3. Promotional standards

- may need to change pods (located in another wing), thus becoming separated from established teacher friends

- may move up to a "high pressure" grade level, (i.e., 1st or 3rd grade)

- may move to a grade level that is not child-centered philosophically

- may change to a grade level and be required to increase class size

Classroom Organizations

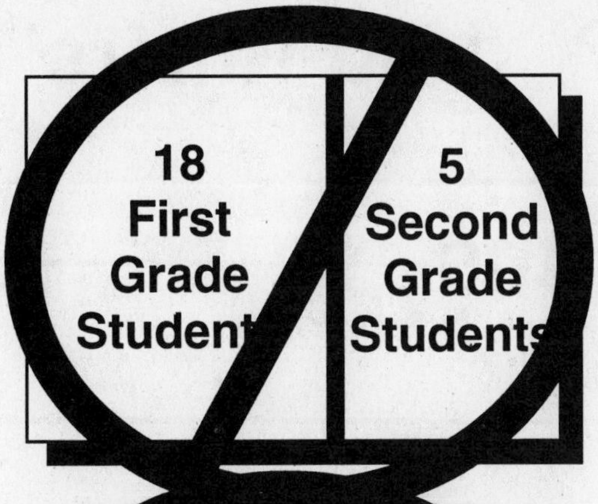

Split Grade Classroom

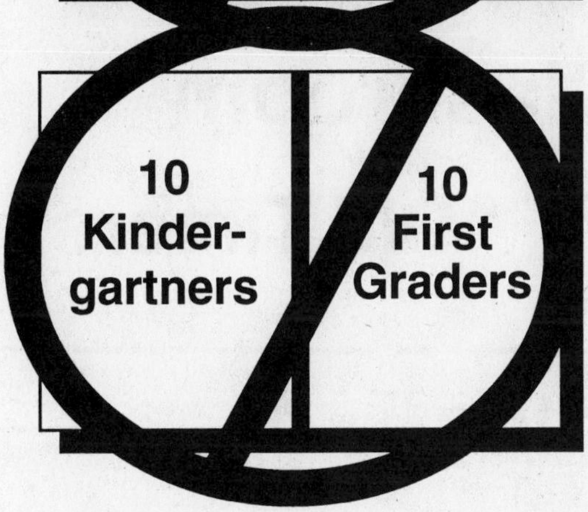

Combination Grade Classroom

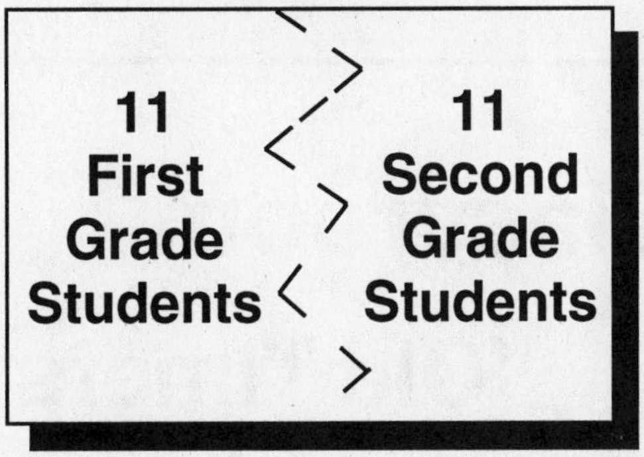

Multiage / Multigrade
Continuous Progress
Classroom

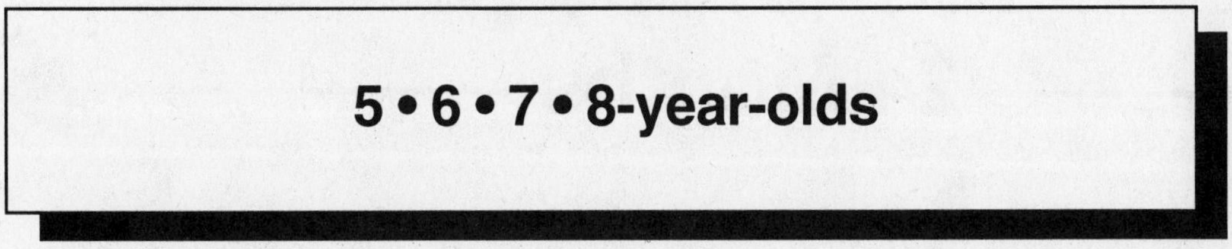

Multiage Ungraded Continuous Progress Classroom

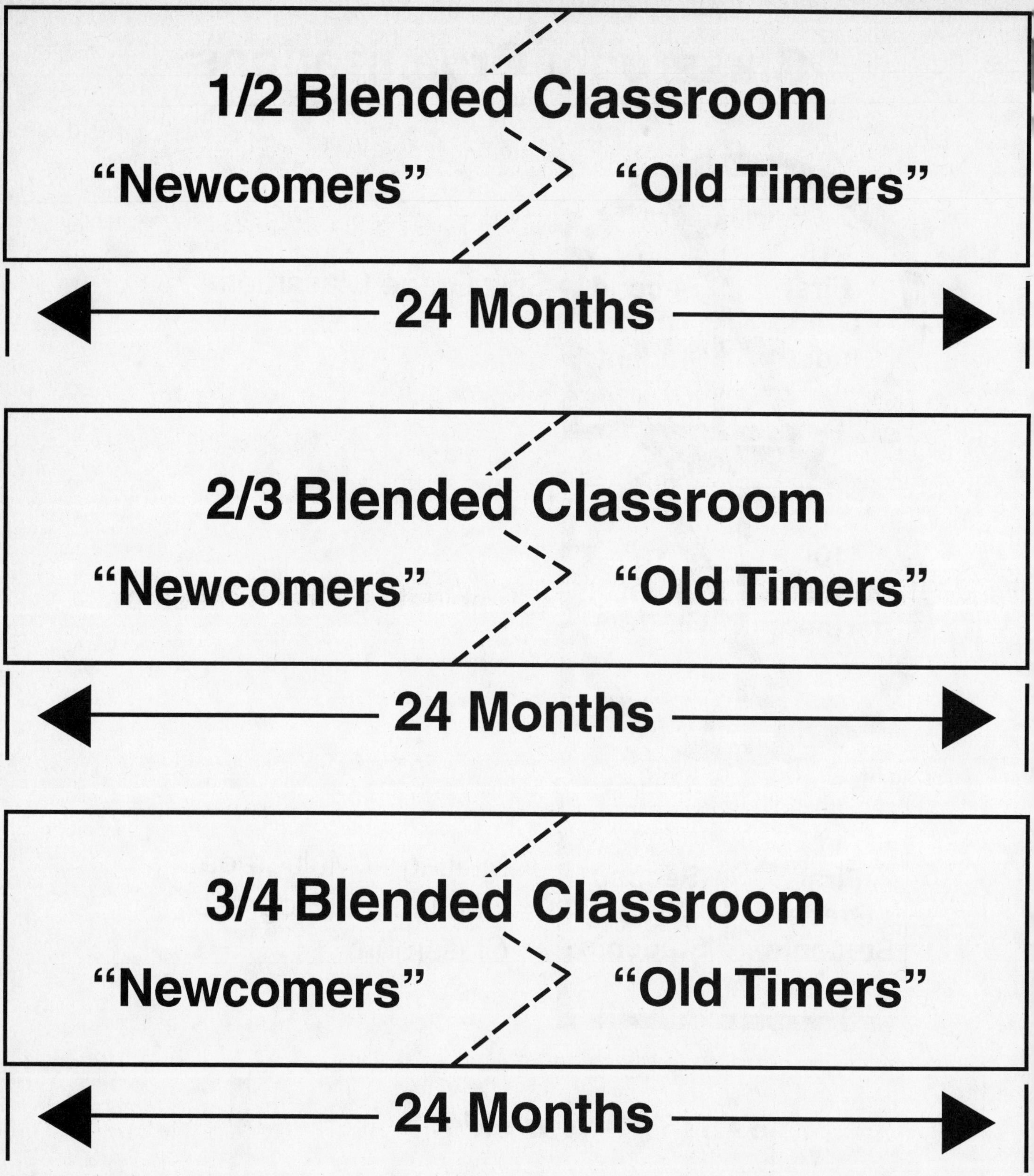

Grade testing and grade specific learner goals for newcomers are transferred to the end of the configuration

Doable Format to Teach Grade Level Mandated Content in a Dual Year Classroom

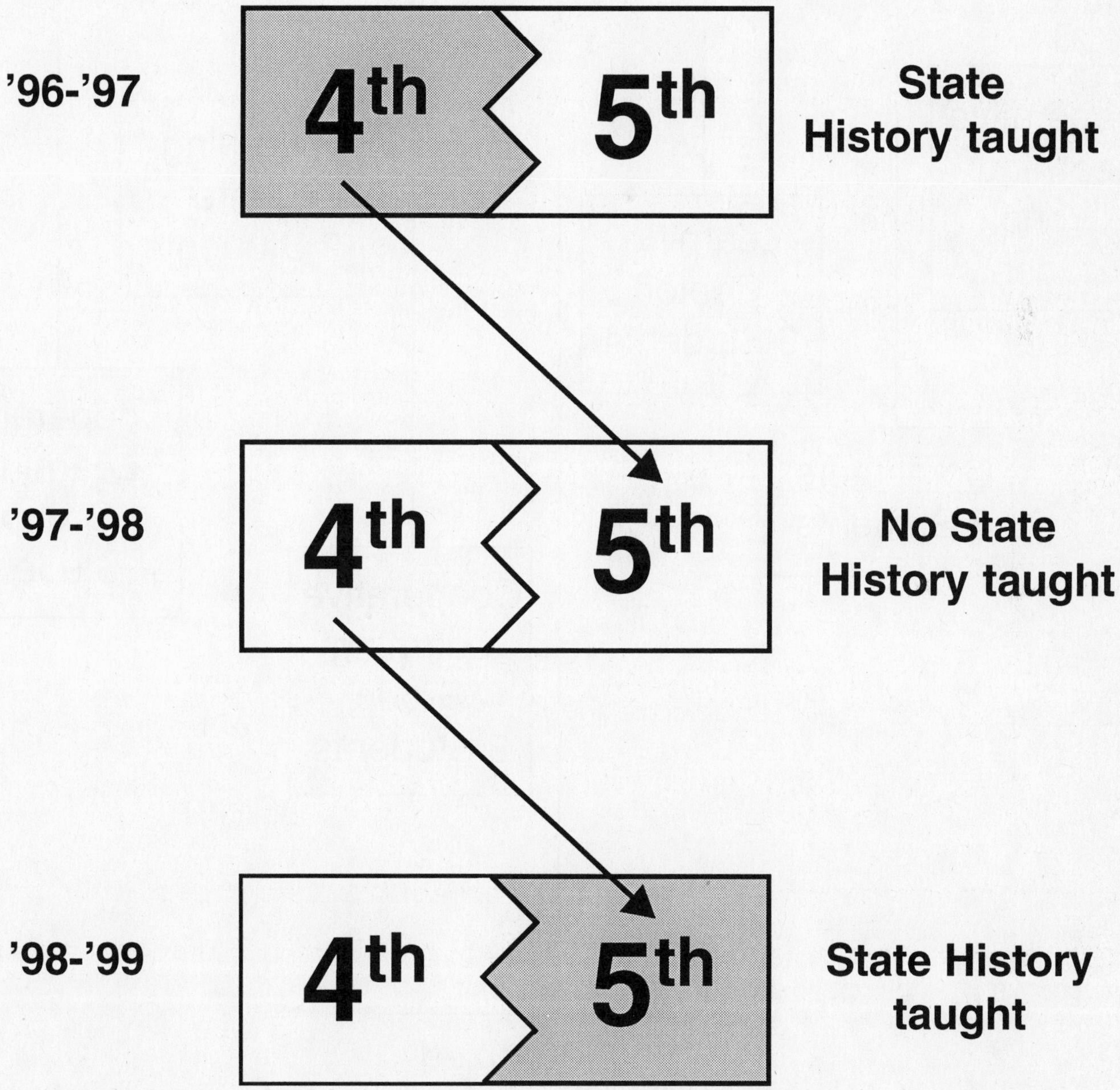

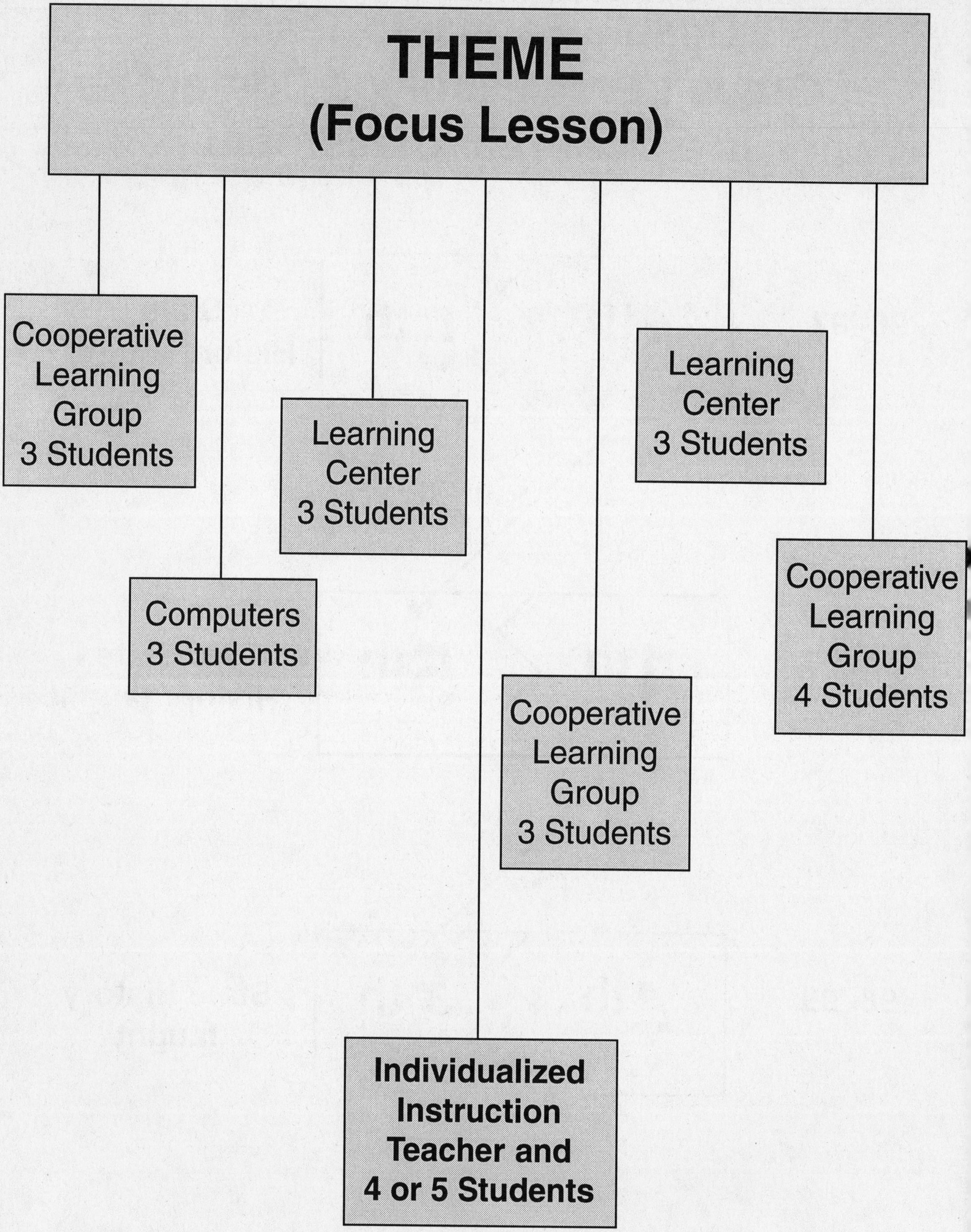
THEME
(Focus Lesson)
Cooperative Learning Group 3 Students
Computers 3 Students
Learning Center 3 Students
Individualized Instruction Teacher and 4 or 5 Students
Cooperative Learning Group 3 Students
Learning Center 3 Students
Cooperative Learning Group 4 Students

MULTIYEAR CURRICULUM CONTINUUM

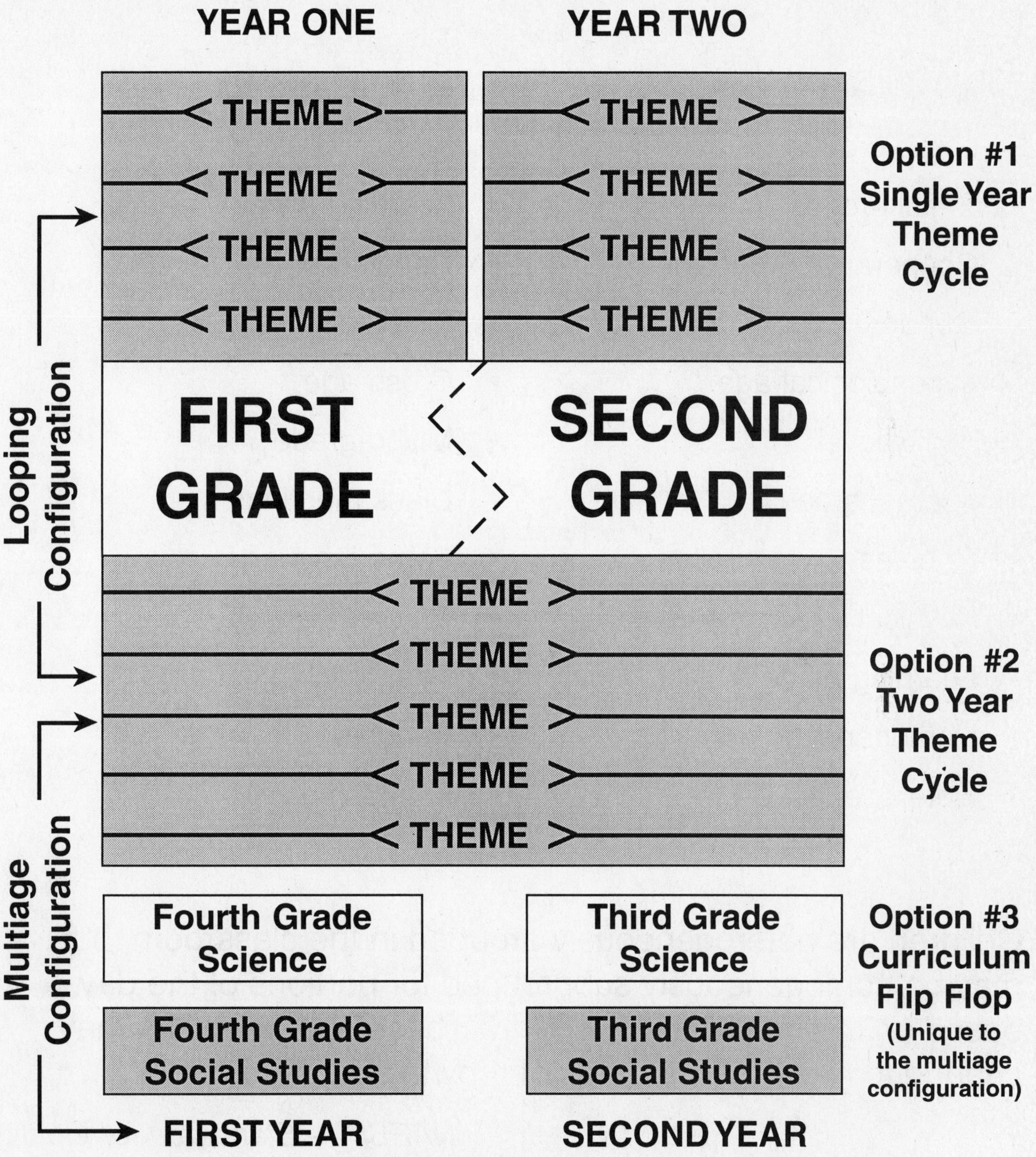

Grouping Strategies

Group Students in a Variety of Ways:

- Individual situations
- Large groups
- Small groups
- Cooperative groups
- Gender
- Chronological age
- Ability level
- Interest areas
- Hobbies
- Physical size
- Learning centers
- Homogeneous
- Heterogeneous
- Skills attainment
- Ad hoc skills groups
- Learning styles
- Reading styles
- Mixed-age
- Cross-age
- Mixed-grade
- Class meetings
- Same language
- Culture
- Peer teaching groups
- Buddies
- Friendships

Children are heterogeneously grouped in the classroom, but may be homogeneously subgrouped for portions of the day, based on the nature of the activity. These subgroupings may change to meet varying rates of growth and development.

NAESP — Standards for Quality Programs for Young Children

Common sense advice on a variety of grouping practices

Tracking by ability and grouping by ability are NOT one and the same thing:

- Students should be instructed in:

Large groups	1/3 of the day
Small groups	1/3 of the day
Individual situations	1/3 of the day

- Name skills groups to reflect the skill(s) being taught:
  - Silent "es"
  - The upper case club
  - Early "goesintos" (3 goes into 5)
  - Late "goesintos" (7 goes into 35)
  - The carriers
  - Handwriting clinic
  - Phonics club
  - Early times table club (0-6)
  - Late times table club (7-12)
  - Punctuation club
  - Double digit addition club
  - The borrowers
  - Keyboard clinic

- Refer to collections of students as groups, clubs, clinics, quads, triads and pairs

- Avoid naming groups: Peacocks, Robins and Buzzards or Shooting Stars, Rising Stars and Falling Stars

- Be careful not to create more groups than you can properly sponsor

Common sense advice about grouping students:

- Group by ability for a specific purpose for a short period of time

- Group some reading and math groups heterogeneously, teaching within a ***"reachable skill range"***

- Group by skills attainment for a specific purpose

- Always keep groups flexible, with "old timers" moving on and "newcomers" joining in

Multiage Classroom Benefits

1. "Old-timers" eavesdrop and revisit concepts taught to newcomers

2. Newcomers eavesdrop on concepts taught to the "old-timers"

3. "Old-timers" model appropriate behavior to newcomers

4. The more knowledgeable students assist the less knowledgeable

5. Extra learning time is provided without the stigma of retention

6. There is a more challenging curriculum

7. The classroom is more inclusionary for differently-abled students

8. There is an opportunity for students to reach "senior citizen" status every two or three years

Times when it's appropriate to separate your multiage class by grade level for a specific purpose

- Annual environmental camp trip
- D.A.R.E. drug programs
- Sex education programs
- Mandated group standardized testing
- Occasionally some types of field trips may require separating the class by age or grade level
- Sometimes an outside sponsored activity by the 4-H club, Boy Scouts, Girl Scouts, Cub Scouts, Brownies, etc. may require dividing classes by age/grade.

Note: Splitting your multiage class on occasion by age/grade level will not undermine the integrity of your program

GIFTED AND TALENTED STUDENTS

Conventional One Year/ Single Grade Classroom

- Extended learning program
- Tutoring opportunities offer a "teaching" role

Multiage Classroom

- Extended learning program
- Tutoring opportunities offer a "teaching" role

AND

- There are younger students to socialize with
- Students can gain "senior citizen" status
- The older more knowledge-able students have the chance to practice being in a leadership role
- Multiage classrooms have a higher ceiling on the curriculum

CLASS SIZE

Compared to large classes:

- small classes ameliorate the effects of large schools;
- fewer students are held back a grade;
- while small classes benefit all students, minority students benefit the most;
- students receive more individual attention;
- smaller classes are friendlier and more intimate;
- there are fewer discipline problems in smaller classes;
- students are more likely to participate in activities.

Consider some potential cost savings from using small classes in grades K-2 or K-3

- There are fewer retentions
- Less need for remediation and/or special education
- Improved behavior
- Increased achievement.

Project Star
Tennessee

Comparisons of Graded and Nongraded Schools

Anderson and Pavan reviewed 64 research studies published between 1968-90 which compared nongraded and graded schools. The studies most frequently favored nongradedness on standardized measures of academic achievement, mental health and positive attitude toward school.

Specifically, regarding **academic achievement:**

58% of the studies favored nongraded groups
33% of the studies showed no difference
9% of the studies showed nongraded groups performed not as well

Regarding, **mental health and positive school attitude:**

52% of the studies favored nongraded groups
43% of the studies showed the groups to be similar in performance
5% of the studies showed nongraded groups performed not as well

The studies also showed that boys, African-Americans, underachievers, and students from lower socioeconomic status were more likely to perform better and feel more positive about themselves and their schools in a nongraded environment.

Sources: *Nongradedness: Helping It To Happen*; Robert H. Anderson and Barbara Nelson Pavan, Technomic Pub. Co., 1992, Page 46.

Managing Complex Change

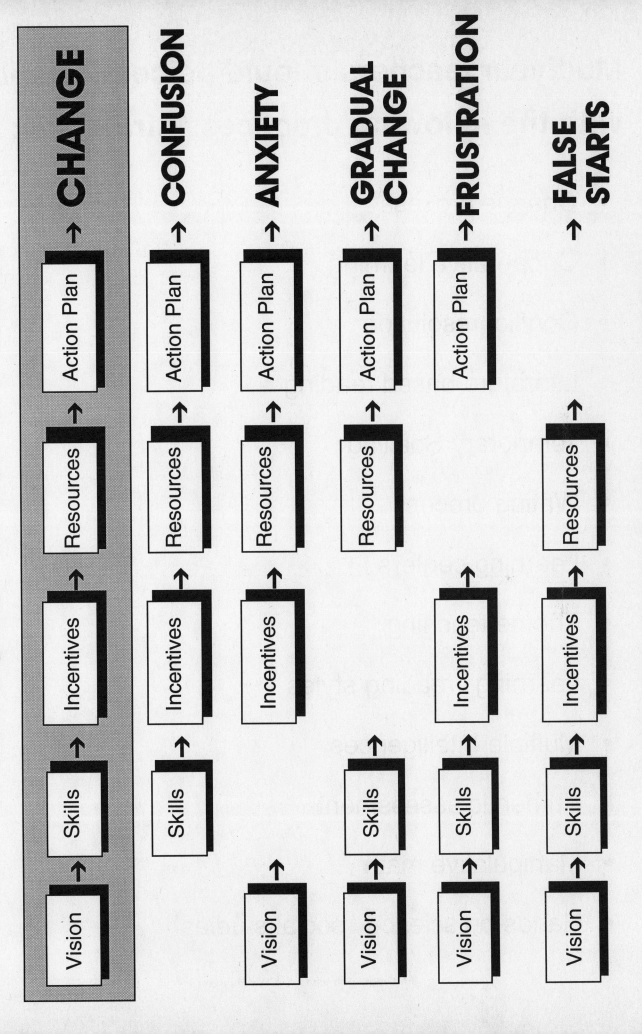

Vision	Skills	Incentives	Resources	Action Plan	**CHANGE**
	Skills	Incentives	Resources	Action Plan	**CONFUSION**
Vision		Incentives	Resources	Action Plan	**ANXIETY**
Vision	Skills		Resources	Action Plan	**GRADUAL CHANGE**
Vision	Skills	Incentives		Action Plan	**FRUSTRATION**
Vision	Skills	Incentives	Resources		**FALSE STARTS**

Multiyear teachers should be comfortable with the following practices / strategies:

- Change process
- Cooperative learning
- Conflict resolution
- Literature-based reading
- Temporary Spelling
- Writing process
- Learning centers
- Theme teaching
- Learning / reading styles
- Multiple Intelligences
- Authentic assessment
- Manipulative math
- Hands-on science / social studies

Perceived Advantages of a Kindergarten/First Grade Blend

- Mixed-age eavesdropping opportunities
- There is a higher ceiling on the curriculum
- There are peer modeling opportunities
- There are over a dozen multiyear placement benefits
- There can be an additional year of learning time without the stigma of "staying back"
- Grade one is afforded more play opportunities
- There is additional time available for "kid watching"
- In some schools kindergartners go home at noon reducing the class size for first grade in the PM
- There are real benefits to proximal development
- There are tutoring opportunities for both groups
- There are 50% fewer new first graders to teach to read

Perceived Disadvantages of a Kindergarten/First Grade Blend

- Kindergartners may be denied play opportunities
- Many of today's kindergartners have very high needs
- Class is too diverse developmentally
- First graders may be shortchanged academically
- Some schools have four-year-olds in kindergarten due to a late entrance date
- The needs of five-year-olds are very different from six-year-olds
- Kindergartners may be overwhelmed by more experienced first graders
- There may not be enough quality kid watching time
- Kindergarten is time intensive to teach
- Some entire kindergarten classes are too disjointed to keep together as a group for multiple years
- Kindergartners who are learning handicapped, yet unidentified, may not qualify for special needs intervention
- If there is an AM and PM kindergarten (2 groups) there may be too much lost time transitioning

Various factors to consider before blending Kindergarten and First Grade

- Class size
- Entrance date
- Program support: Parents, teachers, administrators, school board
- Condition of the student population
- Number of non-English speaking children
- Conflicting mandates from the state, county, and local education officials
- Grade specific curriculum requirements
- Number of identified special needs children
- Number of children with "invisible" disabilities

How to Avoid Disaster in the Multiage Classroom

Notes

1 **Don't Cling to Graded Practices**

2 **Take Your Time When Implementing a Multiage Classroom**

3 **Provide Adequate Staff Development**

4 **Consider Class Size**

5 **Be Willing to Pay for Education Reform**

6 **Avoid Mandating Conflicting Educational Reforms**

7 **Beware of Creating Too Much Student Diversity Within a Multiage Setting**

8 **Pay Attention to School Readiness Issues When Placing a Child**

9 **Create a Shared Vision With All Stakeholders**

10 **Select Students for a Multiage Classroom With Careful Thought**

11 **Don't Start With Too Many Grades**

12 **Offering Parents the Choice of a Multiage Program for Their Child is Essential — But Can Create Problems**

13 **Beware of the Class from the Black Lagoon**

14 **The Multiage Classroom May Not Be the Best Placement for Some Students**

15 **Don't Assume Everyone Can (or Wants to) Teach in a Multiage Classroom**

16 **Allow Enough Planning Time Before Implementation**

17 **Don't Assign a Teacher to Difficult Parents for More Than One Year**

18 **Recognize and Resolve Teacher/Student Personality Conflicts**

19 **Provide Challenges for Gifted Students**

20 **Don't Confuse Combination- or Split-Grade Classrooms With True Multiage Continuous Progress Classrooms**

21 **Don't Expect Multiage Practices to Solve Every Problem in Your Classroom**

22 **Don't Assign a Marginal Teacher to a Multiage Classroom**

23 **Don't Use Inaccurate or Inflammatory Terms When Defining Your Multiage Program**

24 **Don't Turn the Multiage Classroom into a Special Education Room**

25 **Don't Overlook a Student's Potential Learning Disability**

26 **Be Careful Not to Create Staff Dissension**

Guidelines to balancing the multiage classroom

- Equal number of students from each grade level*
- Equal number of boys and girls
- Racially / culturally / linguistically balanced
- Socio-economically balanced
- Equal range of ability levels
- The percent of special needs students is the same as other regular classrooms

Note: Remember, it is not always possible to achieve the above guidelines.

*Does not pertain to single grade looping classrooms

Peterborough Elementary School
Reading and Writing Expectations for **Grade 1**

Midyear — Reading

Can see him/herself as a reader

Reads 50 sight words

Sustains reading for 15 minutes

Fluent at third pre-primer

Uses picture and beginning sound cues

Can focus and participate in shared reading and discussion for 10 minutes

Can generally retell a story

Can draw a picture about a book read

Midyear — Writing

Writes 15-20 minutes at a sitting

Gaining confidence as a writer

Writes two related thoughts

Can read back what he/she has written during the process

Uses inventive spelling

Has concept of word; leaves spaces between words

Shares writing willingly

Third Term — Reading

Knows 75 sight words

Reads 15-20 minutes on his/her own

Uses picture cues, beginning and ending sounds

Can skip unknown words and go on

Can focus and participate in shared reading and discussion for 15 minutes

Can retell a story with details

Can write a sentence about what he/she has read

Third Term — Writing

Writes 20-30 words at a sitting

Writes three or four sentences that are related

Reads what he/she has written after a period of time

Uses inventive spelling, beginning and ending sounds and some sight words

Begins to use punctuation

Writes 15-20 minutes at a sitting

Begins to revise after teacher conference

End of Year — Reading

Fluent at 1.9 level test

Knows 100 sight words

Sustains 20 minutes reading on his/her own

Uses pictures; beginning and ending sound cues

Can skip unknown word and go on, can reread for meaning

Realizes that print constructs meaning

Can focus and participate in shared reading and discussion for 20-25 minutes

Can retell a story with details

Can write about his/her reading

End of Year — Writing

Writes for 40 words at a sitting

Writes four or five sentences

Can read back own writing

Uses inventive spelling, beginning and ending sounds and some sight words

Begins to use capital letters

Begins to use classroom units as ideas for writing

Begins to use punctuation

Can revise a few words after a teacher conference

Reprinted with permission of Sandy Cook and Ann Lessard

Peterborough Elementary School — **Second Grade**

	First Term			Third Term		
	Sept.	Oct.	Nov.	Sept. (baseline)	Jan.	May
Written Samples (words written in ½ hr.)	______	______	______	______	______	______
Average for class	______	______	______	______	______	______
Percentage of words correctly spelled in writing samples	______	______	______	______	______	______
Spelling test — approximate grade equivalents (Morrison McCall)	______	______	______	______	______	______
Class Average on Morrison McCall	______	______	______	______	______	______

FIRST TERM PROFILE

Social

Takes turns and listens to others

Listens and focuses in group discussion (15-20 minutes)

Reading

Knows about 125 sight words

Reads on own for 20 minutes

Uses picture clues plus beginning/ending sounds

Can skip unknown word and go back

Can retell a story read with some details

Can focus and participate in shared reading

Can write two or three sentences about a book s/he's read

Writing

Writes 40-50 words daily

Can write four or five related sentences

Can read what s/he's written

Uses invented spelling with correct beginning/ending and vowel sound

Is using capital at beginning for names and self; periods at end

Can write for 20-25 minutes

Beginning to add or delete words

THIRD TERM PROFILE

Social

Takes turns and listens to others

Listens and focuses in group discussions (15-20 minutes)

Reading

Knows about 200 sight words

Reads on own for 20 minutes

Uses picture clues plus beginning/ending sounds

Can skip unknown word and go back

Can retell a story s/he's read with some details

Can focus and participate in shared reading

Can write two or three sentences about a book s/he's read

Writing

Writes 60-70 words daily

Can write four or five related sentences

Can read what s/he's written

Uses invented spelling with correct beginning/ending and vowel sound

Is using capital at beginning for names and self; periods at end

Can write for 30-35 minutes

Begins to add/delete words for clearer meaning

MONTPELIER PUBLIC SCHOOL SYSTEM
MONTPELIER, VERMONT
READING SKILLS CONTINUUM

Name ______________________________

Date of Birth ______________________________

This continuum lists skills incorporated in the reading programs of the Montpelier Public School System. The skills will coordinate the curriculum in a system where teacher instruction integrates varied methods, materials, and activities.

SCHOOL YEAR	READING / CLASSROOM TEACHER	GRADE

REMEDIAL / SPECIAL

SCHOOL YEAR	READING / CLASSROOM TEACHER	GRADE

DIRECTIONS FOR RECORDING READING PROGRESS:

Place a slash in the space next to the skill introduced. ⧄

When the child shows satisfactory performance on that skill, complete an ☒

Satisfactory performance is 90% – 100%

READING

		K	1	2	3	4
K-3	1. Recognizes name in print					
	2. Recognizes left/right progression					
	3. Blends sounds into words					
	4. Reads/follows printed directions					
	5. Recalls ideas – silent reading					
	6. Finds facts in story					
	7. Knows Dolch — Kucera/Francis words					
	8. Recalls specific details					
	9. Deciphers words in context					
	10. Uses punctuation to get meaning					
	11. Reads words — 3-letter clusters (blends)					
	12. Reads words — Silent letter(s)					
	13. Reads diphthongs					
4	14. Reads manuscript/cursive					
	15. Recognizes main idea					
	16. Reads without vocalizing					
	17. Summarizes (orally)					
	18. Recognizes/uses synonyms/antonyms					
	19. Identifies:					
	A. Character					
	B. Plot					
	C. Setting					
	of passage of reading					

REASONING

		K	1	2	3	4
K-3	20. Draws inferences and conclusions					
	21. Uses context clues to understand the meaning of unfamiliar words					
	22. Distinguishes fact/opinion					
	23. Uses facts to support story interpretation					
	24. Reads passage and sequences events					

LITERATURE

Level	Item	K	1	2	3	4
K-3	25. Interprets feelings of characters					
	26. Recognizes parts of book					
	A. Index					
	B. Table of contents					
	27. Discusses different genre of literature:					
	A. Poetry					
	B. Fiction					
	C. Fables					
	EXPOSED TO AT LEAST TEN OF THE FOLLOWING:					
	28. Mother Goose					
	29. Hans C. Anderson					
	30. Grimm's Fairy Tales					
	31. Kipling's Just So Stories					
	32. Stone Soup					
	33. Little Engine That Could					
	34. Millions of Cats					
	35. Peter Rabbit					
	36. Winnie the Pooh					
	37. Where the Wild Things Are					
	38. Curious George					
	39. Aesop's Fables					
	40. Cinderella					
	41. Little Red Hen					
	42. Chicken Little					
	43. Cat In the Hat					
	44. Laura Ingalls Wilder					
	45. American Folk Tales					
	46. Poetry (Haiku)					
4	47. Identifies/uses figurative language to enhance quality of literature					
	48. Discusses language which creates a different mood					
	49. Distinguishes:					
	Fiction/nonfiction					
	Biography/autobiography					

Literature continued

Level	Item	K	1	2	3	4
4	IS EXPOSED TO THE FOLLOWING:					
	50. Cricket in Times Square					
	51. Charlie and the Chocolate Factory					
	52. Mrs. Frisby and the Rats of Nimh					
	53. Visit from St. Nick					
	54. Poetry					

SPEAKING / LISTENING

Level	Item	K	1	2	3	4
K-3	55. Communicates freely orally					
	56. Speaks 4 word sentences					
	57. Rhymes words					
	58. Tells story using pictures in sequence					
	59. Follows oral directions (3 Step)					
	60. Listens to recall details					
	61. Dictates captions					
	62. Speaks grammatically correctly					
	63. Uses correct punctuation (inflection)					
	64. Uses correct subject/verb agreement					
	65. Gives 3-step oral directions					
	66. Uses telephone for own use					
	67. Uses telephone to get/give messages					
	68. Gives simple introduction(s)					
	69. Listens to get main idea					

MEDIA

Level	Item	K	1	2	3	4
K-3	70. Uses card catalog					
4	71. Locates print and non-print materials on an assigned basis					
	72. Reads newspaper(s)/magazine(s) to learn about current events					

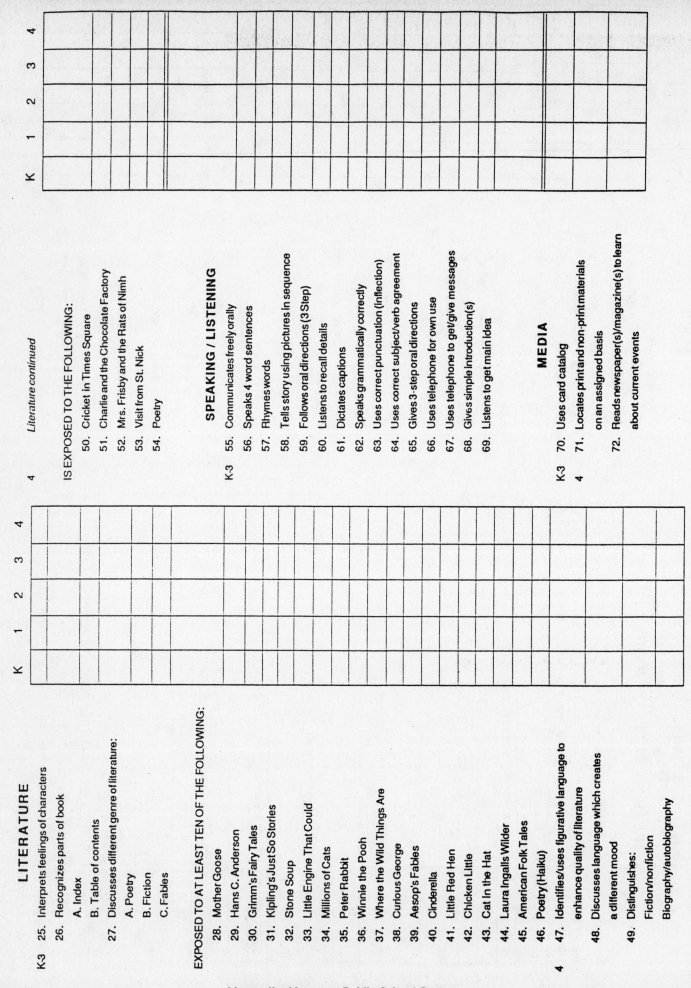

GRAMMAR

		K	1	2	3	4
K-3	73. Uses capital letters at the beginning of sentences					
	74. Reads/understands prefixes un/be/re/dis/en-in					
	75. Reads/understands suffixes s/ed/ing/ly/er/y/es/est/ful/less/able/ness/s/or					
	76. Recognizes plural forms s/es					
	77. Recognizes paragraphs					
4	78. Aware of margins					
	79. Uses plural forms ves/ies					
	80. Recognizes sentence types:					
	Imperative					
	Interrogative					
	Declarative					
	Exclamatory					
	81. Identifies words in sentences as:					
	Nouns					
	Verbs					
	Adjectives					

STUDY

		K	1	2	3	4
K-3	82. Recognizes colors					
	83. Sustains him/herself at task(s)					
	84. Classifies words					
4	85. Sustains him/herself at task(s)					

SPELLING SKILLS

		K	1	2	3	4
K-3	86. Recognizes fine letter likenesses/differences					
	87. Names and recognizes letters					
	88. Spells simple CVC words					
	89. Knows sound/letter correspondence – Long/short vowels					
	90. Knows sound/letter correspondence – Consonants					
	91. Arranges words in alphabetical order (1-3 letters)					
	92. Uses consonant blends/digraphs in encoding					
	93. Recognizes compound words					
4	94. Corrects spelling errors as part of the writing process					
	95. Arranges words in alphabetical order (1-4 letters)					
	96. Uses the dictionary for meanings/spellings of words					
	97. Recognizes and uses homonyms					

WRITING

		K	1	2	3	4
K-3	98. Places name on assigned work					
	99. Writes full name					
	100. Recognizes/writes letters					
	101. Matches lower/upper case letters					
	102. Copies material					
	103. Writes 2-3 complete sentences					
	104. Summarizes (written)					
	105. Writes a short friendly letter					
	106. Uses the possessive form					
	107. Uses correct punctuation (. ! ?)					
	108. Uses steps of writing process appropriate to grade and level***					
4	109. Revises/edits written work					
	110. Writes legibly in manuscript/cursive					

WRITING PROCESS

	K	1	2	3	4
Stimulus					
Prewriting					
Rough Draft					
Rereading					
Responding					
Editing					
Revising					
Final copy					
Evaluating					

Comments:

Teacher: ______________________ Grade: ________

Comments:

Teacher: ______________________ Grade: ________

Comments:

Teacher: ______________________ Grade: ________

Comments:

Teacher: ______________________ Grade: ________

CONTENT

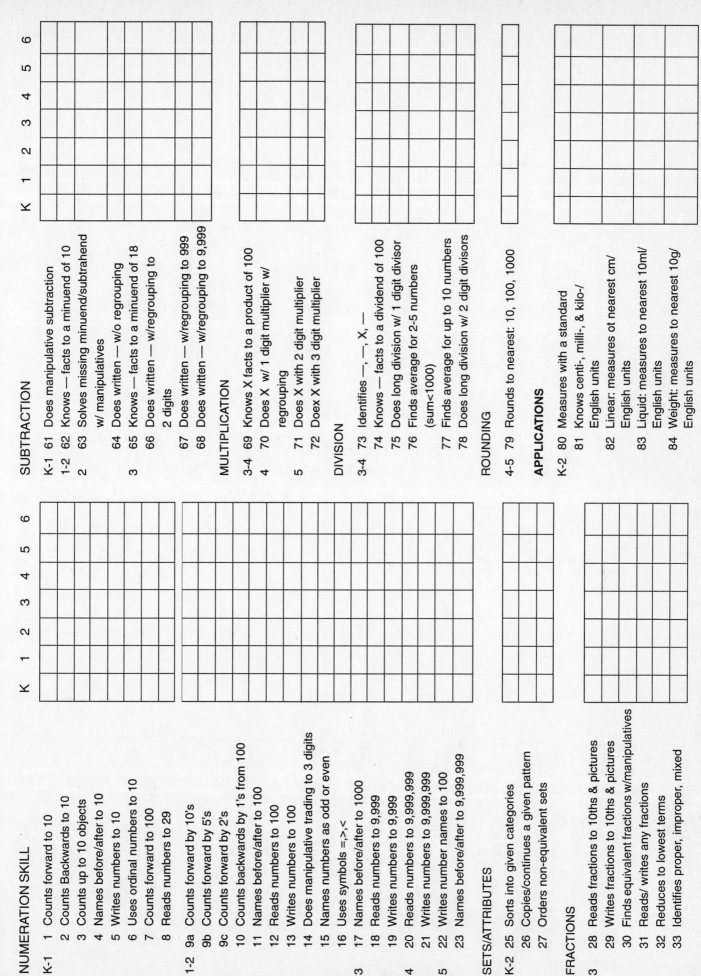

NUMERATION SKILL			K	1	2	3	4	5	6
K-1	1	Counts forward to 10							
	2	Counts Backwards to 10							
	3	Counts up to 10 objects							
	4	Names before/after to 10							
	5	Writes numbers to 10							
	6	Uses ordinal numbers to 10							
	7	Counts forward to 100							
	8	Reads numbers to 29							
1-2	9a	Counts forward by 10's							
	9b	Counts forward by 5's							
	9c	Counts forward by 2's							
	10	Counts backwards by 1's from 100							
	11	Names before/after to 100							
	12	Reads numbers to 100							
	13	Writes numbers to 100							
	14	Does manipulative trading to 3 digits							
	15	Names numbers as odd or even							
	16	Uses symbols =,>,<							
3	17	Names before/after to 1000							
	18	Reads numbers to 9,999							
	19	Writes numbers to 9,999							
4	20	Reads numbers to 9,999,999							
	21	Writes numbers to 9,999,999							
5	22	Writes number names to 100							
	23	Names before/after to 9,999,999							

SETS/ATTRIBUTES			K	1	2	3	4	5	6
K-2	25	Sorts into given categories							
	26	Copies/continues a given pattern							
	27	Orders non-equivalent sets							

FRACTIONS			K	1	2	3	4	5	6
3	28	Reads fractions to 10ths & pictures							
	29	Writes fractions to 10ths & pictures							
	30	Finds equivalent fractions w/manipulatives							
	31	Reads/ writes any fractions							
	32	Reduces to lowest terms							
	33	Identifies proper, improper, mixed							

SUBTRACTION			K	1	2	3	4	5	6
K-1	61	Does manipulative subtraction							
1-2	62	Knows — facts to a minuend of 10							
2	63	Solves missing minuend/subtrahend w/ manipulatives							
	64	Does written — w/o regrouping							
3	65	Knows — facts to a minuend of 18							
	66	Does written — w/regrouping to 2 digits							
	67	Does written — w/regrouping to 999							
	68	Does written — w/regrouping to 9,999							

MULTIPLICATION			K	1	2	3	4	5	6
3-4	69	Knows X facts to a product of 100							
4	70	Does X w/ 1 digit multiplier w/ regrouping							
5	71	Does X with 2 digit multiplier							
	72	Doex X with 3 digit multiplier							

DIVISION			K	1	2	3	4	5	6
3-4	73	Identifies —, —, X, —							
	74	Knows — facts to a dividend of 100							
	75	Does long division w/ 1 digit divisor							
	76	Finds average for 2-5 numbers (sum<1000)							
	77	Finds average for up to 10 numbers							
	78	Does long division w/ 2 digit divisors							

ROUNDING			K	1	2	3	4	5	6
4-5	79	Rounds to nearest: 10, 100, 1000							

APPLICATIONS			K	1	2	3	4	5	6
K-2	80	Measures with a standard							
	81	Knows centi-, milli-, & kilo-/ English units							
	82	Linear: measures ot nearest cm/ English units							
	83	Liquid: measures to nearest 10ml/ English units							
	84	Weight: measures to nearest 10g/ English units							

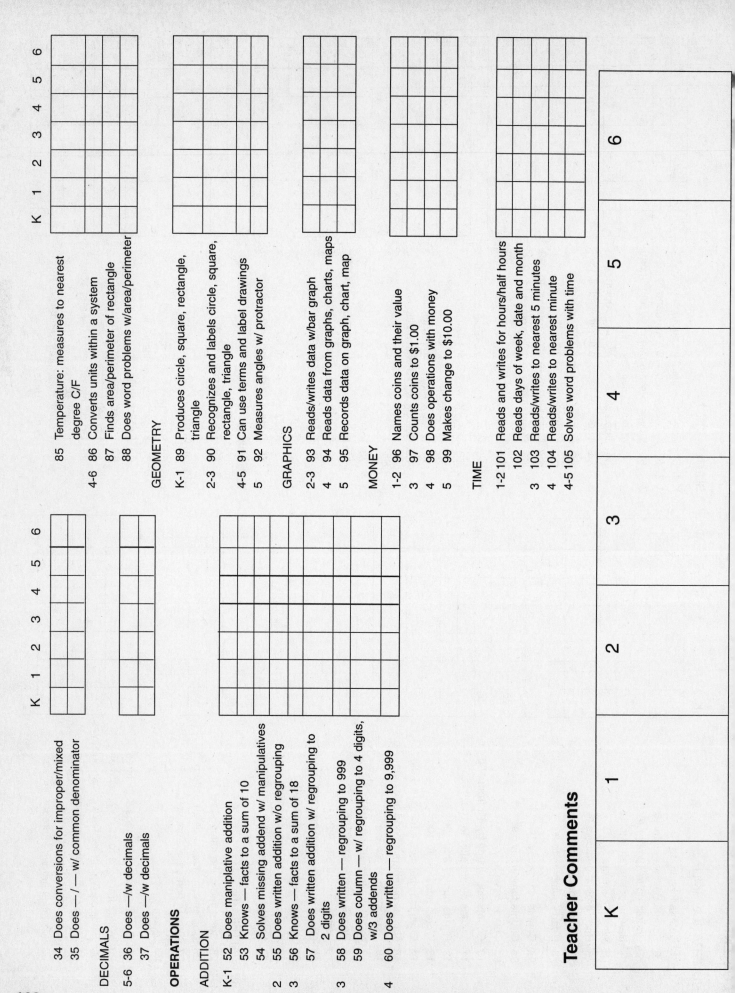

Grade	No.	Skill	K	1	2	3	4	5	6
	34	Does conversions for improper/mixed							
	35	Does — / — w/ common denominator							

DECIMALS

Grade	No.	Skill	K	1	2	3	4	5	6
5-6	36	Does —/w decimals							
	37	Does —/w decimals							

OPERATIONS

ADDITION

Grade	No.	Skill	K	1	2	3	4	5	6
K-1	52	Does maniplative addition							
	53	Knows — facts to a sum of 10							
	54	Solves missing addend w/ manipulatives							
2	55	Does written addition w/o regrouping							
3	56	Knows — facts to a sum of 18							
	57	Does written addition w/ regrouping to 2 digits							
3	58	Does written — regrouping to 999							
	59	Does column — w/ regrouping to 4 digits, w/3 addends							
4	60	Does written — regrouping to 9,999							

Grade	No.	Skill	K	1	2	3	4	5	6
	85	Temperature: measures to nearest degree C/F							
4-6	86	Converts units within a system							
	87	Finds area/perimeter of rectangle							
	88	Does word problems w/area/perimeter							

GEOMETRY

Grade	No.	Skill	K	1	2	3	4	5	6
K-1	89	Produces circle, square, rectangle, triangle							
2-3	90	Recognizes and labels circle, square, rectangle, triangle							
4-5	91	Can use terms and label drawings							
5	92	Measures angles w/ protractor							

GRAPHICS

Grade	No.	Skill	K	1	2	3	4	5	6
2-3	93	Reads/writes data w/bar graph							
4	94	Reads data from graphs, charts, maps							
5	95	Records data on graph, chart, map							

MONEY

Grade	No.	Skill	K	1	2	3	4	5	6
1-2	96	Names coins and their value							
3	97	Counts coins to $1.00							
4	98	Does operations with money							
5	99	Makes change to $10.00							

TIME

Grade	No.	Skill	K	1	2	3	4	5	6
1-2	101	Reads and writes for hours/half hours							
	102	Reads days of week, date and month							
3	103	Reads/writes to nearest 5 minutes							
4	104	Reads/writes to nearest minute							
4-5	105	Solves word problems with time							

Teacher Comments

K	1	2	3	4	5	6

THE MULTIYEAR CONNECTION:

ACTIVITIES TO BRIDGE THE YEARS:

- Summer Reading Logs
- Summer Writing Journals
- Summer Projects
- Scavenger Hunts
- Real World Connections
- Correspondence
- Individualized Review & Extensions
- Skill-Level Maintenance
- Goal-Setting

LONG-TERM PLANNING & DECISION-MAKING CHART

RE: CURRICULUM IN THE MULTIYEAR CLASSROOM

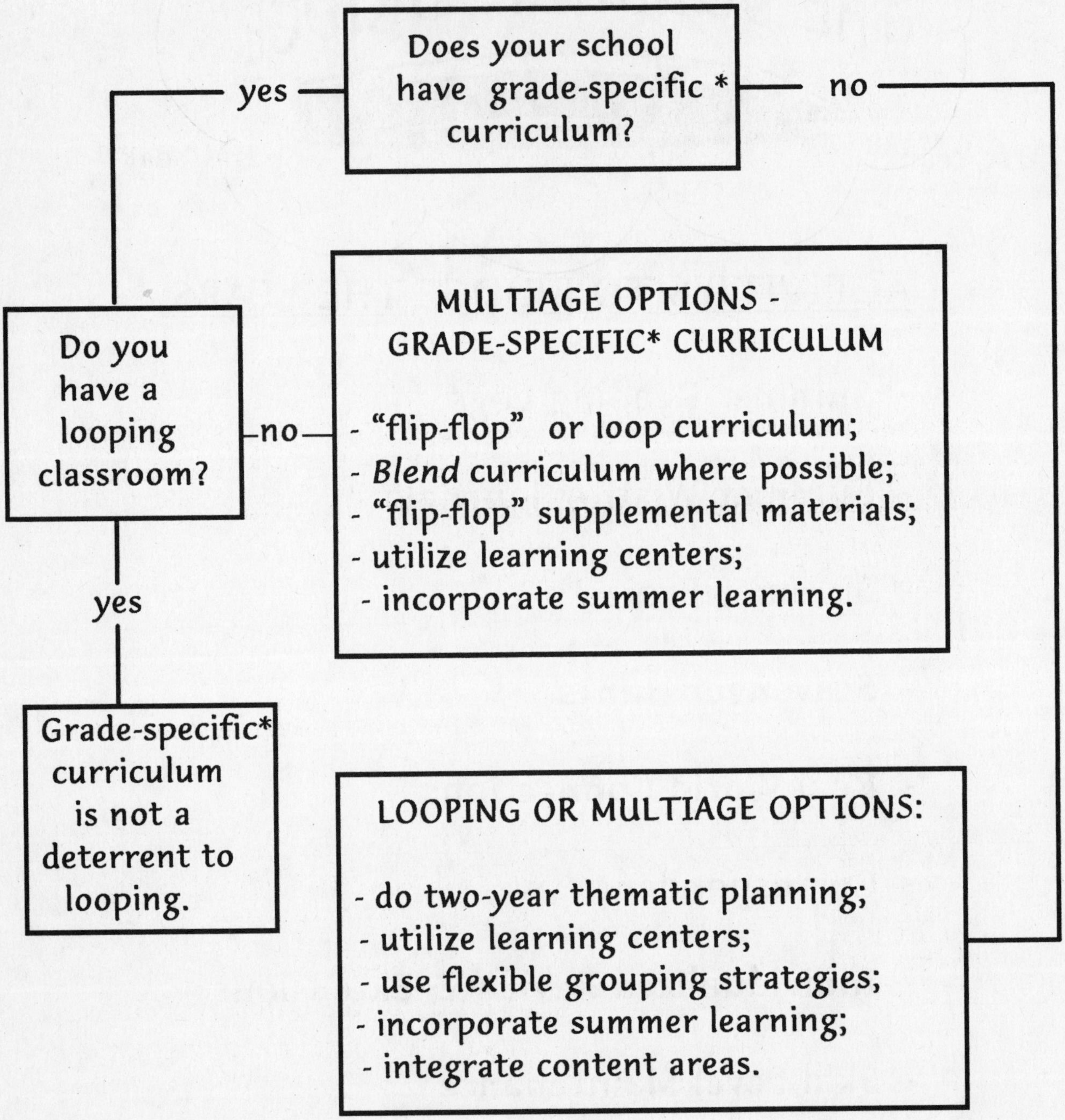

Does your school have grade-specific * curriculum?
yes
no
Do you have a looping classroom?
no
yes
MULTIAGE OPTIONS - GRADE-SPECIFIC* CURRICULUM
- "flip-flop" or loop curriculum;
- *Blend* curriculum where possible;
- "flip-flop" supplemental materials;
- utilize learning centers;
- incorporate summer learning.
Grade-specific* curriculum is not a deterrent to looping.
LOOPING OR MULTIAGE OPTIONS:
- do two-year thematic planning;
- utilize learning centers;
- use flexible grouping strategies;
- incorporate summer learning;
- integrate content areas.

**For discussion purposes, "grade-specific" refers to settings where skills, concepts, and content are assigned to specific grades by school officials*

LONG-TERM PLANNING & DECISION MAKING CHART

RE: ACCELERATE OR ENRICH?

What type of configuration follows your program?

↓

If next setting accelerates, you have the same option or you can enrich.

↓

If next setting does not accelerate, you can enrich through extensions, independent projects, peer tutoring, or mentoring, etc.

COMPONENTS OF A QUALITY INSTRUCTIONAL PROGRAM

Students should be confident learners who value, apply, and communicate their abilities in subjects across the curriculum. They should make real-world connections with their learning.

Thinking: *Creative (open-ended), Analytical (logical), & Critical (evaluative):*

Balanced Language Arts: *(Themes, Genre Studies, & Research Projects, Speaking Activities)*

Reading: *(Guided with Strategies & Skills, Shared, Buddy, Independent, Read Aloud, Vocabulary)*

Writing: *(Writing Process: Pre-Writing, First Draft, Revise, Writing Group, Edit, Edit Group, Teacher Conference, Publication...creative & nonfiction genre.)*

Spelling/Mechanics: *(Strategies & Activities, Skill Groups, Recognition & Application)*

Mathematics: *Problem Solving, Communication, Reasoning, Making Connections, Estimation, Number Sense, Numeration, Whole Number Operations, Geometry & Spatial Sense, Measurement, Statistics & Probability, & Patterns & Relationships) (NCTM Standards)*

Science: *Exploratory, Process Skills, Hands-On, Student-Centered Topics.*

Social Studies: *Integrated Map Skills, Geography, History, Current Events, Real-World Connections.*

"PERMANENT" SUBJECT & REFERENCE CENTERS

Sample Room Plan

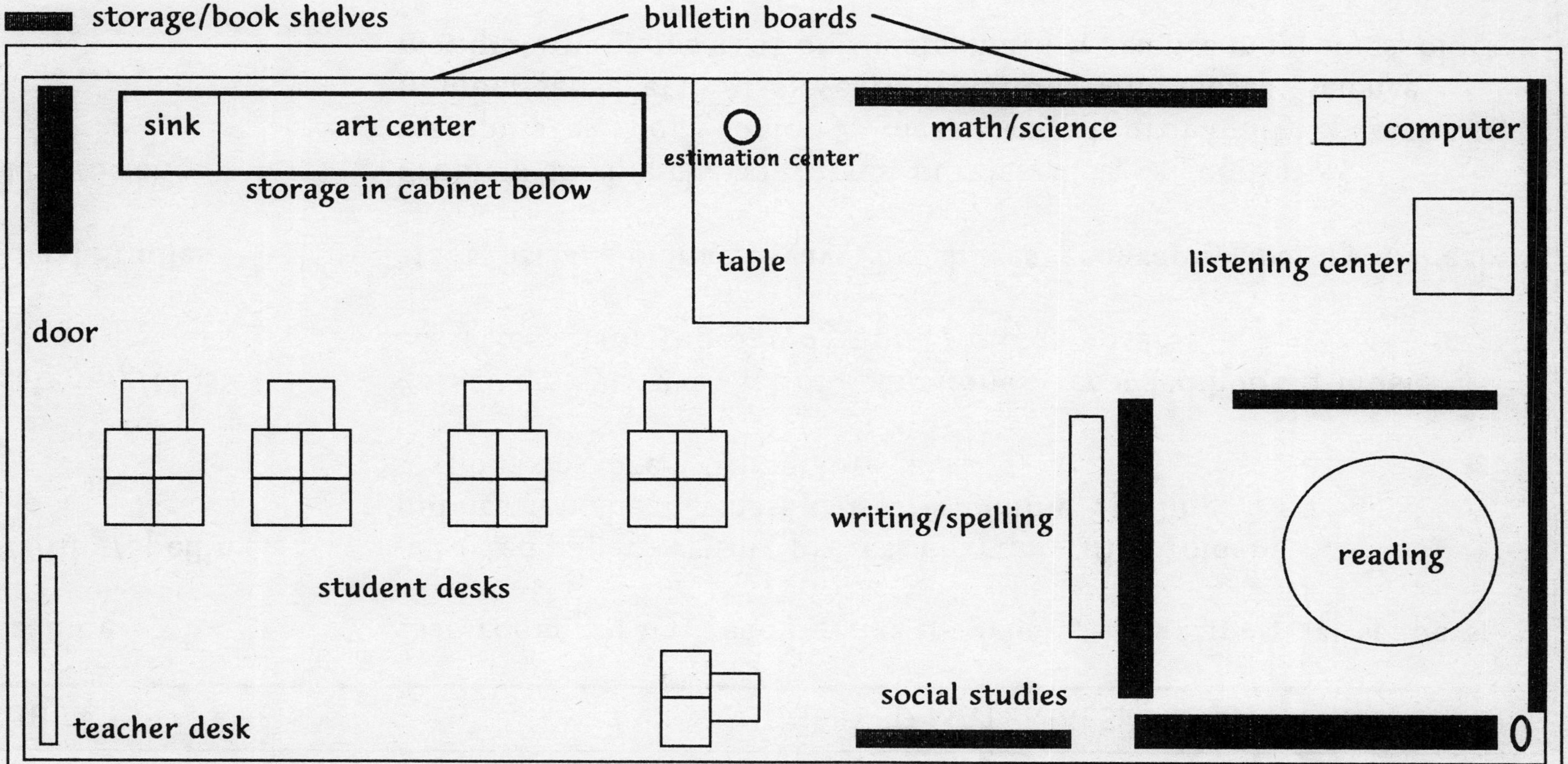

Char Forsten

Society for Developmental Education

1-800-924-9621

"PERMANENT" SUBJECT & REFERENCE CENTERS

SUBJECT:	SUGGESTED MATERIALS:
Reading	Classroom library, reading logs & reviews, magazines, newspapers;
Writing/Spelling	Assorted paper, writing process chart, writing folders, publication sheets, thesauruses, rhyming, spelling, & standard dictionaries, pre-writing materials;
Listening/Music	Cassette player with set of headphones, recorded book & music cassettes, blank tapes, biographies of composers;
Social Studies	Maps, atlas, almanacs, travel brochures, geography/history magazines;
Math/Science	Problem solving charts, games, puzzles, dice, calculators, manipulatives for geometry, measurement, probability & statistics, number sense, etc. Also, weather station, hand lenses, science manipulatives, observation sheets, math & science magazines, blocks;
Art	Assorted paper, crayons, markers, pencils, scissors, glue, paste, paints, recyclables, art prints, artist biographies.

STRATEGIES THAT BUILD CONFIDENCE

- Encourage Child to Change Self Perception
- Teach Positive Self Talk
- Encourage Child to Take Risks
- Make Mistakes OK
- Focus on Improvement
- Note Contributions & Recognize Achievement
- Make Materials Attractive, Concrete, & Helpful
- Acknowledge Difficulty of Task
- Set Time Limit on Tasks
- Teach One Step at a Time

*Permission from: Richard S. Dufresne, MSW Peterborough, NH
(Adapted from *Cooperative Discipline,* by Linda Albert)

Teaching Full Circle:

Organizing Your Instruction & Incorporating Multiple Intelligences

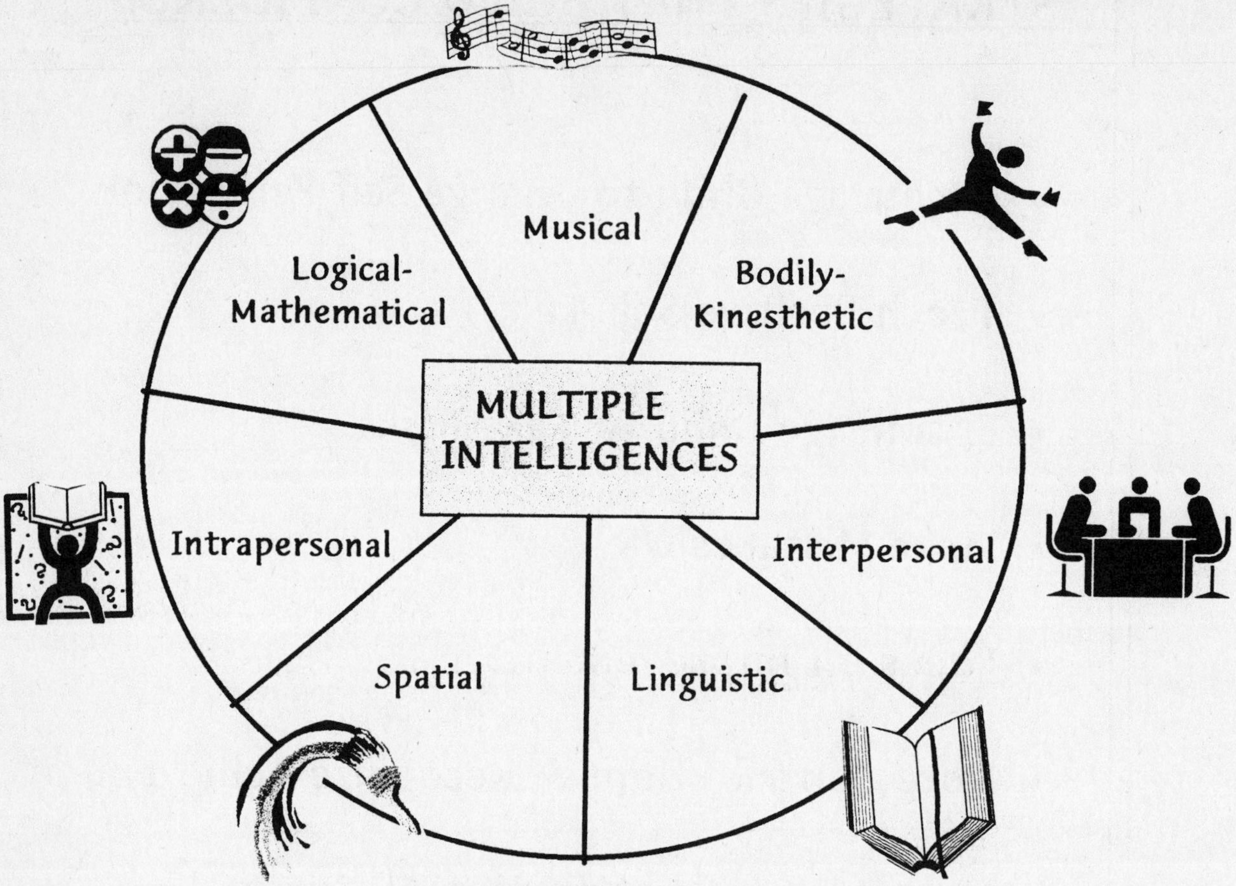

Multiple Intelligences*

As you plan your instruction, incorporate activities that teach to the strengths of a wide range of intelligences among your students. Use this chart to help in your planning:

Logical Mathematical - Numbers, Logic, Puzzles, Scientific Method
Linguistic - Reading, Writing, Speaking, Storytelling, Poetry
Musical - Singing, Music Appreciation, Imagery, Composing, Music Software
Spatial - Charts, Graphs, & Diagrams, Painting & Drawing, Photography, Geometry
Bodily-Kinesthetic - Movement, Skits & Plays, Hands-On Activities, Manipulatives
Interpersonal - Cooperative Groups, Simulations, Conflict Resolution, Clubs
Intrapersonal - Private Space, Journals, Independent Study, Self-Awareness Activities

*Gardner, Howard. *Frames of Mind: The Theory of Multiple Intelligences,* 1983.
__________ *Multiple Intelligences: The Theory in Practice.* Basic Books, 1993.

Example: PRE-PLANNING WORKSHEET FOR THEME OR UNIT OF STUDY

THEME: The Community

DISCIPLINES:	READING	WRITING	SPELLING	SOCIAL STUDIES	MATH	SCIENCE	MUSIC	ART	PE
Concepts/ Content:	(*The Little House*) -non-fiction -biographies -poetry →	-reports -journals -editorials →	-community words -science words -reg. spell. program	(*Hands-On Geography*) -maps -community roles -current events	-scale of miles -measurement -money (economics)	-animal community -food chain/ food web	-original songs - local musicians	-mural & model of community	-food web game
Skills:	-fact & opinion -similes & metaphors -main idea & supporting facts -character traits	-research skills: -business letter -syllables (haiku & limericks) → -rhyme & free verse	-endings "er," "or," & "ar" (roles) -ongoing spell. rules →	-map symbols, key, & scale -cardinal directions -local laws	-linear measure -add/sub money -nonstandard measure	-scientific method -food chain roles	-beats, measure -rhythm	-perspective -proportion	
Multiple Intelligences:	-oral history skits -visit library	-biographical sketch -"Poet Tea" -class newsletter	-word searches -riddles	-make relief maps -dioramas -role playing	-keep checkbook -visit bank -board games	-act out food web -essay on pollution	-write lyrics -compose music	-dioramas -make models	-movement -games
Real World Connections: Roles in Daily Lives	-surveys -debates →	-interview local writers & journalists →	-find words in newspapers →	-community guest speakers →	-field trip to bank →	-report to local conservation com. →	-visit radio station →	-contact local artists →	-community sports →

 Society for Developmental Education 1-800-924-9621

PRE-PLANNING WORKSHEET FOR THEME OR UNIT OF STUDY*

THEME:

DISCIPLINES:	READING	WRITING	MECHANICS SPELLING	SOCIAL STUDIES	MATH	SCIENCE	MUSIC	ART	PE
Concepts/ Content:									
Skills:									
Multiple Intelligences:									
Real World Connections:									

*Recommendation: For better results, enlarge chart on photocopier before using.

PRE-PLANNING WORKSHEET: SPECIFIC LESSONS

*Theme:*____________________________

LESSON	INSTRUCTIONAL STRATEGIES/ GROUPINGS	CORE & SUPPLEMENTAL MATERIALS	ASSESSMENT/ EVALUATION
What will they learn? (Why???)	How & when will they learn it?	What do they/I need?	How will they show what they learned?

DEVELOPING EFFECTIVE STUDY SKILLS

STUDY HABITS

- Present a format that organizes time, materials, & subject matter;
- Organize desks & materials daily;
- Teach one step at a time;
- Start simple, focus on study skills;
- Model! Provide Practice;
- Make Individual Adjustments.

LISTENING

- Eyes on Speaker;
- One speaker at a time;
- "Recapture" before Responding;
- NO "I Don't Know" answers! (Must explain what they don't understand, or take responsibility for not listening.)

INDIVIDUAL WORK - HOMEWORK

- Personal Checklists;
- Engagement Calendars;
- Homework should be meaningful practice/extension;
- Check homework completion each morning;
- Make necessary adaptations.

Char Forsten Society for Developmental Education 1-800-924-9621

STUDY SKILLS LOG

Name:		
Today's Studies Date:		DUE
READING: 		
WRITING: 		
SPELLING: 		
MATH: 		
SOCIAL STUDIES: 		
OTHER:		
REMINDERS: 		

Char Forsten Society for Developmental Education 1-800-924-9621

WHAT ARE LEARNING CENTERS?

Learning centers are classroom areas, settings, or materials that allow students to:

- explore, reinforce, or extend their understanding of subject area material;
- work alone, with a buddy, in small (like or mixed-ability), or in cooperative groups;
- use a variety of learning styles and hands-on materials;

WHY USE CENTERS?...THEY CAN:

- help teachers manage and balance their time by allowing flexible scheduling. Use of centers can fall along a continuum from occasional or supplemental use, to all-day instruction;
- incorporate multiple intelligence theory, learning styles, and student interests;
- support thematic instruction;
- develop, organized, independent learners;
- utilize flexible grouping strategies;
- extend and enrich areas of study;
- provide active, hands-on, exploratory activities;
- make effective use of resource materials;

PORTABLE CENTERS

* Activity Books, Sheets (Puzzle books, word searches, manipulatives, puzzles ...)

* Games (Chess, Scrabble, 24 ,...)

* File Folder Activities

SNOWFLAKE SYMMETRY:

Cut out your own designs, creating fractals in snowflakes.

* "Zip-Lock" Activities

-Directions & materials kept in bag, hanging on a clothesline (space savers)

"Play Pig"

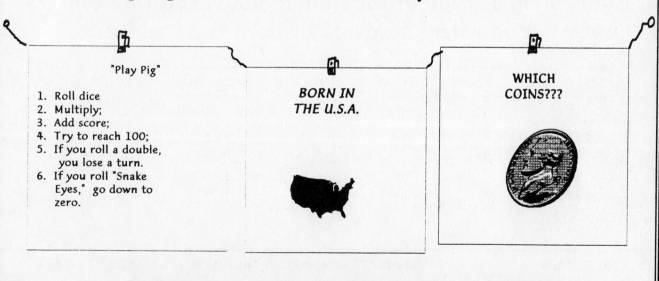

1. Roll dice
2. Multiply;
3. Add score;
4. Try to reach 100;
5. If you roll a double, you lose a turn.
6. If you roll "Snake Eyes," go down to zero.

BORN IN THE U.S.A.

WHICH COINS???

Char Forsten Society for Developmental Education 1-800-924-9621

TEMPORARY CENTERS

- Support themes or units of study;
- Enhance special topics (holidays, monthly themes, interests);
- Develop or reinforce skills & concepts.

Interactive Bulletin Boards - These are teacher-directed centers. The background, title, and directions are clearly presented. Students then complete activity.

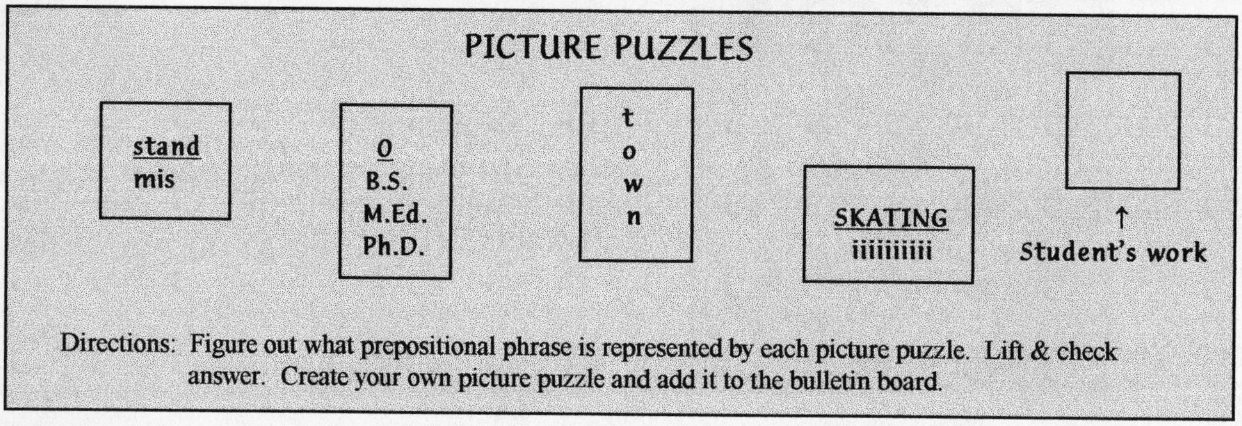

Rotating Centers - Students work in groups for set periods of time on a particular mini-lesson. For example, in a study of the human body, rotating centers can be set up where students explore the 5 senses:

TASTE	TOUCH	SIGHT	SMELL	HEARING	SCHEDULE:
1	2	3	4	5	9:00 - 9:15
2	3	4	5	1	9:15 - 9:30
3	4	5	1	2	9:30 - 9:45
4	5	1	2	3	9:45 - 10:00
5	1	2	3	4	10:00 - 10:15

MY LEARNING CENTER WORK

Name: ______________________ How Did I Do? 

WEEK:	Listening 	Computer 	Math 	Science 	Social Studies 	Reading 	Writing 	Art 	Optional Center
MONDAY									
TUESDAY									
WEDNESDAY									
THURSDAY									
FRIDAY									

Char Forsten Society for Developmental Education 1-800-924-9621

STUDENT ASSESSMENT SHEET

NAME: ________________________ (GROUP:)________________________ WEEK OF ______________________

Directions: Record which centers you attend each day, and write about what you have learned. In the bottom space, describe how well you worked, and back it up with an example.

	MONDAY	TUESDAY	WEDNESDAY	THURSDAY	FRIDAY
C E N T E R (S)					
Work Habits					

FOCUS FRAME

DIRECTIONS: **Use the "Focus Frame" pattern below to cut out pieces of posterboard or another type of heavy weight paper. Cut along the dotted line of frame section "A." Insert "B" into section "A" to form a movable box. Slide the "Focus Frame" to adjust for amount of space needed.**

Student slides focus frame to fit the present problem,

eliminating unnecessary information or distractions →

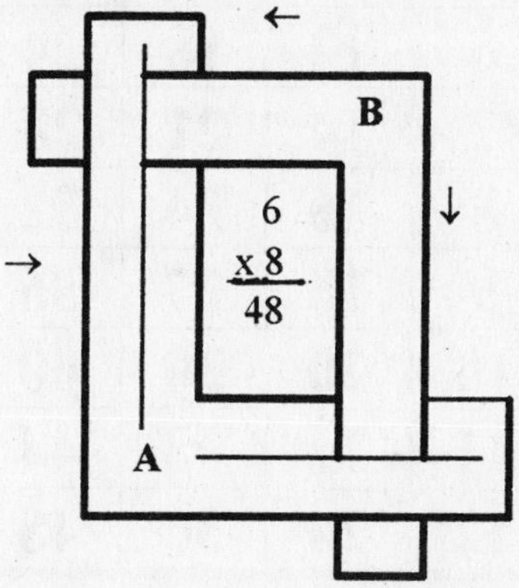

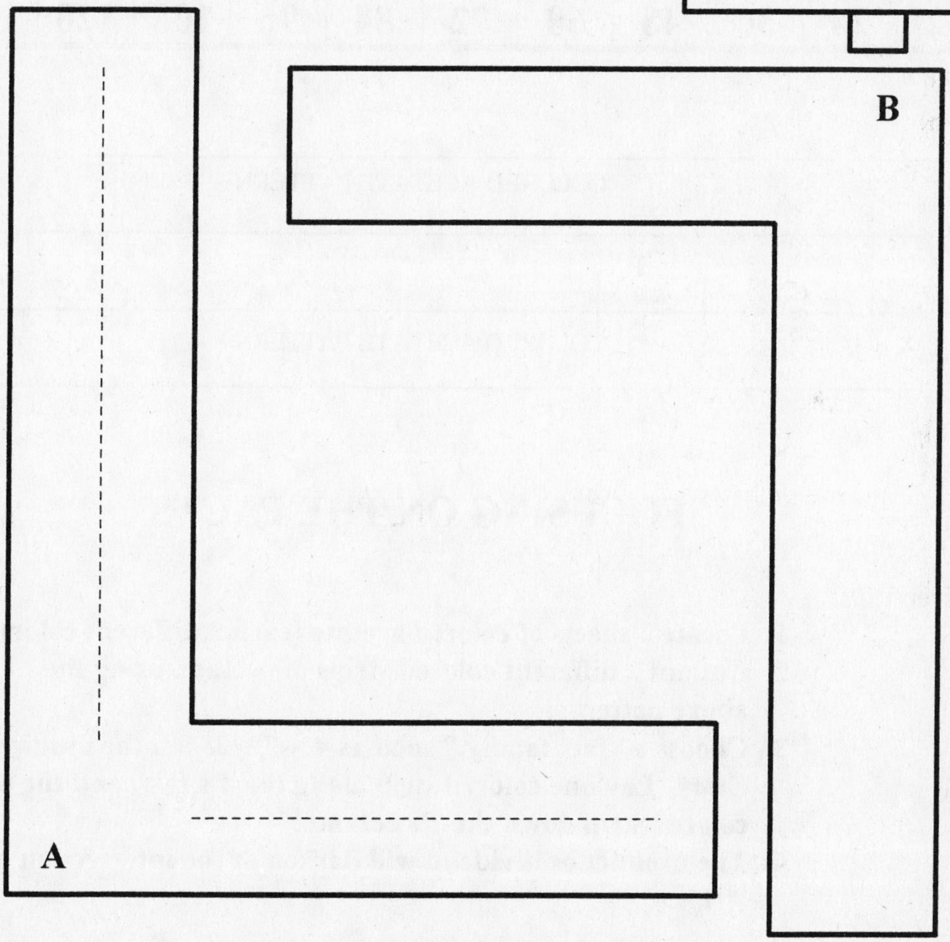

1	2	3	4	5	6	7	8	9	10	11	12
2	4	6	8	10	12	14	16	18	20	22	24
3	6	9	12	15	18	21	24	27	30	33	36
4	8	12	16	20	24	28	32	36	40	44	48
5	10	15	20	25	30	35	40	45	50	55	60
6	12	18	24	30	36	42	48	54	60	66	72
7	14	21	28	35	42	49	56	63	70	77	84
8	16	24	32	40	48	56	64	72	80	88	96
9	18	27	36	45	54	63	72	81	90	99	108
10	20	30	40	50	60	70	80	90	100	110	120
11	22	33	44	55	66	77	88	99	110	121	132
12	24	36	48	60	72	84	96	108	120	132	144

COLORED ACETATE PATTERN

COLORED ACETATE PATTERN

FOCUSING ON THE FACTS

Directions:

1. **Locate 2 sheets of colored acetate (each a different color);**
2. **Cut out 2 different colored strips of acetate, using the above patterns;**
3. **Choose a "fact family," such as *4 × 7 = 28* on the multiplication chart. Lay one colored strip along the 4's row, and the other colored strip down the 7's column.**
4. **The product or dividend will darken at the intersection of the 2 strips.**

ASSESSMENT IDEAS

What is the purpose of assessment? Educators must first consider why they are assessing students, before selecting the method of how it will be done. What is it they hope to learn and how will the results be used? The reason for assessment should guide the decision-making process when choosing what type of tool will be used. Does the tool or method suit the purpose? Some suggestions of reasons and tools for assessment are listed here:

Reasons for Assessment

- Diagnostic Tool
- Student Reporting & Evaluation
- Checking Achievement Level
- Instructional Appraisal
- Evaluation of Program

Assessment Strategies & Methods

- Observations & Anecdotal Records
- Journals
- Homework
- Group Work
- Interviews
- Portfolios
- Authentic Assessment
  - -Presentations & Demonstrations
  - -Letters
  - -Projects
- Running Records, Inventories, etc.
- "Traditional" Tests
- Cassette & Video Tapings

Whole Language vs. Phonics: The Great Debate

Instead of choosing a single approach to reading, we should focus on what works best for the individual child.

MARIE CARBO

Make no mistake: Reading is big business, and the stakes are astronomical. Children who don't read well are in grave danger of doing poorly in school and eventually dropping out. Because success in reading is so important, principals and teachers face unrelenting pressure to produce high test scores—often with pitifully little support.

The high stakes involved in seeing that a nation of children become readers has produced a continuing controversy over the merits of whole language and phonics that seems to bring out the worst in both camps. Products like "Hooked on Phonics" make it appear easy to teach anyone to read. Recently, however, "Hooked on Phonics" was cited by the Federal Trade Commission for false advertising and insufficient research.

Nor do the claims for phonics appear to be based on sound research. Researcher Richard Turner investigated *70 years* of research on phonics and reported that "systematic phonics falls into that vast category of weak instructional treatments with which education is perennially plagued....Perhaps it is time for reading experts to turn away from the debate over systematic phonics in search of more powerful instructional treatments for beginning reading" (Turner 1989).

Marie Carbo is executive director of the National Reading Styles Institute in Syosset, New York.

The truth is that some children do learn to read easily with phonics—and some do not. The same can be said of whole-language programs. Principals need to understand both systems and use the best of both, together with other effective reading programs.

Beware the Pendulum Swing

People have been searching for the single best way to teach children to read for more than a century. But no matter which approach enjoys a spurt of popularity, reading failures persist, disillusionment spreads, and the pendulum swings to yet another approach. The high stakes only make the pendulum swing faster.

The "look-say" reading method held sway for about 30 years (1940–1970) before the pendulum swung to phonics, which was popular for about 20 years (1970–1990) before whole language gained a strong foothold. And now whole language has come under fire, especially by advocates of phonics. Other approaches have been tried for as little as a year or two before being discarded.

The occurrence of these pendulum swings is predictable, and so is their direction. After a global approach to reading enjoys popularity for a time ("look-say," for example), the pendulum swings back to a more analytic approach, such as phonics. With each pendulum swing, heated debates arise as advocates pit one approach against another—sometimes making exaggerated or false claims and counterclaims. In the process, the focus of the debate moves away from where it should be: on the individual child. That is why it is critical for teachers and principals to understand the merits of *both* the analytic and the global methods of teaching reading *(see box)*.

> "CHILDREN WHO DO WELL IN WHOLE-LANGUAGE PROGRAMS ...CAN RECALL WORDS THEY SEE AND HEAR REPEATEDLY IN... STORIES."

It's generally not advisable to use a single approach to reading exclusively. Many combinations are necessary to accommodate the different learning styles for reading that can be found within a single classroom. An extensive body of research on reading styles supports the global approach of whole language as a framework for teaching young children and poor readers—but only as a framework. The strategies within that framework depend on the reading styles of the particular students in the group. Every reading approach demands certain reading style strengths.

Phonics: Who Succeeds? Who Fails?

Youngsters who do well with phonics tend to have strong auditory and analytic reading styles. Children who are auditory can hear and remember letter sounds. If they are also analytic, the logic of phonics makes sense to them, for they proceed naturally from bits of information to the whole. Phonics instruction is usually highly sequential, organized, direct, and predictable—all conditions that appeal to analytics.

But phonics can be confusing and boring to students who are not analytic, who don't learn easily when information is presented in small portions, step by step. Even more serious problems arise for students who are not sufficiently auditory to learn letter sounds. If children cannot *hear* the differences among sounds, they cannot associate those sounds with their corresponding letters. This situation is similar to that of a tone-deaf person who can't repeat a tone. Being sound-deaf can create years of problems if a youngster is exposed primarily to phonics instruction.

Whole Language: Who Succeeds? Who Fails?

Children who do well in whole-language programs tend to have visual, tactile, and global reading styles. They can recall words they see and hear repeatedly in high-interest stories. Lots of experience with story writing helps tactile learners remember words they have felt as they write them. Whole-language programs usually emphasize fun, popular literature, hands-on learning, and peer interactions—all conditions that appeal to global learners.

But whole language can feel disorganized and haphazard to analytic learners. If the modeling of stories is too infrequent, or if the teacher does not provide enough interesting repetition, such youngsters can fall behind quickly. Since the *systematic* teaching of phonics is not emphasized, some children may not develop the tools they need for decoding words. Finally, such strategies as invented spelling may confuse analytic youngsters who want to use correct spellings, and children with memory deficits are likely to persist in using invented spellings long past the early grades.

Recommendations for Teachers

Here are some specific recommendations for improving and combining phonics and whole-language reading programs.

Phonics Programs:

- Balance your reading program by focusing on literature and fun. Read to students often, choral read with them, and give them time to read both alone and in pairs.
- Guard against boredom, a common side effect of phonics. Spend only a few minutes each day on phonics and do no more than one worksheet daily.
- Include many word games in your teaching. For most children, phonics is easier to learn if they are having fun.
- If students are not able to learn phonics easily, try other reading methods, like recorded books or story writing.
- Develop a well-stocked classroom library. Give children time to browse, read, and discuss books.
- Evaluate the stories in your reading series, and exclude the dull or poorly written ones. With the time gained, allow students to read books of their own choice.
- Eliminate or abbreviate skill work whenever appropriate.

Whole-Language Programs:

- Balance your reading program by providing adequate structure and some step-by-step skill work, especially for analytic students, while continuing to emphasize literature and fun.
- Provide sufficient tools for decoding words, using small amounts of direct instruction in phonics for auditory and analytic learners. Try tape-recording phonics lessons so that students can work independently to improve these skills.
- Include games in teaching. Since most young children are tactile, they often learn words and skills quickly with hands-on games.
- Don't use invented spelling for extensive periods with strongly analytic learners or students who have memory problems.
- Provide sufficient modeling of reading aloud before expecting children to read independently, in pairs, or alone. Use

large amounts of shared reading, choral reading, or recorded books if necessary.

Recommendations for Principals

Here are eight ways to improve most reading programs in the shortest possible time. These suggestions combine the best of phonics, whole language, and reading styles.

1. Emphasize the fun of reading. Fill hallway bulletin boards with displays that emphasize reading, such as posters, drawings of book characters, and sign-up sheets for book clubs.

2. Recruit older children to make reading games for younger ones, including phonics games.

3. Don't allow youngsters to be referred to special education classes simply because they can't learn phonics. Make sure other reading approaches are given an honest try first.

4. Help teachers accumulate the books and shelving they need for classroom libraries.

5. Encourage reading aloud to chilc daily. Try to get into classrooms and r to children yourself as often as possi Ask children what their favorite books and how many books they've read. monstrate your enthusiasm for readin

6. Purchase tape players and blank settes to record books so that child can listen to the sounds while lookin the words. This is especially helpful those who have limited proficiency English, who have been read to very li or who simply need repetition to h them learn.

7. Send teachers who are the "mo and shakers" in your school to some g reading seminars. Follow up with s meetings where they can share demonstrate what they learned.

8. Finally, encourage both teachers parents to learn and understand their c dren's reading styles.

Reference

Turner, Richard L. "The 'Great' Deba Can Both Carbo and Chall Be Right?" *Delta Kappan*, December 1989, 276-83.

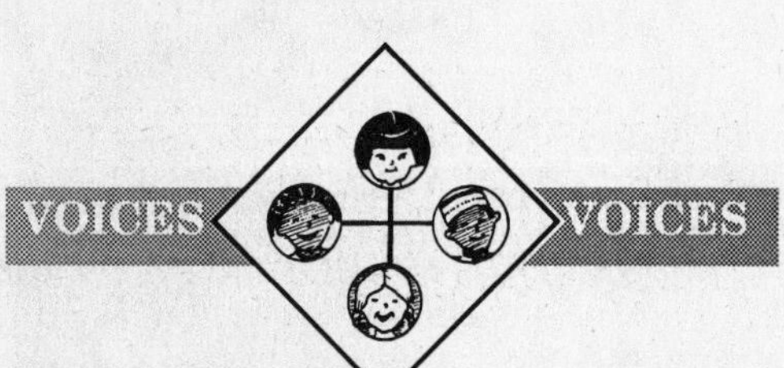

Students who are encouraged to use invented spellings write more than students in a traditional spelling program. Spelling expert Sandra Wilde reports that if you compare these two groups and look only at the percentage of words that are correct, students in a traditional group score a higher percentage. But when you compare the number of words students write, the students using invented spelling actually have more words spelled correctly because they have written so many more words altogether.

This is not surprising. Many of us who teach in the primary grades have had a new student come into our classroom who spells every word correctly. After rejoicing in what on the surface appears to be a competent speller, we quickly find out that these students will only write the words they can spell. Their writing is typically brief, lackluster, and without voice. When correctness is valued above all else in writing, we get students who write correctly but who refuse to take risks or accept challenges.

— Regie Routman, *Literacy at the Crossroads*, Portsmouth, NH: Heinemann, 1996.

Continuum of Modeling Reading Methods

BY MARIE CARBO

An easy-to-follow chart that will enable you to select the most appropriate reading strategy, depending upon the ability of the student

The goal of the modeling strategies on this continuum is reading alone with ease and enjoyment. Moving from bottom to top, each strategy requires increasingly more reading independence of the student and less modeling by the teacher. Teachers should select the strategy that is most appropriate for a student or group. Generally, strategies that provide the most modeling should be used with beginning readers and those who cannot read a particular text with good fluency.

Low Teacher Involvement
High Student Independence

Sustained Silent Reading 	Each person in the classroom, including the teacher, reads alone. The time period for a group can range from 10 to 45 minutes per session, depending on the interests, age and abilities of the students. A strong emphasis is placed on self-selection of reading materials and reading for pleasure.
Paired Reading 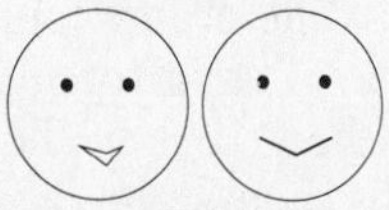	Two students take turns reading a passage or story. Teachers may pair youngsters of similar or dissimilar reading abilities and/or interests, or children may select partners. An emphasis may be placed on reading for pleasure, or students may be given guidelines for assisting or evaluating their partner.
Choral Reading 	Two or more students read a passage in unison. Less able readers try to follow the reading model provided by the more adept readers in the group. Group members may be teachers, parents, students, etc.
Neurological Impress 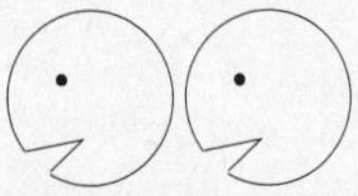	The teachers sits behind the youngster and reads into the child's ear. Both hold the book and read in unison. The child places his/her finger under the line of print being read by the teacher. The purpose is improving reading fluency, and no questions about reading are asked. (Heckelman, 1969)
Repeated Reading 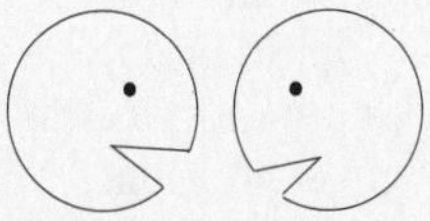	After discussing a passage, the teacher reads it aloud while the student (or group) follows along in the text. Then the teacher reads the first sentence aloud, and the student reads it back. This procedure continues until the passage is completed. In another version, Samuels (1979) recommended repeated, independent practice of easy passages until the student attains a reading rate of 85 wpm.
Recorded Books 	The youngster listens one or more times to a word-for-word recording while following along in the text, and then reads some or all of the book aloud (Chomsky, 1976). Less able readers can listen one to three times to two- to five-minutes segments recorded at a slower-than-usual pace (about 85-90 wpm), and then read the passage aloud. Passages should be recorded with good expression, natural phrasing and clear pronunciation (Carbo, 1989).
Shared Reading 	A high-interest book, often enlarged and containing many pictures and predictable language, is placed in front of students. The teacher reads the story while pointing to the words and pausing to ask questions. After a few readings, youngsters are encouraged to read along with the teacher.

High Teacher Involvement
Low Student Independence

Publishing Young Authors' Work

You've published classroom editions of students' work for years. Now, go one step further and submit it for publication outside the classroom

BY TRUDI MERZ FOSS

For more detailed guidelines regarding manuscript preparation, you may want to refer to Janet Grant's book, Young Person's Guide to Becoming a Writer *(Shoe Tree Press, 1991).*

Most students are probably unaware that children can be "real" authors. While reading other students' published writing might inspire them, there's no greater thrill than seeing one's own words in print! Regardless of whether their work is finally accepted for publication, submitting material for publication can provide continued motivation.

Many local newspapers print children's writings and activities, but national young people's magazines such as *Highlights for Children, American Girl, Cricket, Hopscotch* and *Jack and Jill* also contain work contributed by children. For students who are particularly talented, there are even some book publishers who accept manuscripts written by children.

Sample copies. Juvenile magazines vary in style just as adult magazines do. Some focus on poems and fiction; others prefer stories based on personal experience, or on news about children involved in interesting or unusual activities.

To prepare them for submitting their own work, have students obtain sample copies of various magazines and examine the contents from cover to cover including articles, poems, book reviews, artwork, puzzles, jokes and letters to the editor.

Gathering sample copies and writer's guidelines is easy: students simply write to the editorial departments of the magazines (see opposite page for addresses). They might even want to create a standard request letter on the computer and change the editor's name and address as needed. Be sure, however, to include any necessary payment for the sample issue as well as a self-addressed stamped envelope for return of the guidelines.

When each magazine is received, have the students discuss its contents. Encourage them to identify the magazine and the types of writing with which they are most comfortable. Some children are clearly stronger in fiction writing, while others feel more comfortable in the role of reporter. Of course, they should submit their work to the magazine they feel best suits their style.

Submission of work. Suggest that each child come up with at least one item to send to a magazine, whether it's a story, poem, article, joke, letter-to-the-editor or drawing, and review the magazine's guidelines for manuscript preparation.

Most young author magazines are happy to accept handwritten submissions, but a few require typewritten submissions. The manuscript should include the student's name, address, age, grade and school on the first page, and the student's name and page numbers on additional pages. Some publications require a signature and statement by a parent or teacher certifying that the writing is an original work by the student. Always include a self-addressed stamped envelope of the necessary size with each submission so that the publisher may return the material. Publishers' response times vary from two weeks to six months, so remind students to be patient.

When a student finally receives a letter of acceptance, celebrate! Have an author's party! And for those students whose material is not accepted the first time, remind them of the hundreds of times we adult authors receive rejections before finally being published.

Trudi Merz Foss is a K-12 Speech and Language Specialist in Winters, CA.

MOSTLY STUDENT-CREATED MAGAZINES

Creative Kids: Andrea Harrington, Editor
Prufrock Press
P.O. Box 8813
Waco, TX 76714-8813 (Sample copy $5)
- Talented, gifted, creative children, 8-14 years
- Fiction and non-fiction, 700-1000 words.
- Other: Artwork, photos, games, jokes, puzzles, poetry and filler.

Kid's World: Morgan Kopaska-Merkel, Editor
1300 Kicker Rd.
Tuscaloosa, AL 35404 (Sample copy $1)
- Children ages 2-17 years
- Fiction, to 1500 words
- Other: artwork, arts and crafts activities, comics, jokes, riddles, mazes and puzzles. Poetry to 10 lines.

The McGuffey Writer: Janet Kretschmer, Children's Editor
5128 Westgate Dr.
Oxford, OH 45056 (Sample copy, $3.00)
- Children 5-18 years
- Fiction and nonfiction, to 500 words
- Other: artwork, photos, poetry (to 30 lines), activities and puzzles

Merlyn's Pen: James R. Stahl, Editor
P.O. Box 1058
East Greenwich, RI 02818 (Sample copy $3 with 9x12 SASE $1.44 postage)
- Children ages 12-17
- Fiction and nonfiction to 3000 words
- Other: Artwork, poems, plays, book reviews

Mini-Slush Pile: Sandra Hinojosa, Editor
Junior Friends Publishing
P.O. Box 331635
Corpus Christi, TX 78463 (Sample copy $4.25)
- Children ages 6-12 years
- Fiction and nonfiction, no word limits
- Other: Artwork, poetry, games, activities, jokes, puzzles, book reviews

New Moon: Joe Kelly, Managing Editor
P.O. Box 3587
Duluth, MN 55803-3587 (Sample copy $4.95)
- Girls ages 8-14 years
- Nonfiction to 600 words, must relate to females
- Other: photos, how-to articles about science or math

Stone Soup: Gerry Mandel, Articles/Fiction Editor
Children's Art Foundation
P.O. Box 83
Santa Cruz, CA 95063 (Sample copy $2)
- Children through ages 13
- Fiction and nonfiction, 100-2500 words. Prefers work based on personal experiences rather than classroom assignments.
- Other: Artwork, poetry, book reviews

The Writer's Slate: F. Todd Goodson and Lori Atkins Goodson, Co-Editors
English Department, East Carolina University
Greenville, NC 27858-4353 (Sample copy $5.50)
- Children in grades K-12
- Fiction and nonfiction, word length varies
- Other: artwork, poetry and plays

Young Voices: Char Simons, Editor
P.O. Box 2321
Olympia, WA 98507 (Sample copy $4)
- Children grades K-12
- Fiction and nonfiction, word length varies
- Other: artwork, poetry

Zuzu: Beck Underwood, Editor and Publisher
No. 64
271 E. 10th St.
New York, NY 10009 (Sample copy $1 with 9x12 SASE)
- Children ages 7-12 years
- Primarily nonfiction, word length varies; fiction, 400 to 600 words
- Artwork, contact art department for more information

OTHER MAGAZINES TO TRY

These magazines contain some sections highlighting children's work. Contact the editorial departments at the addresses listed below for writer's guidelines. Sample issues may be found in most public libraries.

American Girl
Pleasant Company
8400 Fairway Pl.
Middleton, WI 53562

Hopscotch
P.O. Box 10
Saratoga Springs, NY 12866

Cobblestone
Cobblestone Publishing Inc.
30 Grove St.
Peterborough, NH 03458

Cricket
Carus Corporation
315 Fifth St.
Peru, IL 61354

Highlights for Children
803 Church St.
Honesdale, PA 18431

Jack and Jill
P.O. Box 567
Indianapolis, IN 46206

National Geographic World
National Geographic Society
17th and M Sts., N.W.
Washington, D.C. 20036

Owl Magazine
c/o Hoot
179 John St.
Suite 500
Toronto, ON M5T 3G5
Canada

READING: READINESS LEVEL

Vocabulary:
- Reads by sight:
  - Own name in print
  - A personal sight vocabulary (high interest)
  - 20 words from the basic sight vocabulary

Word Meaning:
- Understands **beginning** and **end** in relation to:
  - print
  - speech
- When listening, predicts:
  - outcome
  - vocabulary, word, rhyme

Comprehension:
- Knows that:
  - reading makes sense
  - print represents the sounds of the language
- Has a reading attitude.
  - Listens well to stories.
  - Has a desire to read:
    - Looks at books on his/her own
  - Is interested in words and symbols.

Auditory:
- Identifies:
  - beginning sounds
  - ending sounds
  - rhymes
- Discriminates the major consonant sounds.

Visual:
- Has correct directional habits:
  - looks at books from front to back
  - looks at books from left page to right page
  - begins left top
  - proceeds left to right
  - proceeds top to bottom
- Identifies:
  - word
  - letter

Auditory/Visual
- Matches spoken and printed words when someone reads
- Knows most letter names:
  - upper case
  - lower case

Oral Reading
- Attacks words using context and initial letter checked by sense

WRITING: READINESS LEVEL

Fluency:
- Writes independently
- Has confidence as a writer

Composition:
- Expresses thoughts in writing
- Writes telling sentences
- Talks about what he/she has written
- Revises one or more words during conferences

Mechanics:
- Capitalizes:
  - First name and initial of last name
  - I

Handwriting:
- Tries to make recognizable letters

Spelling:
- Own first name
- Uses major consonants: b, d, j, k, l, m, n, p, s, t, z for beginnings of words

SPEAKING

- Expresses his/her needs
- Asks questions
- Responds appropriately to questions
- Maintains the subject line in conversation
- Shares experiences in a group
- Uses complete sentences
- Uses specific vocabulary for objects (book, puzzle, scissors)

Literacy Learning

"Learning to read and to write ought to be one of the most joyful and successful of human undertakings."

"Children learn to listen and to speak in an unbreakable unity of function." [1] Reading and writing are two sides of an integrated learning process. We approach these skills together — and term them literacy learning. Reading is a developmental process starting early in childhood and continuing throughout life.

The essence of reading is to gain meaning from text, and children learn to read by reading. Therefore we teach reading strategies through quality children's literature, rich in human meaning. The joy of reading a novel is superior to using a commercial series for language learning.

The essence of writing is to communicate ideas in written form. Techniques of grammar and spelling are taught after children experience the thrill of expressing themselves in writing. We believe phonics skills need to be taught in order for children to spell correctly and we incorporate these skills as the child is ready.

"Children taught in this way take pride in their work, take pride in themselves, and take joy in communicating from their own writing and reading." [2]

1. Don Holdaway, *The Foundations of Literacy* (Sydney, Australia: Ashton Scholastic, 1979).

2. Marlene J. McCracken and Robert A. McCracken, *Reading, Writing, and Language, A Practical Guide for Primary Teachers* (Winnipeg, Canada: Peguis Publishers Limited, 1979) Foreward, viii.

3 Cue Systems

Meaning
(semantic)

Structure
(grammar / syntax)

Visual
(shapes • sounds • graphophonic)

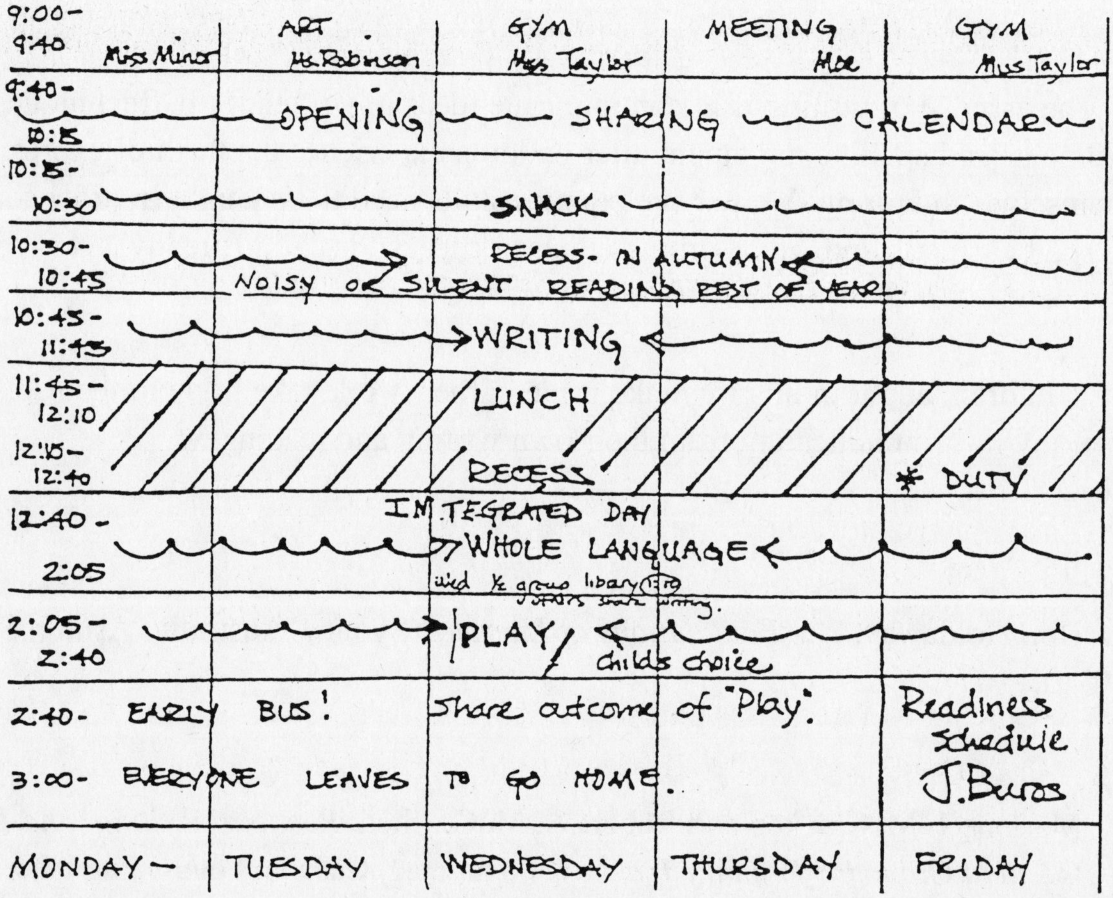
9:00-
9:40
Miss Minor
ART
Ms Robinson
GYM
Mrs Taylor
MEETING
GYM
Mrs Taylor
9:40-
10:15
OPENING
SHARING
CALENDAR
10:15-
10:30
SNACK
10:30-
10:45
RECESS- IN AUTUMN
NOISY OR SILENT READING REST OF YEAR
10:45-
11:45
WRITING
11:45-
12:10
LUNCH
12:15-
12:40
RECESS
* DUTY
12:40-
2:05
INTEGRATED DAY
WHOLE LANGUAGE
2:05-
2:40
PLAY
child's choice
2:40- EARLY BUS!
Share outcome of "Play".
Readiness Schedule
J. Buros
3:00- EVERYONE LEAVES TO GO HOME.
MONDAY-
TUESDAY
WEDNESDAY
THURSDAY
FRIDAY

Whole Language

1. WARM-UP

   Songs

   Poems

   Nursery Rhymes

   Jingles

   Cheers

2. OLD STORY

   Have a child choose the story

3. NEW STORY

   a. Big Book

   b. Good literature on opaque projector or overhead

   c. Student made Big Book

   d. Teacher published Big Book

   e. Song/Poem, chant on chart paper

4. OUTPUT/DEMONSTRATIONS — Student participation in relationship to new story

   1. Wall chart
   2. Student made, published Big Book
   3. Student made small books (copy of large book)
   4. Murals
   5. Puppets

      hand (made out of socks)

      popsicle stick
   6. Flannel board characters and magnetic board characters
   7. Play of story
   8. Innovation of new story (Creating a new story together — probably after it has been read 8-10 times)
   9. Mobile of all the characters in the story
   10. Personal writing about the story — mine and the children's
   11. Field trips to make story come alive
   12. Invite people — to make story come alive (example: teddy bear collector to talk with children)
   13. Share book with a larger audience

Whole Language Block

Monday	Tuesday	Wednesday	Thursday	Friday
		Warm-up		
		Children choose "old" story		
		New story — song — poem — rhyme Teacher's choice from observation of children		
		Demonstration by teacher — Output by children		

Publishing Form

Name: ______________________________________

first middle last

Dedicated: ______________________________________

Because: ______________________________________

Please put an ☒

horizontal ☐ **vertical** ☐

Color:

☐ **Red** ☐ **White**

☐ **Blue** ☐ **Orange**

☐ **Green** ☐ **Pink**

☐ **Yellow** ☐ **Purple**

Print

☐ **small** ☐ **medium**

☐ **large**

Print:

Top of Page

Bottom of Page

Corrected Text:

1
2
3
4
5

About the author:

1
2
3
4
5

______________________________ Observation

______________________________ Date

I looked at: ______________________________

A picture of what I saw:

Here are things I noticed: ______________________________

____

____

____

1 ______________________________
(The Dream)

Where are you today? (in each area listed under (2))	Benchmarks (back plan — include span of time)	If you achieved it how would you know?
(3)	(4)	(2)
A.		A.
B.		B.
C.		C.
D.		D.
E.	(5) Methods you will try. “Be flexible.”	E.
F.		F.

Why Whole Language

by Jay Buros

What do you want children to accomplish by the end of the year?

Drama

Literature – Active Participation

Grandpa, Grandpa
by Joy Cowley
The Wright Group
ISBN 0-86867-186-X

Caps for Sale
by Esphyr Slobodkina
Big Book - Scholastic
ISBN 0-590-71742-1

Mrs. Wishy-Washy and *Return of Mrs. Wishy Washy*
by Joy Cowley
Big Book - Wright Group

The Little Old Lady Who Was Not Afraid of Anything
by Linda Williams
Harper Trophy
ISBN 0-06-443183-5

Literature – Drama

Bony-Legs
by Joanna Cole
Scholastic Inc.
ISBN 0-590-40516-0

Caps for Sale
by Esphyr Slobodkina
Big Book - Scholastic
ISBN 0-590-71742-1

Quack, Quack, Quack
by Joy Cowley
Big Book - Wright Group
ISBN 1-55624-168-2

Hairy Bear (great puppet show)
by Joy Cowley and June Melser
The Wright Group
ISBN 0-86867-219-X

The Lady with the Alligator Purse
by Nadine Bernard Westcott
Little, Brown and Co.
ISBN 0-316-93136-5

The Fourth Little Pig
by Teresa Celsi
Steck-Vaughn
ISBN 0-8114-6740-6

Songs and Poems for Drama

Five Little Monkeys Jumping on the Bed (Puppet show or play)

The Boa Constrictor

Aiken Drum

Pizza Hut

Spider on the Floor
by Ralti
Singable Songs for the Very Young

FAVORITE SONGS, POEMS, AND RHYMES

HEY THERE NEIGHBOR!

Hey there, neighbor!
What do you say?
It's going to be a wonderful day!
Clap your hands and boogie on down.
Give 'em a bump and pass it around!
(or sit on down)

HI! MY NAME IS JOE!

Hi! My name is Joe and I work in the button (doughnut) factory.
I have a wife, a dog, and a family!
One day my boss came to me and said,
"Hey Joe, are you busy?"
I said, "No."
He said, "Well then work with your right hand."

- Repeat each time adding one more body part: left hand, right foot, head

Last line, last time:
I said, "Yes!!!"

TONY CHESTNUT

Toe knee chestnut
Nose eye love you.
Toe knee nose.
Toe knee nose.
Toe knee chestnut nose I love you . . .
That's what toe knee nose.

HI DEE HAY! HI DEE HO!

Leader: *Hi dee hay! Hi dee ho!*
Group: **Hi dee hay! Hi dee ho!**
Leader: *Igglee wigglee wogglee wo!*
Group: **Igglee wigglee wogglee wo!**
Leader: *Raise your voices to the sky.*
Group: **Raise your voices to the sky.**
Leader: *Mrs.________'s class is walking by.*
Group: **Mrs.________'s class is walking by.**
Leader: *Count off!*
Group: **1, 2, 3, 4, 5**
Leader: *Break it on down now!*
Group: **6, 7, 8, 9, 10 . . .**
Leader: *Let's do it all once again!*

COPY CAT

Let's play copy cat just for fun
Let's copy________, she's the one.
Whatever she does we'll do the same,
'cause that's how you play the Copy Cat Game

RISE RUBY RISE!

Down in the valley two by two.
Down in the valley two by two.
Down in the valley two by two.
Rise Ruby Rise!

2nd verse:
We can do it your way two by two.
We can do it your way two by two.
We can do it your way two by two.
Rise Ruby Rise!

3rd verse:
We can do it my way two by two.
We can do it my way two by two.
We can do it my way two by two.
Rise Ruby Rise!

OH! MY AUNT CAME BACK

Oh! my aunt came back
Oh! my aunt came back
from____________.

And she brought me back
And she brought me back
____________________.

Old Japan	old hand fan
Old Algier	a pair of shears
Belgium too	some gum to chew
London Fair	a rocking chair
Holland too	some wooden shoes
Timbuktu	a nut like you

"Whatever you can do or dream you can begin it.
Boldness has genius, power, and magic in it."
Goethe

Music Resources

Greg and Steve
1-800-444-4287
Vol. II, We All Live Together
Playing Favorites
Holidays and Special Times

Charlotte Diamond
Hug Bug Records
c/o Box 58174
Station L
Vancouver, BC
Canada VSP 6CS

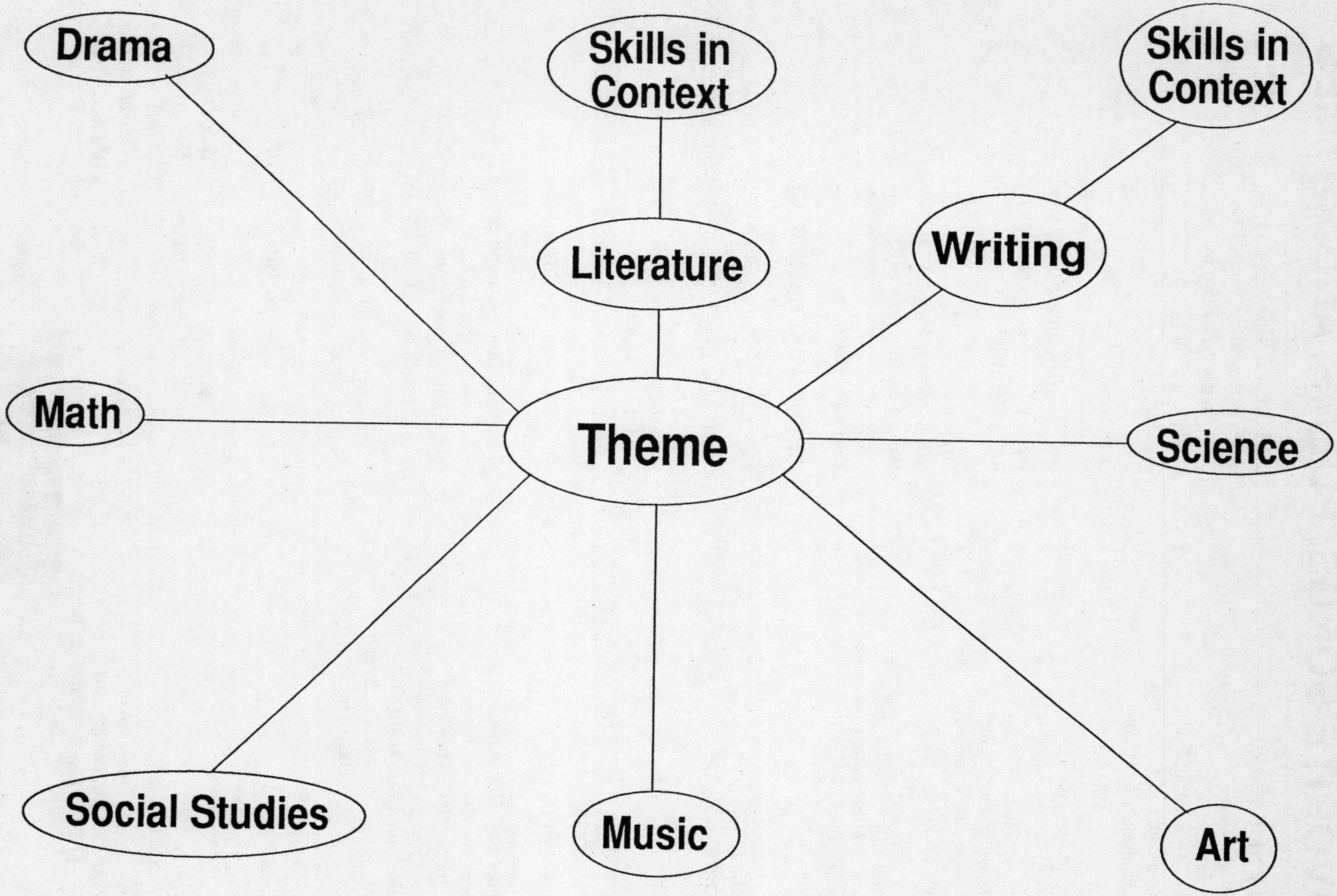

From *Why Whole Language*, by Jay Buros.

Jay Buros

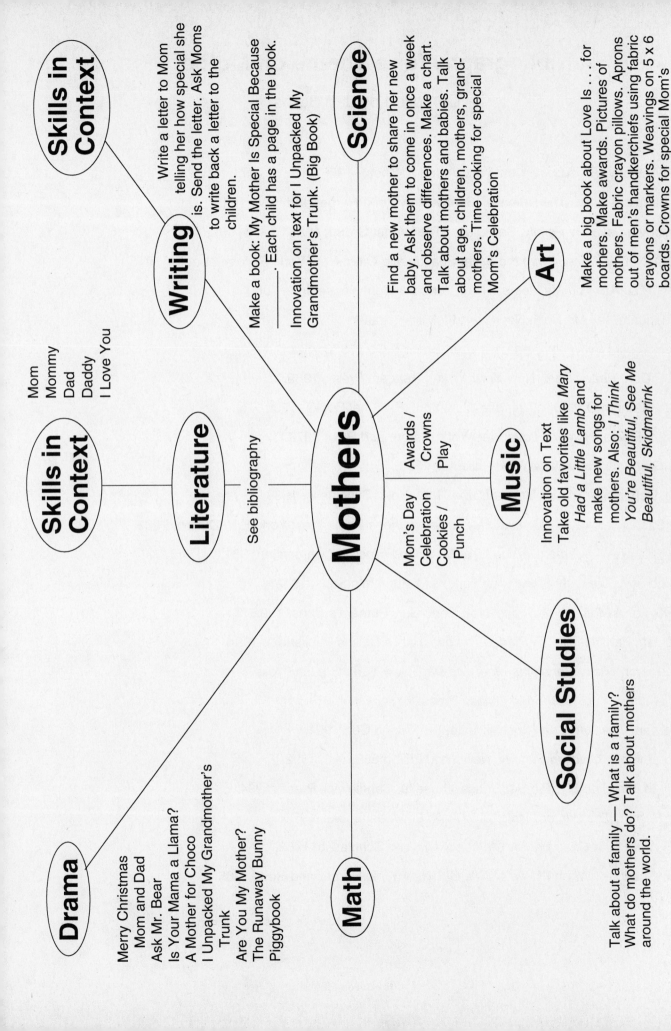

Mothers

Drama

Merry Christmas Mom and Dad
Ask Mr. Bear
Is Your Mama a Llama?
A Mother for Choco
I Unpacked My Grandmother's Trunk
Are You My Mother?
The Runaway Bunny
Piggybook

Skills in Context

Mom
Mommy
Dad
Daddy
I Love You

Literature

See bibliography

Writing

Write a letter to Mom telling her how special she is. Send the letter. Ask Moms to write back a letter to the children.

Make a book: My Mother Is Special Because ________. Each child has a page in the book.

Innovation on text for I Unpacked My Grandmother's Trunk. (Big Book)

Skills in Context

Math

Science

Find a new mother to share her new baby. Ask them to come in once a week and observe differences. Make a chart. Talk about mothers and babies. Talk about age, children, mothers, grandmothers. Time cooking for special Mom's Celebration

Mom's Day Celebration
Cookies / Punch

Awards / Crowns
Play

Social Studies

Talk about a family — What is a family? What do mothers do? Talk about mothers around the world.

Music

Innovation on Text
Take old favorites like *Mary Had a Little Lamb* and make new songs for mothers. Also: *I Think You're Beautiful, See Me Beautiful, Skidmarink*

Art

Make a big book about Love Is . . . for mothers. Make awards. Pictures of mothers. Fabric crayon pillows. Aprons out of men's handkerchiefs using fabric crayons or markers. Weavings on 5 x 6 boards. Crowns for special Mom's Celebration.

From *Why Whole Language* by Jay Buros

Jay Buros

Bibliography for a Theme on Mothers

Compiled by Jay Buros

Browne, Anthony. *Piggybook.* New York: Alfred A. Knopf, 1986.

Brown, Margaret Wise. *The Runaway Bunny.* New York: Harper and Row, 1942.

Cowley, Joy. *I Love My Family.* San Diego: The Wright Group, 1986.

Carlstrom, Nancy White. *Swim the Silver Sea, Joshie Otter.* New York: Philomel Books, 1993.

Eastman, P.D. *Are You My Mother?* New York: Random House, Inc., 1960.

Flack, Marjorie. *Ask Mr. Bear.* New York: McMillan, 1960.

Fox, Mem. *Koala Lou.* San Diego: Harcourt Brace & Co., 1988.

Freeman, Don. *Beady Bear.* New York: Young Readers Press, 1969.

Galbraith, Kathryn O. *Laura Charlotte.* New York: Philomel Books, 1990.

Greenfield, Eloise. *Honey, I Love.* New York: Harper and Row, 1972.

———. *Grandma's Joy.* New York: Philomel, 1980.

Guanno, Deborah. *Is Your Mama a Llama?* New York: Scholastic, 1989.

Hogurt, Susan Ramsay. *I Unpacked My Grandmother's Trunk.* New York: E.P. Dutton, 1983.

Joosse, Barbara M. *Mama, Do You Love Me?* San Francisco: Chronicle, 1991.

Johnson, Tony. *The Quilt Story.* New York: G.P. Putnam's Sons, 1985.

Kasza, Keiko. *A Mother For Choco.* New York: G.P. Putnam's Sons, 1992.

MacLachlan, Patricia. *All The Places To Love.* HarperCollins Publishers, 1994.

Mayer, Mercer, *Merry Christmas Mom and Dad.* New York: Golden Press.

———. *Just For You.* New York: Golden Press.

Mills, Lauren. *The Rag Coat.* Boston: Little, Brown and Co., 1991.

Polacco, Patricia. *Chicken Sunday.* New York: Philomel Books, 1992.

Waddell, Martin. *The Big, Big Sea.* Massachusetts: Candlewick Press, 1994.

Welber, Robert. *The Winter Picnic.* New York: Pinwheel Books, 1973.

Williams, Vera B. *A Chair For My Mother.* New York: Scholastic, 1982.

Zolotow, Charlotte. *When I Have a Little Girl.* New York: Harper and Row, 1965.

Bears

Drama
— Act out "The Three Bears"
— Puppet show / sock puppets — *Hairy Bear* (The Wright Group)
— Act out jumprope chant *Teddy Bear, Teddy Bear*
— Puppet show on tongue depressors of "The Three Bears" or *Ask Mr. Bear*

Skills in Context
— Depends on grade level. —

Skills in Context

Literature
See books on bears, next page.

Writing
— Photograph child with animal. Write about picture.
— Have children write letters to Teddy bears inviting them to school.
— In a Teddy bear shape book have children write about their bears.
— Write a Teddy bear story as a group. Innovate on text or pattern book.

Math
— Teddy bear counters (little plastic bears)
— Teddy Grahams
— Actual Teddy bears
— Teddy bear macaroni

count	estimate
group	weigh
pattern	measure
graph	word problems
add/subtract	
multiply/divide	

Science
— Make Teddy bear cookies.
— Research the Teddy bear.
— Study real bears.
— Make book on tracks in winter (great big book & small book)

Visitors:
— Ask someone who makes Teddy bears to show class how they do it
— Have a bear collector visit room and share collection.

Special Events:
— Teddy bear parade in the entire school, teachers, too.
— Bear Evening – put on plays, make clothes & enjoy.

Social Studies
— Where did the name Teddy bear come from?
— Interview grandparents about their favorite toys.
— What kinds of toys did children play with in the olden days?

Music

Art
— Children make small books (8½ x 11) *Teddy Bear, Teddy Bear*
— Map story of the three bears.

Jay Buros

BIBLIOGRAPHY . . . BEARS!

Compiled by Jay Buros

** A to Z Subject Access to Children's Picture Books. by Caroline Lima, Bowker Co.

* Asch, Frank. *Happy Birthday Moon, Mooncake*. Prentice Hall.
* Berenstein, Stan & Jan. *Bears in the Night, The Bike Ride*. Random House.
Brustlein, Janice. *Little Bears Pancake Party*. Lothrop, Lee & Shepard.
Carlstrom, Nancy. *Jesse Bear, What Will You Wear*?
Cauley, Lorinda. *Bryan, Goldilocks and the Three Bears*. Putnam's Sons.
Craft, Ruth. *The Winter Bear*. Atheneum.
* Dabcovich, Lydia. *Sleepy Bear*. Dutton.
Douglas, Barbara. *Good As New*. Lothrop, Lee & Shepard Co., NY.
DuBois, William. *Bear Party*. Viking.
* Duvoisin, Roger. *Snowy and Woody*. Knopf.
* Flack, Marjorie. *Ask Mr. Bear*. Puffin.
* Freeman, Don. *Beady Bear, Corduroy*. Puffin.
Galdone, Paul. *The Three Bears*. Seabury.
Ginsburg, Mirra. *Two Greedy Bears*. Macmillan.
* Kennedy, Jimmy. *The Teddy Bears' Picnic*.
* Kraus, Robert. *Three Friends*. Windmill Books.
Kuratomi, Chizuko. *Mr. Bear Goes to Sea*. Judson.
* Martin, Bill. *Brown Bear, Brown Bear, What Do You See*? HRW Press.
* Waber, Bernard. *Ira Sleeps Over*.
* Wahl, Jan. *Humphrey's Bear*.
* Ward, Lynn. *The Biggest Bear*.
Yolen, Jane. *The Three Bears Rhyme Book*. HBJ.

CHARTS

Teddy bear, teddy bear, turn around. Teddy bear, teddy bear, touch the ground.
Teddy bear, teddy bear, go upstairs. Teddy bear, teddy bear, say your prayers.
Teddy bear, teddy bear, turn out the light. Teddy bear, teddy bear, say goodnight,
"Goodnight!"

One little, two little, three little Teddy bears, four little, five little, six little Teddy bears, seven little, eight little, nine little Teddy bears, ten little Teddy bears and ___________.

ME AND MY TEDDY BEAR
Me and my Teddy bear
Have no worries have no cares.
Me and my Teddy bear
Just ___________ and ___________ all day.
(play) (play)

Music: **Unbearable Bears** by Kevin Roth
Marlboro Records
845 Marlboro Spring Rd.
Kennet Square, PA 19348

BEARS ARE SLEEPING (Sung to "Frere Jacques" from *More Piggyback Songs*)
Bears are sleeping, bears are sleeping. In their dens, in their dens.
Soon it will be spring, soon it will be spring. Wake up bears, wake up bears!

TEDDY BEAR SONG (Sung to: Mary Had A Little Lamb from *More Piggyback Songs*)
(child's name) has a Teddy bear, Teddy bear, Teddy bear.
______________ has a Teddy bear. It's (brown) and (furry) all over.

I'M GOING ON A BEAR HUNT

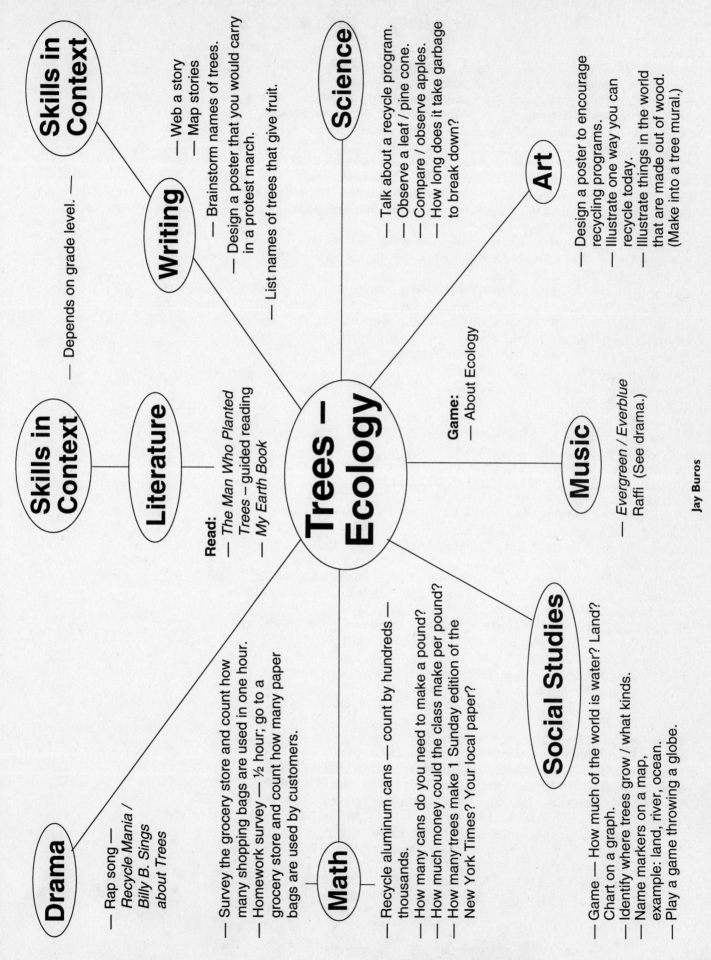

Trees – Ecology

Skills in Context

— Depends on grade level. —

Literature

Read:
— *The Man Who Planted Trees* – guided reading
— *My Earth Book*

Writing

— Web a story
— Map stories
— Brainstorm names of trees.
— Design a poster that you would carry in a protest march.
— List names of trees that give fruit.

Drama

— Rap song — *Recycle Mania / Billy B. Sings about Trees*

— Survey the grocery store and count how many shopping bags are used in one hour.
— Homework survey — ½ hour; go to a grocery store and count how many paper bags are used by customers.

Math

— Recycle aluminum cans — count by hundreds — thousands.
— How many cans do you need to make a pound?
— How much money could the class make per pound?
— How many trees make 1 Sunday edition of the New York Times? Your local paper?

Science

— Talk about a recycle program.
— Observe a leaf / pine cone.
— Compare / observe apples.
— How long does it take garbage to break down?

Game:
— About Ecology

Social Studies

— Game — How much of the world is water? Land? Chart on a graph.
— Identify where trees grow / what kinds.
— Name markers on a map, example: land, river, ocean.
— Play a game throwing a globe.

Music

— *Evergreen / Everblue* Raffi (See drama.)

Art

— Design a poster to encourage recycling programs.
— Illustrate one way you can recycle today.
— Illustrate things in the world that are made out of wood. (Make into a tree mural.)

Jay Buros

Ecology Resources

Books:

* Applehof, Mary. *Worms Eat My Garbage.* Michigan Flower Press, 1982.
* Bare, Edith. *This Is the Way We Go To School.*
  Bonnet, Robert L. *Earth Science — 49 Science Fair Projects.* Tab Books, 1990.
* Brandenberg, Aliki. *The Story of Johnny Appleseed.* NY: Simon and Schuster.
  Byars, Betsy. *The Summer of the Swans.* NY: Puffin Press, 1970.
  Caduto, Michael and Bruchac, Joseph. *Keepers of the Earth.* Fulcrum Inc., 1988.
* Cherry, Lynn. *A River Ran Wild.* NY: Harcourt, Brace Jovanovich, 1992.
  _____. *The Great Kapok Tree.* NY: Harcourt, Brace Jovanovich, 1990.
* Child, Lydia Maria. *Over the River and Through the Wood.* NY: Scholastic, 1974.
* Cook, Janet. *How Things Are Made.* Belgium: Usborne Pub. Ltd., 1989.
* Cooney, Barbara. *Island Boy.*
* Dabcovich, Linda. *Busy Beavers.* NY: Scholastic, 1988.
* dePaola, Tomie. *The Legend of Bluebonnet.* NY: G.P. Putnam's Sons, 1983.
* Donahue, Mike. *The Grandpa Tree.*
  Elkington, Hailes Hill. *Going Green.* NY: Puffin Books, 1990.
  Fiarotta, Phyllis. *Ships, Snails, Walnut Whales: Nature Crafts for Children.* NY: Workman Pub. Co.
* Giono, Jean. *The Man Who Planted Trees.* Chelsea Green Pub., 1985.
* Glaser, Linda. *Wonderful Worms.* The Millbrook Press, 1992.
  Goble, Paul. *I Sing for the Animals.* NY: Bradbury Press, 1991.
* Hallinan, P.K. *I'm Thankful Each Day!* Ideals Pub.
  Herman, Marina. *Teaching Kids to Love the Earth.* Pfeifer-Hamilton, 1991.
* Holling, Holling, C. *Paddle to the Sea.*
  Javna, John. *50 Simple Things Kids Can Do to Save the Earth.* NY: Universal Press.
* Jeffers, Susan. *Stopping by Woods on a Snowy Evening.* NY: Dutton, 1978.
* _____. *Brother Eagle, Sister Sky.* NY: Dial Books, 1991.
  Jeunesse, Gallimard. *The Earth and Sky.* NY: Scholastic, 1992.
* Kindersley, Dorling. *My First Green Book.* NY: Alfred Knopf, 1991.
  Lankford, Marg. *Hopscotch Around the World.*
* Lionni, Leo. *Tico and the Golden Wings.* NY: Alfred Knopf, 1964.
* Lobel, Arnold. *Ming Lo Moves the Mountain.*
* Locker, Thomas. *The Land of the Gray Wolf.* NY: Dial Books, 1991.
* MacDonald, G. *Little Island.*
* Maeno, Itoko. *Mother Nature Nursery Rhymes,* Santa Barbara, CA: Advocacy Press, 1990.
* McLerran, Alice. *The Mountain that Loved the Bird.* Picture Book Studio, 1985.
* Orbach, Ruth. *Apple Pigs.* NY: Philomel Books, 1976.
  Paulsen, Gary. *The Night the White Deer Died.* NY: Delacorte Press, 1978.
* Pearce, Fred. *The Big Green Book.* NY: Grosset and Dunlap, 1991.
  Pinnington, Andrea. *Nature.* NY: Random House, 1991.
* Ray, Deborah Kogan. *Little Tree.* NY: Crown Pub., 1987.
* Ryland, Cynthia. *When I Was Young in the Mountains.*
  Schwartz, Linda. *My Earth Book.* Santa Barbara, CA: The Learning Works, 1991.
* Siebert, Diane. *Hartland.*
* Silverstein, Shel. *The Giving Tree.* NY: Harper and Row, 1964.
* Soutter, Perroti, Andrienne. *Earthworm.* Creative Editions, 1993.
* Speare, Elizabeth George. *The Sign of the Beaver.* NY: Dell Pub. Co., 1983.
* Starr, Susan Bryer. *I Was Good to the Earth Today.* Starhouse Pub., 1992.
  Swartz, Linda. *Earth Book for Kids.* Santa Barbara, CA: The Learning Works Inc., 1990.
* Taylor, Barbara. *Green Thumbs Up!* (Experiments and Activities) NY: Random House, 1954.
* _____. *Hear! Hear!* (Experiments) NY: Random House, 1990.
* _____. *Over the Rainbow.* (Experiments) NY: Random House, 1992.
* _____. *Up, Up and Away!* (Experiments) NY: Random House, 1991.
* Udry, Janice May. *A Tree Is Nice.* NY: Harper and Row Pub., 1986.
* Van Allsburg, Chris. *Just a Dream.* Boston: Houghton Mifflin Co., 1990.

Walker, Colin. *The Great Garbage Mountain.*
_____. *Oceans of Fish.*
_____. *We Need Energy.*
_____. *Our Storehouse Earth.*
_____. *Our Changing Atmosphere.*
_____. *Forests Forever.*
_____. *Food Farming.*
_____. *Ecology — Plants and Animals.*
____. *The Environmental Teacher Guide*, Bothell, WA: The Wright Group, 1992.
White Deer of Autumn. *Ceremony in the Circle of Life.* Beyond Word Pub. Co., 1983.
* Wildsmith, Brian. *Squirrels.* Toronto: Oxford University Press, 1974.
* _____. *The Trunk.*
* Winter, Jeanette. *Follow the Drinking Gourd.*
Wolfman, Ira. *My World and Globe.* NY: Workman Pub., 1991.
Wood, Douglas. *Old Turtle.*
* Yolen, Jane. *Encounter.*
* _____. *Owl Moon.* NY: Philomel Books, 1987.
* Young, Ed. *Birches.* NY: Holt and Co., 1988.

GAME:

About Ecology
Earthwood, Inc.
Keyport, NJ 07735

MUSIC:

Recycle Mania / Billy B. Sings About Trees
P.O. Box 5423
Takoma Park, MD 19912
301-445-3845

PUZZLES, PROJECTS, FACTS AND FUN:

The Learning Works

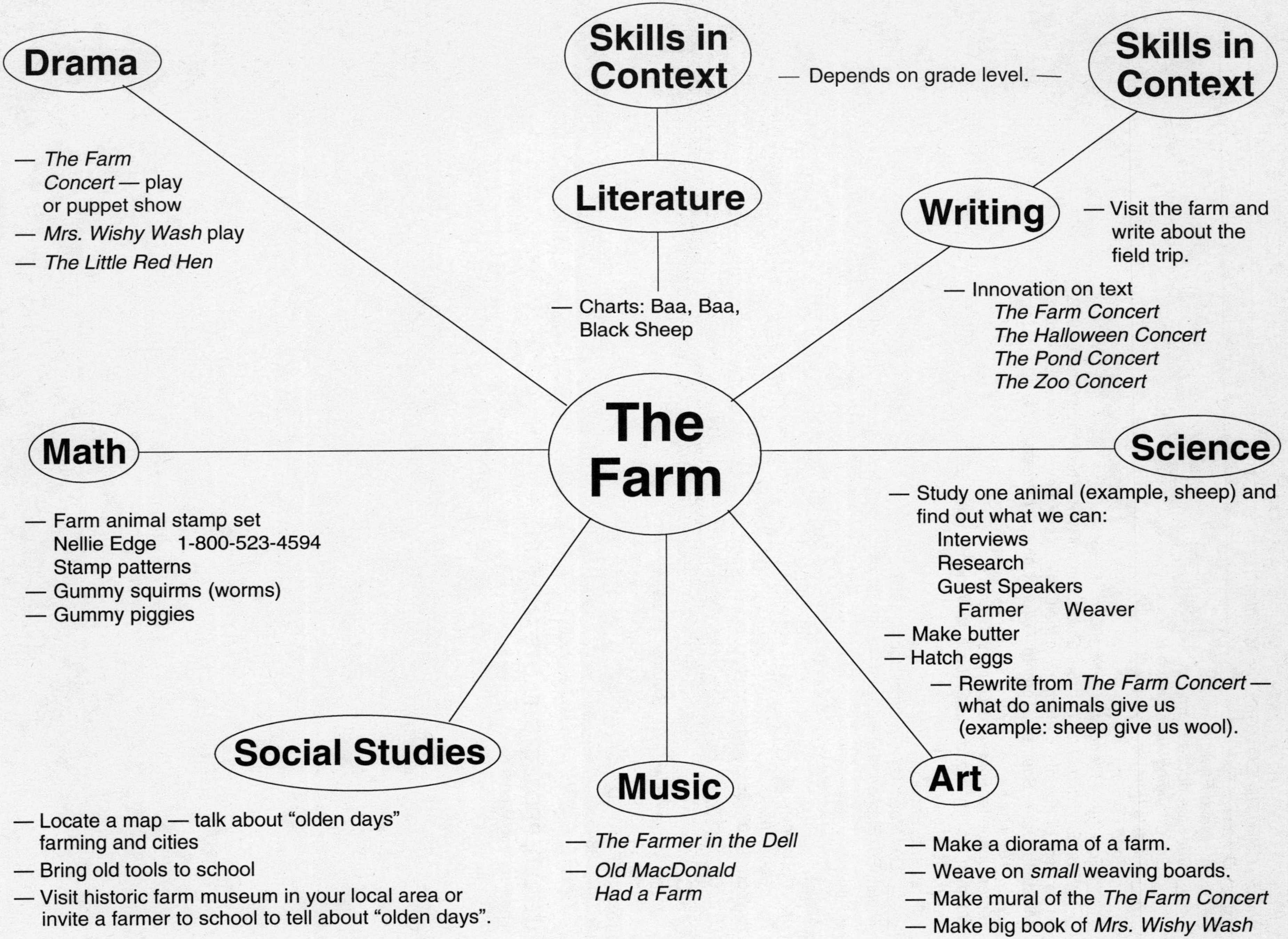
Drama
— The Farm Concert — play or puppet show
— Mrs. Wishy Wash play
— The Little Red Hen
Skills in Context
— Depends on grade level. —
Skills in Context
Literature
— Charts: Baa, Baa, Black Sheep
Writing
— Visit the farm and write about the field trip.
— Innovation on text
The Farm Concert
The Halloween Concert
The Pond Concert
The Zoo Concert
The Farm
Math
— Farm animal stamp set
Nellie Edge 1-800-523-4594
Stamp patterns
— Gummy squirms (worms)
— Gummy piggies
Science
— Study one animal (example, sheep) and find out what we can:
Interviews
Research
Guest Speakers
Farmer Weaver
— Make butter
— Hatch eggs
— Rewrite from The Farm Concert — what do animals give us (example: sheep give us wool).
Social Studies
— Locate a map — talk about "olden days" farming and cities
— Bring old tools to school
— Visit historic farm museum in your local area or invite a farmer to school to tell about "olden days".
Music
— The Farmer in the Dell
— Old MacDonald Had a Farm
Art
— Make a diorama of a farm.
— Weave on small weaving boards.
— Make mural of the The Farm Concert
— Make big book of Mrs. Wishy Wash

Jay Buros

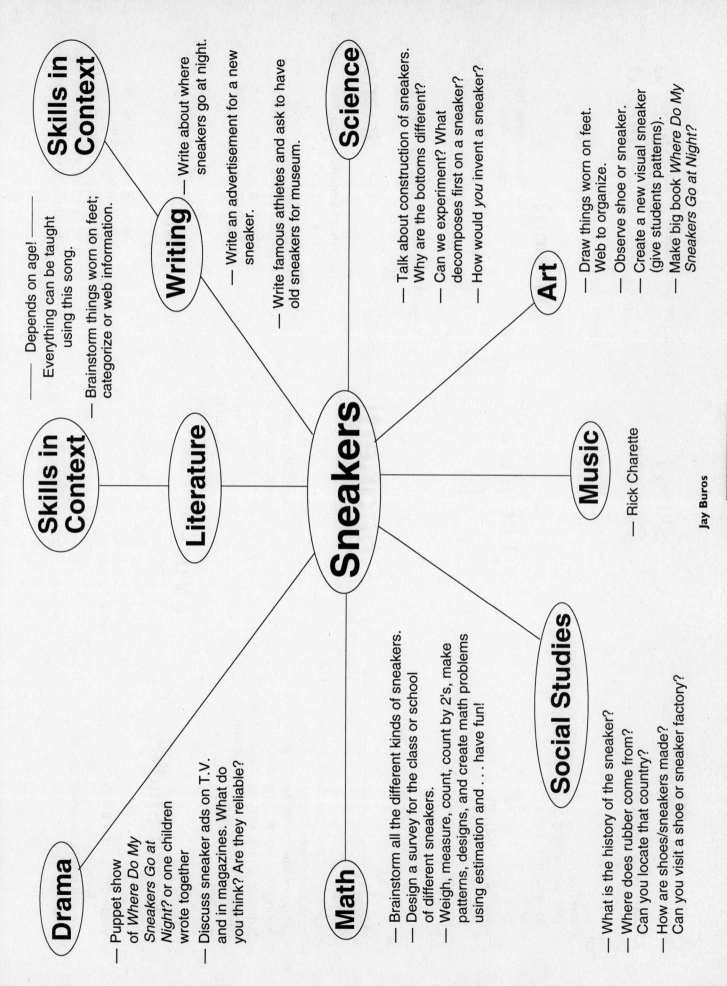

Sneakers

Skills in Context

— Depends on age! —
Everything can be taught using this song.

— Brainstorm things worn on feet; categorize or web information.

Drama

- Puppet show of *Where Do My Sneakers Go at Night?* or one children wrote together
- Discuss sneaker ads on T.V. and in magazines. What do you think? Are they reliable?

Literature

Skills in Context

Writing

Skills in Context

- Write about where sneakers go at night.
- Write an advertisement for a new sneaker.
- Write famous athletes and ask to have old sneakers for museum.

Math

- Brainstorm all the different kinds of sneakers.
- Design a survey for the class or school of different sneakers.
- Weigh, measure, count, count by 2's, make patterns, designs, and create math problems using estimation and . . . have fun!

Science

- Talk about construction of sneakers. Why are the bottoms different?
- Can we experiment? What decomposes first on a sneaker?
- How would *you* invent a sneaker?

Social Studies

- What is the history of the sneaker?
- Where does rubber come from? Can you locate that country?
- How are shoes/sneakers made? Can you visit a shoe or sneaker factory?

Music

— Rick Charette

Art

- Draw things worn on feet. Web to organize.
- Observe shoe or sneaker.
- Create a new visual sneaker (give students patterns).
- Make big book *Where Do My Sneakers Go at Night?*

Jay Buros

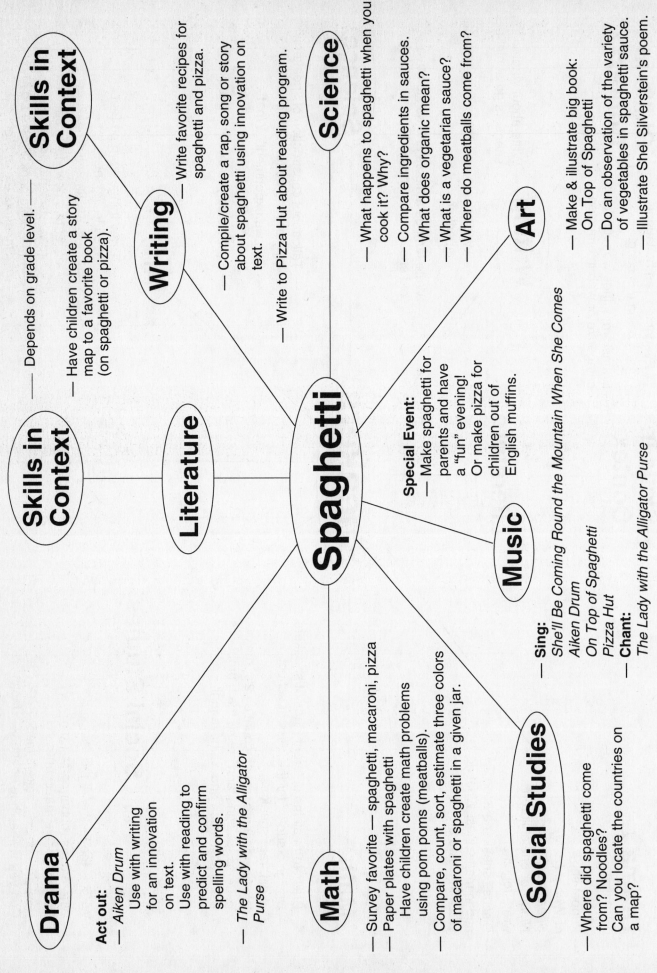

Spaghetti

Drama

Act out:

- *Aiken Drum*
  Use with writing for an innovation on text.
  Use with reading to predict and confirm spelling words.
- *The Lady with the Alligator Purse*

Skills in Context

— Depends on grade level. —

- Have children create a story map to a favorite book (on spaghetti or pizza).

Literature

Skills in Context

Writing

- Write favorite recipes for spaghetti and pizza.
- Compile/create a rap, song or story about spaghetti using innovation on text.
- Write to Pizza Hut about reading program.

Math

- Survey favorite — spaghetti, macaroni, pizza
- Paper plates with spaghetti
  Have children create math problems using pom poms (meatballs).
- Compare, count, sort, estimate three colors of macaroni or spaghetti in a given jar.

Science

- What happens to spaghetti when you cook it? Why?
- Compare ingredients in sauces.
- What does organic mean?
- What is a vegetarian sauce?
- Where do meatballs come from?

Special Event:

- Make spaghetti for parents and have a “fun” evening!
  Or make pizza for children out of English muffins.

Social Studies

- Where did spaghetti come from? Noodles?
  Can you locate the countries on a map?

Music

- **Sing:**
  She'll Be Coming Round the Mountain When She Comes
  Aiken Drum
  On Top of Spaghetti
  Pizza Hut
- **Chant:**
  The Lady with the Alligator Purse

Art

- Make & illustrate big book: On Top of Spaghetti
- Do an observation of the variety of vegetables in spaghetti sauce.
- Illustrate Shel Silverstein's poem.

Developmental Ages and Stages

- 5's — Calm, Cool and Coordinated
- 5 ½'s — Wild and Wooly
- 6's — Teething, Teasing, Temper Tantrums, and Tattling
- 7's — Slow and Sensitive
- 8's — Fast and Sloppy
- 9's — Independent and Competitive
- 10's — Golden Age

Kathryn L. Cloonan

More Success for Struggling Readers

AGENDA

I. Success begins with success
   Finding each child's success points

II. Guided Reading
   What it is . . . and . . . why we need to include it

III. Matching materials to readers' needs

IV. Guided Reading
   Where can it fit in a busy schedule?

V. Guided Reading
   Evaluating reading with running records

VII. Guided Writing
   Helping hesitant writers
   "get something down on paper"

VIII. Guided Writing
   Hands on!

IX. Using favorite children's songs to teach children how to read
   Why music works
   Turning traditional songs into Big books,
   Mini books & Class books

X. Using holiday songs to teach reading and skills

LITERACY PROFILE

1. "Draw a picture and write about it."
2. Progressive Approximation *
3. Developmental Checklist **
4. "Read me a story."
5. Stages of Reading *
6. Initial running record
7. Sight word list
8. Skills checklist

* Whole Language Evaluation for Classrooms – 1992, Orin & Donna Cochrane

** Pegasus program – Kendal Hunt Publishing Company

Progressive Approximation Form

Moving Toward Standard Spelling

Student Name ______________________________ Room __________________

	Text	1st		2nd		3rd		4th	
1.									
2.									
3.									
4.									
5.									
6.									
7.									
8.									
9.									
10.									

Key to Symbols:
+ = moving toward standard spelling
N = no change
– = moving away from standard spelling

Concepts of Print

1. Displays book handling skills
2. Can tell letters from words
3. Has left to right directionality
4. Has some letter / sound connection
5. Knows where to start on a page
6. Can do one-to-one matching

Reading Strategies

1. Semantic — meaning
Illustrations
Prior knowledge
Context of the sentence

2. Syntactic — the structure of our language

3. Graphophonics — phonics
Letter / sound connections
Rhyming words

Supportive Features of Text

Emergent Reading Materials

1. Consistent placement of text
2. Illustrations clearly match text
3. Simple vocabulary using children's natural language
4. Rhythm, rhyme, and repetition
5. Text parallels developmental stages of writing

Early Reading Materials

1. Longer sentence length
2. Book language
3. Variety of genres
4. Pictures enhance but do not consistently match text
5. Less repetition

Fluent Reading Materials

1. Short chapters
2. Increased variety of genres
3. Encourage integrating / utilizing many strategies
4. Encourage development of reading interests
5. Move the reader toward greater independence

Stages of Reading Development

Stage 1

Displays an interest in handling books.
Listens to print read to him for extended periods of time.
Begins to notice print — signs, labels.
Letters may appear in her drawings.
Likes to "name" pictures.

Stage 2

Engages in reading-like activities.
"Reads" or reconstructs content of familiar stories.
Recognizes his name and some other words in environmental context.
Writing may show some letter/sound connection.
Can construct story meaning from pictures.
Cannot pick words out of print consistently.
Can do oral cloze activities.
Rhymes words.
Gives words orally that begin similarly.
Can recall key words.
Begins to internalize story grammer, i.e., "Once upon a time . . . "

Stage 3

Can write and read back her own writing.
Can pick out individual words and letters.
Can read familiar stories. Uses pictures as clues to print.
Words in one context may not be read in another.
Enjoys chants and choral reading.
Can match or pick out words of poems.

Independent Reading Stages

Stage 1

Excited about reading.
Wants to read to you often.
Can read words in new situations.
Reads aloud lots of environmental print.
May focus too much on letters and sounds.
Oral reading may be word-centered rather than meaning-centered.

Stage 2

Understands author's meaning.
Enjoys reading to himself for pleasure.
Reads orally with meaning and expression.
Reads in word-meaning clusters.
Has internalized several genres.
Brings her own experiences to print.

Stage 3

Processes material further removed from his own experiences.
Can use a variety of print forms for pleasure.
Can discuss various aspects of a story.
Can read at varying and appropriate rates.
Can focus on or use varying forms of genre and print.

Components of a Balanced Literacy Curriculum

Reading to Children

Language Experience

Shared Reading

Guided Reading

Independent Reading

Writing

Sharing Responses

Daily Schedule

8:50 Welcome

"Base Groups" — Getting Organized
Teacher — attendance / lunch money, etc.
Managers — Book check, snack table
Independent Writing / Independent Study

9:20 Morning Meeting

9:35 Super Readers

9:45 Literature Block

Shared Reading

Writer's Workshop

mini-lesson
writers' write
teacher conferencing

10:15 Guided Writing

10:30 Recess

10:45 Language Arts Block

Small Group Instruction
Interest or needs or skills

Morning Centers
Buddy Reading

Literature
Extension

11:45 Story / Songs / Book Talk

12:00 Lunch / Recess

12:30 Read Aloud

12:45 Math

Math Centers

and small group instruction

1:15 Thematic Study Science / Social Studies

2:00 Art / Music / P.E.

2:30 Open Centers

3:00 Clean Up / Songs / Story / Discuss the Day

3:20

Kathryn L. Cloonan

Steps in a Literature Block

By Kathryn L. Cloonan

1. **Setup / Background / Semantic Mapping**

2. **Share a piece of literature . . .**
   Story — oral as well as written
   Song
   Flip Chart
   String Story
   Big Book
   Flannel Board Story
   Student Made Book

3. **Personalize It** **READ IT!**

4. **Put It Into Print** **READ IT!**

5. **Model It** **READ IT!**

6. **Expand It — Recreate It**
   Big Book or Class Book
   Mini Books
   Puppets
   Bulletin Board Stories
   Mobiles
   Wall Stories
   Overhead Transparency Stories
   Tutorette Stories
   Masks, Plays, Etc.
   Innovations

7. **Make the Writing Connection**
   Slot Stories
   Signs
   Posters
   Letters to a Character in the Story
   Letter to the Author
   "News" Article
   Adding Another Chapter
   Different Ending, etc.
   Writing Their Own Stories

Steps to Guided Reading for Emergent Readers

1. Select the text

   What are the needs of the children?

   Will the children have a high level of success?

   Does this book support their growth in skills and strategies?

2. Prepare ahead of time

   Look at illustrations.

   Plan the questioning.

3. Setting the scene

   Talk about the cover, author and illustrator.

4. Do a "Picture Walk"

   Read the title page.

   Talk through the illustrations.

5. Let the children read the text.

6. Return to the text.

   Discuss the story.

   Invite them to read their favorite page.

   Have children reread story in pairs.

7. Respond to the text.

   Discussion

   Reread

   Respond with writing, dramatization or arts and crafts.

Steps to Guided Reading with Early Readers

1. Select the text

2. Prepare ahead of time

   Look at illustrations.

   Plan the questioning.

3. Set the scene

   Discuss cover, author and illustrator.

   Semantic / cognitive mapping.

4. Do a "Word Walk"

   Use 'focused questioning'.

   Students 'dip into the text'.

   Read text to find answers and confirm by reading section orally.

5. Review "How can you figure it out?"

6. Students read the story individually.

7. Return to the text.

   Discuss the story.

   Invite them to read their favorite page.

   Have children reread story in pairs.

Running Record Analysis

Name ______________________________ Date ________________ Age _____

Text ______________________________ Level ______________ Seen / Unseen

Running Words: _______________ Accuracy: $\frac{\text{Success}}{\text{Running}}$ x 100 = _______ %

Self Corrections: _________ SC Rate: _______

M.	Meaning	
S.	Syntax	
V.	Visual	

Strategies Used:

Strategies to Coach:

Comprehension:

Kathryn L. Cloonan

Continuous Running Record Summary

Name ______________________________ Date ____________________

Date	Title	Level	Seen/ Unseen	Accuracy	S.C.	Comment

Different Kinds of Writing

Shared Writing

- Model Writing
- Daily News
- Morning Mystery Message
- Language Experience
- Labelling / Captioning

Children's Writing

- Guided Writing
  — Closed & Open-ended Guided Writing
  — Structure Writing
  — Content Writing

- Independent Writing
  — Book Publishing
  — Authors' Tea

Tattletale Application

Name ______________________  Boy ☐  Girl ☐

Address ______________________  ______________

____

______________________ How old are you? ____ years

Grade ______________ Teacher ______________________

School ______________________ Favorite Color ______________

Four (4) nice things about ______________________

1. ______________________________________

2. ______________________________________

3. ______________________________________

4. ______________________________________

Writer's Checklist

Yes, I can . . .

Dates checked

Draw a picture and tell about it.						
Draw a picture and write letters.						
Begin to leave spaces between words.						
Write the first letters in words.						
Write the first and last letters in words.						
Write some middle letters.						
Write some whole words.						

Write sentences.						
Put a period at the end of a sentence.						
Start a sentence with a capital letter.						
Use "super words"						
Give a story a title.						

Use a capital I for myself.						
Use . , ? or ! at the end of a sentence.						
Capitalize the first letter of a name.						
Spell some / most words correctly.						
Proof read my writing.						
Fix some mistakes.						
Find dictionary spelling for some words.						
Use spelling dictionary to correct words.						
Use quotation marks.						
Write paragraphs.						
"Rewrite" to make my best better.						
Write many different types of stories.						

Benefits	Process	Purpose
Encourages self-expression Makes letter-sound connections Builds fluency in ideas	**Writing**	Getting great ideas down on paper
Makes the connection between their ideas and the printed word Supports inventive spelling / corrective spelling	**Conference I**	Communicating ideas Learning new skills in • phonics • decoding skills • grammar • spelling • punctuation • sight words
Builds self-confidence by acceptance Enhances creativity Increases communication skills through making choices and decisions	**Conference II**	Creating, planning, and expressing ideas for a finished product
Encourages further efforts Builds self-respect and self-concept	**Publishing**	Modeling correct spelling, punctuation, sentence formation, and publishing
Builds the connection between print and ideas Encourages sight vocabulary	**Illustrating**	Increasing comprehension Encouraging creativity
Builds sight vocabulary Enhances decoding strategies Builds reading fluency	**Reading**	Building sight vocabulary
	Celebrating	

Celebrating with an Authors' Tea

Encourages a love for reading and writing

Enhances acceptance of others

Increases awareness of "presenting" to others

Enriches sight vocabulary

Builds a collection of readable materials

Encourages learning more about a subject

Builds self-confidence

Enriches organizational and planning skills

Models respect and love for literature

Gives *all* children an arena for success

Offers a completed reading and writing cycle that is relevant to children

AUTHOR'S PLANNING PAGE

Name: ______________________________

Title: ______________________________

Dedicated to: ______________________________

Because: ______________________________

About - Me - The Author: ______________________________

____

____

I would like my book:

Handwritten  ______________

or

Typed  ______________

I would like the words this size:

VERY LARGE   LARGE   SMALL

I would like the color of the cover to be: ______________________________

1. I have chosen my paper: ______________________________
2. I have talked with my Publisher: ______________________________
3. I have a picture of me: ______________________________
4. I have done my illustrations: ______________________________
5. My book is all put together: ______________________________

I DID IT!!!

Kathryn L. Cloonan

Our Authors' Tea Plans

This is our _____________ Authors' Tea.

It will be on _______________. It will start at ___________.

_______________ and _______________ will pass out programs.

_______________ will do the welcome.

_______________ will explain comments.

_______________ will introduce _______________.

Read Comments Applause!

_______________ will introduce _______________.

Read Comments Applause!

_______________ will introduce _______________.

Read Comments Applause!

_______________ will introduce _______________.

Read Comments Applause!

_______________ will introduce _______________.

Read Comments Applause!

Mrs. Cloonan will call all 5 authors up together and give each one a hug and a ribbon.

Applause for our authors!!

Authors will go to their special autograph signing desks.

Parents and teachers can ask for autographs. Boys and girls will start refreshments.

Then parents have refreshments and boys and girls go to authors and ask for autographs.

Especially Honoring

Author of

Autograph

Especially Honoring

Author of

Autograph

"Sing Me a Story, Read Me a Song"

Monday:
1. Teacher introduces a new song on a chart.
2. Sing together
3. Children each get a copy of the song to go in their own books called "Sing That Again".

Tuesday:
1. Teacher introduces the (same) song.
2. Sing together
3. Read together
4. Children illustrate their song.

Wednesday:
1. Sing together
2. Read together
3. Invite a "Leader Reader"
4. "Text Talk" — Discuss skills, pattern, or mechanics. Children can read their songs to a partner and play "Can you find".

Thursday:
1. Sing together
2. "Leader Readers"
3. "Text Talk"
4. Children highlight pattern or skill in their own book. Children take their "Sing That Again" books home to read.

Friday:
1. Sing together
2. "Leader Reader"
3. Plan together — Plan innovations, Big Books or mini-books

SING ME A STORY — READ ME A SONG

INTEGRATING MUSIC INTO THE WHOLE LANGUAGE CLASSROOM

By Kathryn L. Cloonan

PURPOSE

1. Instill a love for reading and music.
2. Make use of simple, delightful materials that have rhythm, rhyme, repetition.
3. To give children early successes in reading.
4. Give children an opportunity to make the connection between print and what they say and sing.
5. Build sight vocabulary by frequently seeing words in meaningful, predictable context.
6. Enrich decoding/reading skills through meaningful print.

STEPS

SHARE IT — Sing Lots of Songs Often
PRINT IT — Print a Favorite on Chart Paper
ILLUSTRATE IT — Make a Big Book, Make Mini Books
READ IT — Let the Children Read It

RESOURCES

Record and Tapes

Sing Me a Story, Read Me A Song, Kathryn Cloonan
Whole Language Holidays — Stories, Chants and Songs, Kathryn Cloonan
Peter, Paul and Mommy, Peter, Paul and Mary
Elephant Show Record, Sharon, Lois and Bram
Special Delivery, Fred Penner
The Cat Came Back, Fred Penner
Learning Basic Skills Through Music, Hap Palmer
We All Live Together, Volumes 1, 2, 3 & 4, Greg Scelse and Steve Millang
Doing the Dinosaur Rock, Diane Butchelor
You'll Sing a Song and I'll Sing a Song, Ella Jenkins
Singable Songs for the Very Young, Raffi
More Singable Songs for the Very Young, Raffi

Resource Books

Sing Me a Story, Read Me a Song, Book I, Kathryn Cloonan. Rhythm & Reading Resources, 1991.
Sing Me a Story, Read Me a Song, Book II, Kathryn Cloonan, 1991.
Whole Language Holidays, Books I and II, Kathryn Cloonan. Rhythm & Reading Resources.

SONGS

WE HAVE A FRIEND

We have a friend and
her name is Amy
Amy is her name
Hello, Amy-Hello, Amy
Hello, Amy
We're so glad you're here.
Innovation:
Change names of children

TWINKLE TWINKLE LITTLE STAR

Twinkle, twinkle little star
How I wonder what you are.
Up above the world so high.
Like a diamond in the sky.
Twinkle, twinkle little star
How I wonder what you are.

HICKORY, DICKORY DOCK

Hickory, Dickory Dock
The mouse ran up the clock
The clock struck one
The mouse ran down
Hickory, Dickory Dock
Innovations:
The clock struck 2, 3, 4, etc.

BAA, BAA, BLACK SHEEP

Baa, Baa Black Sheep
Have you any wool?
Yes sir, yes sir three bags full.

One for my master
One for the dame
One for the little boy
that lives down the lane.

Baa, Baa, Black Sheep
Have you any wool?
Yes sir, yes sir three bags full.
Innovation:
Color Words
Baa, Baa, Purple sheep, etc.

BINGO

There was a farmer
Had a dog and Bingo was his name-o.
B I N G O
B I N G O
B I N G O
And Bingo was his name-o.

ON A SPIDER'S WEB

One elephant went out to play
On a spider's web one day.
He had such enormous fun
He asked another elephant to come.

Two elephants went out to play
On a spider's web one day.
They had such enormous fun
They asked another elephant to come.

Three elephants, four elephants,
Five elephants, six elephants,
Seven elephants, eight elephants,
Nine elephants...............

Ten elephants went out to play
They had such enormous fun
They asked everyone to come.
Innovations: Change with theme or holidays — black cat, Christmas elf, leprechaun, dinosaur, Panda bear, etc.

FIVE SPECKLED FROGS

Five green and speckled frogs
Sat on a speckled log
Eating the most delicious bugs.
YUM! YUM!
One jumped into the pool
where it was nice and cool
Then there were four green speckled frogs.
Four...etc., Three...etc.,
Two...etc., One...etc.
Then there were NO green speckled frogs.

THE WHEELS ON THE BUS

The Wheels on the bus go
round and round
round and round
round and round
The wheels on the bus go
round and round
All through the town.

Innovations:
1. doors . . . open and shut
2. children . . . up and down
3. wipers . . . swish, swish, swish
4. babies . . . wah, wah, wah
5. snakes . . . Sss, Sss, Sss
6. bears . . . growl, growl, growl, etc.

I KNOW AN OLD LADY

I know an old lady who swallowed a fly
I don't know why she swallowed a fly . . .
perhaps she'll die.

I know an old lady who swallowed a spider
(that wiggled and jiggled and tickled inside her)
She swallowed the spider to catch the fly
But I don't know why she swallowed the fly
perhaps she'll die.

I know an old lady who swallowed a bird
She swallowed the bird to catch the spider
(that wiggled and jiggled and tickled inside her)
She swallowed the spider to catch the fly
But I don't know why she swallowed a fly
perhaps she'll die.

I know an old lady who swallowed a cat
She swallowed the cat to catch the bird
She swallowed the bird to catch the spider
(that wiggled and jiggled and tickled inside her)
She swallowed the spider to catch the fly
But I don't know why she swallowed the fly
perhaps she'll die.

I know an old lady who swallowed a dog
She swallowed the dog to catch the cat
She swallowed the cat to catch the bird
She swallowed the bird to catch the spider
(that wiggled and jiggled and tickled inside her)
She swallowed the spider to catch the fly
But I don't know why she swallowed the fly
perhaps she'll die.

I know an old lady who swallowed a goat
She swallowed the goat to catch the dog
She swallowed the dog to catch the cat
She swallowed the cat to catch the bird
She swallowed the bird to catch the spider
(that wiggled and jiggled and tickled inside her)
She swallowed the spider to catch the fly
But I don't know why she swallowed the fly
perhaps she'll die.

I know an old lady who swallowed a horse
She's Full, of course!

Innovations: Change the animals she swallowed

TEN IN THE BED

There were ten in the bed
And the little one said,
"Roll over, Roll over"
So they all rolled over and one fell out
And they gave a little scream
And they gave a little shout

Please remember to tie a knot in your pajamas
Single beds were only made for
1, 2, 3, 4, 5, 6, 7, 8
Nine in the bed, etc.
Eight etc., Seven etc.
Six-five-four-three-two . . . etc.
One in the bed and the little one said,
"I've got the whole mattress to myself"
(repeat last line three more times)
GOOD-NIGHT!

LITTLE COTTAGE IN THE WOODS

"Little cottage in the woods (Touch fingertips of both hands together to form a triangle shape for the house.) "Little man by the window stood." (Form "glasses" shapes with forefinger and thumb of each hand making a circle — put hands up to eyes in that shape, against face.) "Saw a rabbit hopping by" (Make rabbit "ears" by two fingers held up on one hand and "hop" them about.) "Frightened as could be." (Arms held across chest "shake" in mock fear.) "Help me, help me, help me, he said." (Raise arms overhead and down several times.) "Before the hunter shoots me dead: (Form "guns" with forefingers and "shoot.") "Come little rabbit, come inside" (Beckon with hand.) "And happy we will be." (Stroke the back of one hand with the other as though tenderly petting a rabbit.)

LITTLE SKUNK

Oh! I stuck my head in a little skunk's hole — and the little skunk said, "God bless your soul." Take it out! Take it out! Remove it! But I didn't take it out and the little skunk said, "If you don't take it out you'll wish you had." Take it out! Take it out! Psssss — I removed it.

MICHAEL FINNAGIN

There once was a man named Michael Finnagin
He had whiskers on his chin-a-gain
The wind came along and blew them in-again
Poor old Michael Finnagin . . . begin-again.

There once was a man named Michael Finnagin
He went fishing with a pin-again
Caught a whale that pulled him in-again
Poor old Michael Finnagin . . . begin-again.

There once was a man named Michael Finnagin
He was fat and then grew thin-again
Ate so much he had to begin again
Poor old Michael Finnagin . . . begin-again

TINY TIM

I had a little turtle,
His name was Tiny Tim
I put him in the bathtub
To see if he could swim.
He drank up all the water.
He ate up all the soap.
And now he's home sick in bed
With a bubble in his throat.

THE ANTS GO MARCHING

The ants go marching one by one
Hurrah! Hurrah!
The ants go marching one by one
Hurrah! Hurrah!
The ants go marching one by one
the little one stops to suck his thumb
And they all go marching down — into the ground — to get out — of the rain —
BOOM, BOOM, BOOM, BOOM,
BOOM, BOOM, BOOM, BOOM,
two by two . . . tie his shoe
three by three . . . climb a tree
four by four . . . shut the door
five by five . . . jump and dive
six by six . . . pick up sticks
seven by seven . . . wave to heaven
eight by eight . . . climb the gate
nine by nine . . . look behind
ten by ten . . . pat a hen

GOOD-BYE

We have a friend and her name is Amy,
Amy is her name. Good-bye, Amy, good-bye Amy
Good-bye, Amy, we'll see you tomorrow.
Innovation: Change names of children.

HOLIDAY SONGS

TRICK OR TREAT

They'll be Trick or Treating here on Halloween, **Trick or Treat!**
They'll be Trick or Treating here on Halloween, **Trick or Treat!**
They'll be Trick or Treating here,
They'll be Trick or Treating here,
They'll be Trick or Treating here on Halloween, **Trick or Treat!**

2. They'll be knocking at our doors on Halloween, **Knock! Knock!**
3. Ghosts will all go "Boo!" on Halloween, **Boooooooooo!**
4. Black cats all meow on Halloween, **Meeeeeeeeeeow!**
5. We will all have fun on Halloween, **Hurray!**

ONCE I HAD A PUMPKIN

Once I had a pumpkin, a pumpkin, a pumpkin
Once I had a pumpkin with no face at all.
With no eyes and no nose and no mouth and no teeth.
Once I had a pumpkin with no face at all.

Then I made a Jack-o-Lantern, Jack-o-Lantern, Jack-o-Lantern.
Then I made a Jack-o-Lantern . . . with a big funny face.
With big eyes and a big nose and a big mouth and big teeth.
Then I made a Jack-o-Lantern . . . with a big funny face.

DOG HAIR STEW

© 1991 Kathryn L. Cloonan

Ten black cats were left by themselves
on Halloween night with nothing to do.
So they decided to make their own
Dog Hair Stew.

First they got a very large pot
And filled it with water that was extremely hot.
Their goal was to make a horrible brew
More horrible even, than last year's stew.

Cat #1 flicked his tail in a wave
And said, "Here's some slime from a nearby cave."
"And here's some juice from a skunkweed plant."
Said Cat #2 as he joined in the chant.

Cat #3 said, "Heh, Heh, wait till you see what I brought.
The eyes of two dead fish I finally got!"
"Let me add some bat liver oil," meowed Cat #4,
A skinny cat named "Skin and Bones."
Cat #5 said, "Here's a couple of frogs and a snake.
This is my very favorite stew to make."
One by one the cats came by
Adding secret ingredients with a meow and a cry.

The oldest cat carefully stirred it round and round
While the fire crackled with an ominous sound.
The 10th cat hissed with eyes aglow,
"Here's the hair of a dog so stir it in slow."

Now the cats they pranced and danced around their Dog Hair Stew
Then drank every drop of their mysterious brew.
Then all at once the cats gave a very loud wail
And their hair stood up straight from their head to their tail.

"Happy spooky Halloween!", they said with a wink,
"Dog Hair Stew is our favorite drink!"
And for the rest of the year
They had nothing to fear . . .

For each time a dog was seen,
Their hair stood up straight and they looked so mean
Not a dog would dare
give them a scare.

And the cats would wink an eye and say,
A little Dog Hair Stew on Halloween day
Keeps even the meanest dogs away.

SCAT THE CAT

I'm Scat the Cat
I'm sassy and fat
And I can change my colors
Just like that! (Snap)

THIS IS THE CANDLE

This is the candle
This is the candle
That glowed in the jack-o-lantern.

This is the mouse
That lit the candle
That glowed in the jack-o-lantern.

This is the cat
That chased the mouse
That lit the candle
That glowed in the jack-o-lantern.

This is the ghost
That said "BOO!" to the cat
That chased the mouse
That lit the candle
That glowed in the jack-o-lantern.

This is the moon
That shown on the ghost
That said "BOO!" to the cat
That chased the mouse
That lit the candle
That glowed in the jack-o-lantern.
That shouted **"Happy Halloween!"**

ONE LITTLE SKELETON

One little skeleton, hopping up and down
One little skeleton, hopping up and down
One little skeleton, hopping up and down
For this is Halloween!

2. Two little bats, flying through the air.
3. Three little pumpkins, walking in a row.
4. Four little goblins, skipping down the street.
5. Five little ghosties, popping in and out.

FIVE LITTLE PUMPKINS

Five little pumpkins sitting on a gate.
The first one said, "My, it's getting late!"
The second one said, "There are bats in the air".
The third one said, "I don't care!"
The fourth one said, "Let's run, let's run."
The fifth one said, "Halloween is fun!"
OOOOOOOOOOOO went the wind.
Clap out went the lights.
And five little pumpkins rolled out of sight.

BRAVE LITTLE PILGRIM

The brave little Pilgrim went looking for a bear.
He looked in the woods and everywhere.
The brave little Pilgrim found a big bear.
He ran like a rabbit! Oh! what a scare!

FIVE FAT TURKEYS

Five fat turkeys are we.
We slept all night in a tree
When the cook came around
We couldn't be found

Let's fly to the tallest tree
There we'll be safe as safe can be.
From the cook and the oven you see
It surely pays on Thanksgiving days
To sleep in the tallest trees!!

WE WISH YOU A MERRY CHRISTMAS

We wish you a Merry Christmas
We wish you a Merry Christmas
We wish you a Merry Christmas
and a Happy New Year!

Let's all do a little jumping
Let's all do a little jumping
Let's all do a little jumping
and spread Christmas cheer.

Let's all do a little twirling
Let's all do a little twirling
Let's all do a little twirling
and spread Christmas cheer.

We wish you a Merry Christmas
We wish you a Merry Christmas
We wish you a Merry Christmas
and a Happy New Year!

S.A.N.T.A.

There was a man who had a beard.
and Santa was his name-o.
S.A.N.T.A.
S.A.N.T.A.
S.A.N.T.A.
And Santa was his name-o!

There was a man who had a beard.
and Santa was his name-o.
S.A.N.T.Ho!
S.A.N.T.Ho!
S.A.N.T.Ho!
And Santa was his name-o!

(Leave off one more letter and replace it with a "Ho" until the final verse is "Ho, Ho, Ho, Ho, Ho.")

FIVE LITTLE REINDEER

Five little reindeer prancing up and down
Five little reindeer prancing up and down
Five little reindeer prancing up and down
For Christmas time is near.

2. Four little Santa elves trimming up a tree . . .

3. Three little jingle bells ring, ring, ringing . . .

4. Two little snowflakes twirling in the night . . .

5. One little sleigh speeding through the snow . . .

MY DREIDEL

I have a little dreidel.
I made it out of clay.
And when it's dry and ready
My "dreidel" I shall play.

chorus
Oh dreidel, dreidel, dreidel
Oh little top that spins
The children all are happy
When Hanukkah begins.

My dreidel's always playful
It loves to spin all day.
A happy game of dreidel
My friends and I shall play
(repeat chorus)

OH VALENTINE!

© 1991 Cloonan

Oh Valentine! Oh Valentine!
I hope that you'll be mine.
I took my time and wrote this rhyme
Especially for you.

Oh! Valentine! Oh! Valentine!
I hope that you'll be mine.
With crayons, paper, and some glue
I've made this card for you.
Oh Valentine! Oh Valentine!
I hope you'll be mine.
And on this very special day
There's just one thing to say . . .
"I love you!"
"Happy Valentine's Day!"

HERE'S A LETTER

Here's a letter, here's a letter.
One for you.
One for you.
Guess what's in the letter.
Guess what's in the letter.
I love you!
I love you!
(Verses two & three are done in a round)

ONE LEPRECHAUN WENT OUT TO PLAY

One leprechaun went out to play
On a bright St. Patrick's day.
He had such enormous fun
He asked another leprechaun to come.

Two leprechauns went out to play
On a bright St. Patrick's day.
They had such enormous fun
They asked another leprechaun to come.

Three, four, five, six, seven, eight, nine

Ten leprechauns went out to play
On a bright St. Patrick's day.
They had such enormous fun
They asked everyone to come!

LITTLE PETER RABBIT

Little Peter Rabbit
Had a fly upon his nose.
Little Peter Rabbit
Had a fly upon his nose.

Little Peter Rabbit
Had a fly upon his nose.

And he swished until it flew away.
(repeat)

"Sing That Again"

HEY THERE NEIGHBOR!
Hey there, neighbor!
What do you say?
It's going to be a wonderful day!
Clap your hands and boogie on down.
Give 'em a bump and pass it around!
(or sit on down)

HI! MY NAME IS JOE!
Hi! My name is Joe and I work in the button (doughnut) factory.
I have a wife, a dog, and a family!
One day my boss came to me and said,
"Hey Joe, are you busy?"
I said, "No."
He said, "Well, then work with your right hand."
- Repeat each time adding one more body part: left hand, right foot, left foot, head

Last line, last time:
I said, "YES!!!"

TONY CHESTNUT
Toe knee chestnut
Nose eye love you.
Toe knee nose.
Toe knee nose.
Toe knee chestnut nose I love you . . .
That's what toe knee nose.

HI DE HAY! HI DEE HO!
Leader: *Hi dee hay! Hi dee ho!*
Group: **Hi dee hay! Hi dee ho!**
Leader: *Igglee wigglee wogglee wo!*
Group: **Igglee wigglee wogglee wo!**
Leader: *Raise your voices to the sky.*
Group: **Raise your voices to the sky.**
Leader: *Mrs. ____'s class is walking by*
Group: **Mrs. _____'s class is walking by.**
Leader: *Count off!*
Group: **1, 2, 3, 4, 5**
Leader: *Break it on down now!*
Group: **6, 7, 8, 9, 10 . . .**
Leader: *Let's do it all once again!*

RISE RUBY RISE!
Down in the valley two by two.
Down in the valley two by two.
Down in the valley two by two.
Rise Ruby Rise!

2nd verse:
We can do it your way two by two.
We can do it your way two by two.
We can do it your way two by two.
Rise Ruby Rise!

3rd verse:
We can do it my way two by two.
We can do it my way two by two.
We can do it my way two by two.
Rise Ruby Rise!

Mr. Rhythm and Rhyme

1. Mr. Jingle, Mr. Jangle, Mr. Rhythm and Rhyme
   I woke up this morning, I was feeling so fine.
   I went to my mother and my mother said,
   "You've got the rhythm in your head?" tap tap
   I've got the rhythm in my head! tap tap
   You've got the rhythm in your head! tap tap
   We've all got the rhythm in our heads. tap tap
2. hands clap clap
3. hips woo woo
4. feet stamp stamp
5. Mr. Jingle, Mr. Jangle, Mr. Rhythm and Rhyme
   I woke up this morning, I was feeling so fine.
   I went to my mother and my mother said,
   "See if you can do it quiet instead." shh! shh!
   stamp stamp
   woo woo
   clap clap
   tap tap
   shh! shh!
   shh! shh!

Sing That Again is available in both instrumental and vocals versions.

Kathryn L. Cloonan • 5125 N. Amarillo Drive • Beverly Hills, FL 34465

"Sing That Again"

I THINK YOU'RE WONDERFUL
(R & K Grammer)

(Refrain)
I think you're wonderful.
When somebody says that to me,
I feel wonderful,
as wonderful as can be.
It makes me want to say
the same thing to somebody new.
And by the way I've been meaning to say
I think you're wonderful, too.

1. When we practice this phrase
   in the most honest way,
   Find something special
   in someone each day.
   We lift up the world
   one heart at a time.
   It all starts by saying
   this one simple line . . . Refrain
2. When each one of us
   feels important inside
   loving and giving and
   glad we're alive,
   Oh! what a difference
   we'll make in each day.
   All because someone
   decided to say . . . Refrain

* I'M BEING SWALLOWED BY A BOA CONSTRICTOR
(Silverstein)

I'm being swallowed by a boa constrictor
I'm being swallowed by a boa constrictor
I'm being swallowed by a boa constrictor
And I don't like it very much.

Oh, No! Oh, No! He's up to my toe
He's up to my toe, Oh Gee! Oh Gee!
He's up to my knee, he's up to my knee.
Oh fiddle! Oh fiddle! He's up to my middle!
He's up to my middle. Oh Heck! Oh Heck!
He's up to my neck, he's up to my neck!
Oh Dread! Oh Dread! He's up to my _______ slurp!

* A TEEPEE IS MY HOME
A teepee is my home.
Of deerskins it is made.
A place on top where smoke can go.
It stands in forest shade.
The river runs nearby.
And there is my canoe.
I paddle up and down the stream.
Beneath the sky of blue.

GOOD MORNING!!
Leader: *Good Morning!*
Group: **Good Morning!**
Leader: *How are you?*
Group: **How are you?**
Leader:
It's so nice to see you again.
With a one and a two and a How-do-you-do.
DING-DONG
It's so nice to see you again.
Leader: *Here's* ___________
Group: **Hi** ___________
Leader: *Here's* ___________
Group: **Hi** ___________
Leader: *Here's* ___________
Group: **Hi** ___________

All Together:
It's so nice to see you again.
With a one and a two and a How-do-you-do.
DING-DONG
It's so nice to see you again.

Leader: *Here's* ___________
Group: **Hi** ___________
Leader: *Here's* ___________
Group: **Hi** ___________
Leader: *Here's* ___________
Group: **Hi** ___________

All Together:
It's so nice to see you again.
With a one and a two and a How-do-you-do.
It's so nice to see you again.
It's so nice to see you again.

WADDALEE ACHEE

Waddalee Achee
Waddalee Achee

Doodle lee doo
Doodle lee doo (repeat)

It's the simplest song
There isn't much to it.
All you have to do is
Doodle lee doo it.

I know the rest
But the part I like best
Is the doodle lee
Doodle lee — doo!
Woo!

Sing That Again is available in both instrumental and vocal versions.
Kathryn L. Cloonan • 5125 N. Amarillo Drive • Beverly Hills, FL 34465

* Available on SING ME A STORY, READ ME A SONG
▲▲ Available on WHOLE LANGUAGE HOLIDAYS

"Time to get up!"

said the ____________________

Outside My House

by

Inside My House

by

Organize Your Books for Self-Selected Reading

1. Level some of them:

easy/easy
easy/hard
medium/easy
medium/hard
more difficult

emergent
early
early fluent
fluent

2. Group some by author

Books by Tomie de Paola
Books by Eric Carle

3. Group some by topic/genre

Books about fish
Books about Halloween
Books about animals
Poetry books
Fairy Tales
ABC Books

4. Old Favorites or Read Alouds

* use containers
* no more than 10-15 books per container (or fewer)
* present book talks
* use attractive books
* use good literature

Components of the Reading Workshop

(from *Readers' Workshop Real Reading* by Patricia Hagerty)

Mini Lesson (5-10 minutes)

- Procedural
- Strategies and skills
- Literary
- Text responses

Activity Period (30-40 minutes)

Read

- Students read individually selected books
- Students may read alone, in pairs, heterogenous or not

Respond

- Students write responses in a literature log
- Responses can be open or directed
- Write in literature log three times per week

Confer

- Discuss books with children individually
- Use a checklist or anecdotal records for assessment
- Teach one strategy, skill, etc. to individual/small group

Share (10-15 minutes)

- Large group-three or four students share
- Small groups of 3 or 4 members; each member shares

How to Choose a Book
(from Dr. Patricia Hagerty)

Consider the reading level:

Easy:

The book flows for you.
The ideas are easy to understand.
The words are easy for you to read.

Just right:

You understand most of the ideas.
You might not know some words, but you can figure them out or skip them.

Challenge:

The book is hard for you to read.
You don't understand a lot of the ideas.
Many of the words are hard for you.

Other things to think about:

Look at the cover.
Read the inside flap.
Do you know the characters?
Has the book won awards?
What size is the print?
Find someone who's read it.
Do you know the author?
How thick/thin is the book?
Use the five finger rule.

Confer

1. Go to the student
2. Ask student to read aloud. *Assess* reading fluency, problem solving, use of reading strategies.
3. Ask questions, ask what the reader notices or wonders about, ask reader to show understanding of mini-lesson; *assess comprehension.*

student name:

Title: *Level:* *Errors: M S V s/c* *monitoring:* *when stuck:* *fluency:* *comp.*	*Title:* *Level:* *Errors: M S V s/c* *monitoring:* *when stuck:* *fluency:* *comp.:*	
Title: *Level:* *Errors: M S V s/c* *monitoring:* *when stuck:* *fluency:* *comp.:*	*Title:* *Level:* *Errors: M S V s/c* *monitoring:* *when stuck:* *fluency:* *comp.:*	

Reading Skills / Strategies

Name:

Teacher:

Grade:

Key:
N = Not observed
P = Can with prompt
S = Sometimes
H = Habituated

Date				
Tells a story				
Uses reading-like behavior to approximate book language				
Memorizes text				
Recognizes print contains the message				
Controls directionality				
One-to-one matching				
Anchors on known words				
Locates unknown words				
Is learning to read new words:				
uses the picture (meaning cues)				
uses the context of story (meaning cues)				
uses language structure cues				
uses visual cues				
• initial letter cues				
• letter clusters				
• final letter cues				
• links to a known word				
Reads for meaning				
Cross checks and self-corrects				
Re-reads when stuck				
Makes good guesses				
Problem-solves independently / monitors				

Share

1. Large group-circle format; or small groups
2. Reader shares...book, part marked with 'sticky', lit. log, mini-lesson, reminders
3. Reader asks for questions or comments from group
4. Teacher models appropriate discussion questions and *assesses discussion*

Text Responses

- **Double entry diary**
- **Remembering a story**
- **Character report card**
- ***Things we can write about books* chart**
- **Mini-lesson connection**
- **Sentence starters**

  I wonder...
  The title of my book is ____ because...
  The character ____ is (not) a hero/heroine because...
  A place in the story I would (wouldn't) like to be is ...
  I felt ____ when...
  If I were...
  I'm not sure...

- **Skills**

  locate verbs
  fact/opinion
  cause/effect

- **Literary Devices**

  settings
  mood
  main character
  genre

- **Non-fiction**

  K-W-L

  Although I already knew ..., I learned ...

Susan Thomas Kelly

Sources of Information Good Readers Use

(Dr. Marie Clay)

Meaning Cues:

Structure Cues:

Visual Cues:

Julie's Picture

1. Julie painted a picture.	√ <u>paints</u> √ √ painted
2. She painted a face.	√ √ √ √
3. She painted eyes.	√ √ √
4. She painted a big smile.	√ √ √ √ <u>mouth</u> smile
5. She painted long hair.	√ √ <u>like</u> √ long
6. Julie looked at her picture.	√ √ √ <u>the</u> √ her
7. It was a picture of her mom!	√ √ √ <u>painting</u> √ √ √ picture
8. Julie took the picture home after school.	√ √ √ √ √ <u>and</u> √ after
9. "This is for you Mom," said Julie.	<u>That</u> √ √ √ √ √ √ This
10. "It's me!" said Mom. "Thank you, Julie!"	√ √ <u>Mom</u> <u>said</u> said Mom √ √ √

What Do You Do When You're Stuck?

1. Go back and read it again.
2. Think what makes sense.
3. Look at the pictures.
4. Start the word.
5. Make a good guess.

That's what you do when you're STUCK!

Paulette Mansell — Carrollton-Farmers Branch I.S.D.

What to do when young readers get stuck:

1. Wait and see if they work it out.
2. Say, "Try that again."
3. Say, "Look at the picture."
4. Say, "Think about what would make sense."
5. Say, "Read the sentence again and <u>start</u> the tricky word."
6. Tell the word.

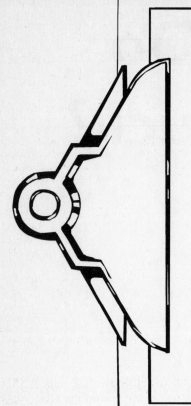

What to do when young readers make a mistake:

1. If the mistakes makes sense, don't worry about it.
2. If the mistake doesn't make sense, <u>wait</u> to see if the reader will fix it.
3. Say, "Try that again."
4. Say, "Did that make sense?"
5. Say, "Did what you read <u>look</u> right and <u>sound</u> right?"
6. Tell the correct response.

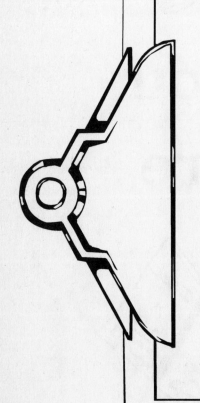

Susan Thomas Kelly

Words and How They Work

Emergent

- Developing concepts about print

- Developing letter/sound knowledge

Early

- Blends

- Digraphs

- Endings

- Vowels

Early Fluent

- Spelling patterns

- Irregular words

Onset	Rime
c	at
sp	ent
tr	ain
bl	ack

Useful rime patterns:

ack	*ice*	*ad*
ick	*ain*	*ide*
ake	*ight*	*ale*
ill	*all*	*in*
am	*ine*	*ame*
ing	*an*	*ink*
and	*ip*	*ank*
ir	*ap*	*ock*
ash	*oke*	*at*
op	*ate*	*or*
aw	*ore*	*ay*
uck	*eat*	*ug*
ell	*ump*	*est*

GUIDED READING

1. *Choose book/story*

- Strategies children control/instructional level
- Interest
- Supportive text

2. *Introduce the book/story*

- Main idea statement
- Let children hear the language of the text.
- Locate one or two important words.

3. *Children read simultaneously-may begin chorally.*

- Teacher scaffolds individually
- Use strategy questions/statements

4. *Re-read together chorally for fluency*

5. *Respond to text*

- Orally
- Written

Book Introductions for Guided Reading Groups

1. Encourage the students to **make predictions** or link the story to prior knowledge.

2. Give a brief (one or two sentence) **overview statement** about the story.

3. **Rehearse any unusual language** or repetitive phrases with the students.

4. Allow students to **browse through the book**, looking at the pictures, and making predictions about the story.The teacher guides the students to the ideas in the story. Browsing can be done as a group or individually.

5. **Locate one or two important words** in the story.

6. All students **read the whole story** with teacher prompting when necessary.

7. **Re-read** chorally for fluency.

Literacy Centers

ABC	Writing	Reading
•alphabet books •magnetic letters •overhead •alphabet stamps •handwriting books •dictionaries •blank books	•blank big books •stencils •stickers •comic strips •poetry box •shape books •writing supplies •story starters	•listening center •poetry books •books of plays •map skill cards •special response sheets •book of finger plays •bean bags
Stretch	**Math**	**Outside**
•encyclopedia •library pass •newspapers •maps •theme books	•number books •math manipulatives •coin stamps •clock stamps •junk boxes •math books •MTW jobs	•blank tapes and recorders •pointers to read walls •permission slips for visits •big books •sing-a-long books and tape

from the primary classroom of Naomi Uribe, Sheffield Elementary School, Carrollton-Farmers Branch I.S.D.

Excerpt from *Teaching Thinking and Problem Solving in Math*, by Char Forsten.

Getting Started by Investigating the Problem

What is a Problem, Exactly?

For many of us, the word *problem* has a negative connotation. Something is wrong that needs to be fixed.

Of course, there are many cases where this is true. When your car makes a suspicious noise, you see dollar signs. At school, when two students argue, you are likely to ask, "What's the problem?"

In mathematics, a problem can be a simple algorithm waiting to be computed or a complex situation with one or more steps and calculations needing to be solved.

I tell students problems are situations that require some kind of action or they go unresolved. If I am hungry, I must decide what to eat, then actually consume the food. If I want to take a vacation, I read about possible locations, then choose one to visit and take the trip. If I face a math problem, I must understand it, decide what to do, then solve it.

A variety of cultures exist in this world because societies solve the problems of food, clothing, shelter, and rules differently. Stop and think about it. An Inuit will solve the problem of needing shelter differently than an aborigine, because the conditions they face are so dissimilar. The fact that each situation reflects different conditions makes problem solving a fascinating adventure.

It is helpful for students to have an expanded view of what a problem is, whether it is a math riddle with one possible answer, or a social issue such as the solid waste program requiring in-depth analysis.

A Model for Problem Solving

Have you ever met someone who seems to know exactly what to do no matter how serious the problem? Such a person confronts an issue, sizes it up, and is at ease making a prompt decision. Most likely, he or she is well-trained or experienced in solving problems. We can help students feel comfortable with problem solving by starting to educate them in logical reasoning processes when they begin school.

In order to accomplish this, we must give students a sequence in which to analyze problems. Children face an overload when confronted with a task that requires them to do many things at once. Certainly complex problems can overwhelm them and leave the door open for a math block to form. That is why it is important to train students to approach problems in a step-by-step fashion.

The following is a problem solving model I use in my teaching:

1. Determine the problem.
2. Identify relevant facts and their relationships to each other.
3. Specify important conditions.
4. Choose a strategy.
5. Solve the problem.
6. Check your results.

Step 1: Determine the Problem

Have you ever walked around with a knot in your stomach and wondered what was bothering you? You know once you figure it out, you can work it through, and be rid of that gnawing feeling.

Determining what the problem is may seem like an easy step, but we should not take for granted that students will always recognize it. This skill requires concentration on the question and the ability to create a mental image of the situation. To help determine the problem:

1. Read, and, if necessary, reread the problem.
2. Create a mental picture of the problem.
3. Find the question and put it in your own words to show understanding.

Allow time for students to practice this skill of determining the problem. By starting out with simple problems, students will be better able to analyze more complex situations.

Step 2: Identify Relevant Facts and Their Relationships to Each Other

Math problems vary according to the amount of information they contain. Students must learn to sift through facts and decide which are necessary to solve the problem. They must also determine their relationships to each other and the order in which they will use them. We have all seen examples that contain too much information such as:

Terry, Larry, and Harry all collect baseball cards. Terry started with thirty-six, gave five to Larry, then bought three from her brother. Larry started with fifty-four. His brother, who collects stamps, gave him another thirteen for his collection. When Larry counted up his cards, he was very upset, because he was missing one of Reggie Jackson. He looked everywhere, but could not find it. Finally, there was Harry, who had the largest collection of seventy-two cards. Last Saturday, he went to a shop and traded three of his cards for five others. How many more cards did Harry have than Larry?

At first glance, this problem is confusing with its rhyming names and juggling of numbers. Students not trained in problem solving are overwhelmed. Those who learn the step-by-step approach would:

1. Determine the problem: In the end, how many more cards did Harry have than Larry?
2. Identify relevant facts and their relationships to each other:

Larry's cards: 54 + 5 + 13 - 1 = 71
Harry's cards: 72 - 3 + 5 = 74

Terry's role in this situation helps students create a mental picture of the problem, and the five cards she gave to Larry must be figured into the math equation. The other number facts about Terry are irrelevant to the solution — they contribute to an understanding of the whole picture, but are not necessary to solve the problem.

Much practice is needed to identify relevant facts correctly. Many students do not have a system for analyzing problems; they manipulate the numbers, come up with an answer which may or may not be reasonable, then move on to the next order of business.

Step 3: Specify Important Conditions

When choosing relevant facts, it is also important to identify conditions that might exist in a problem. In real life, if you want to buy a snack and only have fifty cents, you should immediately eliminate any snacks over this amount. You do not want to waste your time on solutions that are not feasible.

In Chapter Five of this book, I will explain how to do case studies with students. Recognizing conditions becomes a crucial step in these thinking activities. As children become more involved with real-life situations, they must not only look at the problem mathematically, but they also need to consider any conditions that could affect the solution.

If Billy, who is asthmatic, is groping with the dilemma of taking in a stray cat, he must consider both the cost factor of caring for the cat and the condition of his health when making his decision.

Step 4: Choose a Strategy

A variety of strategies used in problem solving are discussed at length in Chapter Three of this book. The ones I have included are: key words to operations; guess and check; make a table or an organized list; draw a picture or use real objects; work backwards or make it simpler; find a pattern; and use logic.

I introduce each strategy separately in a large group setting, provide practice problems, then when all strategies have been taught, give students a variety of problems where they must decide what to do on their own or in their cooperative learning groups. Examples of teaching these applications are provided in Chapter Three.

Step 5: Solve the Problem

This is straightforward — students carry out the plan. Having determined the problem, identified relevant facts and their relationships, recognized conditions, and chosen a strategy, they should now be able to solve the problem mathematically and consider important factors to come up with a logical answer.

Step 6: Check the Results

A few years ago, I had a conference with a parent who is also a high school math teacher. When I discussed my concerns about students' ability to think and solve problems, he told me that if we could just get kids to ask this important question: "Does the answer make sense?," it would make a tremendous difference in their progress in math.

Thus the question, "Is the answer reasonable?" became a critical part of my math lessons. Students know I am going to ask this. In fact, I have a large poster hanging on a wall that constantly poses this evaluative question to the children.

When I ask if the answer is reasonable, I am really directing them to consider whether they used the correct computational approach and backed it up with logical reasoning.

A problem that will demonstrate

whether students are thinking logically is:

There are thirteen kids in an afterschool chess club. They have been invited to a tournament on the other side of the city, and must find adults to drive them. If only four students can ride in each car, how many cars will be needed?

I have seen answers such as 3R.1, which shows the student recognized division as the correct operation, but failed to determine the problem and understand what sort of answer was appropriate.

Other students might suggest only three cars are needed, because the one extra student could sit on someone's lap. This shows an understanding of the problem and creative thinking, but it also demonstrates the student did not recognize given conditions. The answer is not reasonable because the problem stated only four students could ride in each car.

Experience has taught me that many kids tend to use "if only" thinking. "If only the thirteenth student could sit on someone's lap, then only three cars would be needed." When this happens, I acknowledge their use of creative thinking in coming up with an alternative that would save gas and drivers, but I remind them that this problem gave the condition that only four students could ride in each car. There can be no "if only" in this case.

That is why, when dealing with logical thinking in math problems, I remind students they must recognize and adhere to given conditions.

Open-ended problems are another matter. There are times when altering conditions can be a problem. When students change variables in an experiment, they are altering conditions. In order to discover the effects of environmental factors on plant growth, students will vary the conditions in controlled experiments. Open-ended activities and real-life problems encourage students to develop all types of thinking. There are problems where conditions can be altered. Help students see how important conditions are when economists offer ways to control inflation, health workers discover cures for diseases, and environmentalists search for solutions to our solid and toxic waste problems.

When teaching problem solving to elementary students, I usually establish ground rules at the beginning of a session. Later, students are better able to determine which problems are open-ended and which require adherence to given information. When asked whether their answer is reasonable, students must be sure they have determined the correct problem, identified important facts, and recognized given conditions.

Checking results needs to become a habit. Reward students for questioning their answers and praise their movement through each step in the problem solving process.

How can you track the students' progress or identify their weak areas in the problem solving model? A chart that shows their thoughts at each step is a good way to observe growth.

Summary: Charting the Model

As you work through the model, students can fill in a chart to check their progress in problem solving and social skills. They can put the entire model to use with the following problem:

Jack and Jill went up the hill to fetch 2 liters of water. Along the way, they met Ms. Muffet who was collecting spiders. When they finally reached the top and filled their container with water, they turned around and began to run down the hill. Jack fell down and spilled the water everywhere. If Jack was 2 meters ahead of Jill, and Jill was 5 meters from the top, how far down the hill was Jack?

The sample chart on the following page (filled out in the name of John Doe) guides students through the six steps in the problem solving model and helps prevent them from getting stuck.

Learning Problem Solving Strategies

After examining the problem solving model as a whole, it is time to focus on the step of choosing a strategy. In Chapter 3, a variety of strategies will be presented and each will include warm-up activities, math applications, and extensions.

Problem Solving Chart

Name: John Doe **Group:** Challengers **Date:** June 1

Problem: How many meters from the top of the hill was Jack?

Relevant facts: 1.) Jill was 5 meters down the hill.
2.) Jack was 2 meters farther than Jill.

Conditions: Jack was 2 meters farther down the hill than Jill. Jill was not in front of Jack.

Strategy: Draw a picture.

Jack —— Jill —————— top of hill

2m. 5m. = 7m.

Solution: 2m. + 5m. = 7m.

Jack was 7m. down the hill.

Reasonable answer? Yes. Jack was in front of Jill by 2 meters, which would mean he was farther down the hill.

SOCIAL SKILLS

Contributions to group: I drew the picture.

Encouraging words: I told Jill she did a great job of finding important facts.

Ways I cooperated: I let John determine the problem, even though I wanted to do it.

PROBLEM SOLVING CHART

Name:	**Group:**	**Date:**
PROBLEM:		
RELEVANT FACTS:		
CONDITIONS:		
STRATEGY:		
SOLUTION:		
REASONABLE ANSWER?		
SOCIAL SKILLS ASSESSMENT		
CONTRIBUTIONS TO GROUP:		
ENCOURAGING WORDS:		
WAYS WE COOPERATED:		

??????

WHAT ARE PROBLEM SOLVING STRATEGIES ?

* **Guess and Check** [? √] (Learning to ride a bike, shopping)

* **Make a Chart or an Organized List** [1. 2. 3.] (Outlines, Webs, Combinations)

* **Draw a Picture or Use Real Objects**  (Maps, Diagrams, Manipulatives)

* **Work Backward** [←] (Retrace steps, Checking work through inverse operation, Research)

* **Make It Simpler** [2 + 2 = 4] (Anecdotes, Use smaller numbers, Teach younger students, Start Simple!)

* **Find a Pattern** [XOXOX] (Daily Patterns: tides, sunrise & sunset, daily routines, art, nature, rate)

* **Use Logic**  (Analogies, Puzzles, Chess, Brainteasers, etc.)

Char Forsten Society for Developmental Education 1-800-924-9621

Mathematical Awareness, Appreciation, & Attitude:

- *Create a positive climate by:* using humor, creating a visually stimulating classroom, teaching all strands of mathematics, recognizing multiple intelligences in children, and focusing on ways that build confidence in all students.
- *Have you seen any good math lately?* (Use bulletin boards, centers, or large group activities to find math that surrounds us in slides, photos, postcards, and magazine or newspaper pictures; take walking field trips to discover math in and around the school; examine artists' works, such as M.C. Escher, Picasso, & DaVinci; conduct surveys that ask people the role math plays in their daily lives.)
- *Have you heard any good math lately?* (Listen to music or poems to determine notes, beat, and even use of syllables in their composition.)
- *Have you read any good math lately?* (Discuss books, current events, and magazine or newspaper clips that relate to math.)
- *Have you eaten any good math lately?* (Look over menus, examine labels, scrutinize nutritional value of snacks and lunches, list types and amounts of food eaten, such as: 1/2 a grapefruit, 1/3 of a pizza, 4 pieces of bread, etc.)

Thinking!!! (Creative, Analytical, & Critical):

- Creative Concoctions: Take 3 minutes to draw an original vehicle that incorporates at least 4 geometric shapes.
- Logic games (What's My Rule? , 20 Questions, Dominoes)
- Picture puzzles (*Whatzit?*™ - shared first by teacher, then by students.)
- Logic games (*Clue*™, chess, short mysteries, and logic puzzles and software, etc.
- Analogies (Hot is to cold as hard is to soft.)
- "Hink Pink" word game (What do you call a feline who eats too much? (*A Fat Cat*), A tiny numeral? (*midget digit*); 7 minutes after 5? (*prime time*).
- Puzzles (Tangrams, trade books such as: *The Eleventh Hour* and the *I Spy* series.
- Critical Capers: Debates, Editorials, Reviews, & Pro and Con Discussions.

Number Sense:

- Mnemonics (Memory Triggers - acronyms: Division sequence: Divide, Multiply, Subtract, Check, Bring Down...DMSCB Dad, Mom, Sister, Cousin, Brother)
- Dice games (Practice number facts, Games: "*Pig*,' target math, Polyhedral games)
- Card games (*Concentration*, target math, Lola May's "*Make 20 or Make 10*"
- Riddles (What Number Am I?, 20 Questions)
- "Rename the Date" (The answer is the date...what is the question?)
- Exploring properties and operations through manipulatives
- Estimating Opportunities ("Guesstimate...Bestimate," "Predict & Check")
- Daily Number Review ("Up Close and Personal with Today's Number!")
- Real-World Connections (Students, School, Community, World, Architecture, Art, Music, Movement, & Poetry, Newspapers & Magazines, and Nature)

Char Forsten Society for Developmental Education 1-800-924-9621

COMPONENTS OF A QUALITY MATH PROGRAM

Based on the National Council of Teachers of Mathematics *Standards*

Goals

Students should learn to:

- Value mathematics;
- Communicate mathematically;
- Reason mathematically.

Students should become:

- Confident about their ability to do mathematics;
- Mathematical problem solvers.

STRANDS

1. Problem Solving
2. Using Mathematics to Communicate Information
3. Using Mathematics to Reason
4. Making Connections with Mathematics
5. Estimation
6. Number Sense and Numeration
7. Concepts of Whole Number Operations
8. Whole Number Computation
9. Geometry and Spatial Sense
10. Measurement
11. Statistics and Probability
12. Fractions and Decimals
13. Patterns and Relationships

Teachers As Talent Scouts

Joseph S. Renzulli

Originally developed for gifted education programs, the Schoolwide Enrichment Model can be used in an inclusive school that wants to be a laboratory for talent development.

Elaine is a gifted 3rd grader.

When many people hear a statement like that, they raise issues of elitism that have long plagued special programs based on narrow definitions, IQ scores, or other measures of cognitive ability. By labeling some students "gifted," they argue, you relegate all others to the category of "not gifted."

But suppose you say the following: "Elaine is a 3rd grader who reads at the adult level and has a fascination for biographies about women scientists." By focusing on the student's behavioral characteristics, you can make a case for providing the following services:

- Under the guidance of her classroom teacher, Elaine substitutes more challenging books in her interest area for the 3rd grade reader. The schoolwide enrichment teaching specialist helps the classroom teacher locate these books, which are purchased with funds from the enrichment program budget.
- Elaine leaves school two afternoons a month (usually on early dismissal days) to meet with a mentor—a local journalist who specializes in gender issues. The schoolwide enrichment teaching specialist arranges transportation through the parent volunteer group.
- By compacting the curriculum in Elaine's strength areas (reading, language arts, and spelling), the schoolwide enrichment teaching specialist frees time for her to meet with female scientists and faculty members at a nearby university.

© Jeffrey High/IMAGE Productions

Could even the staunchest anti-gifted proponent argue against the logic or the appropriateness of these services? Essentially, such services become opportunities for developing "gifted behaviors" rather than merely finding and certifying them. And when programs focus on developing the behavioral potential of individuals—or of small groups whose members share a common interest—it's no longer necessary to group certain students merely because they all happen to be "gifted 3rd graders."

Tapping Everyone's Potential

Given the opportunity, students like Elaine can develop gifted behaviors in specific areas of learning and human expression, transcending the idea of giftedness as a state of being. This orientation, the basis of the Schoolwide Enrichment Model, can allow many students—not just those labeled gifted—to achieve high levels of creative and productive accomplishments that otherwise would be denied them through traditional program models.

The instructional procedures and programming alternatives that characterize the Schoolwide Enrichment

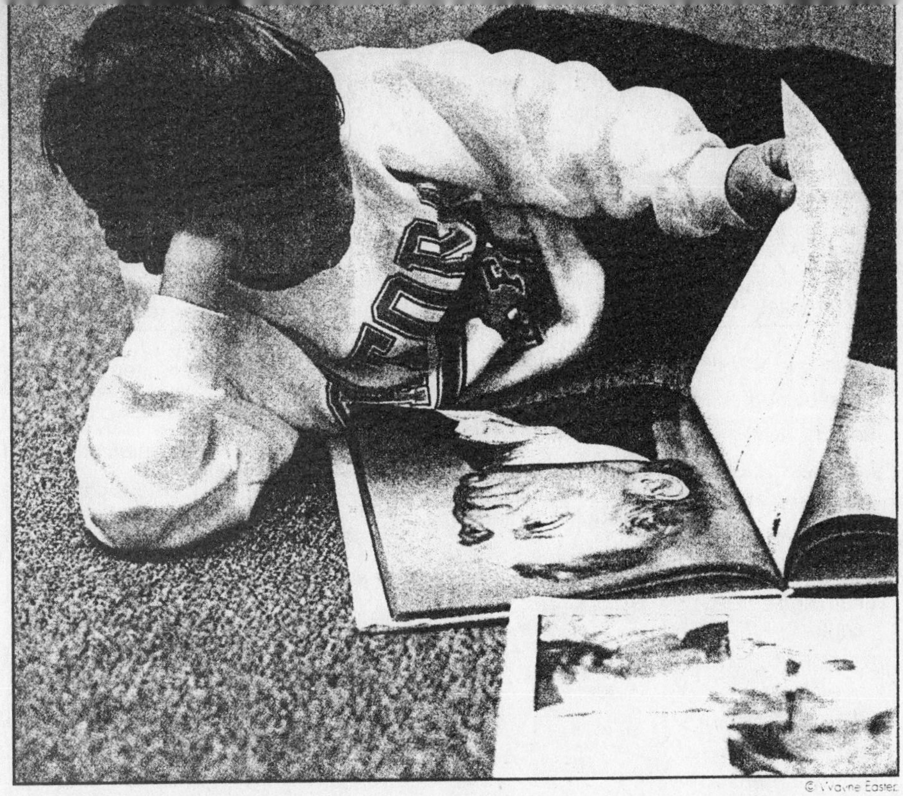

© Wayne Eastep

Model have two objectives:

1. Provide a broad range of advanced-level enrichment experiences for all students.

2. Use the many and varied ways that students respond to these experiences as stepping stones for relevant follow-up.

This approach isn't a new way of identifying who is or isn't gifted. Rather, it identifies how to provide subsequent *opportunities, resources, and encouragement* that will support escalated student involvement in both required and self-selected activities.

True, the model has its roots in special programs for high-potential students. Such programs have proved an especially fertile place for experimentation, because they're usually not encumbered by prescribed curriculum guides or by traditional methods of instruction. Many school improvement concepts that originated in special programs have begun to surface in general education. These include, for example, a focus on concept rather than skill learning, an interdisciplinary curriculum and theme-based studies, student portfolios, cross-grade grouping, and alternative scheduling patterns.

A variety of research on human abilities supports the application of gifted program know-how to general education (Bloom 1985, Gardner 1983, Renzulli 1986, Sternberg 1984). Also, research clearly and unequivocally justifies the broader concept of "talent development" and points to the role that enrichment specialists can play in school improvement.

In addition, the enrichment approach reflects the democratic ideal that schools can accommodate the full range of individual differences. Traditional identification procedures restrict services to small numbers of high-scoring students. Enrichment activities, however, enable schools to help develop the talents of all students who manifest their potentials in many other ways.

Essential Elements

Bringing the Schoolwide Enrichment Model to large segments of the school population requires three components:

1. The Total Talent Portfolio. The model focuses on specific learning characteristics that can serve as a basis for talent development. The approach uses both traditional and performance-based assessment to determine three dimensions of the learner—abilities, interests, and preferred learning styles. This information, which focuses on strengths rather than deficits, is compiled into a form called the Total Talent Portfolio (see fig. 1). Schools use the portfolios to decide which talent development opportunities to offer a particular student through regular classes, enrichment clusters, and special services.

2. Curriculum modification techniques. The Schoolwide Enrichment Model relies upon a curriculum that challenges all students to learn, offers a number of in-depth learning experiences, and injects enrichment opportunities into the school's regular activities. Modifying the curriculum typically involves the following procedures:

- *Curriculum compacting.* Through this process, schools eliminate repetition of previously mastered material, upgrade the challenge level of the regular curriculum, and provide time for enrichment and acceleration activities (Reis and Renzulli 1992). In many ways, curriculum compacting is simply common sense—it imitates the pattern that teachers naturally follow when individualizing instruction or teaching without textbooks.

The first step in curriculum compacting is to define the goals and outcomes of a particular unit or segment of instruction. Next, teachers determine which students have already mastered most or all of a specified set of learning outcomes. They also identify those who are capable of mastering the outcomes in less time than their peers. Lastly, in place of the material that's already been mastered, the school provides more challenging and productive activities. These may include content acceleration, individual or group research projects, peer teaching, or involvement in non-classroom activities. All the options give students some freedom to decide how they'll pursue a particular topic.

- *Textbook analysis.* The textbook *is* the curriculum in the overwhelming majority of today's classrooms. Despite much rhetoric about school and curriculum reform, that situation

Figure 1

Dimensions of the Total Talent Portfolio

Abilities	Interests	Style Preferences			
Maximum Performance Indicators	Interest Areas	Instructional Styles Preferences	Learning Environment Preferences	Thinking Styles Preferences	Expression Style Preferences
Tests ■Standardized ■Teacher-made Course grades Teacher ratings **Product Evaluation** ■Written ■Oral ■Visual ■Musical ■Constructed (Note differences between assigned and self-selected products) Level of participation in learning activities Degree of interaction with others	Fine arts Crafts Literary Historical Mathematical/logical Physical sciences Life sciences Political/judicial Athletic/recreation Marketing/business Drama/dance Musical performance Musical composition Managerial/business Photography Film/video Computers Other (Specify)	Recitation and drill Peer tutoring Lecture Lecture/discussion Discussion Guided independent study Learning/interest center Simulation, role playing, dramatization, guided fantasy Learning games Replicative reports or projects Investigative reports or projects Unguided independent study Internship Apprenticeship	**Inter/Intra Personal** ■Self-oriented ■Peer-oriented ■Adult-oriented ■Combined **Physical** ■Sound ■Heat ■Light ■Design ■Mobility ■Time of day ■Food intake ■Seating	Analytic (school smart) Synthetic/creative (creative, inventive) Practical/contextual (street smart) Legislative Executive Judicial	Written Oral Manipulative Discussion Display Dramatization Artistic Graphic Commercial Service

isn't likely to change soon. As a result, modifying the curriculum will necessarily involve an in-depth analysis of current textbooks, followed by a "surgical removal" of repetitious drills and practices.

Both the analysis and subsequent surgery reinforce the idea that "less is better" when it comes to content selection. The first step in the process might best be described as "textbook triage": Grade-level teams examine each instructional unit and eliminate the material that needlessly repeats skills and concepts covered previously. Teachers then decide which material is necessary for review and which is important enough to cover in either a survey or an in-depth manner.

■ *Expanding the depth of learning.* This third procedure for modifying curriculum is based on the work of Phenix (1964), who found that focusing on representative concepts and ideas is the best way to capture the essence of a topic. Representative ideas—themes, patterns, main features, sequences, and organizing structures—often serve as the basis for interdisciplinary or multidisciplinary studies.

Beyond those concepts, in-depth learning requires increasingly complex information that moves up the hierarchy of knowledge: for example, from facts to trends and sequences, to classifications and categories, to principles and generalizations, and then to theories and structures. The dimension of learning commonly referred to as process or thinking skills is another form of content. These skills form the cognitive structures and problem-solving strategies that endure long after students have forgotten the facts or trends.

Lastly, in-depth learning involves the application of methods to problems. In other words, the student takes on the role of firsthand investigator rather than the more passive learner of lessons.

3. Enrichment Learning and Teaching. The third component needed to put the Schoolwide Enrichment Model into practice is based on the ideas of a philosophers and researchers ranging from William James and John Dewey to Howard Gardner and Albert Bandura. The work of this small but influential group, coupled with our own research, has given rise to the concept of enrichment learning and teaching. Four principles define this concept:

■ Each learner is unique. Therefore, all learning experiences must take into account the abilities, interests, and learning styles of the individual.

■ Learning is more effective when students enjoy what they're doing. Therefore, learning experiences should be designed and assessed with as much concern for enjoyment as for other goals.

■ Learning is more meaningful and enjoyable when content (for example, knowledge) and process (for example,

Figure 2

The Continuum of Services for Total Talent Development

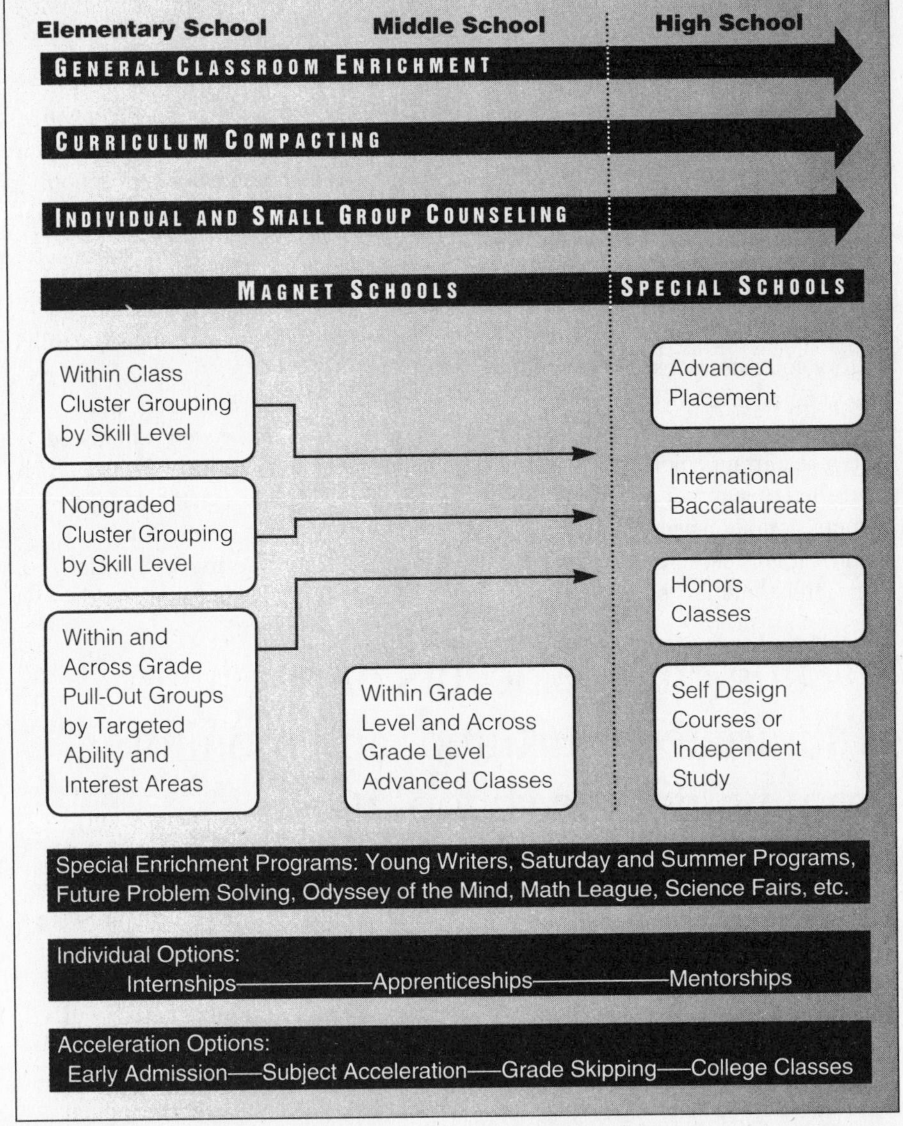

thinking skills) have a real problem as their context. Therefore, students should have some choice in problem selection, and teachers should consider the relevance of the problem for individual students, as well as authentic strategies for addressing the problem.

■ Enrichment learning and teaching focus on enhancing knowledge and acquiring thinking skills. Therefore, *applications* of knowledge and skills must supplement formal instruction.

Implementing the Model

Numerous research studies and field tests in schools with widely varying demographics (Renzulli and Reis 1994) have yielded both research support and practical suggestions for schools wishing to implement the SEM. Here's how the model operates within three types of structures.

1. Regular curriculum. The regular curriculum encompasses the school's goals, schedules, learning outcomes, and delivery systems. Whether traditional, innovative, or in transition, the regular curriculum has one predominant characteristic: Authoritative forces (policymakers, school councils, textbook adoption committees, state regulators, and so forth) have made it the centerpiece of student learning. Our goal with the Schoolwide Enrichment Model is to influence rather than replace the regular curriculum. Still, introducing the model can substantially change content and instructional processes in three ways:

■ Through curriculum compacting and modification of textbook content, the required material challenges students at different levels.

■ Selected, in-depth learning experiences replace the content that's been eliminated.

■ Enrichment activities are integrated selectively into regular curriculum activities (Renzulli 1977).

2. Enrichment clusters. Enrichment clusters bring together nongraded groups of students who share common interests. Like extracurricular activities and programs such as 4-H and Junior Achievement, the clusters meet at designated times and operate on the assumption that students and teachers (or community resource people) want to be there.

Enrichment clusters place a premium on the development of higher-order thinking skills and the creative and productive application of these skills to real-world situations. As a result, the learning environment supports the development of self-concept. To put it another way: *Every child is special if we create conditions in which that child can be a specialist within a specialty group.*

Enrichment clusters revolve around major disciplines, interdisciplinary themes, or cross-disciplinary topics. A theatrical/television production group, for example, might include actors, writers, technical specialists, and costume designers. Clearly the clusters deal with how-to knowledge, thinking skills, and interpersonal relations that apply in the real world. Student work is directed toward producing a product or service. Instead of lesson plans or unit plans, three key questions guide learning:

■ What do people with an interest in this area—for example, filmmaking—do?

■ What knowledge, materials, and other resources do we need to authentically do activities in this area?

■ In what ways can we use the product or service to affect the intended audience?

Schools use enrichment clusters to varying degrees. The Webster Elementary School in St. Paul, Minnesota, for example, has a broad array of interdisciplinary clusters every day. The Southeast School in Mansfield, Connecticut, offers enrichment clusters once each week; teachers and parent volunteers jointly teach the clusters. The superintendent of schools, who is also a licensed pilot, organized one of the most popular clusters: Flight School.

3. Continuum of special services. Although enrichment clusters and the modifications of the regular curriculum help meet individual needs, a program for talent development still requires supplementary services. These services, which challenge the students capable of working at the highest levels of their special interest areas, typically include individual or small-group counseling; direct assistance in facilitating advanced-level work; mentor relationships; and other programs that connect students, families, and out-of-school resources or agencies. (Figure 2 illustrates the continuum of services by education level.)

The schoolwide enrichment teaching specialist—or a team of teachers and parents—has responsibility for providing options for advanced learning. One schoolwide enrichment teaching specialist in Barrington, Rhode Island, estimates she spends two days a week serving as a resource to the faculties of two schools; on the other three days she provides direct services to students.

The schoolwide enrichment coordinator in the LaPorte, Indiana, School Corporation developed a Parent-Teacher Enrichment Guide that describes opportunities in the city and surrounding area. Direct assistance often takes the form of encouraging students, faculty, and parents to participate in programs such as Future Problem Solving, Odyssey of the Mind, and Model United Nations, in addition to essay, mathematics, and history contests sponsored at the state and national levels. Typically, schoolwide enrichment teaching specialists also make arrangements for students interested in summer programs, on-campus courses, special schools, theatrical groups, scientific expeditions, and apprenticeships.

Lasting change occurs only when it's initiated, nurtured, and monitored from within the school itself.

Elements of Reform

The public education system is slowly but surely deteriorating into a massive warehouse of underachievement, unfulfilled expectations, and broken dreams. Yet current reform policies and plans don't appear much different from traditional top-down patterns of school organization or linear/sequential models of learning. If traditional methods have failed to change schools substantially, different models deserve a look. To achieve school improvement, any new model must deal effectively with the three major dimensions of schooling—the act of learning, the use of time, and the change process itself.

■ *Act of learning.* Organizational and administrative structures such as vouchers, site-based management, school choice, ungraded classes, parent involvement, and extended school days are important considerations. They don't, however, directly address how to improve the interaction among teachers, students, and the curriculum.

The Schoolwide Enrichment Model places the act of learning at the center of any recommendations for school improvement. For example, the model looks at the learner's current achievement levels in each area of study, interest in particular topics, and preferred styles of learning (Renzulli 1992).

■ *Use of time.* Educators and laypeople alike are well acquainted with the typical pattern of school organization. Schools teach the major subjects (reading, mathematics, science, language arts, and social studies) five days per week, with special subjects (music, art, and physical education) offered once or twice a week. We've become so accustomed to the rigidity of this schedule that even the slightest hint of changing it meets with a storm of protest from administrators and teachers: "We don't have time *now* to cover the regular curriculum." "How will we fit in the specials?" "They keep adding new things, such as drug education, for us to cover."

By unquestioningly accepting the elementary and secondary school schedule, we lose sight of what happens at the college level. There, where material is ordinarily more advanced and demanding, we routinely drop from meeting five times per week in class to three times (and sometimes even two times). Plus, adhering to the "more time is better" argument ignores research to the contrary. For example, international comparison studies report that 8 of the 11 nations that surpass U. S. achievement levels in mathematics spend less time on math instruction (Jaeger 1992).

© Wayne Eastep

The Schoolwide Enrichment Model addresses the issue of time by selectively borrowing one or two class meetings per month from each major subject area. This approach guarantees that a designated time will be available each week for advanced-level enrichment clusters.

■ *The change process.* Schools are being bombarded with proposals for change, which range from total systemic reform to tinkering with bits and pieces of subjects and teaching methods. Often the proposals seem little more than lists of intended goals or outcomes, with limited direction provided.

Worse yet, policymakers and regulators continue to beam mixed messages to schools at an unprecedented rate. One state, for example, mandated a core curriculum for students—but then evaluated teachers on the basis of generic teaching skills that had nothing to do with the curriculum. Advocates of site-based management encourage teachers to become more active in curriculum development; yet these same schools are rated on the basis of test scores tied to outcome-based competencies specified by the state.

One recent study (Madaus 1992) showed that the most widely used tests measure low-level skills and knowledge. The same study reported that teachers and administrators believe the tests force them to compromise their ideals about good teaching—they feel pressured to emphasize the material covered on the tests. In another study (Olson 1992), researchers asked teachers to evaluate school-reform initiatives in their schools. They replied, "There's nothing but chaos. Our best strategy is to ignore them, close our doors, and go about our business."

The Schoolwide Enrichment Model takes a gentle and evolutionary approach to change. In the early stages of implementation, minimal but specific changes are suggested for existing schedules, textbooks, and curricular activities. These strategies have already demonstrated favorable results in different types of schools and with groups from varying ethnic and economic backgrounds.

Starting Points

Effective and lasting change occurs only when it's initiated, nurtured, and monitored from within the school itself. External regulations and remedies seldom change the daily behaviors of students and teachers. Nor do they deal effectively with solutions to internal school problems (Barth 1990).

The change process recommended in the School Enrichment Model begins with an examination of the major factors affecting the quality of learning in a school. These factors, may be internal (within the school) or external, but all inter-relate. For example, an internal building principal may be externally influenced if central administration makes staffing assignments; state regulations or districtwide textbook policies may externally influence the internal curriculum. The Schoolwide Enrichment Model doesn't replace existing structures but rather seeks to improve them by concentrating on the factors that have a direct bearing on learning. Evaluations indicate that the model is inexpensive to implement and has a common-sense practicality that appeals to professionals as well as laypeople (Olenchak and Renzulli 1989).

Think of an automobile as a metaphor for the Schoolwide Enrichment Model. The school is the car's body—preferably a Porsche—and the principal is the driver—preferably as bold and daring as Mario Andretti. The faculty represents the engine, loaded with power and constantly being tuned-up to become as efficient and effective as possible. Members of the enrichment teams serve as the spark plugs, bringing energy to all activities. And the Schoolwide Enrichment Model specialist is the ignition and the distributor, initiating new developments and directing the flow of resources and energy to appropriate places.

That automobile performs well on the track known as "special programs"—

but the model operates equally well in all schools that wish to be laboratories for talent development. ■

References

Barth, R. S. (1990). *Improving Schools from Within.* San Francisco: Jossey-Bass.

Bloom, B. S., ed. (1985). *Developing Talent in Young People.* New York: Ballantine Books.

Gardner, H. (1983). *Frames of Mind.* New York: Basic Books.

Jaeger, R. M. (1992). " 'World Class' Standards, Choice, and Privatization: Weak Measurement Serving Presumptive Policy." Paper presented at the Annual Meeting of the American Educational Research Association, San Francisco, April 20–24 1992.

Madaus, G. F. (1992). *The Influence of Testing on Teaching Math and Science in Grades 4–12.* Boston College: Center for the Study of Testing, Evaluation, and Educational Policy.

Olenchak, F. R., and J. S. Renzulli. (1989). "The Effectiveness of the Schoolwide Enrichment Model on Selected Aspects of Elementary School Change." *Gifted Child Quarterly* 33, 1: 44–57.

Olson, L. (1992). "Fed up with Tinkering, Reformers Now Touting 'Systemic' Approach." *Education Week* 12, 1: 1, 30.

Phenix, P. (1964). *Realms of Meaning.* New York: McGraw Hill.

Reis, S. M., and J. S. Renzulli. (1992). "Using Curriculum Compacting to Challenge the Above-Average." *Educational Leadership* 50, 2: 51–57.

Renzulli, J. S. (1977). *The Enrichment Triad Model.* Mansfield Center, Conn.: Creative Learning Press.

Renzulli, J. S. (1986). "The Three-Ring Conception of Giftedness: A Developmental Model for Creative Productivity." In *Conceptions of Giftedness,* edited by R. J. Sternberg and J. E. Davidson, pp. 332–357. New York: Cambridge University Press.

Renzulli, J. S. (1992). "A General Theory for the Development of Creative Productivity Through the Pursuit of Ideal Acts of Learning." *Gifted Child Quarterly* 36, 4: 170–182.

Renzulli, J.S., and S. M. Reis. (1994). "Research Related to the Schoolwide Enrichment Model." *Gifted Child Quarterly* 38, 1: 7–19.

Sternberg, R. J. (1984). "Toward a Triarchic Theory of Human Intelligence." *Behavioral and Brain Sciences* 7, 2: 269–316.

Author's note: The Javits Act Program, as administered by the U.S. Department of Education's Office of Educational Research and Improvement, supported the work reported here. The opinions expressed in this article don't reflect the position or policies of the Office of Educational Research and Improvement or the U.S. Department of Education.

Joseph S. Renzulli is Director of the National Research Center on the Gifted and Talented, University of Connecticut, 326 Fairfield Rd., U-7, Storrs, CT 06269-2007.

VOICES VOICES VOICES VOICES VOICES VOICES

Marcel Garber examined the norms of African American infants and found that the average age for mastery of some standard psychomotor tasks vastly preceded those of mainstream youngsters (see Kunjufu). For example, standards such as holding oneself upright appeared at 7 weeks for African American children, compared to 6 months by the mainstream norms; climbing steps at 11 months compared to the mainstream standard of 15 months; and walking to the Gesell box to look inside at 7 months, compared to the mainstream standard of 15 months. Mainstream teachers who are not aware of the norms of motor development among black children are more likely to judge higher activity in the classroom through their own cultural and experiential lens, resulting in a judgment that a child is "hyperactive."*

— Peter Murrell, "Afrocentric Immersion: Academic and Personal Development of African American Males in Public Schools," from *Freedom's Plow: Teaching in the Multicultural Classroom.* Edited by Theresa Perry and James W. Frazer. New York: Routledge Books, 1993.

* Jawanza Kunjufu, *Developing Positive Self-Images and Discipline in Black Children.* (Chicago: African American Images, 1984); *A Talk with Jawanza* (Chicago: African American Images, 1989).

DISCOVERING & INVESTIGATING Rhythm

BY JANET MILLAR GRANT
An Excerpt from Shake, Rattle and Learn

Our lives are filled with rhythm. We feel it as we breathe, as our heart beats, as we walk, skip and run. Students experience rhythm and repetition daily, too. They drum a rhythm with their fingers, hop on a hopscotch and run around the track. Rhythmic and repetitious movement activities allow children to develop body coordination, awareness and an increased ability to sense the beat and rhythm of their experiences.

Children become aware of rhythmical patterns within their own bodies before the patterns become meaningful and real. Most music programs recognize this need for physical awareness of music and include movement. Kinetic experiences link music concepts with physical sensation to clarify relationships between musical ideas. By exploring walking, leaping and galloping students come to know about changes in tempo and rhythm, first knowing in their bodies and then in their minds.

Activities in this chapter encourage students to investigate tempos, durations, pitches and rhythms. By including these in your classroom, you can support your students in developing a working knowledge and vocabulary of musical and movement concepts.

What begins as a teacher-directed activity can quickly develop into a wonderful refocusing and calming activity which the children will want to lead themselves. All of my students wanted to take turns developing a sequence of four repeated movements and leading the class through a patterned dance.

This chapter focuses on rhythm. The children will have an opportunity to practise, dance, observe and discuss rhythms and patterns. They will start with their own body rhythms and rhythmic responses. They will have a chance to note and capture the rhythm of others through movement patterns, accompanying a partner and following the leader. Throughout the activities, students will create simple movement sequences combining basic traveling actions. They will also use different musical forms in their creations, including canon and AB form. Movement —a wonderful way to make music visible!

Repeating Body Movements

Bopping to Contagious Chants

This activity engages students in rhythmic chanting and movement. As they work to create their own chant and Chant Dance, students will develop music skills of rhythm and tempo, and cooperative skills, such as listening, negotiating, integrating ideas, and staying on task.

For this activity, select a book that features a chant. *The Bop* by Irene Hunt contains a chant that is so contagious that children have trouble sitting still. Read the chosen chant and invite children to move as they listen to the words. You can reread the chant and challenge students to move a specific body part to the rhythm of the chant, or use a different movement each time they move. The children will stomp their feet, clap their hands, snap fingers and wriggle on the floor.

You might want to invite students to accompany the chant with planned movement. You can do this by revisiting the chant and discussing its length. Then, ask students to clap the rhythmic pattern and to the syllables on each line. Once students are clear about the pattern of the whole chant, they are ready to begin planning their movement.

Many will choose from the movements they have automatically responded with. You might want to help them by requesting that their movements involve one or two body parts. Have them practise their movements within the chant pattern.

Now they are ready to begin writing. Students can work on their own or with friends to write their own body part bop, keeping the original pattern but changing the words. Throughout the writing process, they may need to keep moving to make certain that their new bop chant will fit their developed bop movement.

Extending the Activity:

After choosing a body part, you can ask the children to move that body part when they feel "moved" and stay still otherwise. Doing this means that during the reading of the chant, children will suddenly come to life in waves of movement. You might choose to let the exploration take the movement impulse into different parts of the body: combining two body parts at once, eventually leading into traveling actions around the room.

Responding Rhythmically

This activity provides an exercise in movement control and in response to rhythmic pattern. The children will learn to analyze and discover rhythmic pattern and use rhythm to convey ideas.

You might begin this activity by reviewing with the class a familiar skipping rhyme. I have found that "Cinderella Dressed in Blue" from *Anna Banana* works well. Whatever rhyme you choose, post it on chart paper for easy reference. Select four movements that can be repeated and create a dance by repeating those four movements to the rhythm of the poem. I started with clapping hands, tapping the floor, shaking hands and stomping feet. Then I created a dance by clapping hands during the first line, tapping the floor during the second, shaking hands on the third and stomping feet during the fourth line. Once you have demonstrated the actions, ask the children to follow your lead.

I had to repeat the movements several times so that students understood the rhythmic pattern clearly. What begins as a teacher-directed activity can quickly develop into a wonderful refocusing and calming activity which the children will want to lead themselves. All of my students wanted to take turns developing a sequence of four repeated movements and leading the class through a patterned dance. They led us through a pattern of four of the following movements.

- swinging
- twisting
- jumping
- tapping
- nodding
- hopping

Extending the Activity:

You can challenge students to explore the possible range of a movement and then to repeat the movement working from small to large and large to small. Working with the first four movements listed above, the children can start with a small swing, increase to a large swing and then return to a small.

You might also incorporate changes in direction into your rhythmic responses. Ask the children to move in a different direction for each pair of lines, traveling forward, backward, sideways and on the diagonal. Another change that you can explore is changing the actual rhythmic pattern. Once the children have played with the pattern extensively, they can change the tempo of the pattern, making it faster or slower. At first, the changes may surprise the children, but they will challenge them to keep up.

Pairing Up for Rhythmic Patterns

Leading and Following Actions

You can encourage children to explore partner relationships, through this leader and follower game. Students will set rhythmic actions to a rhyme, learning listening, analyzing, and selection skills.

Basic everyday gestures can be used to start this activity. Or, you might choose a traditional action game. I used the hand waving game from *Street Rhythms Around the World.*

Invite students to identify a gesture to be used, perhaps stamping, clapping, nodding, bowing or waving. Then, ask students to find partners, and identify the leader and the follower within each group. The leader begins by leading with the chosen gesture; the follower imitates the action. Have the children repeat with changed roles.

I encouraged the children to use different actions each time they led their partner. They tried leading with a different body parts, changing the rhyme from a hand-waving game to a body moving game. The natural extensions were shoulders, hands, head and feet; all moved to they rhythm of the rhyme. Eventually, this activity evolved into a game that we played in the gym class to warm up and begin moving.

Once the children have explored a variety of movements, you can challenge them to follow the leader in canon. Repeating a phase after the leader has just done it may seem easy, but I found that the children were often so eager to follow that they lost the rhythm by not pausing before following.

Making Movement Patterns

Students working with partners will develop their own movement patterns based on sequence, ordering and repetition of movement. As they engage in this activity, they will learn processing skills, and social and group dynamics.

Invite children to work with partners to explore movements on the spot and traveling through space. Ask your students to repeat each movement four times. I found that partners followed each other's lead well as they shared ideas and movements.

You might invite the children to identify four strong movements and repeat each movement four times. When we did this activity, one pair created a pattern of four twists, four jumps, four stretches and four skips. Then have students repeat the four movements, four times in a sequence.

The children will quickly discover a need to choose their actions carefully. Those who choose high-level activities will soon become out of breath. They will need to change their actions to simple movements that they can repeat quickly. When we watched all of the created sequences, the children remarked on the interesting actions and the pattern created by movement and stillness.

Extending the Activity

Some of the children may want to remember the sequences and you may wish to use the sequences in the classroom and in the gym for some physical activity during the day. Ask the children to record their sequences on chart paper. Others might choose some music to accompany their sequence. The music, along with the chart-paper directions, can be used for five-minutes fit breaks in your classroom.

You might introduce the children to the challenge of changing time patterns. Children can speed up and slow down their movement sequences: what starts as a high-level sequence with kicks, leaps and fast arm circles might become a series of stretches, large steps and arm sways. Children might also raise and expand and then lower and reduce the sequenced movements gradually, working with the musical terms *crescendo* and *diminuendo.* The children will feel the changes to the quality of their movements.

Beating an Accompaniment to Movement

Let students work with rhythm instruments and body sounds. As they do, they will develop receiving, listening, interpreting and performing skills.

Have students select a partner to work with. Then, provide each student with a lummi stick. Once the children have explored the sound of the sticks, they should decide which partner will move and which will use the lummi sticks. Now they are ready to accompany an action rhyme. Traditional games serve as good rhyme sources; *Oranges and Lemons* is also a good source of action rhymes.

Read aloud the chosen rhyme and challenge one partner in each pair to move in rhythm, while the other beats the rhythm on the floor with the sticks. Have all students switch roles several times. Encourage movers to create greatly varying movements in response to the changing rhythms. Eventually, you might wish to have the children discard the sticks and keep the rhythm with different body parts. Hand clapping and leg slapping are two ways of doing this.

Extending the Activity

You may find that the children are ready to create and respond to their own independent rhythms. You can give the instrumentalists the job of creating their own rhythmic patterns which challenge the "travelers" to respond with movement. Doing this may lead to the creation of short dances with structured rhythmic accompaniment and movement.

We went beyond the use of body sounds and lummi sticks for our rhythmic accompaniment. My students made their own simple noisemakers, such as drums, whistles, cardboard flutes and shakers. Then we explored sound and stillness in the classroom. Each students was asked to remain still whenever their partner's instrument was silent, but to move to the pattern of the instrument when played. The children enjoyed creating and playing a rhythm on the instrument and seeing what movements their partners used to return the rhythm.

Experiencing Musical Forms

Sending Movement in a Round

Children can experience the form of a round as they create movement sequences. As they do so, they will develop non-verbal communication, receiving and interpreting skills.

This game begins with a simple movement pattern being sent in a round to all classmates. You will need to identify a first sender who must prepare a sequence of three repeated movements and pass the sequence to another person. A hop, skip and jump was sent from person to person in my classroom, as if a bee sting was sent around the class.

This activity began in my classroom by accident. We were messing about with sounds when one child repeated a pattern of three movements, three head taps. Three head taps were sent around the room. The next offered three cheek pats, and the final one suggested three foot stamps. I modeled another pattern of three: three head pats, three elbow taps and three hand drummings. This combination was also sent around the room.

The real challenge began when we sent one sequence around the room, immediately followed by a different sequence; as soon as each student completed a sequence, yet another sequence was sent through the room. Truly a round of movement!

The more movement sequences the children create, the more complex and difficult the sequences become to repeat in a round. You can ask your students to change the number of beats, accenting beats, or the speed of the beats.

The activity leads naturally into a matching (echo) game in which the leader leads the group with a movement pattern and the rest of the students echo that pattern. You might choose to use this as a classroom game to focus the students and to fill in the occasional free moments of the day. You can link the sequences all together and try them. Then you might take turns creating and leading patterns.

Comparing the movement pattern at the beginning of the round with what is performed by the last mover interested me. We tried passing the movement after a few counts and found that to be very difficult but not impossible. As the students become skilled, you can have them pass the movement after two or three movements. Recalling and performing the original movement sequence becomes increasingly difficult.

Identifying the Rhythm Pattern Leader

To encourage the children to observe with focus and take risks, you can introduce a guessing game. This whole-group game supports students in taking turns and staying on task as they learn to observe, locate, and identify movement sources. It can fill small time slots in the classroom.

To begin, ask all students to sit in a circle. Then, send one child from the group out of listening distance and select one member of the group as a leader. Have the leader lead the group with a continual pattern of large movements, such as knee slapping, foot stamping or head tapping. The rest of the group needs to watch and follow the leader closely, changing actions as the leader changes without identifying the leader. You can then invite the remaining child to return to the circle and identify the real movement leader. The trick is for the leader to repeat the pattern many times before changing to a new pattern. If the group is very good at following, they can stump the observer.

Repeat the activity so that all students have a turn at a role.

Extending the Activity

You can ask the leader to lead with a repeated pattern rather than a simple movement. For example, the pattern might be clap, clap, stamp, stamp, stamp. This keeps the class on their toes as they will have to concentrate hard on the following pattern. It also makes it difficult for the leader to change patterns.

Playing with AB Form

To involve students with the exploration of form, you could introduce this composition activity. As students work in small groups, they will develop their skills to identify, organize and synthesize movement and rhythm to present a product.

You will need to identify a round song. "Row, Row, Row Your Boat" works well, but you may have another favourite round song in your classroom that the children would enjoy. To begin the activity, review the chosen song and teach a movement sequence. The movement sequence should have two distinct parts, just as the round song has two parts: A (Row, row . . .) and B (Merrily . . .). The AB form is a combination of two rhythmical and movement patterns. Students joined in as I led them, our arms joined, in swaying side to side for section A and in twirling on the spot for section B.

Invite students to form groups to create their own two movement sequences. You should remind the class that their movements should correspond rhythmically to the pattern and the length of their verse. For the A section, one of my groups developed a stylized rowing movement involving the whole body rocking forward and backward supported by their hands and knees. For the B section, another group of students stretched high and gradually lowered themselves down to their hands and knees.

Once each group has refined and rehearsed their section, you might want to invite them to put the movements and song together. The first time through

ACROSS THE CURRICULUM

DRAMA:
Pantomiming a story
Students can select a character from a known story, such as Peter and the Wolf. Then, you can challenge them to isolate words and actions for their character and put on a silent play, telling about the events through movement only.

MUSIC:
Notating rhythmic patterns
Students can work with rhythm instruments such as lummi sticks, drums, bells, and maracas to create a rhythmic pattern. Then, they can record their pattern on paper with coloured pencils, using symbols such as circles, shapes and lines. You might want to keep a collection of the recorded rhymes and create a class book.

Student can also access recorded instrumental and vocal music to listen for rhythmic patterns. They can listen for long and short sounds and for the overall pattern, and record the patterns on paper.

VISUAL ART:
Piecing rhythm together
Students can collect pictures in magazines and books that feature a pattern. They can make mosaics by cutting small squares of coloured paper and gluing the paper pieces in a colour pattern on paper. For a textured effect, they could cut the mosaic squares out of several materials, such as glossy paper, coloured paper, foil, wallpaper, and acetate.

LANGUAGE ARTS:
Finding patterns in books
Let students explore pattern books in the classroom language arts program. Gather together a text set of pattern books and immerse students in them for awhile. Soon they will be comparing the patterns in each book and creating their own pattern books.

MATH:
Manipulating patterns
There are countless math manipulatives that can be used to explore patterns in our world. Students can pattern common classroom materials, such as pattern blocks and building blocks, according to colour, size, shape . . . They enjoy recording their own patterns using noodles, beans and other objects and can challenge one another to try to continue their patterns.

PHYSICAL EDUCATION:
Playing with rhythm
Small physical education equipment, such as bean bags and rhythm balls, provide some wonderfully clear chances to develop rhythm patterns. You can have students create repeated patterns on their own, working with a ball or bean bag, and listen to the sound pattern created. For example, while working with a ball, "bounce and catch and throw and catch, dribble round and round" creates a wonderful sound pattern on the floor.

children can dance and sing simultaneously. Later, you could challenge them to repeat the sequences in a round. The visual effect is stunning!

Creating Variations on a Theme

Patterns and variations in words and music provide a great source of learning experiences for children. As students explore and combine the patterns, they develop organizing, interpreting, sequencing and producing skills.

As you prepare for this activity, select a class pattern book. *Charlie Parker Played Be Bop* by Chris Raschka is a wonderful book for this activity. Although it is simple to read, the patterns and variations that are introduced provide some interesting opportunity for exploration for all levels.

Now, invite students to identify a repeating pattern sentence in your chosen book. In our case, "Charlie Parker played Be Bop" was the obvious choice. With the class, talk about the length of the chosen sentence and have them listen to the sentence's beat as you read it. Then, each student should work individually to create a movement sequence for that sentence. Although the sequences will vary, they should all be the same length. You might want to take some time for children to share their sequences with a friend and talk about the interesting points of each sequence. In my classroom, one child tried to capture the travel of sound, beginning with a large wide shape, bursting through space and changing shape as he ran and slowly stopped in a small wide shape.

Returning to the book, ask the students to select two of the pages that appealed to them. Challenge students to create a movement sequence for both pages, beginning with the sequence developed earlier for the chosen sentence. They should somehow base the two new sequences on the original sequence. In my class, one sequence became a wide shape moving low to the ground, then traveling low through space with a slow stop down on the floor. Once students have three movement sequences, the original and two variations, they are ready to put them all together.

The original sequence now becomes the chorus movement during the sentence and the variation movements represent changes and expansions of the chorus. Once the children have rehearsed all sequences and are familiar with the pages that inspired their two new phrases, they are ready for the finale. Read the book and invite all students to move through their original sequences as they hear the sentence and to perform their own sequences as their selected pages come up. The result: A theme and variation creation!

Reprinted with permission from *Shake, Rattle and Learn*, by Janet Millar Grant. York, ME: Stenhouse ©1995.

VOICES VOICES VOICES VOICES VOICES VOICES

Strong self-esteem in the flower and fruit of active involvement, emerging competence, exposure to appropriate challenge, and willingness to risk. When we nurture curiosity, creativity, and opportunities for genuine success, self-esteem blooms.

— Priscilla L. Vail, *Emotion: The On-Off Switch for Learning.* Rosemont, NJ: Modern Learning Press, 1994.

Bridging Home and School Through Multiple Intelligences

Judith C. Reiff

Judith C. Reiff is Associate Professor, Department of Elementary Education, University of Georgia, Athens.

Children's learning styles are as different as the colors of the rainbow. All people have different, distinct personalities, preferences and tastes. When we understand the various ways in which children learn, we are better able to 1) prevent discipline problems, 2) communicate with parents, 3) reduce teacher burn-out and parent frustration, 4) organize the classroom and 5) help children reach their potential (Reiff, 1992).

Howard Gardner's theory of multiple intelligences (1987, 1993) enables us to discuss positive strengths in all children and to plan appropriate learning strategies for a more effective classroom environment. Gardner maintains that intelligence is something more complex than can ever be reflected by a test score, and that the Western education system overemphasizes the linguistic and logical/mathematical intelligences. At least five other intelligences are present in everyone to some degree; therefore, our classrooms should include activities, materials and assessment that respond to all intelligences (Faggella & Horowitz, 1990; Lazear, 1992).

By sharing this information with parents and involving them in the learning process, parents are recognized and valued as collaborators in their children's education. Teachers can explain these intelligences or domains to parents in a brochure or pamphlet (Reiff, 1995), at an Open House or during a parent/teacher conference. The specific terms are not as important as the idea that all of us need to be appreciated for our strengths, which might be in different areas. Parents should be encouraged to provide different activities to discover and nurture their child's own intelligences. This article provides the classroom teacher with instructional strategies for each domain and additional activities for parents.

Linguistic Learners

These children have a sensitivity to the meaning, sounds and rhythms of words. They enjoy storytelling, wordplay and creative writing. They love reading, poetry, tongue twisters, puns and humor, and find pleasure in working puzzles and solving riddles. Teachers should be sensitive to the language and questioning patterns used in the home.

Suggestions for teachers. Activities for linguistic learners could include reading/writing workshops, book sharing, dialogue writing, book-tape stories, word processing and newspaper activities.

Suggestions for parents. Read with your children. Listen intently to their questions, concerns and experiences. Provide ample books and paper for reading and writing activities. Encourage your children to tell you about the stories they read or to share something they have written. A tape recorder is a helpful aid. Provide opportunities to visit the public library and local bookstores. Games such as Scrabble™, Hangman, Boggle™ and Yahtzee™ are ideal for linguistic learners.

Logical-Mathematical Learners

These children enjoy number games, problem solving, pattern games and experimenting. They have strong reasoning skills and ask questions in a logical manner. Activities that are more ordered and sequential appeal to these children.

Suggestions for teachers. Challenge these children with problem solving and patterning activities. They will enjoy experiments, computer instruction and syllogism. Use graphic organizers, number sequences and pattern games, and show relationships to help them learn.

Suggestions for parents. Let your children experiment! Invite them to help you bake a cake or make new colors by mixing paints. Show them how to use a calculator. Allow your children to help with the family budget and to budget their own allowances. Setting the table, sorting clothes or organizing the desk drawer are ideal activities. Games such as UNO™, checkers and chess will tap a logical-mathematical intelligence.

Spatial Learners

Spatial learners respond to visual cues and are image-oriented. They often are daydreamers and have a talent for art. These children like to invent and design. They enjoy creating visual patterns and need visual stimulation. Visual word cues assist these individuals. Maps, charts, diagrams, puzzles and mazes are excellent resources. Provide opportunities to create with various arts and crafts.

Suggestions for teachers. Use color in your activities. Verbs could be blue, nouns red, antonyms orange and synonyms purple, for example. Mathematical symbols could be color-coded as well. Provide manipulatives and use guided imagery and mind-mapping.

Suggestions for parents. Provide opportunities for solving puzzles or inventing. Let children with spatial intelligence choose the colors for their bedrooms and design the furniture arrangement. A spatial learner will enjoy mapping the bedroom to show where everything belongs or arranging items on a table or shelf. Visiting art museums and taking photographs are appropriate activities. Provide a variety of art mediums such as paints, crayons and magic markers. Play games such as Pictionary™ or cards.

Musical Learners

These children thoroughly enjoy playing instruments, singing songs, drumming, etc. They like the sounds of the human voice, environmental sounds and instrumental sounds. They can learn easier if things are set to music or to a beat.

Suggestions for teachers. "Note" the volume and pitch of your voice. Use descriptive and rhythmic words to enhance communication. Use a variety of music in the classroom as background and to teach skills. Play musical chairs, have listening centers and tape-record storybooks. Be attentive to environmental sounds and how they might interfere with children's learning.

Suggestions for parents. Allow musical children to select a recording at the local music store. Encourage your children to sing along or clap to the rhythm. If possible, involve your children in some type of music lessons. Provide opportunities to attend concerts and musicals. Have sing-alongs.

Bodily-Kinesthetic Learners

These children are athletic and active. They enjoy creative dramatics, role-playing, dancing and expressing themselves with movement and bodily action. These children derive much of what they learn through physical movement and from touching and feeling. They use movement, gesture and physical expression to learn and solve problems. They may touch while talking.

Suggestions for teachers. Provide physical exercise and hands-on activities. Walk through difficult problems and ideas, such as subtraction and addition. Use materials such as fabric, clay, blocks and other manipulatives.

Suggestions for parents. Involve your children in dancing, acting or sports activities. Provide a variety of manipulatives for experimentation. Walk, jog, hike, play tennis, bowl or bike as a family. These children will enjoy swings, riding toys and slides. Play games such as charades, Simon says and hide-and-seek. Provide chores such as sweeping, setting the table and emptying the trash cans.

Interpersonal Learners

These children are very social and intuitive about others' feelings. They are "people persons" because they can "read" others' feelings and behaviors. They are excellent leaders, have empathy for others, enjoy being part of a group and are street smart. They can help peers and work cooperatively with others.

Suggestions for teachers. Arrange for these children to be peer tutors or buddies to younger children. These children would enjoy skits, plays, group work, discussions, debates or cooperative learning.

Suggestions for parents. Play a family game. Encourage your children to participate in group activities. Encourage discussions and problem solving.

Intrapersonal Learners

Intrapersonal children like to work independently. They "march to a different drummer" and are very self-motivated, preferring solitary activities. They have the ability to understand their own feelings, motivations and moods. They may be daydreamers.

Suggestions for teachers. Provide a quiet area for independent work, encourage writing in a personal journal, discuss thinking strategies, facilitate metacognition techniques and suggest independent projects.

Suggestions for parents. Give your children quality time to work or play alone because individual time is very important to these children. Ask them to make something for the whole family to enjoy. Provide a time for reflection. Encourage your children to keep a diary or journal.

Conclusion

Teachers must recognize and admit that schools traditionally value certain intelligences over others. Some children identified as "at risk" might be considered gifted in a different situation or context. It is important, therefore, to carefully observe each child to identify where their key intelligences lie. A profile representing the child's spectrum of intelligences can be a valuable resource at a parent/teacher conference (Krechevsky, 1991). Parents can help teachers by providing insight into the domains in which the child excels at home. The goal of education should be to provide an equitable environment for all children; one way of accomplishing this is to value the multiple intelligences in all of us.

Children should not be "tracked" according to a specific intelligence, nor should they be excluded from enjoying activities in other intelligences. Instead, all children must be provided an equal opportunity for succeeding within the context of the classroom.

References

Faggella, K., & Horowitz, J. (1990). Different child different style. *Instructor, 100*(2), 49-54.

Gardner, H. (1987). *Multiple intelligences: The theory in practice.* New York: Basic Books.

Gardner, H. (1993). *Frames of mind* (rev. ed.). New York: Basic Books.

Krechevsky, M. (1991). Project spectrum: An innovative assessment alternative. *Educational Leadership, 48*(5), 135-138.

Lazear, D. (1992). *Teaching for multiple intelligences.* Bloomington, IN: Phi Delta Kappa.

Reiff, J. (1992). *What research says to teachers: Learning styles.* Washington, DC: National Education Association.

Reiff, J. (1995). *Multiple intelligences: Different ways of learning.* Pamphlet for parents. Wheaton, MD: Association for Childhood Education International.

VOICES VOICES VOICES VOICES VOICES VOICES

Animal and passionate, children — more than adults — are on the nature end of the nature-culture continuum. Schools rightly intend to pull children toward culture, but in long school days respect must be paid to the nature part of children for them to stay healthy. And nature, according to contemporary physics, is matter and energy in continual motion — that is, a typical second grader. Conceived in motion, we are born to move and learn from moving. Playing outdoors is generally more active than being in the classroom . . . .

. . . It is remarkable in the late-20th century that being too active, hyperactive, or as we now shorthand it, hyper, *is the affliction of so many, particularly boys. Is it possibly, in part, a cultural disease that if children were not as confined as they are, their activity level would not seem so disruptive? If very active children were permitted more time in a safe, interesting outdoor setting, would their behavior during indoor time be more tolerable to adults?*

— Mary S. Rivkin, *The Great Outdoors: Restoring Children's Right to Play Outside*. Washington, D.C.: National Association for the Education of Young Children, 1995.

Professional Voices/Classroom Portrait

POSITIVE CHANGES FOR CHILDREN

Therese M. Bialkin

Third-grade teacher, Jackson Academy, East Orange, New Jersey

Michele Giordano

Third-grade teacher, Jackson Academy, East Orange, New Jersey

Is that all there is? That song title, made famous decades ago, comes very close to summing up the way we felt about our teaching just a few years ago. As beginning, primary grade teachers, our enthusiasm and excitement could not be rivaled. We expected hard work and we approached it eagerly. We worked hard to learn all that we could about our students and their community, to acquaint ourselves with school and district expectations, and to establish ourselves as professionals. As graduates of local teacher education programs, we felt reasonably well prepared. Yet, as with most beginning teachers, those early years posed enormous challenges for us.

We both began teaching more than a decade ago, a time when school districts throughout the United States were heavily focused on the basics. Urban school districts, such as ours, were under tremendous pressure to improve student performance on standardized tests. Many felt that the surest and quickest way to raise test scores was to offer a curriculum that emphasized isolated skills and teacher-centered, direct instruction with strict time constraints for each curriculum area. It was not uncommon for us to leave school at the end of the day, loaded down with totebags full of worksheets and workbooks. We were working hard! Our students were working hard! Indeed, most of them *were* acquiring the skills that we presented. Unfortunately, much of the learning was devoid of a sense of purpose and joy—elements we knew were essential to the creation of lifelong learners. We knew there must be a better way.

Ironically, it was only after our routines settled into place and we felt a growing sense of confidence about ourselves as professionals, that we both—quite independently—began to question some of our teaching practices. We knew that our students were capable. Yet, the curriculum we were providing did not allow them to demonstrate their abilities to the fullest. We also knew that we were capable of more creative and inspired teaching. Yet, in many ways, the curriculum we had worked so hard to master seemed to discourage individual teacher creativity and initiative. We began to explore possibilities—together. Now, as third grade teachers, two years into our journey of change, the initial excitement and enthusiasm we felt as beginning teachers has returned, but in a very different way.

First Steps

It was easy to identify the first problem we would tackle together. We both had difficulty apportioning the time available in a typical school day among all the subjects we were required to teach. In order to reduce the time spent on some subjects without reducing the quality of the instruction, we devised a form of "semi-departmentalization." We divided the curriculum between us with one of us teaching science and math to both classes and the other teaching social studies and language skills. With classrooms right next door to each other, this was a relatively easy innovation.

After a year's experimentation, it was clear that our teaching had changed dramatically. Narrowing our focus gave us time to make our lessons more exciting and challenging. In general, we were better prepared. Moreover, teaching this way required us to communicate with each other frequently in order to coordinate our activities. Still, we were not satisfied. Our collaboration and discussion led us to realize that we could improve our lessons even further by working together to integrate the subjects we were teaching, rather than teaching them in isolation. Having some familiarity with whole language, we felt that this was the direction that would offer us the most help. We also knew that we had a lot to learn.

Moving toward Whole Language

Over the years, we had attended several workshops dealing with various aspects of whole language philosophy and practice. We continued to attend as many workshops as we could. We also shared articles with one another; and we talked with other professionals about what they were doing. We enlisted and received the administrative support of our principal, Gladys Calhoun. From the very beginning, her support has been an essential part of our success.

One of the most important activities affecting our change was the initiation of a whole language study group by our district reading and language arts supervisors, Norma Nichols and Ruth Gillman. The group was established to provide support to teachers, like ourselves, who were interested in changing their teaching. We met once a month to discuss new insights, ideas, and problems encountered as we attempted to move toward the use of whole language. We read and discussed Regie Routman's *Invitations: Changing as Teachers and Learners*. These meetings helped us to know that the concerns we were experiencing were not unique to us. Our ideas about integrating the subject areas with the language arts were reinforced. During the summer of 1992, we began to do some serious planning.

Teaching through Themes

During our initial planning, we selected five theme topics, established goals for each theme, and brainstormed ideas for integrating subject areas and for establishing a learning environment that was natural and flowing, not forced. We decided to use a variety of children's literature (tradebooks), rather than a text-

We collaborate with students to list on the map the subjects and content we expect to cover in the unit.

book, as the major source of reading material. A story related to the theme would serve as the catalyst for framing our work.

Acquiring the literature we needed proved to be our first major challenge. We wanted a minimum of one book per child for each of the five themes. The challenge was met through a series of collaborative efforts. Our principal and the Office of Curriculum provided partial funding. Additional funds came through the use of monies allocated for the purchase of workbooks; a student-managed plant sale; and through the use of bonus points earned through student book clubs, such as Troll and Scholastic. Other teachers donated excess tradebooks and several publishers sponsored us through the donation of trial materials. Once we had obtained the necessary literature, we began each theme using a variety of instructional techniques.

Mapping the theme. We usually start each theme unit with a brainstorming activity. This involves the creation of a semantic map of the theme we are going to explore. We collaborate with students to list on the map the subjects and content we expect to cover in the unit. Copies of the map are distributed to students and referred to as we move through the unit.

Introducing the theme story. Each story is introduced with a prediction activity. For example, students may be asked to observe only the illustrations in the literature. A prediction list is then created from ideas that students volunteer, such as where they think the story takes place, what might occur in the story, and so on. These ideas are compiled on a chart. Students are required to justify their predictions with evidence gathered from the pictures or story title. After reading the story, the chart is used to evaluate all of the predictions made.

Reading the story. In order to accommodate the various reading abilities of individual students, we employ a number of different reading strategies. One of us may read the story aloud to the less proficient readers before they read it on their own. More able students may be initially assigned to read independently, while other students may be linked with a reading partner.

Reading is done in an informal setting with students lying on the carpet or gathered around the teacher in comfortable positions. After the reading, students respond to the story in their literature logs. These responses are later shared and discussed in small groups. The discussions focus on subject-area content, reading comprehension, and literary understandings in an integrated way.

Follow-through and follow-up. The brainstorming and story-reading activities serve as a commonly shared experience for all of the students. This is followed by a variety of lessons and experiences that may involve the whole group, small groups, and individuals. Here are three examples:

Extended reading and writing. Each day, we read aloud to students from materials related to the current theme. Students are also given time for independent reading in theme-related materials. The reading is followed by discussion as well as opportunities to write. Each child has a journal and a literature response log to write down their reactions to the reading, create a poem or story, or to record some interesting facts. Students are given time and assistance for the revision and editing of material that will eventually be published. Whenever possible, computers are used to publish books using different word-processing programs.

Cooperative learning. We use a variety of cooperative learning strategies throughout each unit. One cooperative learning technique we employ is called "Envelope." Varied levels of comprehension questions relating to the literature (or content) under study are written on the front of the envelopes. Students work together to discover the evidence in the story that supports the answer to the question written on the front of the envelope. The answers are written down and placed inside the envelope, which is then rotated to another group for evaluation. This is followed by a very high level class discussion, as students verify or challenge certain answers and return to the text for supporting evidence. Most often the questions are originated by the teacher, but as students become more familiar with the process, they enjoy developing questions themselves as a small-group or homework activity.

Grouping for specific strategies and skills. Strategies and skills, such as vocabulary or word analysis, are integrated into the various lessons. Based on our observation of student needs, skill groups in these areas are formed. Groups are changed daily as students progress. The literature always forms the nucleus of these lessons. For example, one skill lesson originated from our observation that a number of students were having trouble recognizing and reading dialogue. A lesson addressing this problem consisted of helping children to identify specific lines of dialogue in the story. Having demonstrated that they could isolate the dialogue from the remaining text, we had them choose characters, identify all the dialogue for their character, practice reading it, and perform it as a play.

Pulling It All Together

Providing an integrated curriculum for students, while keeping track of the various disciplines, is a common dilemma for teachers using theme-based instruction. What follows are some examples of science, social studies, math, and language integration for a theme commonly taught in third grade. For purposes of record keeping and accountability, we labeled the activities in terms of specific subject areas. However, each activity overlapped into all the others.

Science. During our unit on Native Americans, students learned the importance of corn for the survival of many tribes. Students were shown real, fully grown corn plants. They learned the parts of the corn plant, grew their own corn, dissected corn seeds and looked at the baby plant under a microscope.

Language arts. After reading a number of Native American legends in class, students worked in groups to create their own legends, complete with illustrations. The stories were bound and made into books for everyone's reading enjoyment.

Social studies. Students investigated Native American homes, crafts, and tools. They created their own simulations using various materials and then wrote about them.

Mathematics. Students used corn seeds to conduct estimation activities.

All Day Learning Stations

Every Friday, we institute what we call our "All Day Learning Stations." Students are rotated through a series of learning stations, working cooperatively in small groups. They are grouped heterogeneously. This, in itself, is unusual in our school, where students are typically divided into groups according to academic ability. Our third grade classes contain a mixture of students with varying academic abilities, ranging from very fluent readers to several students who are more than a grade level behind in reading.

The make-up of each group is not absolutely fixed throughout the year. As we see fit, students are moved to different groups to allow them to gain experience working with other members of the class as well as to allow us to find the combination of students that produces the best results academically and socially.

Station assignments for the whole day are written on the board. Due to the size of each class, ten stations are required to keep group sizes to a maximum of six students.

At a station, each group is required to complete a task associated with our theme and requiring the use of children's literature. The tasks are designed so that they can be generally completed within the fifty minutes allotted to each group. While the students are working diligently at their stations, we act as facilitators, moving from station to station, monitoring progress, and offering assistance. After the time is up, groups rotate to the next station to begin a new task. Students are able to work through three stations in the morning, and then complete two more stations after lunch. On the following Friday, the remaining five stations are completed, using the same routine.

This scheduling leaves about thirty minutes at the end of the day to get together with the entire two classes and reflect on the day's progress. We use this time to discuss solutions to problems that may have occurred, share opinions of tasks assigned, listen to feedback from teacher observations, and sometimes use our journals to log personal evaluations. These sessions have proven to be invaluable in improving the listening skills of our students and ourselves.

A very bold innovation for us and for our school, the "All Day Learning Stations" have opened our eyes to what children can do when they are given greater control over their own learning. The children are learning more; they are thoroughly engaged in their tasks; and, contrary to what most teachers would think, there are virtually no discipline problems.

Assessment

Student evaluation is an ongoing process. As the need arises, students are given formal tests concerning information and skills taught within our theme. Daily classwork is also assessed by observing student behaviors and by measurable academic progress. In addition, we keep anecdotal records of academic and social progress for discussion in parent, student, and teacher conferences.

Reflections

These past two years have been enormously challenging and rewarding. It is true that our teaching has changed. But perhaps more importantly, we have changed the way we view ourselves as professionals. Taking greater control over what we do has meant that we work much harder, but we believe we also work much better. As we look back there are several things that really account for the success we have had so far. Our commitment to individual accountability and team planning is essential. We spend time together planning our weekly lessons and our Friday sessions so that we both understand the entire learning program and how it all fits together. Planning initially took a great deal of time. As the program developed, we found that less time had to be spent once the framework was in place.

Another key element is the support and talent of some of our colleagues. Gwendolyn Cottingham, our librarian, has proved to be an essential part of our program. She has created, at our request, a list of books available in our library covering our chosen theme. She also helps to provide literature for classroom read-alouds, silent reading, and student research projects. She even supplied her personal slides taken on her trip to Africa when we were studying African folktales.

The Music, Art, French, and Physical Education teachers also make themselves available to enhance the learning process. With advance notice, these professionals will develop their lessons specifically to relate to our current theme. The special talents of all these people are invaluable to our program.

We feel that we have progressed a long way toward achieving our goals and we are continuing to plan some interesting new activities for the upcoming school year. We are aware that research has shown that it can take as many as five years to develop a comprehensive whole language program. Keeping this in mind, we continue to monitor and adjust our learning environments to make them the best they can be for our student learners and for ourselves as professionals, continuing to learn. We are excited about what the future holds because we know that the change has been a positive one.

Friday Schedule for "All Day Learning Stations"

9:00–9:30	All students meet in one room for whole group conference (station directions, etc.). Each group is assigned to one of the ten areas.
9:30–12:00	Students rotate through three of the 40-minute stations with five-minute clean-up between each.
12:00–12:30	Lunch
12:30–2:00	Students rotate through two additional stations.
2:00–2:30	Whole group processing (discussions and reactions about the day's activities)
2:30–2:35	Dismissal

A repeat of the same ten stations will occur the following Friday in order for students to work through all of them. Below is an example of some possible station arrangements. Stations vary as they relate to our chosen theme.

1. Computer Station: Teacher selected integrated software
2. Listening Station with headphones
3. Arts & Crafts Station
4. Hands-On Science Lab Experiments
5. Writing and Publishing Center
6. Computer Station: Free choice from network menu
7. Social Studies Research
8. Math Manipulative Station
9. Reading/Language Strategies
10. Student/Teacher Writing Conferences

Classroom Floor Plans for "All Day Learning Stations"

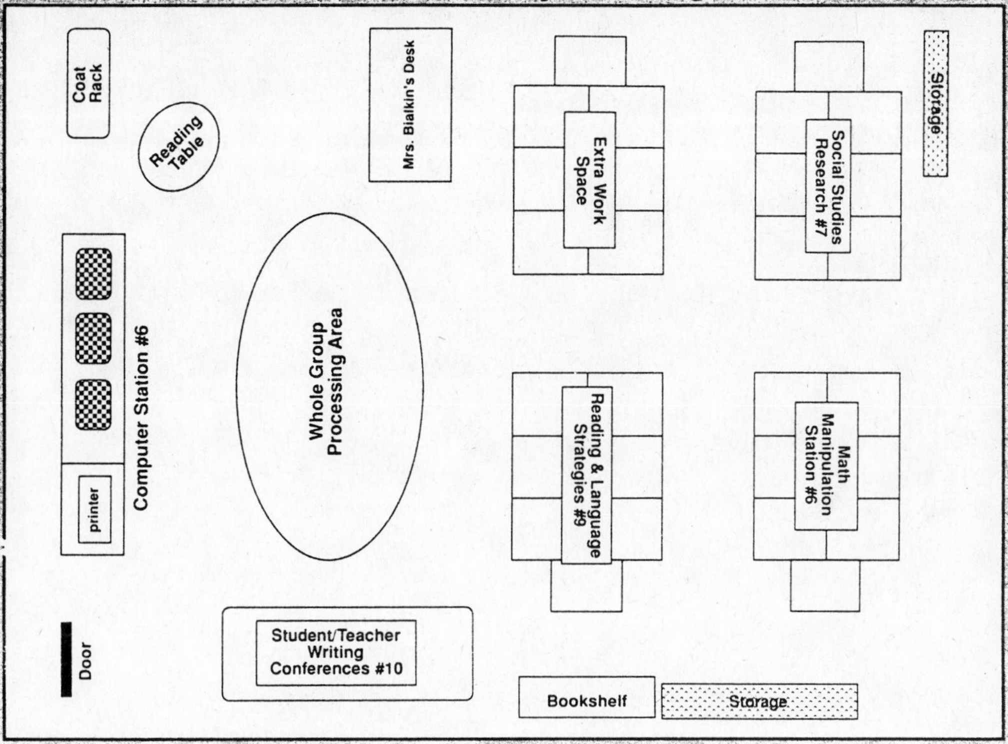

Mrs. Bialkin's Classroom

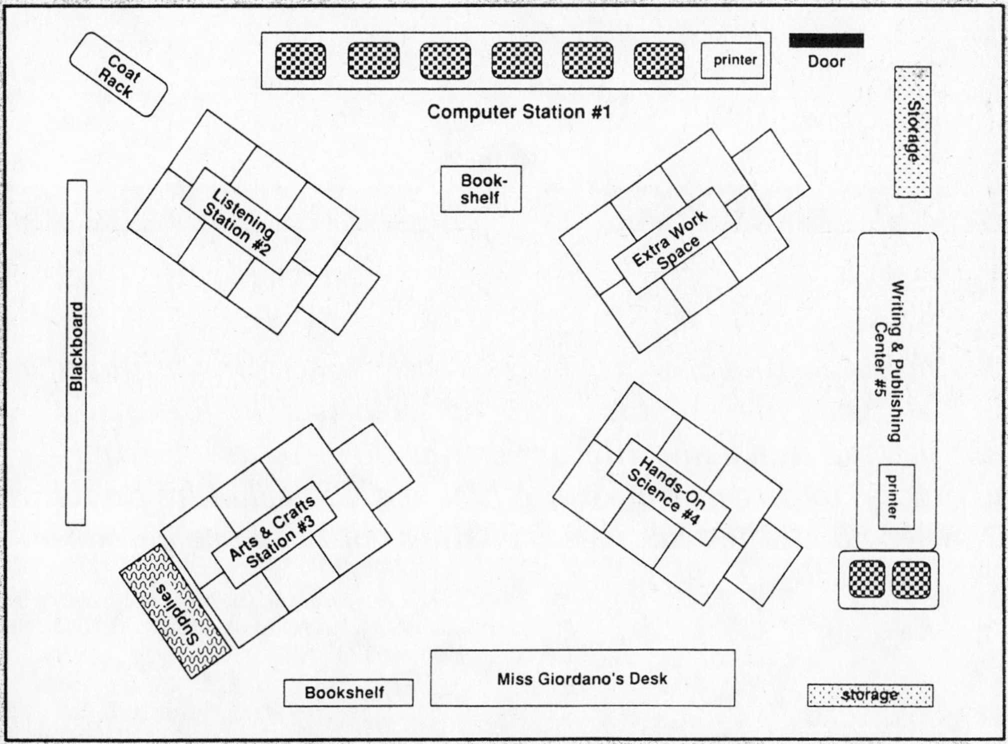

Miss Giordano's Classroom

Lingering Questions

1. Should a successful innovation created by classroom teachers be implemented across a school district? If so, under what circumstances and how?

2. How can children, who are only familiar with teacher-centered classrooms, be helped to adjust to the expectations of a whole language classroom?

3. How can teachers reconcile the need to encourage children to make their own choices with the need to maintain quality time on task during independent activities?

Resources That Supported Our Change

Glazer, S. (1992). *Reading comprehension.* New York: Scholastic Professional Books.

Goodman, K. (1986). Basal readers: A call for action. *Language Arts, 63* (4), 358–363.

Johnson, W., & Johnson, R. (1991). *Cooperating in the classroom.* Edina, MN: Interaction Book Company.

Newman, J., & Church, S. (1990). Myths of whole language. *The Reading Teacher, 44* (1), 1–7.

Routman, R. (1991). *Invitations: Changing as teachers and learners.* Portsmouth, NH: Heinemann.

VOICES VOICES VOICES VOICES VOICES VOICES

I am suggesting that teachers of every discipline might ask students to think and write as scientists, historians, mathematicians, and literary critics do — to use writing — as process to discover meaning just as these scholars do when they go about the real, messy business of thinking on paper.

— Nancie Atwell, editor. *Coming to Know: Writing to Learn in The Intermediate Grades.* Portsmouth, NH: Heinemann, 1990.

Excerpt from: ***CREATING & MANAGING LEARNING CENTERS: A Thematic Approach***
by Phoebe Bell Ingraham

AR
CENTERS

ART CENTERS SUGGESTED MATERIALS

- two tables of differing size
- at least one easel
- a large shelf for supplies
- a small shelf or cart for materials specific to a project
- a hanging rack or shelf for laying work to dry
- close proximity to a sink, if at all possible
- scrap boxes for paper, material, fake fur, plastic-type materials
- hole punches: officetype and the new cute shapes are nice
- markers, crayons, colored pencils, chalk, paint, finger paint, payons (paint crayons)
- newsprint, draw ing paper, finger paint paper, construction paper, tissue paper, wrapping paper, wallpaper
- sponge shapes and small sponges on clothespins for painting
- paint brushes of all sizes
- lots of miscella- neous junk: buttons, rickrack, ribbon, feathers, cotton-balls, confetti shapes, glitter
- butcher paper to cover tables
- wall space for hanging finished products
- empty cans and plastic containers for holding small objects for projects
- yarn of various colors and thick- nesses
- glue, colored glue, glue sticks, tape, colored tape, paste
- glue brushes, Q-tips for fine work
- moist clay, playdough, self-hardening clay
- plastic mats for working with messy materials
- eyedroppers
- tongue depressors and popsicle sticks
- paper towels

Musical Instruments

SPECIFIC SKILLS
- creative thinking
- patterns
- rhythm
- listening skills
- following directions
- problem solving

Make a variety of musical instruments with various materials. Create a music store where students can buy the instruments. Write ads for them and display them around the school. Create music to use with the instruments, forming a band.

Some suggested instruments and the materials to use might include:

- a drum from an empty can with ends cut from a paper grocery bag. Put rice, corn or beans in the can to make a different shaker sound.
- maracas from empty film canisters filled with dried beans, rice, or corn; pencils can be stuck into ends for holders.
- lace bells with yarn and beads for bands worn around the wrists or ankles
- rubber bands stretched across a box to make a stringed instrument
- rubber bands wrapped around an embroidery hoop. Place the top hoop over the bands to hold them in place to make a small string instrument
- sandpaper wrapped around a block of wood to make scratch boards
- bells glued or tied to tongue depressors for a bell shaker

Decorate each instrument with markers or puffy paints.

Murals

SPECIFIC SKILLS
- fine motor control
- applying knowledge
- cooperative work strategies
- creative thinking
- reading for information

Create a mural of the zoo, an ocean, a tropical rainforest, or a farm using a variety of art media, such as finger painting and tissue paper collage.

Utilize a bulletin board or an entire corner of the room. Hang streamers from the ceiling for vines, build trees up the wall with large paper stuffed with old newspapers. Make rocks or coconuts from stuffed paper bags. Fill the space with objects. Ask the children for suggestions. Add to it little by little as children work in the art center.

Multiple Stage Activities!

SPECIFIC SKILLS
small and large motor development
creative thinking
perspective
beginning abstract thinking

Create art experiences that go along with your thematic units and utilize a variety of materials. These can be created in two separate stages; as the first step dries, the second step is completed on another day, or in another area.

FOR EXAMPLE:

1) Paint paper one day with a thinned blue paint wash. Add cotton ball clouds to create pictures during a weather unit.

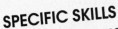

2) Paint paper with watercolors of all colors. Add shapes cut from wallpaper scraps to complete a picture of animals living in a rain forest. Try to create a camouflage effect with the paint and wallpaper.

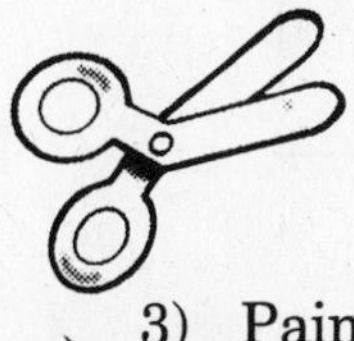

3) Paint paper with watered down glue, then lay tissue paper scraps of all colors all over the paper. Later, color a picture with black crayons. This might be used in a unit about the solar system, colors, or nutrition (draw fruits and veggies).

Easel Experiences!

SPECIFIC SKILLS
small and large motor development
creative thinking
perspective
beginning abstract thinking

Use a variety of materials at the easel. Try such things as:

- painting with evergreen branches
- dipping chalk in saltwater before drawing
- using two mediums, such as paint and crayons
- cutting paper long and thin, square, round, triangular
- using crayon chunks made of old melted crayon pieces melted in tins
- finger paint at the easel with sponge "brushes"

The Grid Game

The object of the game is to be the first to complete the organization of colors on the grid according to the specifications listed:

- Colors: Red, Blue, Yellow, Green
- Quantity: 4 of each color
- Arrangement: no two of the same color may be used in the same horizontal, vertical, or major diagonal line on the grid.

There are many correct ways to accomplish this task.

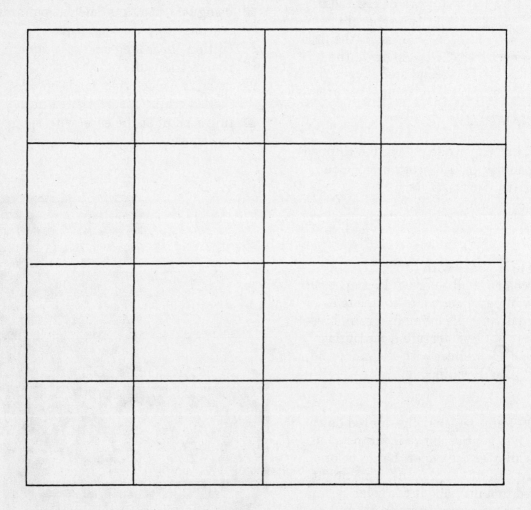

Stephanie Noland

The Mathematical Mind set

Things to consider when organizing for mathematics in the Primary Classroom

NCTM Goals for Students

√ Learn to value mathematics

√ Become confident in ability to do mathematics

√ Learn to communicate mathematically

√ Become mathematical problem solvers

√ Learn to reason mathematically

Math Processes Taught in Early Childhood

- identifying
- classifying
- estimating
- generalizing
- hypothesizing
- recognizing
- representing
- predicting
- explaining
- communicating

By taking a close look at these listed goals and processes, we realize that they are not limited only to the mathematics classroom. We could replace the math terminology in the goals and apply them to all aspects of learning. Additionally, by comparing the process verbs to our objectives, we find the same language in behavioral objectives for all subject areas.

Science in Early Childhood Classrooms

"Imagination is more important than knowledge." - *Albert Einstein*

Dr. Einstein said that young children engage in thinking and investigation that is truly scientific and that their strong curiosity is similar to that of great scientists.

Children are natural scientists. They have a sense of wonder and curiosity that is the beginning of a scientific attitude. The teacher must provide an environment where children are encouraged to develop the scientific attitude.

Any child can be taught facts if he can memorize. The idea of teaching science is to introduce concepts and allow the learner to <u>experience</u> the facts. Facts only make sense if they are clearly related to a concept. We all know that E = mc2 but, few of us understand the concept behind the math. Concepts are enriched and broadened by facts.

Elementary science education should place more stress on the attitudes and aptitudes it develops than on content. The development of attitudes involves continued participation. If children are to develop a scientific attitude, they must have personal science experiences which are enjoyable (Herbert Zim).

"In teaching children to read, we must begin with the experiences of the child." - *Marie Clay*

By giving our children hands - on opportunities to explore science materials, not only are we encouraging a scientific attitude, we are also enabling the child to begin to read and understand scientific material. When the child experiences, his mental setting enlarges -- then those experiences support the child in dealing with a print setting.

SCIENCE PROCESSES TAUGHT IN EARLY CHILDHOOD

•Observation - gathering of information
•Comparison - noticing similarities and differences
•Classifying - sorting and grouping according to common attribute
•Measuring - use of standard and non-standard units
•Communication - telling about an event
•Inferring - using observations to venture a guess
•Predicting - using information to anticipate future events
•Hypothesizing - If... then...

Stephanie Noland

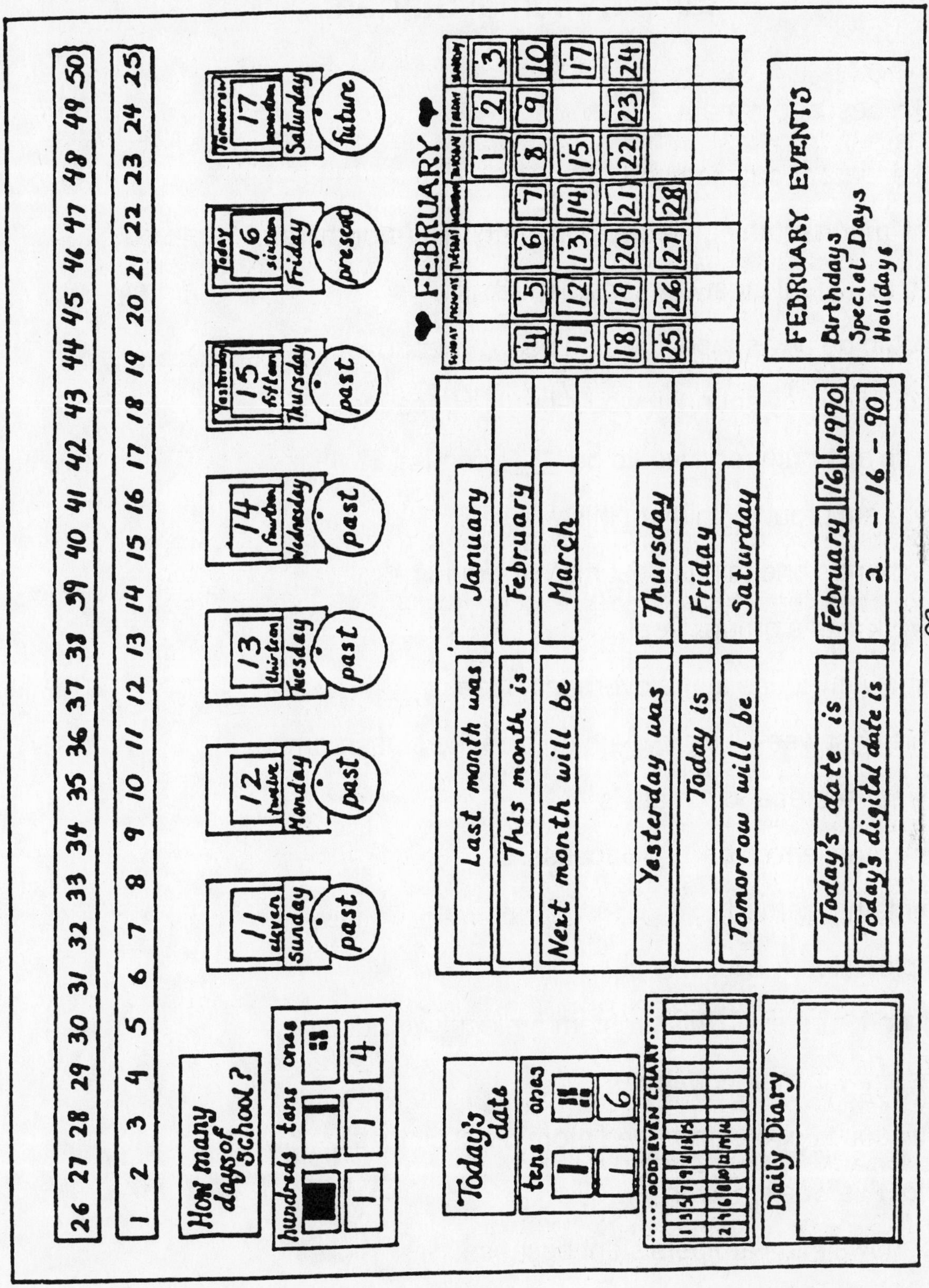
26 27 28 29 30 31 32 33 34 35 36 37 38 39 40 41 42 43 44 45 46 47 48 49 50
1 2 3 4 5 6 7 8 9 10 11 12 13 14 15 16 17 18 19 20 21 22 23 24 25
How many days of school?
hundreds tens ones
1 1 4
11 eleven Sunday past
12 twelve Monday past
13 thirteen Tuesday past
14 fourteen Wednesday past
Yesterday 15 fifteen Thursday past
Today 16 sixteen Friday present
Tomorrow 17 seventeen Saturday future
♥ FEBRUARY ♥
SUNDAY MONDAY TUESDAY WEDNESDAY THURSDAY FRIDAY SATURDAY
1 2 3
4 5 6 7 8 9 10
11 12 13 14 15 17
18 19 20 21 22 23 24
25 26 27 28
FEBRUARY EVENTS
Birthdays
Special Days
Holidays
Today's date
tens ones
1 6
ODD-EVEN CHART
1 3 5 7 9 11 13 15
2 4 6 8 10 12 14
Daily Diary
Last month was January
This month is February
Next month will be March
Yesterday was Thursday
Today is Friday
Tomorrow will be Saturday
Today's date is February 16, 1990
Today's digital date is 2 - 16 - 90

♡ Tom Wrightman. Used with permission.

Stephanie Noland

WRITING IN MATHEMATICS
Sample Journal Starters

What I like best about math is...

What I like least about math is...

The most important thing I learned in math this (month) is...

The math that I feel most comfortable with is...

If math could be any shape, it would be ___ because...

If math could be any sound, it would be ___ because...

If I could be any number, I would be ___ because...

One thing I am proud of in math this week is...

If I could change one thing about math it would be...

When I work with a group, I feel...

When I show my ideas at the overhead, I feel...

During this past week, I used math outside the classroom to...

My best kept secret about math is...

I make my most errors on ___ because...

Today in math I learned...

An example of today's lesson is...

If I could work further on this problem/project I would...

What was easy in math today is...

What I still don't understand/need more practice in is...

My goal for this week in math is...

My work shows that I am persistent because...

Steps Used in the Scientific Method of Investigaton

Problem:

Hypothesis:

Materials:

Procedure:

Data:

Conclusion:

Stephanie Noland

Learning Centers

What is a learning center?

Individual children or small groups working and playing cooperatively or alone on projects they have selected themselves or are guided to by the teacher. Materials and activities are concrete, real, and relevant to children's lives. (NAEYC, 1987)

Component parts of learning centers

Each center needs:

1. **a title and clear instructions -** The learning center should be identified or titled. The instructions should be presented to the entire class or be simple enough so that all students can figure out the instructions independently. The students should be shown how to use the center appropriately.

2. **all necessary equipment and materials necessary to complete the center** - The center should be created so that materials are readily available to the students. Students should know how the materials should be stored so that other students may use the center.

3. **a variety of activities** - The activities in the center should be related to a topic being studied, provide the opportunity to explore an area of interest, or provide practice of a skill. The center should be able to accommodate a variety of ability levels. Open-ended activities do a good job at achieving this goal.

4. **assessment** - The students should know how their work will be evaluated and where to put their completed work. Students may also be given a standard of work and then judge the quality of their own work or the work of their peers.

5. **to be visually attractive** - This seems insignificant, but students will want to work in a center that is attractive.

6. **to have a purpose -** Centers should be more than a replacement for "busy work" or "seatwork". Students should be able to apply what they have learned both in the centers and as a result of working with the centers.

REMEMBER: Many behavior issues are really management issues. If students know what is appropriate -- they're on task and behaving.

adapted from *Learning Centers handout developed by Irv Richardson*

Stephanie Noland

The Developmentally Appropriate Classroom: What Does It Look Like?

When establishing a work environment that is appropriate for young children - especially those of mixed ages, there are many things to consider. Take a look at your own classroom and ask yourself the following questions.

Questions to Consider:

- Are there large spaces for the whole group to meet comfortably?

- Are there medium spaces for small group instruction? If team teaching, are these far enough apart to reduce interference noise?

- Are there small spaces for 2-3 kids to work in together?

- Are there quiet spaces for individual tasks?

- Does table space and arrangement promote cooperation?

- Are there spaces for hands-on science and manipulative-based math? If not, does your routine allow for designating floor or table space for these materials?

- Is safety considered in available supplies?

- Are writing materials, art supplies, and books openly and readily available?

- Are kid spaces and materials well identified? (labels - Kids can make these!)

- Are there soft spaces with rugs, pillows, etc...

- Are kid messages at kid-eye level?

- Is the environment print-rich?

- Is the work/print displayed meaningful to the children?

- Is the print current?

- Do the children participate in organizing the space?

Remember:
Give the children TIME to adjust to any new arrangements!

Learning Center Choices And Multiple Intelligence

Verbal Linguistic
Writing
Reading
Listening

Logical/Mathematical
Pattern Blocks
Multi-links
Puzzles

Bodily/Kinesthetic
Blocks
Clay
Pattern Blocks
Multi-links
Puppets
Sand/Water Table

Intrapersonal
Writing

Spatial
Blocks
Pattern blocks
Multi-links
Invention
Easels
Markers
Water Colors
Stencils
Tangrams
Puzzles

Musical
Listening
Instruments
Poetry

Interpersonal
Puppets
Dramatic Play/Theatre
Home Living
Dress Up Boxes

Natural
Science
Weather
Animal/Pet
Garden

Adapted from Sherry Egllngton and Kathryn Fischer

Center Time is....... LEARNING TIME!!!

Through blocks, a child:
- has opportunity for using large muscles
- chooses sizes and shapes
- learns to use his own ideas
- may enjoy conversation
- learns to put materials away

Through Dramatic Play, a child:
- plays out home experiences
- develops muscular coordination in imitating home actions
- has opportunity to play alone
- has opportunity to "help"
- role plays life like situations
- may begin to cooperate with others
- reveals thoughts and attitudes through conversation
- develops his imagination
- may develop thinking and reasoning skills

Through table games, a child:
- enjoys a sense of achievement
- learns to solve problems
- learns to work independently
- has opportunity for choices
- may enjoy conversation
- develops coordination and fine motor control
- learns to manipulate materials
- forms mathematical concepts

Through Art Materials, a child:
- enjoys sensory experiences
- has opportunity to plan and think for himself
- enjoys manipulation by squeezing, pounding, brushing, and cutting
- experiences creative ways of using materials
- has opportunity for releasing emotional tensions and frustrations
- experiments with color and texture
- learns responsibility for cleaning up

Through Library Materials, a child:
- may enjoy handling and looking at books
- learns to listen to stories
- increases attention/interest span
- develops new concepts and adds to previous experiences
- learns to visually attend to activities
- begins to take responsibility for orderliness

Through Science, a child:
- learns to appreciate beauty
- enjoys sensory experiences
- becomes more aware of his surroundings
- learns to help care for plants and animals
- develops interest in experimentation
- learns to draw conclusions
- accepts change

Through Woodworking, a child:
- has opportunity to plan and carry out ideas
- uses large muscles
- learns to share materials
- has opportunity for releasing emotional tension and aggression
- experiences creativity
- contributes to problem solving activities
- learns measurement principles

Through cooking, a child:
- has opportunity to contribute to the well being of others
- learns concepts of measurement, time, and space
- may enjoy sharing and taking turns
- associates experiences with tangible rewards
- enjoys sensory experiences
- shares cultural background
- develops language

S. Noland, 1995.

Three Grouping Strategies

Whole Class

Group conferences
Appropriate group lessons
Introductions
Reading to class
Instructional games
Etc.

Small Group Instruction

Group	Other students
Skills development	Contracts
Interest	Centers
Work habits	Stations
Social	Peer tutoring
Random	Parent volunteers
Task/Activity	Choices

Individual Instruction

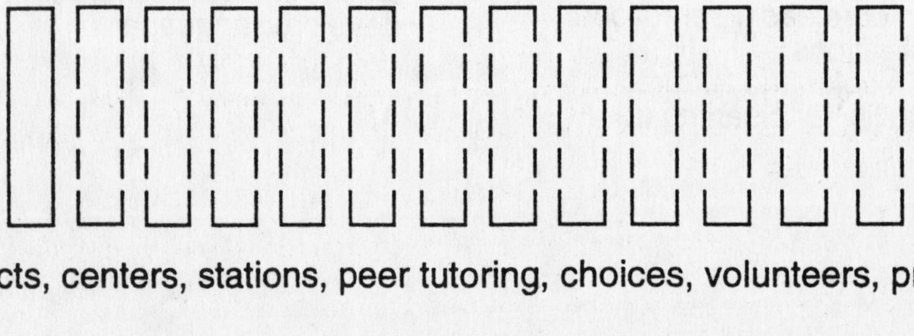

Contracts, centers, stations, peer tutoring, choices, volunteers, projects

New Twists on Old Tales

Center Ideas to Add to Your Existing Program

Compiled by Stephanie Mullins Noland

• Book Order - What a great way to recycle and use all those book club orders we receive in the mail. The teacher gives a certain amount of money to spend on the book order. Kids place their order and calculate change. The add difficulty to the math task, the teacher may also want to specify the number of books for minimum purchase.

• Cold and Flu - Include empty over the counter medicine boxes. Kids write about being absent/sick. What kind of medicine did they take? Also have paper for other s to make get well cards for the absent child to pick up when they return to school.

• Coupon - Laminate coupons of different values. Children select a few coupons, compute the amount of money the coupons total in "savings" and then stamp that amount onto a recording sheet using rubber stamp coins and dollars.

• Gripes/Tattles/Wishes/Miracles - This is probably the best center I have ever heard of. The teacher who shared this with me said that it got the most use right after recess... You know when the kids hit the door wanting to complain about something that happened outside? Well, send them to the center to write about it. Other times, kids can wish and dream.

• Humor - Put joke books, comic books, comic strips (both intact for reading and cut apart for sequencing). Use single frame cartoons for a "create a caption" activity. Kids read and write jokes, comic strips, and humorous stories.

• Sports - Create this center with supplies like sports books, the sports section from the local newspaper, etc... Children can write articles on sporting events and don't forget to include writing scripts for sports casters. Add trading cards for the designated sports. Use school picture photocopies and let kids create their own trading cards. (Can you imagine the stats they will create for themselves?) Also, be sure to add information on the local high school activities.

• Treasure Map - While at recess, the child chooses a spot/item/whatever. After returning to the room, the child creates a treasure map for others to try and find what he has designated.

• Unscramble - Put a child's school pictures on the front of an envelope and write the name on the back of the envelope. Place the letters of the name, cut apart, inside. Kids try to unscramble the name by looking at the photo, name, or perhaps even just by looking at the letters. This could also be used for high frequency vocabulary or spelling words.

• Window Watch - This center is located by the window with a notebook available for a class observation log. A child draws and writes about what he observes at a specific time of day. You could also document the time of day when the observation took place.

• Wellness and Fitness - The school nurse would be a great resource for supplies for this center. The children can learn to take their resting and working heart rates. Include timers, stethoscopes, exercise equipment like a step-aerobic bench, posters with health tables and information listed, and of course, paper to record information.

For more ideas, send a self addressed, stamped (with two stamps) envelope to my home - 500 Laurel Lane, Nicholasville, Kentucky 40356.

My Experiment Sheet

My Name:____

Name of my experiment ________________________________

My Predictions:____________________________________

My Observations:

My Conclusions and What I Learned:

Teacher's Rating and Comments on the Process:

1= Correctly completed task and explained concept

2= In the process of understanding the concept

3=No understanding of the concept or of the process

Stephanie Noland

Responding to My Reading

Name ______________________________ Date ___________

Book Title ____

Author ____

Illustrator ____

My rating of the book:

My favorite part was _________________________________

____

Here is a picture of my favorite part:

____________________________ should read this book next.

Stephanie Noland

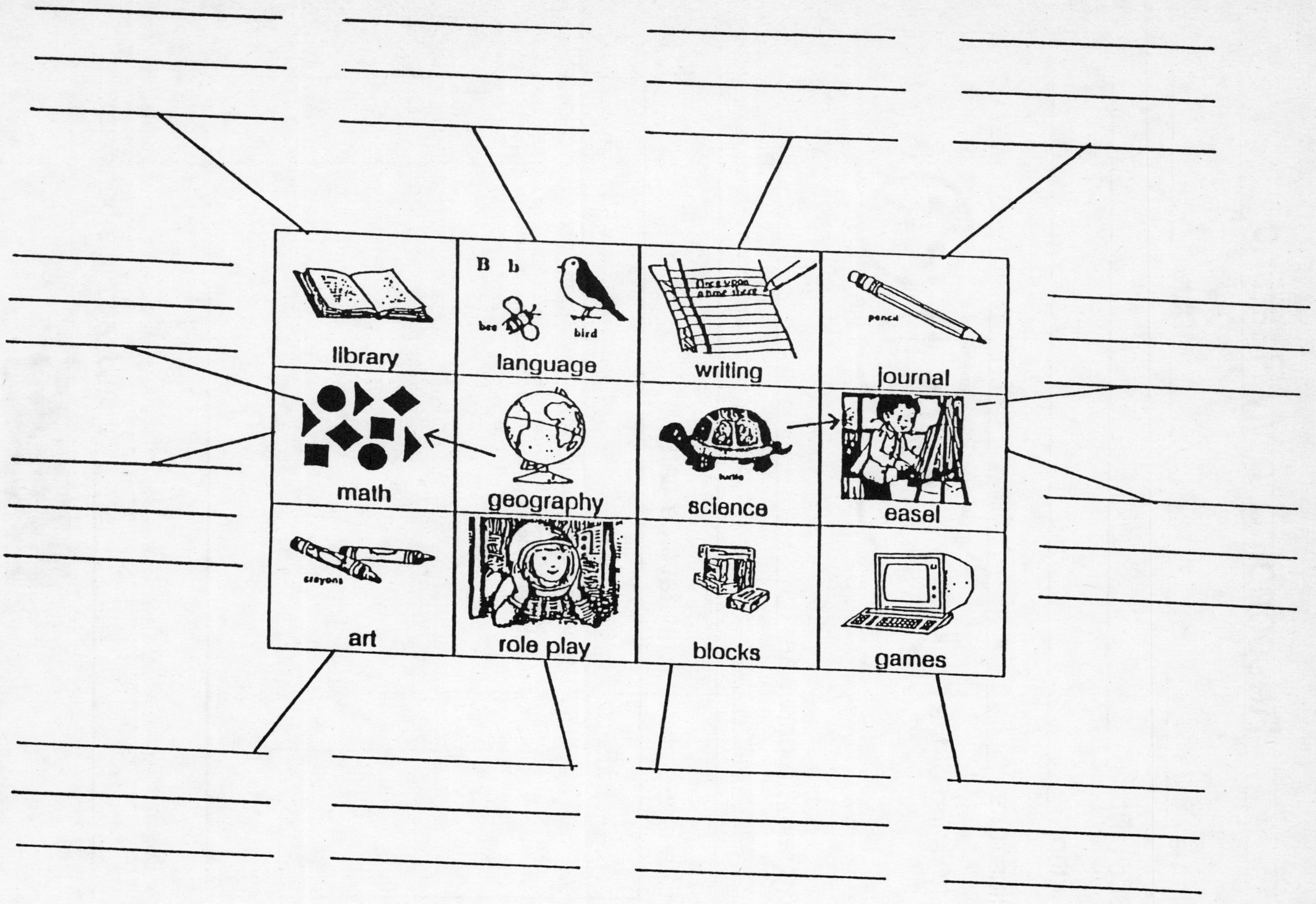

Stephanie Noland

Reprinted courtesy of Phoebe B. Ingraham

______________________'s Contract   Date ______________________

______________ Theme Task Sheet

1	Library: Book: ______________ Author: ______________	6	Art:
2	Writing:	7	Journal:
3	Math:	8	Computer:
4	Science:	9	Cooking:
5	Geography:	10	Small Group Project:

Stephanie Noland

How do I write an integrated unit?

This format is not the only way to create and develop an integrated thematic unit of instruction. Be flexible.

1. Determine the length of time for your unit. - Keep in mind that if you are tuned into the children's interests and needs as well as your curriculum guidelines that your plan may not be the final time line.

2. Look over content area objectives and try to find some logical connections. - View your listed objectives like you would look at a menu at a restaurant. Pick and pull things together that make sense to you and your situation.

3. Come up with a unit topic or title. - Give your unit a focus that you and the children can emphasize.

4. Brainstorm any/all objectives, activities, projects, etc... you could address in all subject areas. - Jot down these ideas on a curriculum web. Be sure to include learning centers, higher order thinking, and even the subjects you don't teach. You'd be surprised at how physical education, music, and art can tie in and how these teachers would love to be a part of your classroom experience.

5. Develop guiding questions. - These are some overall concepts that you want the kids to discover during the course of the study. You could post them and refer to them during the study -- finding out how much more we know about this now...

6. Plan integrated lessons. - Attempt in planning to include at least two subject areas in the lesson. Avoid designing lessons in only one curriculum area.

Stephanie Noland

Curriculum Web

Theme

Stephanie Noland

Tic - Tac - Toe Homework

An alternative homework strategy

Purpose and Rationale

To offer homework assignments that are: 1. integrated across the curriculum , 2. opportunities for student choice under teacher direction and 3. to be completed over several days' time.

In doing so, children see connections between otherwise discreet disciplines and have some voice in selecting assignments (and , therefore, more motivation to do the work). The teacher can maximize use of planning time -- organizing for one generic assignment rather than several daily ones.

Strategy and Preparation

Generate desired list of activities. Arrange them on a tic-tac-toe grid so that, regardless of the child's choices, a variety of content will be addressed in the assignment.

Assign the project and give several days for completion. The children choose the activities they want to work on -- with the understanding that they must do 3 in a row.

Suggested Activities

- Read and discuss a story for ___ minutes.
- Practice math facts for ___ minutes with parents.
- Put spelling words in alphabetical order (on the back of this).
- Use 2 non-standard units of measurement. Measure _______ (one item) and compare findings. Record all information.
- Find things in your home that are _______.
- Find all the holidays/Saturdays/etc... in the month. Write the dates 3 different ways.
- Count all the teeth/windows/whatever in your house. Get a total.
- List the ingredients of a recipe. Sequence the preparation events.
- Use the class newsletter. Find all the words that _____________.
- Look in the newspaper. Find (number) of adjectives/ nouns/ etc...
- Measure _____ items using standard units of measurement.
- Look at food labels. Compare nutritional information on ___ products from dinner.
- Using colors, properties, etc... describe a room in your house.
- Look for/create a pattern.

Stephanie Noland

Integrated Theme: ____________________________________

Name: ________________________ Date: ______________

One big idea from this theme was:

New vocabulary words I can use:

1. _______________ 2. _______________ 3. _______________

I discovered that ____________________________________

____

____

My favorite activity was ______________________________

Books You Can Count On

Compiled by Stephanie Mullins Noland

Aker, Suzanne. *What Comes in 2's, 3's, and 4's?* (skip counting)
Briggs, Raymond. *Jim and the Beanstalk.* (measurement)
Brown, Margaret Wise. *Goodnight Moon.* (time)
Carle, Eric. *The Grouchy Ladybug.* (time)
Carle, Eric. *The Secret Birthday Message.* (geometry and shapes)
Carle, Eric. *The Very Hungry Caterpillar.* (days of the week)
Clement, Rod. *Counting on Frank.* (estimation and large numbers)
Crews, Donald. *Light.* (look for the clocks!)
Crews, Donald. *Ten Black Dots.* (counting)
Dee, Ruby. *Two Ways to Count to Ten.* (skip counting)
DePaola, Tomie. *Pancakes for Breakfast.* (time)
Ehlert, Lois. *Fish Eyes — A Book You Can Count On.* (addition)
Emberly, Ed. *Ed Emberly's Picture Pie.* (fractions)
Giganti, Paul Jr. *Each Orange Had 8 Slices.* (multiplication)
Giganti, Paul Jr. *How Many Snails?* (counting)
Hamm, Diane Johnston. *How Many Feet in the Bed?* (counting)
Harshman, Marc. *Only One.* (counting backwards)
Hooper, Meredith. *Seven Eggs.* (days of the week)
Hulme, Joy N. *Sea Squares.* (multiplication and squaring)
Hutchins, Pat. *Changes, Changes.* (shapes and geometry)
Hutchins, Pat. *Clocks and More Clocks.* (time)
Hutchins, Pat. *1 Hunter.* (counting and patterns)
Hutchins, Pat. *The Doorbell Rang.* (division)
Inkpen, Mick. *One Bear at Bedtime.* (counting)
Kasza, Keiko. *The Wolf's Chicken Stew.* (100s)
Kitchen, Bert. *Animal Numbers.* (counting to 100)
Lionni, Leo. *Inch by Inch.* (measuring)
Lottridge, Celia Barker. *One Watermelon Seed.* (counting to 100)
McGrath, Barbara Barbieri. *The M&M Counting Book.* (counting)
Macmillian, Bruce. *Eating Fractions.* (fractions)
Macmillian, Bruce. *Time To . . .* (time)
Martin, Bill Jr. *The Happy Hippopotami.* (time)
Merriam, Eve. *Train Leaves the Station.* (time)
Merriam, Eve. *12 Ways to Count to 11.* (number concepts)
Pinczes, Elinor. *One Hundred Hungry Ants.* (counting to 100, skip counting)
Rees, Mary. *Ten In A Bed.* (counting and subtraction)
Schwartz, David M. *How Much is a Million?* (counting)
Schwartz, David M. *If You Made a Million.* (money)
Sloat, Teri. *From 1 to 100.* (counting to 100 and skip counting)
Thornhill, Jan. *The Wildlife 1-2-3.* (counting to 1000)
Viorst, Judith. *Alexander Who Used To Be Rich Last Saturday.* (money)
Wiesner, David. *Tuesday.* (time)

LITERATURE FOR THE SCIENCE CURRICULUM

Listed below are several titles for commonly explored scientific topics as well as one terrific way to include parents and home reading in the content connections.

Birds

Ehlert, Lois. Feathers for Lunch.
Heller, Ruth. Chickens Aren't The Only Ones.
Hutchins, Pat. Good Night Owl.
Oppenheim, Joanne. Have You Seen Birds?
Pallotta, Jerry. The Bird Alphabet Book.
Yolen, Jane. Owl Moon.

Ecology

Brown, Ruth. The World That Jack Built.
Cherry, Lynne. The Great Kapok Tree.
Cowcher, Helen. Rain Forest.
Dorros, Arthur. Rain Forest Secrets.
Gibbons, Gail. Recycle!
Greene, Carol. The Old Lady Who Liked Cats.
Jeffers, Susan. Brother Eagle, Sister Sky.
Kellogg, Steven. Island of the Skog.
Kraus, Robert. How Spider Stopped the Litterbugs.
Livingston, Myra Cohn. Earth Songs.
Peet, Bill, The Wump World.
Rand, Ted and Gloria. Prince William.
Yolen, Jane. Welcome to the Greenhouse.

Insects and Spiders

Brown, Ruth. If At First You Do Not See.
Carle Eric, The Grouchy Ladybug.
— The Very Busy Spider.
— The Very Hungry Caterpillar.
— The Very Quiet Cricket.
Dorros, Arthur. Ant Cities.
Pallotta, Jerry. The Icky Bug Alphabet Book.
Parker, Nancy Winslow. Bugs.

Oceans and Ocean Life

Cole, Joanna. The Magic School Bus on the Ocean Floor.
Gibbons, Gail. Whales.
Kalan, Robert. Blue Sea.
Pallotta, Jerry. The Ocean Alphabet Book.
—The Underwater Alphabet Book.
Sheldon, Dyan. The Whale's Song.

Plants

Bash, Barbara. Desert Giant.
Behn, Harry. Trees.
Carle, Eric. The Tiny Seed.
Ehlert, Lois. Planting A Rainbow.
— Growing Vegetable Soup.
Guilberson, Brenda. Cactus Hotel.
Heller, Ruth. Plants That Never Ever Bloom.
— The Reason For a Flower.
Lobel, Anita. Alison's Zinnia.
Merrill, Claire. A Seed is A Promise.
Pallotta, Jerry. The Flower Alphabet Book.
— The Victory Garden Alphabet Book.

Space

Asch, Frank. Happy Birthday Moon.
— Moondance.
— Mooncake.
Barton, Byron. I Want To Be An Astronaut.
Brown, Margaret Wise. Goodnight Moon.
Carle, Eric. Papa, Please Get the Moon For Me.
Cole, Joanna. The Magic School Bus: Lost in the Solar System.
Moche, Dinah. What's up There?
Simon, Seymour. Jupiter.
— The Moon.
— Saturn.
— Stars.
— The Sun.

The Science Backpack - Its purpose is to allow students to independently explore scientific concepts and draw conclusions. Topics could range from those listed to weather, inventions, rocks, and the list goes on and on. Included with the books in the backpack are related activities and necessary materials for the student to work on at home with the parent.

Stephanie Noland

Additional Resources For Today's Session

Expository Trade Books to Add to the List...

Aardema, Verna. *Bringing the Rain to Kapiti Plain*
Allen, Pamela. *Mr. Archimedes' Bath*
Baylor, Byrd. *Everybody Needs A Rock*
Carle, Eric. Papa, *Please Get the Moon for Me*
Clifton, Lucille. *Some of the Days of Everett Anderson*
Cole, Johanna. *The Magic School Bus on the Ocean Floor*
Dunrea, Olivier. *Eppie M. Says...*
Hutchins, Pat. *The Wind Blew*
Konigsburg, E. L. *Samuel Todd's Book of Great Inventions*
McMillian, Bruce. *Mouse Views*
Seuss, Dr. *Bartholomew and the Oobleck*
Singer, Marilyn. *Nine O'Clock Lullaby*
Tafuri, Nancy. *Have You Seen My Duckling?*

Where to Find...

Box It and Bag It	The Math Learning Center Salem, Oregon (503) 370-8130
Pennies, Papers and Ice Cubes Discover the World... Minds on Math	SRA/McGraw Hill (800) 843-8855
AIMS activities	AIMS Educational Foundation Fresno, California (209) 255-4094
ScienceArts (also other science and math resources)	Crystal Springs Books Peterborough, NH 1-800-321-0401
Wonder Science (magazine)	American Chemical Society (800) 8 724-5463

Do You Bolster Children's *Self-Esteem* or Promote **Selfishness?**

Find out if your classroom practices help kids develop healthy self-esteem or turn their attention excessively inward

By LILIAN G. KATZ

If there is one thing educators agree on, it's this: Helping children to feel good about themselves is an important goal. Pick up curricula guidelines, teacher kits, and education journals, and you're likely to find it mentioned.

But many of the current practices intended to enhance self-esteem are more likely to foster preoccupation with oneself and the way one appears to others. And the distinction between praise and flattery is often blurred.

As we'll see in this article, practices that engage children in investigating real environments—instead of turning their attention inward—are more likely to help them develop true self-esteem and learn to cope with occasional frustration or negative feedback.

1 THE PRACTICE: Feel-Good Posters

A poster hanging in the entrance hall of a suburban school declares: WE APPLAUD OURSELVES, surrounded by pictures of clapping hands. Other posters at schools around the country feature Person of the Week, Super Spellers, or Handwriting Honors. Over the principal's office in one urban elementary school, a sign states: WATCH YOUR BEHAVIOR, YOU ARE ON DISPLAY! A small northeastern school's cafeteria sign reads: DO *YOURSELF* A FAVOR. COMPLIMENT SOMEONE TODAY! Below it, a smiling rabbit dripping yellow paint on itself while painting a sunburst says: "It's hard to spread sunshine without spilling a little on yourself!"

LILIAN G. KATZ, PH.D., *is professor of early childhood education at the University of Illinois and director of the ERIC Clearinghouse on Elementary and Early Childhood Education.*

THE EFFECT:

While the WE APPLAUD OURSELVES sign might seek to help children "feel good about themselves," it does so by urging self-congratulation. The poster makes no reference to other ways of deserving applause, such as considering the feelings or needs of others. And the person-of-the-week posters encourage showing off.

While the behavior incentive sign may be intended to encourage appropriate conduct, it does so by directing children's attention to how they *appear* to others, rather than to appropriate behavior. Along the same lines, the smiling rabbit encourages readers to compliment others as a favor to *oneself* rather than as an act of kindness toward *others* and a virtue in and of itself.

All of these practices inadvertently produce excessive preoccupation with oneself instead of a deep and meaningful sense of self-confidence. Why, therefore, are they popular today in schools? Some teachers may be trying to correct an earlier tradition that discouraged complimenting children for fear they would become conceited. Others may hope to compensate for what they believe may be the lack of strong and healthy attachment experiences in children's early years that some research says is necessary for the development of self-esteem.

BETTER WAYS TO GO:

While a large body of evidence indicates that children benefit from positive feedback, general praise is not the only option. Another kind is *appreciation*—positive feedback related explicitly and directly to the *content* of the child's interest and effort. To show appreciation in response to a question raised by a child, for example, a teacher might bring a reference book to class, or share his or her reflections. In this way, the teacher responds to students' questions and concerns with respect, deepening their interest in the issues raised and providing positive feedback. When students see that their teacher follows up on their interests, they will be more likely to raise questions and problems during future class discussions and to take their own ideas seriously. School hallways, therefore, might feature a narrative display of children's investigations into seasonal changes observed in the school yard.

2 THE PRACTICE: Stars and Stickers

In schools across the country, teachers give students positive feedback in the form of gold stars, smiling faces, stickers, and trophies.

THE EFFECT:

Awarding children gold stars is unlikely to make an enduring contribution to the development of their self-esteem, especially if such feedback is frequent. Although gold stars provide children with positive feedback, they can deflect the child's and the teacher's attention from the content of the work at hand. The reason is this: Rewards only work if students keep an eye on them. If they're keeping one eye on the reward, they only have one eye—and not all their attention and concentration—to keep on their work.

BETTER WAYS TO GO:

Instead of mainly relying on direct feedback from the teacher, children can be helped to develop and apply their own evaluation criteria. For example, teachers can ask students to collect their work in a special folder for a week or more. Then after discussing with them some criteria they might use for selection, teachers can invite kids to pick one item they wish to take home. The emphasis should not be on whether the student likes a piece of work, but instead on whether it is complete, clear, or accurate; whether it shows progress; and so on. Also teachers can help parents engage in fruitful discussion with their children about the criteria they use to select work. This helps children understand that the evaluation of their own work is something to be taken seriously by themselves, teachers, and parents.

Students can also be helped to evaluate and assess project work. Rather than drawing attention to themselves, to the image they project, or to how

Illustrations: Pat Porter

others see them, applying criteria to their own efforts helps children engage their minds in their work and growing competence.

Children should also be encouraged to discuss what they might do the next time they undertake a certain investigation (this helps them vary their strategies and use their own experience as data).

3 THE PRACTICE: Behavior Kudos

In their eagerness to reinforce cooperative behavior, teachers often praise young children's efforts by saying: "I was glad to hear you use words to get your turn instead of grabbing" or "It made me happy to see you share."

THE EFFECT:

Such strategies may be useful when introducing children to using verbal strategies for conflict resolution. However, frequent praise of such behavior may be taken by children to mean that the praised behavior is not expected. And it may imply that the rationale for the desirable behavior is merely to please the teacher.

BETTER WAYS TO GO:

It seems more appropriate for teachers to exercise a calm authority by stating clearly and respectfully what behavior is expected as occasions arise. When children squabble about materials, the teacher can calmly and firmly suggest phrases to use if they have not yet acquired them, or remind them in a low-key but authoritative manner to use approaches they already know.

4 THE PRACTICE: Learning About Me

In one first-grade class, each child produced a booklet titled "All About Me," consisting of dittoed pages prepared by the teacher on which the child provided information about him- or herself. The first page asked for information about the child's home and family. Subsequent pages covered "What I like to eat," "What I like to watch on TV," "What I want for a present," "Where I want to go on vacation," and so forth.

THE EFFECT:

The teacher's intention was to make children "feel good about

How much self-esteem is enough?

In one school I visited, a banner in the hallway read: THERE'S NO SUCH THING AS TOO MUCH SELF-ESTEEM! This message is misleading, if not incorrect. A generally beneficial characteristic may be most valuable when it is present at an optimum rather than at a minimum or maximum level. Therefore, parents and teachers should seek to help children achieve optimum self-esteem. There are bound to be ups and downs in behavior, competence, and feedback, so self-esteem fluctuates, but should do so within a narrow range. To help children cultivate a consistent sense of self-worth, keep the following guidelines in mind.

While many schoolchildren have less than optimum self-esteem, telling them otherwise is unlikely to have much effect. Feelings cannot be learned from direct instruction. Furthermore, constant messages about how wonderful one is may raise doubts about the credibility of the message and the messenger.

Self-esteem is most likely to be fostered when children are esteemed. Esteem is conveyed when significant adults and peers treat children respectfully, acknowledge their views and preferences (even if they do not always accede to them), and provide opportunities for real choices. For example, a teacher reported that during creative-writing time one boy was unable to generate more than half a sentence. She acknowledged his "writer's block" and suggested that he return to the task later in the day. By the afternoon, his ideas flowed into two-and-a-half pages about which he expressed real satisfaction.

themselves." However, the "All About Me" booklets directed children's attention toward their own inner gratification and put them in the role of consumers of food, entertainment, gifts, and recreation.

BETTER WAYS TO GO:

To shift children's attention from their own consumer gratification, the teacher might ask them to write about topics that encourage their curiosity about others *and* themselves, as well as topics that can further the intellectual work of the classroom. For example, children could pool, graph, and analyze class data on height, weight, eye color, and family size in a project entitled "All About *Us.*" A British preschool classroom I visited did just this, creating a display titled "We Are a Class Full of Bodies." Below the title was the heading "Here Are the Details." Underneath were bar graphs of the children's birth dates, weights and heights, numbers of lost teeth, shoes sizes, and so forth.

5 THE PRACTICE: What I Like

In a kindergarten classroom, a bulletin board displayed comments made by children about their visit to a dairy farm. Each of the 47 children's sentences began with the words "I liked": "I liked the cows," "I liked the milking machine," "I liked the chicks," and so on.

THE EFFECT:

These comments focus children exclusively on their own individual gratification rather than on worthwhile discoveries and questions stimulated by the visit.

BETTER WAYS TO GO:

Instead of turning their attention inward, the teacher could help students bring out features of the farm visit that aroused their curiosity and could spark further investigations. For example, students might complete statements that begin: "What surprised me was…," "What I am curious about is…" or "What I want to know more about is…," "What I want to explore, find out, solve, figure out…," or even "What I want to make…." These questions

Self-esteem is unlikely to be fostered by easy success on a series of trivial tasks. Young children are more likely to benefit from real challenge and hard work than from frivolous one-shot activities. It is a good idea to incorporate project work that provides children with ample opportunity for decision making, initiative, negotiation, compromise, and self-evaluation.

Educational practices that foster mutual cooperation are also likely to foster self-esteem. Processes that foster healthy self-esteem require that individual work be balanced with group work in which each child has a chance to make a contribution. One such practice is mixed-age grouping, in which the teaching and other kinds of assistance provide opportunities for children to see clearly their real contributions to others.

Editor's Note: For more on multi-age grouping, see "Straight Talk from Multi-Age Classrooms," Instructor, *March 1995, page 64.*

One of the primary goals of building students' self-esteem is to help them cope with failures. When children are engaged in challenging and significant activities, they are bound to experience some failures. Parents and teachers have an important role not in helping kids avoid such events, but in helping them cope constructively when they fail to get what they want—whether a turn on the playground or success at a task. An adult might say, "I know you're disappointed, but you can try again tomorrow." Accepting the child's feelings and responding respectfully helps the child learn from the incident. Also it's helpful if teachers encourage children to recall a time when they struggled and eventually mastered a task.

put the child in the role of producer, investigator, initiator, outreacher, explorer, experimenter, puzzler, wonderer, or problem-solver.

6 THE PRACTICE: I'm Special

A display at one school included nine identical, large, paper doll–like figures, each with a speech bubble containing a sentence stem beginning "I am special because...." The sentences depicted in the display read "I am special because I can color," "...I can ride a bike," "...I like to play with my friends," "...I know how to play," and so forth.

THE EFFECT:

Although there is certainly value in these skills, traits, or activities, there is danger in *stressing* that children's specialness is dependent on these comparatively trivial things, rather than on more enduring skills and traits such as the ability to persist in the face of difficulty and the desire to help classmates. Although there is little doubt that many children arrive at school with less than optimum self-esteem, merely telling them they're special is not likely to change that, and at worst it sounds phony to kids.

BETTER WAYS TO GO:

While children may not be harmed by exercises that tell them they are special, they are more likely to achieve real self-esteem from experiences that provide meaningful challenges and opportunities for real effort. For example, a teacher watching her pupils build a model school bus noted that their efforts were hampered when more than six children

worked on it at once. She shared her observations and suggested that the children work out a schedule so that no more than four or five of them at a time were working on the project. The children eagerly accepted her challenge and developed a workable schedule to their great satisfaction. Instead of giving students empty praise, the teacher acknowledged the students' exemplary problem-solving effort. ■

Before You Praise: Questions to Ask

Before you praise a child—or have your class try an activity designed to boost self-esteem—ask yourself these questions:

- **Is the praise I'm about to offer significant and meaningful?** If not, reconsider what you're saying to children and why.
- **Is my praise frequent and trivial?** If so, it loses value; children may dismiss it as empty teacher talk. Furthermore, when children are accustomed to frequent and easy praise, its inevitable occasional absence may be experienced by some children as a rebuke. Also if a child's sense of self-worth can be raised by simple flattery from one person, it probably can be just as easily deflated by criticism from another. Positive feedback that is specific and informative is more beneficial than general praise.
- **Can children's minds be engaged by the exercises I'm asking them to do?** Will the exercises strengthen students' desire to explore and investigate worthwhile topics? Activities that provide children with a sense of accomplishment bolster their self-esteem.
- **What's the best way to convey to my students that I respect and value their views?** This is important because it prompts children to further explore and therefore see their own progress as researchers and learners.

RESOURCES

"Distinctions Between Self-Esteem and Narcissism: Implications for Practice" by Lilian G. Katz, Ph.D., ERIC/EECE, 1993. See address below. The article above is based on this 80-page monograph.

Talks with Teachers of Young Children and Engaging Children's Minds: The Project Approach by Lilian G. Katz, Ph.D. (Ablex, 1995 and 1989). Call (201) 767-8455.

For additional resources on this topic, contact ERIC/EECE, University of Illinois, 805 W. Pennsylvania Ave., Urbana, IL 61801-4897; (217) 333-1386; e-mail: riceece@ux1.cso.uiuc.edu

TEACHING KIDS *about* GENDER *Stereotypes*

BY MERRYN RUTLEDGE

Boys are doctors; girls are nurses" a kindergartner tells her teacher. Fourth grade boys yell "sissy" at a playmate who tries to cross gender borders on the playground. American Association of University Women surveys that preceded *How Schools Shortchange Girls* showed that girls' self esteem plummets in the middle school years, and no wonder.[1] As these primary school children show, both boys and girls suffer from gender role stereotyping.

Teachers in the Vermont Equity Project are inventing new strategies that help children understand how they come to be gendered and how sex roles lead to harmful stereotypes.

Class explorations begin with gathering information about children's perceptions. For example, write "girl" and "boy" on the board, asking students to brainstorm about what comes to mind for each word. One teacher, curious about a well-known assignment, asked her third graders to write an essay in which they imagine that they wake up tomorrow changed into a person of the other sex. As a Colorado study based on this assignment found, boys often express chagrin at being girls, and girls feel boys have greater freedom.[2]

Most teachers . . . deny the possibility that we show gender bias until we see ourselves teaching. Invite a colleague to videotape or observe a discussion class. How many girls and how many boys are called on? How many boys and how many girls receive follow up questions in which you coax or coach them to respond? Do you consistently enforce "wait time" after asking a question?

Such opening activities must be followed by others that help children understand that they are born with a sex, male or female, but that to a large extent we learn gender, and stereotyping is a natural, albeit dangerous, outgrowth of becoming gendered. Students can ask, are there any "mostly boy" or "mostly girl" spaces and activities in their home? Do bedroom decorations reflect gender? How about toys? Kids can investigate allowance pay among their classmates, or ask whether boys and girls perform chores that correlate with gender role stereotypes they identify. To feed discussions about how gender roles change, children can also interview parents or older community members about their memories of growing up a boy or girl.

Such projects are most effective when they are extensions of ongoing units. For example, when you read and talk about a story, invite reflection about the gender of the characters. Even in animal stories, do children assume the gender of the characters? Try rereading some stories, changing names or pronouns. When Adrienne crossed out "his" and wrote in "her" in her second grade scrawl, she meant to be remaking Nathaniel Benchley's story *Red Fox and His Canoe.* Now a **girl** pleads with **her** father to build a bigger canoe for larger adventures. Red Fox now models an adventurous heroine. [3]

Teachers can also help students to understand their culture by exploring the visibility of women and men. One class kept records of the number of women and men on the sports page. At the end of a month, they tallied their results and made bar graphs that clearly showed men outnumbering women. Children can count books on their reading shelves and count the number of female protagonists.[4]

One sixth grade teacher in the Vermont Equity Project encouraged her middle schoolers to survey books in the literature units of the neighboring elementary school. The children were surprised to find many more male protagonists than female.

Children need to discuss their feelings about such discoveries. James Banks, writing about multicultural schools, says that in the most mature multicultural curriculum, isolated events like Women's History Month celebrations give way to multicultural themes woven into the fabric of a curriculum that encourages children to act upon discoveries and connections to their community. [5]

So when children express bewilderment or anger at discovering the invisibility of women in their books, unfair sports coverage or stereotyping, students can make bulletin board displays, write letters to school officials and the newspaper. Besides teaching critical thinking skills like distinguishing between fact and opinion, such activities teach civic responsibility, show kids that they do have choices and model constructive ways of acting upon feelings.

Elementary school students will not, of course, be able to trace declines in their own self-esteem, but we can bolster their self image by constantly re-examining our course materials and interactions.

Most teachers, myself included, deny the possibility that we show gender bias until we see ourselves teaching. Invite a colleague to videotape or observe a discussion class. How many girls and how many boys are called on? How many boys and how many girls receive follow up questions in which you coax or coach them to respond? Do you consistently enforce "wait time" after asking a question? Girls, as Deborah Tannen has pointed out, often wait until the floor is open or until they perceive it is their turn, while boys are accustomed to jumping in to seize the floor. [6]

One teacher I observed taught herself to call on a girl and a boy alternately. To allow sufficient wait time, she might say, "I'd like to wait until I see more hands."

Since our assumptions about gender are reflected in the language we use, we need to listen to ourselves. One teacher announced to her students that she wanted to stop calling them all "guys." When they caught her, she would chuckle and say simply, "Oops, did it again!" Students soon learn that mistakes give us all a chance to learn.

We can also watch the way we praise or criticize. One kindergartner's father recently reported that at a school ceremony, boys received prizes for being thinkers, imaginative and eager, while girls were complimented for being sweet, cute, good sharers, well mannered and helpful. Such praise reinforces stereotypes that boys are smart and active while girls are cooperative, even docile, and need to be physically attractive. Suggest that your staff make a brainstorming list of words they use to characterize children's behavior and achievement; then explore which words reinforce stereotypes about girls and boys.

We need also to assess classroom materials for the roles boys and girls, women and men play in math problems, storybooks and examples we give orally. When inviting parents to speak about their careers, one teacher made sure to invite a pharmacist and carpenter who are women. Teachers can invite their students to explore their preconceptions by asking them, upon beginning an electricity unit, for example, to draw a picture of an electrician.

In an American history unit, teachers encouraged fifth grader Marian to choose Dolly Madison for a research project. She could only find very old books that showed Madison as a bride, hostess and mother. I asked Marian how she would feel if her life were so summarized. "I'd be insulted," she said, so I suggested that she write a postscript to her report. "I wanted to find out about Dolly her own self," she wrote.

Teachers like Marian's who are chagrined by limited resources might ask children to imagine who else was around at that time and to picture their lives. I asked Rachel, who was doing a report on Alexander Hamilton, to imagine who made his tea. Who grew the cotton in his shirt and sheared the wool for his coat?

Peggy McIntosh, in her essay on assessing curriculum for gender bias, contends that most of the human race is engaged in making and mending life, and our study of history will be gender fair once we reflect this way of defining human experience. [7]

The Women's History Project is a terrific resource for books, posters and videos, and if money is tight, remember the philosopher's encouragement that a journey of a thousand miles advances by single steps. [8]

Staffs can set a school goal of agreeing that each teacher will assess and revise one unit each year. At staff meetings, share before and after versions of a unit, and keep a summary on file for new teachers.

Such recreated curricula support helping our children to X-ray both the school and the wider culture for attitudes and behavior that perpetuate gender bias. Curriculum that invites children to understand the culture's ongoing conversation about gender frees them to become the men and women they choose to be.

1. "Shortchanging Girls, Shortchanging America," Greenberg-Lake poll of girls and boys ages 9-15, commissioned by American Association of University Women Educational Foundation, January, 1991, was one study that led to *How Schools Shortchange Girls*. AAUW and National Education Association (1992).
2. Baumgartner-Papageorgiou, Alice (reprinted 1992). "My Daddy Might Have Loved Me." Sex Equity/Title IX Sex Desegregation Project, New Hampshire Department of Education.
3. Benchley, Nathaniel (1964.) *Red Fox and His Canoe*. New York: Harper and Row, Publishers.
4. Crawford, Susan Hoy (1996.) *Beyond Dolls and Guns: 101 Ways to Help Children Avoid Gender Bias*. Portsmouth, New Hampshire: Heinemann.
5. Banks, James (1989.) "Integrating the Curriculum with Ethnic Content: Approaches and Guidelines," in J. Banks and C. Banks, eds., *Multicultural Education: Issues and Perspectives*. Boston, Massachusetts: Allyn and Bacon.
6. Tannen, Deborah (May/June, 1992.) "Language, Gender and Teaching." *ReThinking Schools*. Milwaukee, Wisconsin.
7. McIntosh, Peggy (1983.) "Interactive Phases of Curricular Re-Vision: A Feminist Perspective." Wellesley Center for Research on Women, Working Paper No. 124.
8. National Women's History Project, 7738 Bell Road, Windsor, California 95492-8518. Tel 707 838-6000.

Merryn Rutledge is the founder and director of the Vermont Equity Project, a fifteen-week series serving teachers in eight Burlington, Vermont schools. She gives gender equity workshops at state conferences and in school districts throughout Vermont. She is also the founder of ReVisions, giving workshops and consultations in interpersonal communication, conflict management, group process, and men and women in the workplace, and is an instructor in communications, gender and communication, and diversity and communication at Champlain College in Burlington, Vermont.
She may be reached at:
ReVisions Workshops
233 Van Patten Parkway
Burlington, VT 05401
Tel 802 863 7084
FAX 802 860 7183
e mail merryn@cameng.com

VOICES VOICES VOICES  VOICES VOICES VOICES

"...I became increasingly convinced that education is a seamless web, that one level of learning relates to every other, and that the most promising prospects for educational reform are in the first years of formal learning."

— Ernest Boyer, The Basic School: A Community for Learning. Princeton, NJ: The Carnegie Foundation for the Advancement of Learning, 1995.

How's Your Attitude Toward Accommodating Differently-Abled Students?

	I have arrived!	I am working on this	I do not believe this is possible	I am not prepared to deal with this
1. I respect students with disabilities as individuals with differences as I respect all children in my classroom.	☐	☐	☐	☐
2. I am aware of the individual capabilities of students and adapt accordingly.	☐	☐	☐	☐
3. I establish routines appropriate for students with disabilities (establish settings so children know what is consistently expected).	☐	☐	☐	☐
4. I employ classroom management strategies that are effective with students with disabilities (e.g., time out, point systems, etc.).	☐	☐	☐	☐
5. I consciously provide reinforcement and encouragement (e.g., encourage effort, provide support if student gets discouraged, emphasizing positive gains).	☐	☐	☐	☐
6. I attempt to determine student interests and strengths and connect personally with students.	☐	☐	☐	☐
7. I help students of all abilities learn to find appropriate avenues to express feelings and needs (drawings, sign language, time outs, etc.).	☐	☐	☐	☐
8. I am comfortable communicating with students with disabilities (plan frequent, short, one-on-one conferences, discuss potential modifications).	☐	☐	☐	☐

How's Your Attitude Toward Accommodating Differently-Abled Students?

	I have arrived!	I am working on this	I do not believe this is possible	I am not prepared to deal with this
9. I am comfortable communicating with the special education teacher (e.g., write notes back and forth, talk informally, collaborate during allotted prep time).	☐	☐	☐	☐
10. I communicate with parents of students with or without disabilities (e.g., write notes back and forth, talk informally, encourage them to provide support for student's education).	☐	☐	☐	☐
11. I expect the best from all students in the classroom and am aware of their capabilities.	☐	☐	☐	☐
12. I am able to make adaptations for students when developing long-range (yearly/unit) plans (e.g., establish realistic long-term objectives).	☐	☐	☐	☐
13. I consciously make adaptations for students when planning daily activities, being aware of potential problems before they occur.	☐	☐	☐	☐
14. I plan assignments and activities that allow students with and without disabilities to be successful (structure assignments to reduce frustration).	☐	☐	☐	☐
15. I strive to allot time for teaching successful strategies as well as content material (test-taking skills, note-taking skills).	☐	☐	☐	☐
16. I adjust the physical arrangements of room for students with disabilities (modify seating arrangements, provide space for movement).	☐	☐	☐	☐

How's Your Attitude Toward Accommodating Differently-Abled Students?

	I have arrived!	I am working on this	I do not believe this is possible	I am not prepared to deal with this
17. I construct study guides, tape-record readings, provide skeletal outlines, and hands-on activities for classroom members.	❐	❐	❐	❐
18. I am able to use alternative materials for learners (variety of textbooks, supplemental readers, calculators).	❐	❐	❐	❐
19. I encourage students to use computers for word processing or skill development.	❐	❐	❐	❐
20. I allow time to monitor the students' understanding of directions and assigned tasks (ask children to repeat or demonstrate what I have asked them to do, check in with students to be sure they are performing assignments correctly).	❐	❐	❐	❐
21. I observe students' understanding of concepts presented in class (attend to, comment on and reinforce understanding of vocabulary, abstract ideas, key words, time sequences, and content organization).	❐	❐	❐	❐
22. I provide individual instruction for students as needed (plan for one-on-one sessons after school, allocate time for individual instruction during class, provide cross-age tutoring).	❐	❐	❐	❐
23. I pair students of all abilities with peers to assist with assignments, projects, provide role models for behavior, academics and social interaction.	❐	❐	❐	❐

How's Your Attitude Toward Accommodating Differently-Abled Students?

	I have arrived!	I am working on this	I do not believe this is possible	I am not prepared to deal with this
24. I involve students in active learning and in cooperative learning groups of mixed abilities.	☐	☐	☐	☐
25. I encourage students of all abilities to participate in whole-group instructions.	☐	☐	☐	☐
26. I consciously provide extra time for students to process information and complete tasks.	☐	☐	☐	☐
27. I am comfortable breaking down assignments into smaller chunks to lessen frustration and ensure success.	☐	☐	☐	☐
28. I observe students in groups and individually, documenting progress and interaction.	☐	☐	☐	☐
29. I collect a variety of work samples from students which reflect progress and growth.	☐	☐	☐	☐
30. I conference with students to provide one-to-one feedback regarding individual achievement.	☐	☐	☐	☐
31. I adapt assessment prodedures as needed to ensure success (oral test, open book test, shortened test, more time for completion).	☐	☐	☐	☐
32. I am comfortable employing individual criteria for student assessment.	☐	☐	☐	☐
33. I present material to a variety of learning modalities within the classroom (auditory, visual, kinesthetic, tactual).	☐	☐	☐	☐

How's Your Attitude Toward Accommodating Differently-Abled Students?

	I have arrived!	I am working on this	I do not believe this is possible	I am not prepared to deal with this
34. I am comfortable collaborating with support personnel.	☐	☐	☐	☐
35. I am comfortable with support services provided in my classroom.	☐	☐	☐	☐
36. I am able to share gifts, talents and needs of my students with colleagues.	☐	☐	☐	☐
37. I see the job description of "teacher" as one who facilitates learning for children of all learning ability levels.	☐	☐	☐	☐
38. I embrace the philosophy that each child is important and worthwhile, demonstrating fulfillment of individual responsibilities while supporting one another.	☐	☐	☐	☐
39. I believe that all children belong and are capable of learning in the mainstream of school and community.	☐	☐	☐	☐
40. I value all children and their contributions to society.	☐	☐	☐	☐

Goodman, Gretchen. *Inclusive Classrooms from A to Z.* Peterborough, NH: Cyrstal Springs Books, 1994.

Suggested books to use with acceptance activities:

Be Good to Eddie Lee
By Virginia Fleming

Big Al
By Andrew Clements Yoshi

Boastful Bullfrog
By Keith Faulkner

Chrysanthemum
By Kevin Henkes

Crowboy
By Taro Yashima

Do I Have To Go To School Today?
By Larry Shles

Elephant and the Rainbow
By Keith Faulkner

I Like Me
By Nancy Carlson

I Wish I Were A Butterfly
By James Howe

Josh: A Boy with Dyslexia
By Caroline Janover

Kids Explore the Gifts of Children with Special Needs
By Westridge Young Writers Workshop

Kittens Who Didn't Share
By Keith Faulkner

Little Rabbit Who Wanted Red Wings
By Carolyn Sherwin Bailey

Mama Zooms
By Jane Cowen-Fletcher

Me First and the Gimme Gimmes
By Gerald G. Jampolsky & Diane V. Cirincione

My Buddy
By Audrey Osofsky

My Sister is Different
by Betty Ren Wright

Original Warm Fuzzy Tale
By Claude Steiner

Our Brother Has Down's Syndrome
By Shelley Cairo

Owl and the Woodpecker
By Brian Wildsmith

People
By Peter Spier

Rainbow Fish
By Marcus Pfister

Reach for the Moon
By Samantha Abeel

Santa's Book of Names
By David McPhail

Stellaluna
By Janell Cannon

Table Where Rich People Sit
By Byrd Baylor

That's What a Friend Is
By P.K. Hallinan

What Do You Mean I Have a Learning Disability?
By Kathleen M. Dwyer

When Learning is Tough
By Cynthia Roby

Tacky the Penguin
By Helen Lester

We Can Do It
By Laura Dwight

TOOT What Do I Do?

	M	T	W	Th	F
1. Desk Clean	☐	☐	☐	☐	☐
2. Classroom Job	☐	☐	☐	☐	☐
3. Get Lunchbox & Backpack	☐	☐	☐	☐	☐
4. Take Home Folder	☐	☐	☐	☐	☐
5. Put a SHARPENED pencil on your shelf	☐	☐	☐	☐	☐
6. Hat, Coat, Mittens	☐	☐	☐	☐	☐

For Older Students:

Assignment Notebook
Check Calendar

Three Cueing Systems

Guessing
Word callers

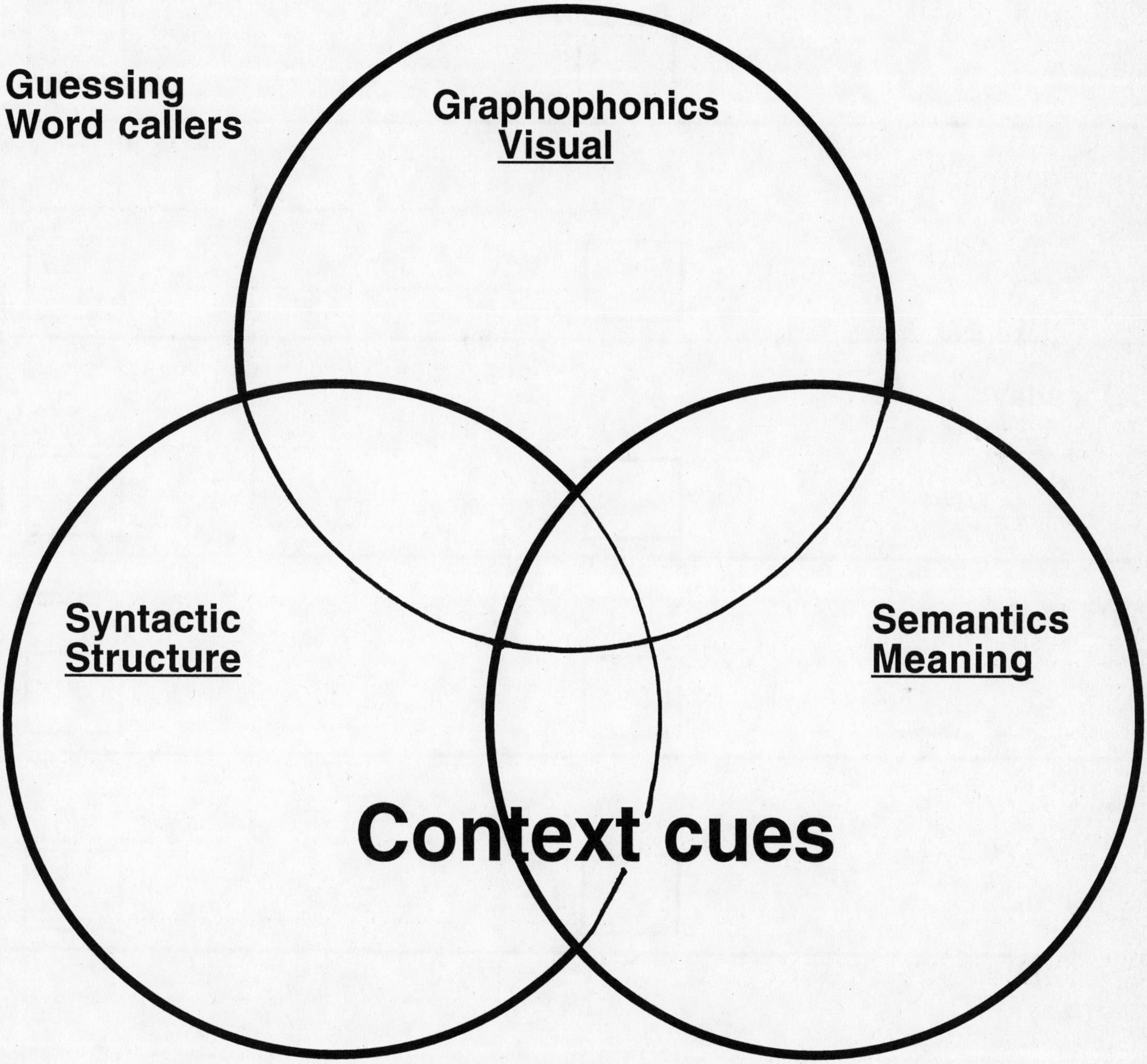

Making up story with no regard to text

Looking at pictures

Home and School Reading Contract

	Independent	Read Aloud
Monday	☐	☐
Tuesday	☐	☐
Wednesday	☐	☐
Thursday	☐	☐
Friday	☐	☐
Saturday	☐	☐
Sunday	☐	☐

1.

2.

3.

4.

Name ______________________ Date ____________________

Title of Book ____

Author ____

What was your favorite part? __________________________

____

____

____

____

____

Name: Date:

Title:

Author:

Illustrator:

This book was about

My favorite part was

SDE Reproducible Page
For Classroom Use

Patricia Pavelka, M.Ed.

Cover 2

Look 1

Write 3

check

1 2 3

Patricia Pavelka, M.Ed.

Name ______________________ Date _________

1. How do you feel about reading?

2. Do you think you are a good reader? Why?

3. What was the last book you read?

4. Do you think it is important to be a good reader?
   Why?

5. What do you do when you come to a word you can't read?

6. Do you read at home?

Patricia Pavelka, M.Ed.

7. **How do you feel about writing?**

8. **Do you think you are a good writer? Why?**

9. **What was the last thing you wrote?**

10. **Do you think it is important to be a good writer? Why?**

11. **What do you usually do after school when you get home?**

12. **Is there anything you would like me to know that would help you have a good year at school?**

Patricia Pavelka, M.Ed.

Help Children Work through Emotional Difficulties—

Sand Trays Are Great!

Rebecca Wheat

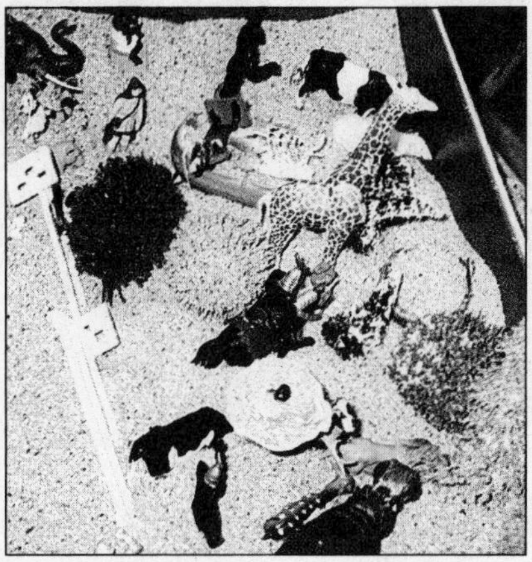

© Rebecca Wheat

Violence is everywhere

Everywhere! It concerns us all. The statistics are staggering. We live in fear for the children in our care. We live in fear for ourselves. There is probably not one of us, in an urban setting, who has not worked directly with families and children dealing with the tragic consequences of violence. Sometimes the violence in our society seems so overwhelming that we feel powerless to combat it. But we are not powerless. Each of us can make a concerted effort to do one or two specific things to mitigate violence—**to help children who *feel* violent find *non*violent ways of dealing constructively with their distress.**

In the Early Childhood Education Department of the Berkeley Unified School District, we have instituted three concepts that work effectively to reduce violence among our children. Two are widely utilized programs: the antibias curriculum and the conflict-resolution curriculum. Both of these programs have been very successful; you can read about them elsewhere. In this article I will focus on our third endeavor—our highly successful project with sand-tray boxes.

Rebecca Wheat, *Ed.D., is a teacher and administrator in Berkeley, California, and has worked with many children with emotional difficulties. She considers sand trays one method of helping children that really works and is very "do-able."*

Sand-tray boxes are one antidote

We all know that many of the children we work with have significant problems. Many times we recommend therapy, but a great number of our children never receive the therapy they need. We have found sand play to be extremely therapeutic! Teachers were introduced to this method of working with children by a local therapist, Dorothy Giller, who explained how she has used the trays in her own work. The boxes are kept in teachers' classrooms, and every child has a chance to work in the box on a rotating, scheduled basis. The box is approximately 2' x 4' x 6" deep and is filled with fine-textured sand. Next to the box are approximately 70 figures, representing animals, people, household figures, construction figures, nature symbols, domestic animals, wild animals, trees, buildings, symbols of good and evil, and so on.

Ms. Giller showed teachers slides of the progression of sand-tray boxes from a variety of children. For example, one series of slides concerned a child who was a serious behavioral problem in school. All that was known of his background was that his mother had died. In the beginning of the sand-box sessions, the child arranged the figures in chaotic scenes. Later there were scenes of grieving. In the last sessions with the therapist, the figures were arranged in a peaceful setting. The tray scene depicted the boy standing at his mother's grave, surrounded by flowers. The child had found some sense of peace after this tragic incident.

Our teachers have learned how to set up the sand trays. The child works by herself for approximately 30 to 60 minutes at a time each week. There is a schedule that includes every child in the class. The teacher observes, if possible—at least intermittently. The very process of working with the sand tray regularly has helped some children immensely.

Teachers have discussed how they have watched children work through sadness, anger, and disappointment and finally return to the group in a much more relaxed state. For example, one teacher said that one of the children in her class is under great stress at home. This child lives in a home with unusually high expectations. When the child feels tense at his after-school program, he works in the sand tray. He usually returns to

For information on the sand-tray boxes and for pictures of play figures, please contact

Playrooms
Toys for Therapists
P.O. Box 2660
Petaluma, CA 94953
707-763-2448

An excellent booklet about the sand tray, which describes how to set one up is available from therapist and teacher Cherie Chichester-Glasse. Please write to

Cherie Chichester-Glasse
14 Camino Del Diablo
Orinda, CA 94563

For direct training in the sand-tray process and how to use it in the classroom, please contact

Dorothy Giller
630 Lexington Avenue
El Cerrito, CA 94530
510-528-3272

Many children come to us feeling angry and upset. Sometimes this makes them behave violently. We have found some ways of helping children work through violent and other disturbing feelings.

the group relaxed. Another teacher commented on how she has learned so much from the children by watching what figures and scenes they put in the trays. Some scenes are chaotic, others peaceful. Some sessions begin with chaotic scenery and end with figures arranged peacefully. Other sand-tray sessions remain with figures chaotically placed.

Another teacher told us,

> A child recently created 2 "gardens," each with its own set of animals inside the fences. This child has been adjusting to a new co-parenting situation, and it seems she was working out some of her feelings by creating the two "gardens." In instances such as this, the sand tray has been an invaluable part of my classroom. I also find this form of quiet and meditative self-expression balances out the other "louder" activities happening in the room.

And another teacher who has a child in her room with a manic-depressive mother notes,

> A young girl in my classroom, who lives in a highly dysfunctional family where any sense of order is absent, has truly led me to value the sand tray as a wonderful possibility for a child to create a perfect world of harmony and walk away with a greater sense of self.

I also had Ms. Giller discuss the sand-tray technique with the graduate students I teach at a local university. She had each graduate student select several figures (from approximately 200) and explain why they selected these figures. The experience was profoundly powerful. Each graduate student was amazed when the group discussed the figures each had selected. They realized that they had selected figures that symbolized people or events that were important in their lives. It gave the graduate students a much clearer idea of the process the children go through when they select figures for the boxes.

Next year our early childhood teachers will be meeting with Ms. Giller three to four times throughout the year to discuss our work with the boxes. She will give feedback on our use of the boxes and offer ideas for further use.

Already a graduate student at a local university is planning to conduct her graduate thesis on the way that the boxes help children deal with their emotions. We hope that her project will generate additional interest in sand trays and disseminate more information on them to local educators, thereby benefitting many children.

The cost of setting up a sand-tray project is approximately $600 per class, plus the consulting time of our therapist. We consider this an excellent investment in time and money. We know that the use of these sand trays is helping our children.

* * *

Implementing therapeutic sand play is one important step in helping children deal with their emotions and thereby attain inner peace. Working together, one step at a time, we can lessen the emotional effects of violence and create peace in the lives of our children.

VOICES VOICES VOICES VOICES

There is debate whether a child should be forced to do school work in class. Personally, I feel such coercion would interfere with his choosing learning for his own benefit. I support the right of a child to withhold consent to learn during class if he sits quietly and does not interfere with others learning. It is also important not to rescue the child by persuading him to learn or by interfering with natural consequences when he has nothing completed for evaluation. My experience has been that few children will sit for more than two days without re-engaging themselves in the learning process if the classroom has something worth learning and the teacher is actively engaged with the rest of the class. At this point, the child becomes a self-directed learner.

— Diane Chelsom Gossen, *Restitution: Restructuring School Discipline*. Chapel Hill, NC: New View Publications, 1993.

ERIC® Clearinghouse on Elementary and Early Childhood Education

University of Illinois • 805 W. Pennsylvania Ave. • Urbana, IL 61801-4897
(217) 333-1386 • (800) 583-4135 • ericeece@ux1.cso.uiuc.edu

ERIC DIGEST
1990 • EDO-PS-90-10

Positive Discipline

How do young children learn self-control, self-help, ways to get along with others, and family and school procedures? Such learning occurs when parents and teachers of infants, toddlers, or preschoolers are continuously involved in setting limits, encouraging desired behaviors, and making decisions about managing children.

When making these decisions, caregivers often ask themselves these questions: Am I disciplining in a way that hurts or helps this child's self-esteem? Will my discipline help the child develop self-control? This digest suggests methods and language that can be used in handling common situations involving young children.

Methods of Discipline That Promote Self-Worth

1. Show that you recognize and accept the reason the child is doing what, in your judgment, is the wrong thing:

> "You want to play with the truck but..."
>
> "You want me to stay with you but..."

This validates the legitimacy of the child's desires and illustrates that you are an understanding person. It also is honest from the outset: The adult is wiser, in charge, not afraid to be the leader, and occasionally has priorities other than those of the child.

2. State the "but":

> "You want to play with the truck, *but Jerisa is using it right now*."
>
> "You want me to stay with you, *but right now I need to (go out, help Jill, serve lunch, etc.)*."

This lets the child know that others have needs, too. It teaches perspective taking, and may lead the child to develop the ability to put himself in other people's shoes. It will also gain you the child's respect, for it shows you are fair. And it will make the child feel safe; you are able to keep him safe.

3. Offer a solution:

> "Soon you can play with the truck."

One-year-olds can begin to understand "just a minute" and will wait patiently if we always follow through 60 seconds later. Two- and three-year-olds can learn to understand, "I'll tell you when it's your turn," if we always follow through within two or three minutes. This helps children learn how to delay gratification but does not thwart their short-term understanding of time.

4. Often, it's helpful to say something indicating your confidence in the child's ability and willingness to learn:

> "When you get older I know you will (whatever it is you expect)."
>
> "Next time you can (restate what is expected in a positive manner)."

This affirms your faith in the child, lets her know that you assume she has the capacity to grow and mature, and transmits your belief in her good intentions.

5. In some situations, after firmly stating what is not to be done, you can demonstrate *how we do it*, or *a better way*:

> "We don't hit. Pat my face gently." (Gently stroke).
>
> "Puzzle pieces are not for throwing. Let's put them in their places together." (Offer help).

This sets firm limits, yet helps the child feel that you two are a team, not enemies.

6. Toddlers are not easy to distract, but frequently they can be redirected to something that is similar but OK. Carry or lead the child by the hand, saying,

> "That's the gerbil's paper. Here's your paper."
>
> "Peter needs that toy. Here's a toy for you."

This endorses the child's right to choose what she will do, yet begins to teach that others have rights, too.

7. Avoid accusation. Even with babies, communicate in respectful tones and words. This prevents a lowering of the child's self-image and promotes his tendency to cooperate.

8. For every *no*, offer two acceptable choices:

> "No! Rosie cannot bite Esther. Rosie can bite the rubber duck or the cracker."
>
> "No, Jackie. That book is for teachers. You can have this book or this book."

This encourages the child's independence and emerging decision-making skills, but sets boundaries. Children should never be allowed to hurt each other. It's bad for the self-image of the one who hurts and the one who is hurt.

9. If children have enough language, help them express their feelings, including anger, and their wishes. Help them think about alternatives and solutions to problems. Adults should never fear children's anger:

> "You're mad at me because you're so tired. It's hard to feel loving when you need to sleep. When you wake up, I think you'll feel more friendly."
>
> "You feel angry because I won't let you have candy. I will let you choose a banana or an apple. Which do you want?"

This encourages characteristics we want to see emerge in children, such as awareness of feelings and reasonable assertiveness, and gives children tools for solving problems without unpleasant scenes.

10. Establish firm limits and standards as needed. Until a child is 1-1/2 or almost 2 years old, adults are completely responsible for his safety and comfort, and for creating the conditions that encourage good behavior. After this age, while adults are still responsible for the child's safety, they increasingly, though extremely gradually, begin to transfer responsibility for behaving acceptably to the child. They start expecting the child to become aware of others' feelings. They begin to expect the child to think simple cause/effect thoughts (provided the child is guided quietly through the thinking process). This is teaching the rudiments of self-discipline.

11. To avoid confusion when talking to very young children, give clear, simple directions in a firm, friendly voice. This will ensure that children are not overwhelmed with a blizzard of words and refuse to comply as a result.

12. Remember that the job of a toddler, and to some extent the job of all young children, is to taste, touch, smell, squeeze, tote, poke, pour, sort, explore, and test. At times toddlers are greedy, at times grandiose. They do not share well; they need time to experience ownership before they are expected to share. They need to assert themselves ("No," "I can't," "I won't," and "Do it myself"). They need to separate to a degree from their parents, that is, to individuate. One way they do this is to say no and not to do what is asked; another is to do what is not wanted.

If adults understand children in this age range, they will create circumstances and develop attitudes that permit and promote development. Self discipline is better learned through guidance than through punishment. It's better learned through a "We are a team, I am the leader, it's my job to help you grow up" approach than through a "me against you" approach.

Creating a Positive Climate Promotes Self-Discipline

Creating a positive climate for the very young involves

- spending lots of leisurely time with an infant or child;
- sharing important activities and meaningful play;
- listening and answering as an equal, not as an instructor (for example, using labeling words when a toddler points inquiringly toward something, or discussing whatever topic the two-year-old is trying to tell you about);
- complimenting the child's efforts: "William is feeding himself!" "Juana is putting on her shoe!" (even if what you are seeing is only clumsy stabs in the right direction); and
- smiling, touching, caressing, kissing, cuddling, holding, rocking, hugging.

Harmful, Negative Disciplinary Methods

Criticizing, discouraging, creating obstacles and barriers, blaming, shaming, using sarcastic or cruel humor, or using physical punishment are some negative disciplinary methods used with young children. Often saying, "Stop that!" "Don't do it that way!" or "You never..." is harmful to children's self-esteem. Such discipline techniques as removal from the group, or isolation in a time-out chair or a corner, may have negative consequences for the child.

Any adult might occasionally do any of these things. Doing any or all of them more than once in a while means that a negative approach to discipline has become a habit and urgently needs to be altered before the child experiences low self-esteem as a permanent part of her personality.

Good Approaches to Discipline

- increase a child's self-esteem,
- allow her to feel valued,
- encourage her to feel cooperative,
- enable her to learn gradually the many skills involved in taking some responsibility for what happens to her,
- motivate her to change her strategy rather than to blame others,
- help her to take initiative, relate successfully to others, and solve problems.

Note: This digest was adopted from an article that appeared in the November, 1988 issue of *Young Children* (pages 24-29).

For More Information

"Ideas That Work with Young Children: Avoiding Me Against You Discipline." *Young Children* (November, 1988): 24-29.

This publication was funded by the Office of Educational Research and Improvement, U.S. Department of Education, under contract number OERI 88-062012. Opinions expressed in this report do not necessarily reflect the positions or policies of OERI. ERIC Digests are in the public domain and may be freely disseminated.

ERIC® Clearinghouse on Elementary and Early Childhood Education

University of Illinois • 805 W. Pennsylvania Ave. • Urbana, IL 61801-4897
(217) 333-1386 • (800) 583-4135 • ericeece@ux1.cso.uiuc.edu

ERIC DIGEST
June 1994 • EDO-PS-94-7

Violence and Young Children's Development

Lorraine B. Wallach

Violence in the United States has claimed thousands of lives and annually costs hundreds of millions of dollars in medical care and lost wages. In the context of this digest, the term *violence* is used to refer to child abuse or other domestic conflict, gang aggression, and community crime, including assault. One of the most pernicious consequences of violence is its effect on the development of children. This digest examines the developmental consequences for children who are the victims of, or witnesses to, family and community violence.

Violence in the Preschool Years

Children growing up with violence are at risk for pathological development. According to Erikson's classical exposition of individual development, learning to trust is the infant's primary task during the first year of life. Trust provides the foundation for further development and forms the basis for self-confidence and self-esteem. The baby's ability to trust is dependent upon the family's ability to provide consistent care and to respond to the infant's need for love and stimulation. Caregiving is compromised when the infant's family lives in a community racked by violence and when the family fears for its safety. Parents may not give an infant proper care when their psychological energy is sapped by efforts to keep safe (Halpern, 1990). Routine tasks like going to work, shopping, and keeping clinic appointments take careful planning and extra effort.

When infants reach toddlerhood they have an inner push to try newly gained skills, such as walking, jumping, and climbing. These skills are best practiced in parks and playgrounds, not in crowded apartments. But young children who live in communities racked by crime and menaced by gangs are often not permitted to be out-of-doors. Instead, they are confined to small quarters that hamper their activities, and that lead to restrictions imposed by parents and older family members (Scheinfeld, 1983). These restrictions, which are difficult for toddlers to understand and to obey, can lead in turn to disruptions in their relationships with the rest of the family.

During the preschool years, young children are ready to venture outside of the family in order to make new relationships and learn about other people (Spock, 1988). However, when they live in neighborhoods where dangers lurk outside, children may be prevented from going out to play or even from accompanying older children on errands. In addition, preschoolers may be in child care programs that are located in areas where violent acts occur frequently.

Violence: The School Years

Although the early years are critical in setting the stage for future development, the experiences of the school years are also important to children's healthy growth. During the school years, children develop the social and academic skills necessary to function as adults and citizens; violence at home or in the community takes a high toll.

- When children's energies are drained because they are defending themselves against outside dangers or warding off their own fears, they have difficulty learning in school (Craig, 1992). Children traumatized by violence can have distorted memories, and their cognitive functions can be compromised (Terr, 1983).
- Children who have been victimized by or who have seen others victimized by violence may have trouble learning to get along with others. The anger that is often instilled in such children is likely to be incorporated into their personality structures. Carrying an extra load of anger makes it difficult for them to control their behavior and increases their risk for resorting to violent action.
- Children learn social skills by identifying with adults in their lives. Children cannot learn nonaggressive ways of interacting with others when their only models, including those in the media, use physical force to solve problems (Garbarino et al., 1992).
- To control their fears, children who live with violence may repress feelings. This defensive maneuver takes its toll in their immediate lives and can lead to further pathological development. It can interfere with their ability to relate to others in meaningful ways and to feel empathy. Individuals who cannot empathize with others' feelings are less likely to curb their own aggression, and more likely to become insensitive to brutality in general. Knowing how some youths become emotionally bankrupt in this way helps us understand why they are so careless with their own lives and with the lives of others (Gilligan, 1991).
- Children who are traumatized by violence may have difficulty seeing themselves in future roles that are

meaningful. The California school children who were kidnapped and held hostage in their bus were found to have limited views of their future lives and often anticipated disaster (Terr, 1983). Children who cannot see a decent future for themselves have a hard time concentrating on present tasks such as learning in school and becoming socialized.

- Children need to feel that they can direct some part of their existence, but children who live with violence learn that they have little say in what happens to them. Beginning with the restrictions on autonomy when they are toddlers, this sense of helplessness continues as they reach school age. Not only do they encounter the constraints that all children do, but their freedom is restricted by an environment in which gangs and drug dealers control the streets.
- When children experience a trauma, a common reaction is to regress to an earlier stage when things were easier. This regression can be therapeutic by allowing the child to postpone having to face the feelings aroused by the traumatic event. It is a way of gaining psychological strength. However, when children face continual stress they are in danger of remaining psychologically in an earlier stage of development.

Individual Differences and Resilience

Not all children respond to difficult situations in the same way; there are many factors that influence coping abilities, including age, family reaction to stress, and temperament. Younger children are more likely to succumb to stress than school-age children or adolescents. Infants can be shielded from outside forces if their caregivers are psychologically strong and available to the baby.

Children who live in stable, supportive homes have a better chance of coping because they are surrounded by nurturing adults. If grown-ups are willing to listen to children's fears and provide appropriate outlets for them, children are better able to contend with the difficulties in their lives. Children are more resilient if they are born with easy temperaments and are in good mental health. If they are lucky enough to have strong parents who can withstand the stresses of poverty and community violence, children also have a better chance of growing into happy and productive adults (Garmezy & Rutter, 1983).

Adaptability in Children

Although what happens to them in the early years is very important, many children can overcome the hurts and fears of earlier times. For children living in an atmosphere of stress and violence, the ability to make relationships and get from others what they miss in their own families and communities is crucial to healthy development.

The staff in schools, day care centers, and recreational programs can be resources to children and offer them alternative perceptions of themselves, as well as teaching them skills for getting along in the world. With time, effort, and skill, caregivers can provide children with an opportunity to challenge the odds and turn their lives in a positive direction.

NOTE: This digest is the first in a series of two digests on violence in children's lives.

References

Bell, C. (1991). Traumatic Stress and Children in Danger. *Journal of Health Care for the Poor and Underserved* 2(1): 175-188.

Carnegie Corporation of New York. (1994). Saving Youth from Violence. *Carnegie Quarterly* 39(1, Winter): 2-5.

Craig, S.E. (1992). The Educational Needs of Children Living with Violence. *Phi Delta Kappan* 74(1, Sep 10): 67-71. EJ 449 879.

Garbarino, J., N. Dubrow, K. Kostelny, and C. Pardo. (1992). *Children in Danger: Coping with the Consequences of Community Violence.* San Francisco: Jossey-Bass. ED 346 217. Not available from EDRS.

Garmezy, N. and M. Rutter, Eds. (1983). *Stress, Coping, and Development in Children.* New York: McGraw Hill.

Gilligan, J. (1991). Shame and Humiliation: The Emotions of Individual and Collective Violence. Paper presented at the Erikson Lectures, Harvard University, Cambridge, MA, May 23.

Halpern, R. (1990). Poverty and Early Childhood Parenting: Toward a Framework for Intervention. *American Journal of Orthopsychiatry* 60(1, Jan): 6-18.

Kotlowitz, A. (1991). *There Are No Children Here.* New York: Doubleday.

Scheinfeld, D. (1983). Family Relationships and School Achievement among Boys in Lower-Income Urban Black Families. *American Journal of Orthopsychiatry* 53(1, Jan): 127-143.

Spock, B. (1988). *Dr. Spock on Parenting.* NY: Simon & Schuster.

Terr, L. (1983). Chowchilla Revisited: The Effects of Psychic Trauma Four Years after a Schoolbus Kidnapping. *American Journal of Psychiatry* 140: 1543-1550.

Wallach, L. (1993). Helping Children Cope with Violence. *Young Children* 48(4, May): 4-11. EJ 462 996.

Zero To Three. (1992). *Can They Hope To Feel Safe Again?: The Impact of Community Violence on Infants, Toddlers, Their Parents and Practitioners.* Arlington, VA: National Center for Clinical Infant Programs. ED 352 161.

Zinsmeister, K. (1990). Growing Up Scared. *Atlantic Monthly* 256(6, Jun): 49-66.

References identified with an ED (ERIC document) or EJ (ERIC journal) number are cited in the ERIC database. Most documents are available in ERIC microfiche collections at more than 825 locations worldwide, and can be ordered through EDRS: (800) 443-ERIC. Journal articles are available from the original journal, interlibrary loan services, or article reproduction clearinghouses, such as: UMI (800) 732-0616; or ISI (800) 523-1850.

This publication was funded by the Office of Educational Research and Improvement, U.S. Department of Education, under contract no. DERR97002007. The opinions expressed in this report do not necessarily reflect the positions or policies of OERI.

Getting Ready for Young Children with Prenatal Drug Exposure

Shirley Cohen and Christina Taharally

The appearance of crack cocaine in 1984 precipitated a dramatic increase in women of childbearing age who abuse drugs. Many of these women are polydrug users, combining heroin, methadone, cocaine, marijuana and alcohol (Feig, 1990). As a result, the numbers of young children prenatally exposed to drugs are increasing. Moreover, for many of these young children, prenatal drug exposure is but one of multiple risk factors present before and after birth (The Future of Children, 1991).

While the effects of prenatal drug exposure appear to vary with the type of drugs used, the amount and timing of drug use and differences in fetuses, the research indicates mild-to-moderate developmental delays and behavioral differences in some young children (Rodning, Beckwith & Howard, 1989). Young infants with prenatal drug exposure often experience problems. Their sleep patterns may be irregular; they may cry frequently, appear agitated and be difficult to console. They may also be deficient in the social engagement skills (e.g., eye gaze and reciprocal smiling) necessary for early attachment (Schneider, Griffith & Chasnoff, 1989). Initial injury to the fetus from prenatal drug exposure and other risks may be compounded by environmental factors that inhibit sensitive and skilled caregiving.

The growing population of young children with prenatal drug exposure raises concern about special education referrals. In fact, referrals of 5-year-olds for special education evaluations are increasing in New York City and other urban areas, a phenomenon at least partially attributed to greater use of drugs by pregnant women during the '80s (Daley, 1991).

The authors take the position that the education of young children with prenatal drug exposure is not primarily the responsibility of special education. The behavior of such children varies greatly, and most do not appear to have severe disabilities. For the most part, their IQs are in the normal range (Rodning, Beckwith & Howard, 1989; Viadera, 1992), and generally they are not characterized by severe sensory, motor or health impairments. Moreover, the field of special education is moving toward integration of special needs children into the education mainstream, particularly at the early childhood level (Burton, Hains, Hanline, McLean & McCormick, 1992). An appropriate response, therefore, is to strengthen early childhood education and develop collaborative relationships with special education, allowing effective care without special placements. Only a small percentage of these children are likely to need or be better served in separate special education programs during the preschool years.

Although prenatal exposure to crack cocaine has attracted the greatest attention during the last few years, exposure to alcohol affects an even greater number of young children (Streissguth et al., 1991). Four-year-old children whose mothers engaged in even moderate social drinking during pregnancy were less attentive, less obedient and more fidgety than children of nondrinkers (Spohr & Steinhausen, 1987). Children identified as having fetal alcohol syndrome (1 of every 600-700 live births) and children with fetal alcohol effects (1 of every 300-350 live births) often display impulsivity, poor attention and difficulty in making transitions (Burgess & Streissguth, 1990). Many of these children are now in early childhood programs. To be effective, the programs require greater awareness of such children's needs, modifications in instructional strategies and additional supports for the children and their families.

Shirley Cohen is Professor, Department of Special Education, Hunter College, New York, New York. Christina Taharally is Associate Professor, Department of Curriculum and Teaching, Hunter College.

Issues in Practice

An *American School Board Journal* article asked: "When crack babies are ready for school (and the first cohort will arrive sooner than you think) will your schools be ready for them?" (Rist, 1990). Many teachers of pre-kindergarten and kindergarten classes, along with their colleagues in Head Start and day care, are answering "No." A veteran kindergarten teacher in the Bronx reported her recent experience: "The first few days of school . . . when I came home from work, I just fell down I was so tired. I kept thinking, 'What is going on here?'" (Daley, 1991).

Data on the characteristics of preschool children with prenatal drug exposure are scarce. Most research has focused on infancy. Information about preschool children comes largely from anecdotal reports by preschool personnel, parents and other caregivers. This anecdotal literature describes children who are having difficulty in selected areas of development, including relationships/attachments, communication, attention and play. Some of them may experience mood changes and distress more frequently than other children, and display aggressive behavior without apparent provocation.

One must remember, however, that the anecdotes focus on children presenting difficulties or causing problems, not on those who are developing satisfactorily and may constitute a large percentage of this population. Furthermore, anecdotal material does not distinguish between children exposed to other risk factors (e.g., low birth weight and inadequate or erratic caregiving during the first three years) and those who are not. Preschool personnel cannot wait for research results, however; they are confronting the problems now. The remainder of this article suggests ways of serving these children without violating core early childhood principles and premises.

Preschool personnel cannot wait for research results, however; they are confronting the problems now.

Developmentally Appropriate Practices

The National Association for the Education of Young Children guidelines for developmentally appropriate practices (Bredekamp, 1987) can serve as a framework for establishing preschool programs for children with prenatal drug exposure. The most relevant ones relate to adult-child interaction. Some of these guidelines are discussed here.

▪ *Guideline: Adults respond quickly and directly to children's needs, desires, and messages and adapt their responses to children's differing styles and abilities* (Bredekamp, 1987, p. 9). Children with prenatal drug exposure may need extra help forming relationships. The literature (Rodning, Beckwith & Howard, 1989) suggests that some of these children may not have formed secure attachments to caregivers. Furthermore, anecdotal reports refer to lack of discrimination between familiar and unknown adults; some children show inappropriate interest and affection toward strangers. One appropriate response might be "specialing" by an adult in the classroom (not necessarily the teacher) whose style seems best suited to a particular child. The "specialing" adult would provide physical proximity, instructional assistance and comforting.

Comforting may be important because some children appear to be difficult to console. Techniques developed to console drug-exposed infants include swaddling the infant in a blanket and rocking slowly (Schneider & Chasnoff, 1987). Preschoolers who are difficult to console might be calmed by age appropriate equivalents of these techniques; e.g., by enveloping children in their nap blankets and gently pushing them in a child-size rocking chair within a set-off, quiet area of the room. Teachers need to be aware of variation in children's responses to physical contact. Some children seek physical signs of affection and are comforted best by being held on a teacher's lap; others distance themselves and need to be comforted without close physical contact, at least while developing a relationship.

Children with prenatal drug exposure may be subject to mood changes or distress without easily recognizable catalysts. One such instance observed by the authors involved a 4-year-old girl who became distressed at the slight overlapping of two oaktag letters the teacher had placed in sequence to form the child's name. Even after the letters were separated, the child continued to whimper for several minutes. When offered the responsibility of distributing cups for juice, however, she quickly recovered.

▪ *Guideline: Adults provide many varied opportunities for children to communicate* (Bredekamp, 1987, p. 10). One of the most commonly reported characteristics of children with prenatal drug exposure is poor language development. Some children acquire speech late, while others speak infrequently. To develop their communication skills, stimulation of conversation should take place throughout the day and in virtually every activity. Teacher directives do not usually encourage discourse, while questions that ask "what," "where," "who," "how" and "why" do—even in children with delayed language whose responses are partially gestural.

Some children may receive services from a speech therapist. Therapy, however, is no substitute for stimulation through natural classroom activities and interactions. Formal language development strategies should supplement peer modeling, peer interaction, teacher modeling and gentle encouragement. Care should be taken, however, not to bombard children with rapidly delivered speech or speech that has little communicative value.

▪ *Guideline: Adults facilitate the development of self-control in children* (Bredekamp, 1987, p. 11). Another characteristic commonly attributed to children with prenatal drug exposure is aggressiveness, particularly unanticipated aggression. Thus, it is necessary to help the child gain an understanding of what constitutes both appropriate and inappropriate behavior and to develop controls that enable the child to act in accordance with these guidelines.

Clear limits, redirection, modeling of appropriate behavior and verbalization of feelings are the major tools for facilitating self-control. Children with particular difficulty in this area may require additional guidance in the form of more specific directions, a more limited range of choices at any one time, more clearly bounded play areas and more ongoing teacher assistance with peer interactions. Teachers must recognize that these children may not yet have developed skill in relating to peers in ways that support the forming of friendships. They may also require more private work space and materials than are commonly provided in early childhood programs. Some children will also need alternative activities during large group instructional periods.

One of the most commonly reported characteristics of children with prenatal drug exposure is poor language development.

▪ *Guideline: Adults facilitate a child's successful completion of tasks by providing support, focused attention, physical proximity and verbal encouragement* (Bredekamp, 1987, p. 10). Children with prenatal drug exposure are often described as hyperactive and easily distracted. Some, however, have no difficulty concentrating on selected tasks. Those children who do will need extra support, attention, encouragement and proximity to an adult.

Early childhood teachers also have to reappraise the placement and storage of materials. Maintaining attention to a particular activity may be easier if irrelevant materials are not within the child's visual field or reach. Recently, the authors observed a class for children with prenatal drug exposure where the teacher had great difficulty holding children's interest during storytime. They were distracted by a nearby shelf with puppets, records and picture books. Many years ago, one of the authors installed "curtains" over open shelves in her classroom for emotionally disturbed children and found it helped the children focus their attention on the activity in progress.

Administrative Supports

Without administrative supports, early childhood programs will not be able to effectively serve the population of children whose prenatal drug exposure has left them at particular risk of developmental delay and educational failure. The NAEYC guidelines on "policies essential for achieving developmentally appropriate early childhood programs" recognize the significant role of administrative supports. Critical among these supports is adult-to-child ratios.

> Implementation of developmentally appropriate early childhood programs requires limiting the size of the group and providing sufficient numbers of adults to provide individualized and age-appropriate care and education. (Bredekamp, 1987, p. 14)

For 4- and 5-year-olds, NAEYC recommends a ratio of 2 adults to 20 children. Yet some urban school systems, like that of New York City, often have kindergarten classes of 25 or more students, sometimes with only one teacher and no other adult. These same urban schools are most likely to include children with prenatal drug exposure in their kindergartens. School systems must restructure resources to provide at least two full-time adults for every kindergarten and lower-grade class and limit class size to a maximum of 20 children. Even this ratio is far too high; ways must be found to enlist the assistance of other adults. Without such restructuring, it will be impossible to effectively serve many drug-exposed or otherwise seriously at-risk children in the education mainstream.

Apart from the critical issue of adult-to-child ratios, administrators who want to serve drug-exposed children in mainstream programs need to become knowledgeable about new trends in using special education resources. They also need to encourage early childhood personnel to expand their knowledge and skill to include teaching children with special needs arising from prenatal drug exposure and other risk factors.

Accessing Special Education Services

Some young children with prenatal drug exposure may benefit from special education resources and supports. Many of these resources can be made available to children in mainstream early childhood programs, although a referral for special education evaluation and a determination that a child is in need of special education services may first be required. The Individualized Education Program (IEP) and Individualized Family Service Plan (IFSP) are the critical tools in determining services and in placing the child. The IEP or IFSP can mandate the services of a consultant teacher, resource teacher, speech/language therapist or assistant teacher to work with the child in the mainstream class, and other personnel to work with the parent or family.

With special education moving toward redefinition as a support system for mainstream education, newer administrative arrangements are appearing that combine special education and early childhood education staff. The New York City public school system is pilot-testing such a model at the Pre-K level. This model involves collaborative teaching teams of early childhood and special education staff serving groups of about 18 children, one-third of whom have been identified as needing special education services.

Another model was put into practice by an upstate New York nonprofit agency that formerly operated a special education preschool program. The agency placed its former students in mainstream early childhood settings, assigning its special education staff as consultant teachers, resource teachers and assistant teachers. These new administrative arrangements may be particularly advantageous for children with prenatal drug exposure needing more than an early childhood program.

Personnel Preparation Programs

Recently the authors were approached by an undergraduate interested in a program that prepared teachers to work with young drug-exposed children. This student verbalized an assumption that may be quite common; namely, young children with prenatal drug exposure are distinctly different from other young children, including those who have special needs or are at risk of developmental delay. The available data do not support this view.

A strong case can be made for preservice programs that combine special education with early childhood education, including special knowledge accumulated over two decades of experience with Head Start and other programs serving children of poverty (Miller, 1992; Schutter & Brinker, 1992). The goal of such preparation programs would be to serve the greatest possible percentage of children in early childhood mainstream programs, including children with prenatal drug exposure. While some universities have initiated such programs, most state certification systems do not support such preparation; they do not offer a certificate in early childhood special education.

Inservice education can serve as a lifeline for those early childhood educators who ask, as did the teacher quoted earlier, "What is going on here?" For such teachers, the focus of inservice activities would be to:

- Develop an understanding of developmental and functional changes in the kindergarten population
- Acquire additional strategies, some adapted from special education, for coping with behavior that doesn't respond to standard early childhood strategies
- Share and gain support from others who are also experiencing shock and searching for new answers.

After several sessions of observing 3- and 4-year-olds in a program for children with prenatal drug exposure, the authors selected six skills as examples of important points of focus for inservice programs:

- Skill in designing classroom environments that encourage independence and autonomy while supporting self-control and that respond to children's need for safety, personal space and quiet retreats to balance stimulating activities
- Skill in adapting and modifying the typical schedule and format of activities in early childhood classrooms to better meet the learning and behavioral needs of a particular group, and of individual students in that group
- Skill in recognizing nonverbal cues to children's emotions and determining when supportive intervention is needed
- Skill in responding to a wide spectrum of child behavior, including sudden mood changes and inappropriate attempts to engage other children
- Skill in recognizing "teachable moments" and selecting teaching strategies that match these opportunities
- Skill in working in supportive and complementary ways with assistant teachers, speech therapists, social workers and family assistants.

Conclusion

This is a time of challenge, a time to expand and seek new collaborations. Historically, early childhood education programs have responded most directly to student needs and, over the past 25 years, have focused increasingly upon children of poverty. The influx of children prenatally exposed to drugs, therefore, does not represent a change in direction; rather, it presents a heightened challenge. Early childhood educators need to seek new collaborations, joining forces with whatever support systems are available and redesigning administrative structures to respond more effectively to children with prenatal drug exposure.

References

Bredekamp, S. (Ed.), (1987). *Developmentally appropriate practice in early childhood programs serving children from birth through age 8.* Washington, DC: National Association for the Education of Young Children.

Burgess, D. M., & Striessguth, A. P. (1990). Educating students with fetal alcohol syndrome or fetal alcohol effects. *Pennsylvania Reporter, 22*(1), 1-3.

Burton, C. B., Hains, A. H., Hanline, M. F., McLean, M., & McCormick, K. (1992). Early childhood intervention and education: The urgency of professional unification. *Topics in Early Childhood Special Education, 11*(4), 53-69.

Daley, S. (1991, February 7). Born on crack, and coping with kindergarten. *The New York Times*, pp. A1, A13.

Feig, L. (1990). *Drug exposed infants and children: Service needs and policy questions.* Washington, DC: U. S. Department of Health and Human Services, Office of Human Services Policy, Division of Children and Youth Policy.

The Future of Children. (1991). Special Issue: Drug exposed infants, 1(#1).

Miller, P. S. (1992). Segregated programs of teacher education in early childhood: Immoral and inefficient practice. *Topics in Early Childhood Special Education, 11*, 39-52.

Rist, M. C. (1990). The shadow children. *The American School Board Journal, 177*(1), 18-24.

Rodning, C., Beckwith, L., & Howard, J. (1989). Characteristics of attachment organization and play organization in prenatally drug-exposed toddlers. *Development and Psychopathology, 1*, 277-289.

Schneider, J. W., & Chasnoff, I. J. (1987). Cocaine abuse during pregnancy: Its effects on infant motor development—a clinical perspective. *Topics in Acute Care and Trauma Rehabilitation*, 2(1), 59-69.

Schneider, J. W., Griffith, D. R., & Chasnoff, I. J. (1989). Infants exposed to cocaine in utero: Implications for developmental assessment and intervention. *Infants and Young Children*, 2(1), 25-36.

Schutter, L. S., & Brinker, R. P. (1992). Conjuring a new category of disability from prenatal cocaine exposure: Are the infants unique biological or caretaking casualties? *Topics in Early Childhood Special Education, 11*(4), 84-111.

Spohr, H. L., & Steinhausen, H. C. (1987). Follow-up studies of children with fetal alcohol syndrome. *Neuropediatrics, 18*, 13-17.

Streissguth, A. P., Aase, J., Clarren, S. K., Randels, S. P., LaDue, R. A., & Smith, D. F. (1991). Fetal alcohol syndrome in adolescents and adults. *Journal of the American Medical Association, 265*(15), 1961-1967.

Viadero, D. (1992, January 29). New research finds little lasting harm for 'crack' children. *Education Week, XL* (19), 1, 10.

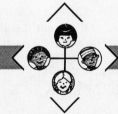

VOICES VOICES VOICES VOICES VOICES VOICES

"As educators we never do know who sits before us or where they can go. Only through education can we clear the many paths that lie before each and every student. We have the knowledge and the skill to unlock the closed doors that stand in the way of our children's development. Our attitude is the key. Actions speak far louder than words. Our lessons and materials are an integral part of our schools. But it is our philosophy of teaching and our behavior that have the greatest impact on our students.

Educators play a crucial role in determining the future of our society. We must understand this responsibility and open our hearts and minds to all students. Their souls are in our hands."

— Sandra McBrayer, 1994 National Teacher of the Year

Attention Deficit Disorders: A Guide for Teachers

Prepared by the Education Committee of CH.A.D.D. (Children With Attention Deficit Disorders)

Recommendations for Giving Instructions to Students:

1. Maintain eye contact with the ADD student during verbal instruction.
2. Make directions clear and concise. Be consistent with daily instructions.
3. Simplify complex directions. Avoid multiple commands.
4. Make sure ADD student comprehends before beginning the task.
5. Repeat in a calm, positive manner, if needed.
6. Help ADD child to feel comfortable with seeking assistance (most ADD children won't ask).
7. These children need more help for a longer period of time than the average child. Gradually reduce assistance.
8. Require a daily assignment notebook if necessary.
   a. Make sure student correctly writes down all assignments each day. If the student is not capable of this then the teacher should help the student.
   b. Parents and teachers sign notebook daily to signify completion of homework assignments.
   c. Parents and teachers may use notebook for daily communication with each other.

Recommendations for Students Performing Assignments:

1. Give out only one task at a time.
2. Monitor frequently. Use a supportive attitude.
3. Modify assignments as needed. Consult with special education personnel to determine specific strengths and weaknesses of the student. Develop an individualized educational program.
4. Make sure you are testing knowledge and not attention span.
5. Give extra time for certain tasks. The ADD student may work more slowly. Don't penalize for needed extra time.
6. Keep in mind that ADD children are easily frustrated. Stress, pressure and fatigue can break down the ADD child's self-control and lead to poor behavior.

Recommendations for Behavior Modification and Self-Esteem Enhancement

Providing Supervision and Discipline

a. Remain calm, state infraction of rule, and don't debate or argue with student.
b. Have pre-established consequences for misbehavior.
c. Administer consequences immediately and monitor proper behavior frequently.
d. Enforce rules of the classroom consistently.
e. Discipline should be appropriate to "fit the crime," without harshness.
f. Avoid ridicule and criticism. Remember, ADD children have difficulty staying in control.
g. Avoid *publicly* reminding students on medication to "take their medicine."

Recommendations for the Proper Learning Environment:

1. Seat ADD student near teacher's desk, but include as part of regular class seating.
2. Place ADD student up front with his back to the rest of the class to keep other students out of view.
3. Surround ADD student with "good role models," preferably students that the ADD child views as "significant others." Encourage peer tutoring and cooperative collaborative learning.
4. Avoid distracting stimuli. Try not to place the ADD student near:
   air conditioner
   heater
   high traffic areas
   doors or windows
5. ADD children do not handle change well so avoid:
   transitions
   changes in schedule
   disruptions
   physical relocations (monitor closely on field trips)
6. Be creative! Produce a "stimuli-reduced study area." Let all students have access to this area so the ADD child will not feel different.
7. Encourage parents to set up appropriate study space at home with routines established as far as set times for study, parental review of completed homework, and periodic notebook and/or book bag organized.

Using Medication in the Treatment of Attention Deficit Disorders

The use of medication alone in the treatment of ADD is *not* recommended. As indicated earlier, a multimodal treatment plan is usually followed for successful treatment of the ADD child or adolescent. While not all children having ADD are prescribed medication, in certain cases the proper use of medication can play an important and necessary part in the child's overall treatment.

Excerpt from prepared material. For more information on ADD, contact CH.A.D.D., 499 NW 70th Ave., Suite 308, Plantation, FL 33317, 1-305-587-3700.

Temperament

Natural Disposition

As many as 15% of all children are born with a difficult temperament

Learning Style

Sensory
Cultural
Perceptual

Developmental

Slower than average social/emotional growth

Unmet Needs

Love
Attention
Power
Stability/Security

Prenatal Conditions

Drug/Alcohol Exposed

As many as 18% of America's children

Other Conditions

Attention Deficit/Hyperactivity
Learning Problems
Physical/Emotional Abuse

DISCIPLINE: PUNISHMENT OR TEACHING?

PUNISHMENT	=	**Anger**
		Resentment
		Revenge
		Sadness
		Negativity
TEACHING	=	**Responsibility**
		Alternative Behaviors
		Actions/Consequences
		Good Judgment
		Values

SIX STEPS TO A SOLUTION

1. Identify <u>one</u> behavior you wish to work on.

2. Identify possible <u>causes</u> of problem.
   (seating? emotional needs? instructional issue?)

3. Identify possible <u>interventions</u> that address the cause as well as the disruptive behavior.

4. Identify <u>resources and support</u> as needed.

5. Implement the interventions and support with understanding that <u>there are no guarantees</u> that things will change quickly or that you have chosen the appropriate intervention.

6. Take a deep breath and <u>go back to number 3.</u>

Esther Wright, 1995

A REMINDER . . .

STUDENTS NEED

TO BE LOVED

TO BE HEARD

TO BE RESPECTED

TO BE SUPPORTED

TO BE ACKNOWLEDGED

TO BE SUCCESSFUL

TEACHERS NEED

TO BE LOVED

TO BE HEARD

TO BE RESPECTED

TO BE SUPPORTED

TO BE ACKNOWLEDGED

TO BE SUCCESSFUL

Esther Wright

What Does This Student Need?

This is the most important question to ask when dealing with chronic, persistent misbehavior. Use the following list as a menu — remembering that different students respond to different interventions based on their needs and the causes of their inappropriate behaviors.

Does This Student Need:

_______ More success and validation?

_______ Opportunities to be a leader?

_______ Opportunities to serve and contribute to others (special projects in school or community/ cross age tutoring)?

_______ More specific or clear guidelines for behavior?

_______ A behavior management contract?

_______ A buddy or mentor?

_______ An opportunity to express emotions and feelings appropriately (journal, art, counseling, physical activity?

_______ More rigorous consequences? (only after natural/logical consequences have failed)

_______ Good role models?

_______ More one-to-one attention? (volunteer, instructional aide)

_______ Shorter assignments? (for student with short attention span or cognitive delays)

_______ More choices regarding the instructional program? (alternatives for assignment, classroom activities)

_______ Parental support?

_______ More tangible rewards for appropriate behavior?

_______ A special "quiet place" to do work?

_______ Conflict resolution skills? (taught through role play, stories, discussion)

Implement one or more of these interventions until you discover the one that is effective for the student. How you implement these actions is as important as choosing the right one. Be calm, confident and positive. Make sure the student experiences these interventions as support rather than punishment.

♡ Loving Discipline Pledge ♡

- ♡ I promise to serve, support, and teach every child in my classroom.
- ♡ I promise to be a good role model for my students.
- ♡ I promise to exhibit positive attitudes and behaviors in this classroom.
- ♡ I promise to develop caring and respectful relationships with my students.
- ♡ I promise to bring out the goodness in my students throughout the school day.
- ♡ I promise to give students the opportunity to experience their ownership and responsibility for the classroom.
- ♡ I promise to help students develop empathy and compassion for each other.
- ♡ I promise to listen to my heart when managing disruptive students.
- ♡ I promise to use quiet, calm, and positive discipline interventions.
- ♡ I promise to respond, rather than react, when disciplining students.
- ♡ I promise to speak to my students as if they are future Harvard scholars.
- ♡ I promise to remember that my students want to be responsible and successful learners.
- ♡ I promise to value each student's unique self-expression.
- ♡ I promise to welcome parents as my partners.
- ♡ I promise to continue learning and growing in my classroom.
- ♡ I promise to be the best teacher I can be.
- ♡ I promise to remember that human beings cannot always keep their promises, and I will lovingly forgive myself when I am being human.

Teaching From The Heart

1-800-798-2686

Dear Parent(s),

This is your child's I CAN READ poetry folder. It is a vital part of your child's reading program as it contains the familiar print from the poems, songs and rhymes we have been learning in our classroom.

Each poem, rhyme, or song is first learned orally. This gives the oral language to call upon when we later connect the poem, song or rhyme to enlarged print during our Shared Reading time. Once the children are familiar with the print, they receive their own individual copy of the passage so that it can be illustrated and added to their notebook. Each week children will add 2-3 new passages to their notebook. By the end of the year your child will successfully read this wonderful collection.

Your child takes home this notebook once a week for reading pleasure and practice. It is helpful if a family member reads the passage first, if needed. That way your child again hears the flow of language and is better able to predict unknown words. A natural part of your child's reading development is memorization. As children practice reading the passages, they continue to recognize more words in print and also gain fluency. It is helpful to guide your child's hand or finger along the print while reading, so the oral language continues to be connected to print.

Children need help with their reading when they are having difficulty. The type of help we give is important. We want to keep children thinking as they are reading and teach them problem-solving strategies when they encounter unknown words.

These reading and thinking strategies include:

- Giving children "think time" to see what they attempt to do themselves.
- Asking children what would make sense there.
- Using the picture to figure the word out.
- Skipping the word and coming back to it, using initial and or final sounds.
- Going back to the beginning of the sentence and trying again after completing the reading.
- Substituting another word that makes sense.
- Telling children the word.

We find the least useful strategy for children (especially beginning readers) is to "sound it out." This stops the flow of the reading process and no longer enables children to read for meaning.

Once you and your child have enjoyed the notebook at home, return it to school the next morning. Please remind your child to return the folder in good condition, and it always needs to be transported to and from school in a bookbag!

Your role as Parents as Partners in Developing Literacy is so appreciated. Due to our work together, your child will celebrate the pleasure and joy in becoming a lifelong reader.

Sincerely,

Kathy Skinner

STRATEGIES FOR TEACHING READING

- **Big Books:** Whole group participation.
- **Book Sets:** (Multiple copy sets) Whole group and partner reading.
- **Basals:** (Choose the good stories!) Whole group and partner reading.
- **Poetry Theatre:** 10-15 minutes daily. Excellent for establishing one-to-one correspondence, phonetic and sight word skills and expression of language and self!
- **D.E.A.R. Time:** 10-15 minutes daily of silent reading (or observing!) that is self-selection.
- **Author Study:** Introduce and expose students to various authors and illustrators throughout the year.
- **Chapter Books:** To increase listening comprehension, attention span, vocabulary and exposure to good literature!
- **Mini Groups:** Based on interests and skill level.
- **D.O.L.** (Daily Oral Language) mini English lessons, whole group 5-10 minutes daily on the chalkboard.
- **Magic Letter:** Whole group, excellent tool for providing sight words, phonetic skills, English skills, Reading Recovery strategies.
- **Science / Social Studies Text:** Whole group, partner or individual reading.
- **Songs:** Good for memorization, one-to-one correspondence, expression and building confidence as a reader!
- **Reader's Choice**: (Ultimate goal!) Self-selection, reading at an independent level!

Reader's Choice Conference Sheet

NAME: ____________________

Date	Book Title	Comments

Kathy Skinner

Sample Monthly Reading/Writing Schedule

Whole Group Reading (one hour)	Writing Activities (30 minutes)
Week 1 Big Book — 15 min. Songs/Chants — 15 min. Basal Story — 30 min.	**Week 1** Class Big Books
Week 2 Magic Letter — 15 min. Author Focus — 15 min. Book Set — 30 min.	**Week 2** Individual Small Books (extensions springboards)
Week 3 Big Book — 15 min. Author Focus — 15 min. Reader's Choice — 30 min.	**Week 3** Individual Small Books
Week 4 Big Book — 15 min. Mini-Groups/Readers' Workshop — 45 min.	**Week 4** Class Big Book (with cross-grade pals)

STRATEGIES FOR TEACHING WRITING

JOURNALS: (diary style) Student directed.

"SHORT STUFF" BOOKS: Teacher directed. (Completing an idea.)

BOOK EXTENSIONS: The teacher models the writing process using books as models and springboards.

CLASS BIG BOOKS: Teacher/Student directed.

WRITER'S WORKSHOP: (The ultimate goal!) Student is self-selecting, brainstorming, and independently going through the steps of the writing process.

DEFINITION OF STAGES

(Creative Writing)

EMERGENT: Pictures, random and isolated letters, are telling a story. Student can verbalize complete thoughts.

EARLY: Begins to write 2 or 3 sentences on a subject.

FLUENT: Beginning to write stories with a distinct beginning, middle, and ending.

WEEKLY POETRY ROUTINE

Day One: Introduce new poem. Pass out copies to students and read poem to class. Read chorally and practice using expression. Discuss particular skill using highlighter markers, highlighter tape or crayons and the poem on chart paper.

Day Two: Practice previously introduced poem. Have students read lines or verses individually or by category. ("Read the next verse if you are wearing tennis shoes today.")

Day Three: Introduce new poem following the same routine as day one. Discuss particular skill using overhead projector and "magic" paddle.

Day Four: Review and practice previously introduced poems. Discuss vocabulary and related skills. Have students illustrate both poems.

Day Five: Poetry Theatre. Allow student volunteers to read or recite poems of their choice in front of the class. Give volunteers positive feedback and suggestions for improvement.

HAVE-A-GO

1ST ATTEMPT	2ND ATTEMPT	STANDARD SPELLING

Kathy Skinner

FEELINGS FORMULA

I feel ______________________________

when_______________________________

because____________________________

and I wish __________________________

Self-Evaluation Sheet for Writing

Name: ____________________ Date: ____________

What score do you give this piece of writing? (circle one)

1 2 3 4 5

Why did you give yourself this score?

____

____

____

Would you do anything differently on your next piece of writing?

____

____

____

Kathy Skinner

School Wide Transitions

- Progressive reports
- Increasing vocabulary by modeling
- Short-stuff books, chapter books, poetry, D.E.A.R. time
- Wee-Deliver postal program
- Cross-Grade Pals
- Math Their Way
- Feelings formula and feelings centers
- Free play and structured play
- Themes at each grade level
- Keeping the same group of students together each year

Paradigm Shifts

Dependent:

All do the same thing
Standardized
Teacher approval

Independent:

Do your own thing
Creative Writing
Responsibility

Interdependent:

Both one and connected
Unity
Inclusion

Kathy Skinner

Building Community

1. *Know Your Students*
    - basic needs met vs. needs not met
2. *Teach Social Skills*
    - helpful and kind
    - express gratitude
    - get attention from others in positive ways
    - assertiveness
3. *Build Trust, Love and Respect*
    - LOVE unites
    - FEAR separates

Life in the 90's
Factors Affecting Today's Children

- Divorce
- Developmentally Delayed Children
    - — "Crack" babies
    - — Fetal Alcohol Syndrome (FAS)
    - — Substance abuse
- Dysfunctional Families
- Violence
    - — home
    - — school
    - — community
- Homeless Children
- Latch-Key Children
- Transient Population
- Poor Quality Day Care
- Abused and Neglected Children
- Discrimination
- TV
- Poverty
- Hungry Children

NEEDS

EXTROVERTS

Time with others

Feedback

People to help them think

INTROVERTS

Time alone

Physical space

Time to reflect

Uninterrupted work time

EXTROVERTS

Draw their energy from others.

Talk, share ideas and experiences immediately

They have to tell you all that's happening and will follow you around and keep talking non-stop.

IDENTIFICATION

Gregarious and outgoing

Enjoys others and is energized by a group

Wants to share immediately

Thinks by talking

Talks a lot and easily initiates conversations

Hates being sent to room to be alone and comes to "cheer you up"

Lets you know what she's thinking and feeling

Needs lots of approval

INTROVERTS

Get their energy by being alone or with one or two special people.

Prefer to interact with world on the inside by reflecting on thoughts and feelings before sharing.

You have to ask questions because they don't readily share information.

IDENTIFICATION

Prefers to watch or listen before joining in

Prefers doing things by self or with best-friend

Becomes grouchy if around people too long

Being with strangers is draining

Doesn't like to discuss days' events until later

Strong sense of personal space

Doesn't mind going to room to sit alone

Difficult to share feelings

Guests or substitutes are "invasive"

May talk a lot with family members but is quieter among outsiders

TEMPERAMENT TRAITS

Intensity

Persistence

Sensitivity

Perceptiveness

Adaptability

Regularity

Energy

First Reaction

Mood

Kathy Skinner

Ways to Set Children Up to Succeed

- Acceptance
- Love
- Emphasize the good
- Take them seriously
- Be specific
- Healthy role model
- Reasonable expectations
- Tolerance
- Responsibility
- Be available
- Don't be petty
- Discipline vs. punishment
- Assume the best
- Show respect
- Ask for their help vs. Telling them

Old Negative Labels	New Exciting Labels
Manipulative	Charismatic
Impatient	Compelling
Anxious	Cautious
Explosive	Dramatic
Picky	Selective
Whiny	Analytical
Distractible	Perceptive
Stubborn	Assertive, a willingness to persist in the face of difficulties
Nosy	Curious
Wild	Energetic
Extreme	Tenderhearted
Inflexible	Traditional
Demanding	Holds high standards
Unpredictable	Flexible, a creative problem solver
Loud	Enthusiastic and zestful
Argumentative	Opinionated, strongly committed to one's goals

EXTROVERTS: A SUMMARY

Extroverted spirited children need to hear:

You're outgoing.

You share your thoughts and feelings easily.

You enjoy being with people.

You make others feel comfortable.

If you are an extrovert too:

Avoid isolating yourself at home with small children. Plan outings with other parents and children. Recognize that you need time with other adults in order to refuel.

Take time to talk through problems and issues with others before making a decision.

Let others know you need feedback. You aren't nagging.

Kathy Skinner

INTROVERTS: A SUMMARY

Introverted spirited children need to hear:

You think before you talk.

You enjoy spending time by yourself.

You need time alone to recharge.

You form deep and lasting relationships.

If you are an introvert too:

Recognize your need for time alone in order to refuel.

Let others know you need time to think before you can respond.

Appreciate your observation skills.

Kathy Skinner

Teaching Tips:

EXTROVERTS:	INTROVERTS:
Your extroverted child needs other people to help her recharge.	Make sure your introverted child has an opportunity to pull out of the action and refuel by being alone.
Provide her with lots of feedback.	Help your child to understand that she needs space and can ask for it without pushing others away.
Spend time talking with her to help her think through problems.	Allow your introverted child time to think before you expect a response.
Understand that her need for people and feedback is not a reflection of low self-esteem.	Avoid interrupting her when she is working.

Kathy Skinner

INTENSE SPIRITED KIDS NEED TO HEAR PHRASES LIKE:

You are enthusiastic.

You are expressive and lively.

You are easily frustrated.

You are very upset, but you are not dying.

Being intense does not mean being aggressive.

I think you are feeling anxious, angry, sad (or whatever the emotion might be).

When kids hear these messages over and over again, they are able to turn them into "I" messages.

AN INTENSE SPIRITED KID CAN LEARN TO TELL HIMSELF:

I am getting upset.

I can be angry without hurting someone.

I am really excited.

I like being enthusiastic.

My blood is starting to boil. I can't stand it in here.

I'm feeling crabby.

The rubber bands inside of me are starting to stretch.

Kathy Skinner

Multiage Organizations

National Alliance of Multiage Educators (N.A.M.E.)
Ten Sharon Road, Box 577
Peterborough, NH 03458
1-800-924-9621

N.A.M.E. is a networking organization for educators who want to share ideas, information, and experiences with others who have a similar interest in multiage and continuous progress practices. N.A.M.E. is also a source of information on books and audiovisual materials about multiage. Membership is open to those considering multiage as well as those already teaching and supervising it.

n.a.m.e.
NATIONAL ALLIANCE OF MULTIAGE EDUCATORS sm
Ten Sharon Road, PO Box 577
Peterborough, NH 03458

Membership Application

SB 9 1996-97

Name ____________________

Position ____________________

Grade/age levels taught ____________________

Home Address ____________________

Town/City ____________________ State __________ Zip __________

Home phone ____________________

School phone ____________________

Name of School ____________________

School Address ____________________

Town/City ____________________ State __________ Zip __________

N.A.M.E. membership will be under (circle one) individual school

___ I want to join N.A.M.E. My membership fee is enclosed.($15 individual, $30 school)

For school membership, photocopy and complete this form for each of the 3 members.

International Registry of Nongraded Schools (IRONS)
Robert H. Anderson, Co-director (with Barbara N. Pavan)
PO Box 271669
Tampa, FL 33688-1699

IRONS is housed at the University of South Florida. It has been established to gather information about individual schools or school districts that are either in the early stages of developing a nongraded program or well along in their efforts. Its purpose is to facilitate intercommunication and research efforts. There is a phase one membership and a full membership.

Multiage Classroom Exchange
Teaching K-8
40 Richards Ave.
Norwalk, CT 06854

The Multiage Classroom Exchange puts teachers in contact with others who are interested in swapping ideas, activities, and experiences relating to the multiage, progressive classroom.

To join, send your name, address, age levels you teach, years of experience with multiage education, and a self-addressed, stamped envelope to the address listed. You'll receive a complete, up-to-date list of teachers who are interested in exchanging information.

California Alliance for Elementary Education
Charlotte Keuscher, Program Consultant
California Department of Education
721 Capitol Mall, 3rd Floor
Sacramento, CA 95814

The Elementary Education Office and the California Alliance for Elementary Education have published the second and third installments of The Multiage Learning Source Book.

The second installment is a guide for teachers, principals, parents, and community members who are involved and interested in multiage learning. It contains descriptions of what multiage learning is and is not, questions staffs and parents need to explore before and during the implementation stage, samples of how schools have communicated to their communities about multiage learning, classroom curriculum vignettes, anecdotes from schools that have successfully implemented multiage learning under a variety of conditions, descriptions of multiage programs throughout the state, and current and relevant research and articles.

The third installment deals with evaluation of a multiage program and assessment in multiage classrooms. Copies of the Source Book are distributed free of charge to California Alliance for Elementary Education members.

California Multiage Learning Task Force
(see California Alliance for Elementary Education)

Much of the multiage learning effort in California is guided by the Multiage Learning Task Force, which is made up of California Alliance for Elementary Education teachers, principals, parents, board of education members and university professors. The group has provided guidance and material for The Multiage Learning Source Book and are practitioners of multiage learning.

Networks supporting multiage education are being developed throughout California, coordinated by the Elementary Education Office, which assists the startup of the groups. Once started the groups operate independently.

Under Construction
Jane Meade-Roberts
202 Riker Terrace Way
Salinas, CA 93901
Phone (408) 455-1831 (to leave message)

Under Construction's goal is to assist teachers, parents and administrators in gaining an understanding of how children and adults construct knowledge, and to support experienced teachers who are working to understand constructivist theory and its implications for teaching. (Constructivism is a scientific theory of learning, based on Piaget's theory of cognitive development, that explains how people come to build their own knowledge and understand the things and people in their own world.)

The organization feels that multiage classrooms are wonderfully suited for helping adults learn more about how children develop and construct knowledge. Many of the teachers and parents in the group are currently involved in multiage classrooms or are interested in developing their understanding of constructivism so that they may begin a multiage learning environment for children in their own school.

Under Construction is an umbrella for several groups working toward this end. The Constructivist Network of Monterey County, which meets monthly, is largely composed of university personnel and some school teachers. The network provides a speaker series for the community. A focus group includes teachers involved in coaching and classroom visitations. The organization is collaborating with the local adult school to provide classes for parents of children in multiage classrooms, and has just begun to work with a new local university, with the object of working with people in the community. An advisory board oversees the organization.

The organization is funded by the Walter S. Johnson Foundation.

OTHER ORGANIZATIONS

Center of Excellence for Research in Basic Skills
Tennessee State University
330 Tenth Avenue North, Suite J
Nashville, TN 37203
(615) 963-7238

Contact *Jayne Zaharias* for more information on the Student/Teacher Achievement Ratio Project (Project STAR). The project has studied the effect of class size on learning.

FairTest
National Center for Fair & Open Testing
342 Broadway
Cambridge, MA 02139-9745
(617) 864-4810

The National Center for Fair & Open Testing has literature discussing the serious inequities involved in standardized testing and offers information about alternative, authentic assessment.

Research Concepts
1368 Airport Road
Muskegan, MI 49444

Research Concepts offers a readiness checklist developed by psychologist John Austin.

NEWSLETTER

MAGnet Newsletter
805 W. Pennsylvania
Urbana, IL 61801-4897

The MAGnet Newsletter provides information about schools that have implemented multiage practices.

ERIC

ERIC (Educational Resources Information Center) is a clearinghouse or central agency responsible for the collection, classification, and distribution of written information related to education. If you need help finding the best way to use ERIC, call ACCESS ERIC toll-free at 1-800-LET-ERIC. If you need specific information about multiage education, call Norma Howard at 1-800-822-9229.

A Value Search: Multiage or Nongraded Education is available for $7.50 and can be ordered from Publication Sales, ERIC Clearinghouse on Educational Management, 5207 University of Oregon, Eugene, OR 97403-5207. A handling charge of $3.00 is added to all billed orders.

Workshops and Conferences

The Society For Developmental Education
Ten Sharon Road, Box 577
Peterborough, NH 03458
1-800-462-1478

The Society For Developmental Education (SDE) presents workshops and conferences throughout the year and around the country for elementary educators on multiage, inclusion education, multiple intelligences, character education, discipline, whole language, authentic assessment, and related topics.

SDE sponsors an International Multiage Conference each July. For information on dates and location, write or phone SDE at the address or number listed above.

Child Advocacy Organizations

Children's Defense Fund
25 E. St. NW
Washington, DC 20077-0176

Inclusive Education Resources

A.D.D. Warehouse
300 Northwest 70th Ave. Suite 102
Plantation, FL 33317
1-800-233-9273
FAX: (954) 792-8545
Internet: www.addwarehouse.com
Books, tapes, videos on ADD and hyperactivity

Paul H. Brookes Publishing Co. (catalog available)
P.O. Box 10624
Baltimore, MD 21285-0624
1-800-638-3775

Centre for Integrated Education and Community
24 Thome Crescent
Toronto, Ontario M6H 2S5

CH.A.D.D. (Children with Attention Deficit Disorder)
499 NW 70th Ave., Suite 308
Plantation, FL 33317
(305) 587-3700

The Council for Exceptional Children
1920 Association Drive
Reston, VA 22091-1589
(703) 620-3660
(publishes *Exceptional Children, Teaching Exceptional Children* and *CEC Today*.)

Down Syndrome News
National Down Syndrome Congress
1605 Chantilly Dr., Suite 250
Atlanta, GA 30324
1-800-232-6372

Exceptional Children's Assistance Center
PO Box 16
Davidson, NC 28036
(704) 892-1321
1-800-962-6817 (NC only)
FAX: (704) 892-5028

The Exchange
The Learning Disabilities Network
72 Sharp St., Suite A-2
Hingham, MA 02043
(617) 340-5605

Impact
Publications Office
Institute on Community Integration
University of Minnesota
109 Pattee Hall, 150 Pillsbury Dr. S.E.
Minneapolis, MN 55455
(612) 624-4512

Inclusion Press International
24 Thome Crescent
Toronto, Ontario M6H 2S5
(416) 658-5363
FAX: (416) 658-5067
e-mail: Compuserve: 74640, 1124
Web Page: http: //inclusion.com

Learning Disabilities Association (LDA)
4156 Library Rd.
Pittsburgh, PA 15234
(412) 341-1515
FAX: (412) 344-0224

MPACT (Missouri Parents Act)
8631 Delmar, Suite 300
St. Louis, MO 63124
1-800-995-3160

PEAK (Parent Center, Inc.)
6055 Lehman Dr., Suite 101
Colorado Springs, CO 80918
(719) 531-9400
FAX: (719) 531-9452
Inclusion resources, practical tools for educating ALL students in general education classrooms

Whole Language Hotline

In the fall of 1991, the Center for the Expansion of Language and Thinking (CELT) began sponsoring a crisis hotline to support teachers and administrators who come under attack for their child-centered practices.

For further information, contact:
The Center for Establishing Dialogue in Teaching and Learning (CED)
325 E. Southern Ave., Suite 107-108
Tempe, AZ 85282
1-602-894-1333 • FAX 602-894-9547

Publications

Children's Literature

Book Links: Connecting Books, Libraries and Classrooms
American Library Association
50 Huron St.
Chicago, IL 60611

The Bulletin of the Center for Children's Books
University of Illinois Press
1325 S. Oak St.
Champaign, Il 61820

CBC Features
Children's Book Council
568 Broadway, Suite 404
New York, NY 10012

Children's Literature and Reading
(special interest group of the International Reading Association)
Membership: Dr. Miriam A. Marecek
10 Marchant Rd.
Winchester, MA 01890

The Horn Book Magazine
11 Beacon St., Suite 1000
Boston, MA 02105

The Horn Book also publishes *The Horn Book Guide to Children's and Young Adult Books*, a semi-annual publication reviewing nearly 4000 hardcover trade books each year.

Journal of the Children's Literature Council of Pennsylvania
226 East Emaus St.
Middletown, PA 17057

Journal of Children's Literature
Children's Literature Assembly
Membership: Marjorie R. Hancock
2037 Plymouth Rd.
Manhattan, KS 66503

The Kobrin Letter (reviews nonfiction books)
732 Greer Rd.
Palo Alto, CA 94303

The New Advocate
Christopher-Gordon Publishers, Inc.
480 Washington St.
Norwood, MA 02062

Reading Is Fundamental (RIF)
600 Maryland Ave. S.W.
Suite 600
Washington, D.C. 20024-2569
(202) 287-3220
For information on starting a RIF program or for parent brochures.

The WEB (Wonderfully Exciting Books)
The Ohio State University
Room 200 Ramseyer Hall
29 West Woodruff
Columbus, OH 43210

Early Childhood / Developmental Education

Childhood Education
Journal of the Association for Childhood Education International
Suite 315
11501 Georgia Ave.
Wheaton, MD 20902

Early Childhood News
Peter Li, Inc.
330 Progress Road
Dayton, OH 45449
(513) 847-5900

Early Childhood Today
Scholastic, Inc.
555 Broadway
New York, NY 10012

Young Children
National Association for the Education of Young Children (NAEYC)
1509 16th St. NW
Washington, DC 20036-1426
1-800-424-2460

General Education — Classroom Focus

Creative Classroom
Children's Television Workshop
P.O. Box 53148
Boulder, CO 80322-3148

Instructor Magazine
Scholastic, Inc.
555 Broadway
New York, NY 10012-3999

Learning
1607 Battleground Avenue
Greensboro, NC 27408

Teaching K-8
40 Richards Ave.
Norwalk, CT 06854

General Education — Issues/Research Focus

The American School Board Journal / Executive Educator
National School Boards Association
1680 Duke St.
Alexandria, VA 22314

Democracy and Education
The Institute for Democracy and Education
College of Education
313 McCracken Hall, Ohio University
Athens, OH 45701-2979

Education Week
P.O. Box 2083
Marion, OH 43305
Editorial:
4301 Connecticut Ave. NW #250
Washington, DC 20008

Educational Leadership
Journal of the Association for Supervision and Curriculum Development (ASCD)
1250 N. Pitt St.
Alexandria, VA 22314-1403

Phi Delta Kappan
Eighth and Union
P.O. Box 789
Bloomington, IN 47402
Journal of Phi Delta Kappan International
The professional fraternity in education

Principal
National Association of Elementary School Principals (NAESP)
1615 Duke St.
Alexandria, VA 22314-3483

The Responsive Classroom: A Newsletter for Teachers
Northeast Foundation for Children
71 Montague City Rd.
Greenfield, MA 01301
1-800-360-6332

The School Administrator
American Association of School Administrators
1801 North Moore St.
Arlington, VA 22209

Teaching Voices
The Massachusetts Field Center for Teaching and Learning
University of Massachusetts
100 Morrissey Blvd.
Boston, MA 02125

TIP (Theory into Practice)
Subscription Dept.
The Ohio State University
174 Arps Hall
1945 N. High St.
Columbus, OH 43210-1172

Language *(See also Whole Language, this section)*

Language Arts
National Council of Teachers of English
1111 W. Kenyon Rd.
Urbana, IL 61801-1096

Literacy
The International Institute of Literacy Learning
Box 1414
Commerce, TX 75429

Primary Voices K-6
National Council of Teachers of English
1111 W. Kenyon Rd.
Urbana, IL 61801-1096

The Reading Teacher
International Reading Association
P.O. Box 8139
Newark, DE 19714-8139
(IRA also publishes *Journal of Adolescent and Adult Literacy, Reading Today, Reading Research Quarterly; Lectura y Vida* — a Spanish language journal.)

Math and Science

Science and Children
National Science Teachers Association
1840 Wilson Blvd.
Arlington, VA 22201-3000

Teaching Children Mathematics
National Council of Teachers of Mathematics
1906 Association Dr.
Reston, VA 22091

Whole Language

The Whole Idea
The Wright Group
19201 120th Ave. NE
Bothell, WA 98011

Whole Language Network
Teaching K-8
40 Richards Ave.
Norwalk, CT 06854

The Whole Language Teachers Association Newsletter
P.O. Box 216
Southboro, MA 01772

WLSIG Newsletter
Whole Language Umbrella

President: Sharon Murphy
Faculty of Education
Ross Building, York University
4700 Keele St.
North York, ON M3J 1P3 Canada
(416) 650-8059
FAX (416) 650-8097

Send membership inquiries to: Whole Language Umbrella - Membership
Ross Building, York University
4700 Keele St.
North York, ON M3J 1P3 Canada
(416) 650-8059
FAX (416) 650-8097

Newsjournal: Jane and Jerry Bartow
520 Kingsview Lane
Plymouth, MN 55447

Sources of Multiage Materials

Crown Publications
546 Yates Street
Victoria, British Columbia
Canada V8W 1K8
Phone: (604) 386-4636
FAX: (604) 386-0221
Distributes books and videos for the Province of British Columbia Ministry of Education.

Crystal Springs Books
Ten Sharon Road
PO Box 500
Peterborough, NH 03458
Phone: 1-800-321-0401
FAX: 1-800-337-9929

Big Book Publishers

Creative Teaching Press, Inc.
P.O. Box 6017
Cypress, CA 90630-0017
1-800-444-4287

Richard C. Owen Publishers, Inc.
P.O. Box 585
Katonah, NY 10536
1-800-336-5588

Sundance Publishing
P.O. Box 1326
Littleton, MA 01460
1-800-343-8204

The Wright Group
19201 12th Ave. NE
Bothell, WA 98011
1-800-523-2371

Materials

Big Book Materials

Sticky pockets — Demco Library Supplies and Equipment, 1-800-356-1200

Velour paper — Dick Blick Art Supply, 1-800-345-3042

Grommets — Hardware stores

Alphabet & number stickers — Childcraft Education Corp., 1-800-631-5652

"Scribbles" Glitter Writers — Arts and crafts stores or Duncan Hobby, (209) 291-2515

Binding Machines and Spiral Binding

General Binding Corporation
One GBC Plaza
Northbrook, IL 60062
(847) 723-1500

Scholastic, Inc. — 1-800-724-6527

Book Racks/Easels

Fixturecraft Corp.
443 East Westfield Ave.
P.O. Box 292
Roselle Park, NJ 07204-0292
1-800-275-1145

Chart Paper/Sentence Strips

School Specialty – New England Division
P.O. Box 3004
Agawam, MA 01101-8004
1-800-628-8608

J.L.Hammett Company
P.O. Box 859057
Braintree, MA 02185-9057
1-800-333-4600

Computer Programs

Print Shop
Broderbund
500 Redwood Blvd.
P.O. Box 6121
Novato, CA 94948-6121
1-800-521-6263

SuperPrint
Scholastic
P.O. Box 7502
Jefferson City, MO 65102
1-800-724-6527

Educational Records Center

Catalog for Songs
3233 Burnt Mill Drive, Suite 100
Wilmington, NC 28403-2655
1-800-438-1637

Highlight Tape

Available through Crystal Springs Books
1-800-321-0401

Kinesiology

Brain Gym®
Developmental activities to help children learn more effectively
Educational Kinesiology Foundation
P.O. Box 3396
Ventura, CA 93006-3396
1-800-356-2109

Manatee Adoption

Save the Manatee Club
500 N. Maitland Ave., Suite 210
Maitland, FL 32751
(407) 539-0990
($10.00/year)

Math Books & Products

Creative Publications
5623 W. 115th Street
Worth, IL 60482-9931
(800) 624-0822

Crystal Springs Books
Ten Sharon Road, PO Box 500
Peterborough, NH 03458
(800) 321-0401

Cuisenaire
PO Box 5026
White Plains, NY 10602-5026
(800) 237-0338

Dale Seymour Publications
PO Box 10888
Palo Alto, CA 94303-0879
(800) 872-1100

Dandy Lion Publications
3563-L Sueldo
San Luis Obispo, CA 93401
(800) 776-8032

Delta Education
PO Box 3000
Nashua, NH 03061-9912
(800) 442-5444

Interact (Simulation Units)
1825 Gillespie Way, #101
El Cajon, CA 92020-1095
(800) 359-0961

The Math Shop
Quantexx
PO Box 694
Canfield, OH 44406
(800) 798-MATH

National Council of Teachers of Mathematics
PO Box 25405
Richmond, VA 23260-5405
(800) 235-7566

Scholastic, Inc.
2931 E. McCarty Street
Jefferson City, MO 65101
(800) 325-6149

Educational Electronics (Calculator Dist.)
70 Finnell Drive
Weymouth Landing, MA 02188
(617) 331-4190

Metal Shower Curtain Rings

Department Stores

Plastic Rings/Bird Bands

Farm Feed Stores

Ribbons and Awards

Hodges Badge Company, Inc.
1-800-556-2440

Sea Monkey Eggs

Sea Monkeys
Transcience Corporation
P.O. Box 809
Bryans Road, MD 20616

Stencil Machines

The Ellison LetterMachine
Ellison Educational Equipment, Inc.
P.O. Box 8209
Newport Beach, CA 92658-8209
1-714-724-0555

Touch phonics Reading Systems

Manipulative Phonics System
4900 Birch Street
Newport Beach, CA 92660
(714) 975-1141
(800) 92-TOUCH (928-6824)
FAX (714) 975-1056

Whale Adoption

Whale Adoption Project
International Wildlife Coalition
634 N. Falmouth Highway
P.O. Box 388
N. Falmouth, MA 02556-0388
($15.00/year)

Wikki Stix

Available through Crystal Springs Books
1-800-321-0401

More Than Books

Expanding Children's Horizons Through Magazines

Publication Subscription Address	Interest Area/Age Group
Big Book Magazine Scholastic, Inc. P.O. Box 10805 Des Moines, IA 50380-0813 1-800-788-7017	General Interest 4-7
Boys' Life Boy Scouts of America 1325 Walnut Hill Lane P.O. Box 152079 Irving, TX 75015-2079	General Interest 7-18
The C.A.R.E. Package (Children's Authors Make Reading Exciting) Apple Peddler 25112 Woodfield School Rd. Gaithersburg, MD 20882-3715	Children's Authors 5-10
Classical Calliope 7 School St. Peterborough, NH 03458-1454	World History 9-16
Cobblestone 7 School St. Peterborough, NH 03458-1454	American History 8-14
* *Creative Kids* P.O. Box 8813 Waco, TX 76714-8813 1-800-998-2208 FAX: 1-800-240-0333 e-mail: Creative_kids@prufrock.com Submissions: Attn: Submissions Editor P.O. Box 6448 Mobile, AL 36660	Student Art/Writing 8-14
* *Cricket* P.O. Box 7433 Red Oak, IA 51591-4433 Submissions: 315 5th St., P.O. Box 300 Peru, IL 61354	Literature/Art 9-14
Faces 7 School St. Peterborough, NH 03458-1454	World Cultures 8-14
* *Highlights for Children* P.O. Box 269 Columbus, OH 43216-0269 Submissions: 803 Church St. Honesdale, PA 18431	General Interest 2-12
KIDS Discover P.O. Box 54209 Boulder, CO 80321-4209	Science/General Interest 5-12
Kids Life and Times Kids Life Submissions: Children's Television Workshop One Lincoln Plaza New York, NY 10023	Entertainment/Education 6-12

Publication Subscription Address	Interest Area/Age Group
Ladybug Red Oak, IA 51591	Literature 2-6
* *Merlyn's Pen* The National Magazines of Student Writing, Grades 6-12 P.O. Box 1058 East Greenwich, RI 02818	Student Writing 12-16
National Geographic World P.O. Box 2330 Washington, DC 20013-2330	Science/General Interest 8-14
* *Odyssey* 7 School St. Peterborough, NH 03458-1454	Space Exploration/ Astronomy 8-14
Plays 120 Boylston St. Boston, MA 02116-4615	Drama 6-18
Ranger Rick National Wildlife Federation 8925 Leesburg Pike Vienna, VA 22180-0001	Science/Wildlife Nature, Environment 6-12
* *School Mates* 186 Route 9W New Windsor, NY 12553	Chess for Beginners 7 and up
Scienceland 501 Fifth Ave. Suite 2108 New York, NY 10017-6107	Science 5-11
Sesame Street Magazine P.O. Box 52000 Boulder, CO 80321-2000	General Interest 2-6
Sports Illustrated for Kids P.O. Box 830609 Birmingham, AL 35283-0609	Sports 8-13
* *Stone Soup* The Magazine by Young Writers and Artists P.O. Box 83 Santa Cruz, CA 95063	Student Writing/Art 6-14
Storyworks Scholastic 555 Broadway New York, NY 10012-3999	Literature 8-11
3-2-1 Contact P.O. Box 51177 Boulder, CO 80321-1177	Science 8-14
Your Big Backyard National Wildlife Federation 8925 Leesburg Pike Vienna, VA 22184	Animals/Conservation 3-5

***encourages children's submissions**

Paperback Book Clubs

The Trumpet Club
P.O. Box 604
Holmes, PA 19043
1-800-826-0110

Troll Book Club
2 Lethbridge Plaza
Mahwah, NJ 07430
1-800-541-1097

Bibliography

Anti-Hurrying

Elkind, David. *All Grown Up & No Place to Go.* Reading, MA: Addison-Wesley, 1984.

———. *The Hurried Child.* Reading, MA: Addison-Wesley, 1981.

———. *Miseducation: Preschoolers at Risk.* New York: Alfred A. Knopf, 1987.

National Education Commission on Time and Learning. *Prisoners of Time.* Washington, DC: U.S. Government Printing Office, Superintendent of Documents, 1994.

Packard, Vance. *Our Endangered Children.* Boston: Little, Brown & Co., 1983.

Uphoff, James K. *Real Facts From Real Schools: What You're Not Supposed To Know About School Readiness and Transition Programs.* Rosemont, NJ: Modern Learning Press, 1990, 1995.

Uphoff, James, K.; Gilmore, June; and Huber, Rosemarie. *Summer Children: Ready (or Not) for School.* Middletown, OH: The Oxford Press, 1986.

Attention Deficit Disorder (ADD) / Attention Deficit Hyperactivity Disorder (ADHD)

Bain, Lisa J. *A Parent's Guide to Attention Deficit Disorders.* New York: Dell, 1991.

Copeland, Edna D., and Love, Valerie L. *Attention Without Tension: A Teacher's Handbook on Attention Disorders (ADHD and ADD).* Atlanta, GA: 3 C's of Childhood, 1990.

Hallowell, Edward M., and Ratey, John J. *Driven to Distraction.* New York: Touchstone, 1994.

Hartmann, Thom. *Attention Deficit Disorder: A Different Perception.* Penn Valley, CA, and Lancaster PA: Underwood-Miller, 1993.

Moss, Deborah. *Shelley, the Hyperactive Turtle.* Rockville, MD: Woodbine House, 1989.

Moss, Robert A., and Dunlap, Helen Huff. *Why Johnny Can't Concentrate: Coping with Attention Deficit Problems.* New York: Bantam Books, 1990.

Parker, Harvey. *The ADD Hyperactivity Handbook for Schools.* Plantation, FL: Impact Publications, 1992.

———. *The ADD Hyperactivity Workbook for Parents, Teachers, and Kids.* Plantation, FL: Impact Publications, 1988.

———. *The ADAPT Accommodation Planbook for Teachers.* Plantation, FL: Impact Publications, 1992.

———. *The ADAPT Student Planbook.* Plantation, FL: Impact Publications, 1992.

Quinn, Patricia O., M.D., and Stern, Judith M., M.A. *Putting on the Brakes: Young People's Guide to Understanding Attention Deficit Hyperactivity Disorder (ADHD).* New York: Magination Press, 1991.

———. *The "Putting on the Brakes" Activity Book for Young People With ADHD.* New York: Magination Press, 1993.

Rief, Sandra. *How to Reach and Teach ADD/ADHD Children.* West Nyack, NY: The Center for Applied Research in Education, 1993.

Shapiro, Lawrence E. *Sometimes I Drive My Mom Crazy, But I Know She's Crazy About Me.* King of Prussia, PA: The Center for Applied Psychology, inc., 1993.

Taylor, John F. *Helping Your Hyperactive/Attention Deficit Child.* Rocklin, CA: Prima Publishing, 1994.

Assessment

Anthony, Robert. *Evaluating Literacy.* Portsmouth, NH: Heinemann, 1991.

Baskwill, Jane, and Whitman, Paulette. *Evaluation: Whole Language, Whole Child.* New York: Scholastic. 1988.

Batzle, Janine. *Portfolio Assessment and Evaluation: Developing and Using Portfolios in the K-6 Classroom.* Cypress, CA: Creative Teaching Press, 1992.

Belanoff, Pat, and Dickson, Marcia, eds. *Portfolios: Process and Product.* Portsmouth, NH: Heinemann, 1991.

Clay, Marie. *An Observation Survey of Early Literacy Achievement.* Portsmouth, NH: Heinemann, 1993.

———. *Sand* and *Stones: "Concepts About Print" Tests.* Portsmouth, NH: Heinemann, 1980.

Clemmons, J.; Laase, L.; Cooper, D.; Areglado, N.; and Dill, M. *Portfolios in the Classroom: A Teacher's Sourcebook.* New York: Scholastic, Inc., 1993.

Cochrane, Orin, and Cochrane, Donna. *Whole Language Evaluation for Classrooms.* Bothell, WA: The Wright Group, 1992.

Daly, Elizabeth, ed. *Monitoring Children's Language Development.* Portsmouth, NH: Heinemann, 1992.

Goodman, Kenneth, ed. *The Whole Language Evaluation Book.* Portsmouth, NH: Heinemann, 1988.

Goodman, Yetta et al. *Reading Miscues Inventory: Alternative Procedures.* New York: Richard C. Owen Publishers, 1987.

Graves, Donald, and Sustein, Bonnie, eds. *Portfolio Portraits.* Portsmouth, NH: Heinemann, 1992.

Harp, Bill, ed. *Assessment and Evaluation in Whole Language Programs.* Norwood, MA: Christopher Gordon Publishers, 1993.

Kamii, C., ed. *Achievement Testing in the Early Grades: The Games Grownups Play.* Washington, DC: National Association for the Education of Young Children, 1990.

Keshner, Judy. *The Kindergarten Teacher's Very Own Student Assessment and Observation Guide.* Rosemont, NJ: Modern Learning Press, 1996.

Lazear, David. *Multiple Intelligence Approaches to Assessment: Solving the Assessment Conundrum.* IRI/Skylight Publishing, Inc., 1994.

Parsons, Les. *Response Journals.* Portsmouth, NH: Heinemann, 1989.

Picciotto, Linda. *Evaluation: A Team Effort.* Ont.: Scholastic, 1992.

Sharp, Quality Quinn. *Evaluation in the Literature-Based Classroom: Whole Language Checklists Grades K-6.* New York: Scholastic, 1989.

Tierney, Robert J.; Carter, Mark A.; and Desai, Laura E. *Portfolio Assessment in the Reading-Writing Classroom.* Norwood, MA: Christopher Gordon, 1991.

Traill, Leanna. *Highlight My Strengths.* Reed Publications, 1993.

Behavior / Discipline

Albert, Linda. *An Administrator's Guide to Cooperative Discipline.* Circle Pines, MN: American Guidance, 1989.

———. *Cooperative Discipline: How to Manage Your Classroom and Promote Self-Esteem.* Circle Pines, MN: American Guidance Service, 1996.

———.*Linda Albert's Advice for Coping With Kids.* Tampa, FL: Alkorn House, 1992.

Bluestein, Jane. *21st Century Discipline—Teaching Students Responsibility and Self-Control.* New York: Scholastic, 1988.

Burke, Kay. *What to Do with the Kid Who ... Developing Cooperation, Self-Discipline and Responsibility in the Classroom.* Palatine, IL: IRI/Skylight Publishing, 1992.

Coletta, Anthony. *What's Best for Kids: A Guide to Developmentally Appropriate Practices for Teachers & Parents of Children Ages 4-8.* Rosemont, NJ: Modern Learning Press, 1991.

Curwin, Richard L., and Mendler, Allen N. *Discipline with Dignity.* Alexandria, VA: Association for Supervision and Curriculum Development, 1993.

———.*Am I in Trouble? Using Discipline to Teach Young Children Responsibility.* Santa Cruz, CA: Network Publications, 1990.

Glasser, William, M.D. *Control Theory: A New Explanation of How We Control Our Lives.* New York: HarperPerennial, 1984.

———.*The Quality School: Managing Students Without Coercion.* New York: HarperPerennial, 1992.

———.*The Quality School Teacher: A Companion Volume to the Quality School.* New York: HarperPerennial, 1993.

Kohn, Alfie. *Punished by Rewards: The Trouble with Gold Stars, Incentive Plans, A's, Praise, and Other Bribes.* Boston: Houghton Mifflin, 1993.

Kreidler, William. *Creative Conflict Resolution: Strategies for Keeping Peace in the Classroom.* Glenview, IL: Scott, Foresman, & Co., 1984.

Kurchinka, Mary Sheedy. *Raising Your Spirited Child.* New York: Harper, 1991.

Kuykendall, Crystal. *From Rage to Hope: Strategies for Reclaiming Black & Hispanic Students.* Bloomington, IL: National Educational Service, 1992.

Mendler, Allen. *Smiling at Yourself: Educating Young Children About Stress and Self-Esteem.* Santa Cruz, CA: Network Publications, 1990.

———.*What Do I Do When? How to Achieve Discipline with Dignity in the Classroom.* Bloomington, IL: National Educational Service, 1992.

Nelson, Jane, Ed.D. *Positive Discipline.* New York: Ballantine Books, 1987 by Jane Nelson.

Nelson, Jane; Lott, Lynn; and Glenn, Stephen. *Positive Discipline in the Classroom.* Rocklin, CA: Prima Publishing, 1993.

Reider, Barbara. *A Hooray Kind of Kid.* Folsom, CA: Sierra House Publishing, 1988.

Vail, Priscilla. *Emotion: The On-Off Switch for Learning.* Rosemont, NJ: Modern Learning Press, 1994.

Wright, Esther. *Good Morning, Class — I Love You!* Rolling Hills, CA: Jalmar Press, 1988.

———.*Loving Discipline A to Z.* San Francisco: Teaching From the Heart, 1994.

Cooperative Learning

Cohen, Dorothy. *Designing Groupwork: Strategies for the Heterogeneous Classroom.* New York: Teachers College Press, 1994.

Curran, Lorna. *Cooperative Learning Lessons for Little Ones: Literature-Based Language Arts and Social Skills.* San Juan Capistrano, CA: Resources for Teachers, Inc., 1992.

DeBolt, Virginia, with Dr. Spencer Kagan. *Write! Cooperative Learning and The Writing Process.* San Juan Capistrano, CA: Kagan Cooperative Learning, 1994.

Ellis, Susan S., and Whalen, Susan F. *Cooperative Learning: Getting Started.* New York: Scholastic, 1990.

Fisher, Bobbi. *Thinking and Learning Together: Curriculum and Community in a Primary Classroom.* Portsmouth, NH: Heinemann, 1995.

Forte, Imogene, and MacKenzie, Joy. *The Cooperative Learning Guide and Planning Pak for Primary Grades: Thematic Projects and Activities.* Nashville, TN: Incentive Publications, 1992.

Johnson, David, and Johnson, Roger. *Cooperation and Competition: Theory and Research.* Edina, MN: Interaction Book Company, 1989.

———.*Learning Together and Alone.* Englewood Cliffs, NJ: Prentice Hall, Inc, 1991.

Kagan, Spencer. *Cooperative Learning.* San Juan Capistrano, CA: Resources for Teachers, Inc., 1994.

Shaw, Vanston, with Spencer Kagan, Ph.D. *Communitybuilding In the Classroom.* San Juan Capistrano, CA: Kagan Cooperative Learning, 1992.

Slavin, Robert. *Cooperative Learning.* Englewood Cliffs, NJ: Prentice-Hall, 1989.

———. *Cooperative Learning.* Boston: Allyn and Bacon, 1995.

Curriculum — Overview

Bredekamp, Sue, and Rosegrant, Teresa, eds. *Reaching Potentials: Appropriate Curriculum and Assessment for Young Children,* Vol. 1. Washington, DC: NAEYC, 1992.

Dodge, Diane Trister; Jablon, Judy R.; and Bickart, Toni S. *Constructing Curriculum for the Primary Grades.* Washington, DC: Teaching Strategies, Inc., 1994.

Fogarty, Robin. *The Mindful School: How to Integrate the Curricula.* Palatine, IL: Skylight Publishing, 1991.

National Association of Elementary School Principals. *Standards for Quality Elementary and Middle Schools: Kindergarten through Eighth Grade.* Alexandria, VA, 1990.

Rowan, Thomas E., and Morrow, Lorna J. *Implementing the K-8 Curriculum and Evaluation Standards: Readings from the "Arithmetic Teacher."* Reston, VA: National Council of Teachers of Mathematics, 1993.

Short, Kathy, and Burke, Carolyn. *Creating Curriculum.* Portsmouth, NH: Heinemann, 1981.

Stevenson, S. Christopher and Carr, Judy F. *Integrated Studies in the Middle School: Dancing Through Walls.* New York: Teachers College Press, 1993.

Whitin, D.; Mills, H.; and O'Keefe, T. *Living and Learning Mathematics: Stories and Strategies for Supporting Mathematical Literacy.* Portsmouth, NH: Heinemann, 1990.

Curriculum — Integrated Activities (see page 366 for math section)

Bauer, Karen, and Drew, Rosa. *Alternatives to Worksheets.* Cypress, CA: Creative Teaching Press, 1992.

Brainard, Audrey, and Wrubel, Denise H. *Literature-Based Science Activities: An Integrated Approach.* New York: Scholastic, 1993.

Cherkerzian, Diane. *The Complete Lesson Plan Book.* Peterborough, NH: Crystal Springs Books, 1993.

Chertok, Bobbi, et al. *Learning About Ancient Civilizations Through Art.* NY: Scholastic, 1992.

Cochrane, Orin, ed. *Reading Experiences in Science.* Winnipeg, Man.: Peguis, 1985.

Goin, Kenn; Ripp, Eleanor; and Solomon, Kathleen Nastasi. *Bugs to Bunnies: Hands-on Animal Science Activities for Young Children.* New York: Chatterbox Press, 1989.

Hiatt, Catherine; Wolven, Doug; Botka, Gwen; and Richmond, Jennifer. *More Alternatives to Worksheets.* Cypress, CA: Creative Teaching Press, 1994.

Huck, Charlotte, and Hickman, Janet, eds. *The Best of the Web.* Columbus, OH: Ohio State University, 1982.

Irvine, Joan. *How to Make Pop-ups.* New York: Beech Tree Books, 1987.

———. *How to Make Super Pop-ups.* New York: Beech Tree Books, 1992.

Jorgensen, Karen. *History Workshop.* Portsmouth, NH: Heinemann, 1993.

Julio, Susan. *The Complete Geography Project & Activity Book.* NY: Scholastic, 1993.

Kohl, MaryAnn, and Potter, Jean. *ScienceArts: Discovering Science Through Art Experiences.* Bellingham, WA: Bright Ring Publishing, 1993.

McCarthy, Tara. *Literature-Based Geography Activities: An Integrated Approach.* New York: Scholastic, 1992.

Ritter, Darlene. *Literature-Based Art Activities (K-3).* Cypress, CA: Creative Teaching Press, 1992.

———. *Literature-Based Art Activities (4-6).* Cypress, CA: Creative Teaching Press, 1992.

Rothstein, Gloria Lesser. *From Soup to Nuts: Multicultural Cooking Activities and Recipes.* New York: Scholastic, 1994.

Ruef, Kerry. *The Private Eye. Looking/Thinking by Analogy: A Guide to Developing the Interdisciplinary Mind.* Seattle: The Private Eye Project, 1992.

Spann, Mary Beth. *Literature-Based Multicultural Activities.* New York: Scholastic, 1992.

———. *Literature-Based Seasonal and Holiday Activities.* New York: Scholastic, 1991.

Developmental Education / Readiness

Ames, Louise Bates. *What Do They Mean I'm Difficult?* Rosemont, NJ: Modern Learning Press, 1986.

Ames, Louise Bates; Baker, Sidney; and Ilg, Frances L. *Child Behavior (Specific Advice on Problems of Child Behavior).* New York: Barnes & Noble Books, 1981.

Ames, Louise Bates, and Chase, Joan Ames. *Don't Push Your Pre-Schooler.* New York: Harper & Row, 1980.

Ames, Louise Bates, and Haber, Carol Chase. *He Hit Me First (When Brothers and Sisters Fight).* New York: Dembner Books, 1982.

———. *Your Seven-Year-Old (Life in a Minor Key).* New York: Dell, 1985.

———. *Your Eight-Year-Old (Lively and Outgoing).* New York: Dell, 1989.

———. *Your Nine-Year-Old (Thoughtful and Mysterious).* New York: Dell, 1990.

Ames, Louise Bates, and Ilg, Frances L. *Child Behavior.* New York: Barnes & Noble Books, 1955.

———. *The Child from Five to Ten.* New York: Harper & Row, 1946.

———. *Your Two-Year-Old (Terrible or Tender).* New York: Dell, 1980.

———. *Your Three-Year-Old (Friend or Enemy).* New York: Dell, 1980.

———. *Your Four-Year-Old (Wild and Wonderful).* New York: Dell, 1980.

———. *Your Five-Year-Old, Sunny and Serene.* New York: Dell, 1979.

———. *Your Six-Year-Old, Loving and Defiant.* New York: Dell, 1979.

———. *Your Ten-to-Fourteen Year-Old.* New York: Dell, 1981.

Ames, Louise Bates; Ilg, Frances L.; and Haber, Frances L. *Your One-Year-Old (The Fun-Loving 12-to-24-month-old).* New York: Delacorte, 1982.

Ames, Louise Bates, et al. *The Gesell Institute's Child from One to Six.* New York: Harper & Row, 1946.

Bluestein, Jane. *Being a Successful Teacher—A Practical Guide to Instruction and Management.* Belmont, CA: Fearon Teacher Aids, 1988.

Boyer, Ernest. *The Basic School: A Community for Learning.* Ewing, NJ: Carnegie Foundation for the Advancement of Learning, 1995.

———. *Ready to Learn: A Mandate for the Nation.* Princeton, NJ: The Foundation for the Advancement of Teaching, 1991.

Brazelton, T. Berry. *To Listen to a Child: Understanding the Normal Problems of Growing Up.* Reading, MA: Addison-Wesley, 1986.

———. *Touchpoints: The Essential Reference. Your Child's Emotional and Behavioral Development.* Reading, MA: Addison-Wesley, 1994.

Bredekamp, Sue, ed. *Developmentally Appropriate Practice in Early Childhood Programs Serving Children From Birth Through Age 8,* expanded edition. Washington, DC: National Association for the Education of Young Children, 1987.

Coletta, Anthony. *Kindergarten Readiness Checklist for Parents.* Rosemont, NJ: Modern Learning Press, 1991.

Elovson, Allanna. *The Kindergarten Survival Book.* Santa Monica, CA: Parent Ed Resources, 1991.

Grant, Jim. *Childhood Should Be a ~~Pressure~~ Precious Time.* (poem anthology) Rosemont, NJ: Modern Learning Press, 1989.

———. *Developmental Education in the 1990's.* Rosemont, NJ: Modern Learning Press, 1991.

———. *"I Hate School!" Some Common Sense Answers for Parents Who Wonder Why, Including the Signs and Signals of the Overplaced Child.* Rosemont, NJ: Programs for Education, 1994.

———. *Jim Grant's Book of Parent Pages.* Rosemont, NJ: Programs for Education, 1988.

———. *Worth Repeating: Giving Children a Second Chance at School Success.* Rosemont, NJ: Modern Learning Press, 1989.

Grant, Jim, and Azen, Margot. *Every Parent's Owner's Manuals. (Three-, Four-, Five-, Six-, Seven-Year- Old).* Rosemont, NJ. Programs for Education.

Hardin, Sonya, and Ridgley, Linda. *Ready, Set, Go! to Kindergarten.* Helping children transition from preschool to kindergarten. Video. Doulos Productions, P.O. Box 1351, Hickory, NC 28603-1351. 1-800-354-9982.

Healy, Jane M. *Endangered Minds: Why Children Don't Think and What We Can Do About It.* New York: Simon and Schuster, 1990.

———. *Your Child's Growing Mind: A Guide to Learning and Brain Development From Birth to Adolescence.* New York: Doubleday, 1987.

Karnofsky, Florence, and Weiss, Trudy. *How to Prepare Your Child for Kindergarten.* Carthage, IL: Fearon Teacher Aids, 1993.

Lamb, Beth, and Logsdon, Phyllis. *Positively Kindergarten: A Classroom-proven, Theme-based Developmental Guide for the Kindergarten Teacher.* Rosemont, NJ: Modern Learning Press, 1991.

Mallory, Bruce, and New, Rebecca, eds. *Diversity and Developmentally Appropriate Practices: Challenges for Early Childhood Education.* New York: Teachers College Press, 1994.

National Association of Elementary School Principals. *Early Childhood Education and the Elementary School Principal.* Alexandria, VA: NAESP, 1990.

National Association of State Boards of Education. *Right from the Start: The Report of the NASBE Task Force on Early Childhood Education.* Alexandria, VA: NASBE, 1988.

Northeast Foundation for Children. *A Notebook for Teachers: Making Changes in the Elementary Curriculum.* Greenfield, MA, 1991.

Reavis, George H. *The Animal School.* Rosemont, NJ: Modern Learning Press, 1988.

Singer, Dorothy, and Revenson, Tracy. *How a Child Thinks: A Piaget Primer.* Independence, MO: International University Press, 1978.

Wood, Chip. *Yardsticks: Children in the Classroom Ages 4-12.* Greenfield, MA: Northeast Foundation for Children, 1994.

Grade Replacement

Ames, Louise Bates. *What Am I Doing in This Grade?* Rosemont, NJ: Modern Learning Press, 1985.

———. *Is Your Child in the Wrong Grade?* Rosemont, NJ: Modern Learning Press, 1978.

Ames, Louise Bates; Gillespie, Clyde; and Streff, John W. *Stop School Failure.* Rosemont, NJ: Modern Learning Press, 1972.

Grant, Jim. *I Hate School: Common-Sense Solutions for Teachers & Parents Who Wonder Why.* Rosemont, NJ: Modern Learning Press, 1986.

———. *Worth Repeating.* Rosemont, NJ: Modern Learning Press, 1989.

Hobby, Janice Hale. *Staying Back.* Gainesville, FL: Triad, 1990.

Moore, Sheila, and Frost, Roon. *The Little Boy Book.* New York: Clarkson N. Potter, 1986.

Grade Replacement — Audio/Video

(All from Modern Learning Press, PO Box 167, Rosemont, NJ 08556. 1-800-627-5867)

Ames, Louise Bates. *Part I: Ready Or Not: Here I Come!* and *Part II: An Evaluation of the Whole Child,* video. 1983.

Gesell Institute of Human Development. *Ready or Not Here I Come!* Video/16 mm film. 1984.

Grant, Jim. *Do You Know Where Your Child Is?* Video. 1985.

———. *Grade Replacement.* Audiotape. 1988.

———. *Jim Grant Live.* Audiotape. 1985.

———. *Worth Repeating.* Video. 1988.

Inclusion / Differently Abled / Learning Disabilities

Dudley-Marling, Curtis. *When School is a Struggle.* New York: Scholastic, 1990.

Bailey, D.B, and Wolery, M. *Teaching Infants and Preschoolers with Handicaps.* Columbus, OH: Merrill, 1984.

Dunn, Kathryn B., and Dunn, Allison B. *Trouble with School: A Family Story about Learning Disabilities.* Rockville, MD: Woodbine House, 1993.

Fagan, S.A.; Graves, D.L.; and Tressier-Switlick, D. *Promoting Successful Mainstreaming: Reasonable Classroom Accommodations for Learning Disabled Students.* Rockville, MD: Montgomery Couny Public Schools, 1984.

Goodman, Gretchen. *I Can Learn! Strategies and Activities for Gray-Area Children.* Peterborough, NH: Crystal Springs Books, 1995.

———. *Inclusive Classrooms from A to Z: A Handbook for Educators.* Columbus, OH: Teachers' Publishing Group, 1994.

Harwell, Joan. *Complete Learning Disabilities Handbook.* New York: Simon & Schuster, 1989.

Lang, Greg, and Berberich, Chris. *All Children are Special: Creating an Inclusive Classroom.* York, ME: Stenhouse Publishers, 1995.

McGregor, G., and Vogelsberg, R.T. *Transition Needs Assessment for Parents.* Philadelphia, PA: Temple University, 1989.

Perske, R. and Perske, M. *Circle of Friends.* Nashville, TN: Abingdon Press, 1988.

Phinney, Margaret. *Reading with the Troubled Reader.* Portsmouth, NH: Heinemann, 1989.

Rainforth, Beverly; York, Jennifer; and McDonald, Cathy. *Collaborative Teams for Students with Severe Disabilities.* Baltimore: Paul H. Brookes, 1992.

Rhodes, Lynn, and Dudley-Marling, Curtis. *Readers and Writers with a Difference: A Holistic Approach to Teaching Learning Disabled and Remedial Students.* Portsmouth: Heinemann, 1988.

Society For Developmental Education. *Creating Inclusive Classrooms: Education for All Children.* Peterborough, NH: 1994.

Stainback, S., and Stainback, W. *Curriculum Considerations in Inclusive Classrooms: Facilitating Learning for All Students.* Baltimore: Paul H. Brookes, 1992.

———. *Support Networks for Inclusive Schooling.* Baltimore: Paul H. Brookes, 1990.

Stainback, S, Stainback, W., and Forest, M., eds. *Educating All Students in the Mainstream of Regular Education.* Baltimore: Paul H. Brookes, 1987.

Vail, Priscilla. *About Dyslexia.* Rosemont, NJ: Programs for Education, 1990.

———. *Smart Kids with School Problems.* New York: E.P. Dutton, 1987.

Villa, R., et al. *Restructuring for Caring and Effective Education: Administrative Strategies for Creating Heterogeneous Schools.* Baltimore: Paul H. Brookes, 1992.

Language Arts

Atwell, Nancie. *Coming to Know: Writing to Learn in the Middle Grades.* Portsmouth, NH: Heinemann, 1990.

———. *In the Middle: Writing, Reading, and Learning with Adolescents.* Portsmouth, NH: Heinemann, 1987.

———. *Side by Side: Essays on Teaching to Learn.* Portsmouth, NH: Heinemann, 1991.

Barron, Marlene. *I Learn to Read and Write the Way I Learn to Talk.* Katonah, NY: Richard C. Owen Publishers, 1990.

Baskwill, Jane, and Whitman, Paulette. *A Guide to Classroom Publishing.* Toronto: Scholastic TAB, 1988.

———. *Moving On: Whole Language Sourcebook for Grades 3 and 4.* Toronto, Ont.: Scholastic TAB, 1988.

———. *Whole Language Sourcebook: Grades K-2.* Toronto: Scholastic TAB, 1986.

Beeler, Terri. *I Can Read! I Can Write! Creating a Print-Rich Environment.* Cypress, CA: Creative Teaching Press, 1993.

Bromley, Karen. *Journalling: Engagements in Reading, Writing, and Thinking.* New York: Scholastic, 1993.

Buros, Jay. *Why Whole Language?* Rosemont, NJ: Programs for Education, 1991.

Calkins, Lucy M. *The Art of Teaching Writing.* Portsmouth, NH: Heinemann, 1986.

———. *Lessons from a Child: On the Teaching and Learning of Writing.* Portsmouth, NH: Heinemann, 1983.

———. *Living Between the Lines.* Portsmouth, NH: Heinemann, 1990.

Cambourne, Brian. *The Whole Story.* New York: Scholastic, 1988.

Cambourne, Brian, and Brown, Hazel. *Read and Retell.* Portsmouth, NH: Heinemann, 1990.

Cambourne, Brian, and Turbill, Jan. *Coping with Chaos.* Portsmouth, NH: Heinemann, 1988.

Clay, Marie. *Becoming Literate.* Portsmouth, NH: Heinemann, 1991.

———. *Observing Young Readers.* Portsmouth, NH: Heinemann, 1982.

———. *Reading Recovery: A Guidebook for Teachers in Training.* Portsmouth, NH: Heinemann, 1993.

Cloonan, Kathryn L. *Sing Me A Story, Read Me a Song* (Books I and II). Beverly Hills, FL: Rhythm & Reading Resources, 1991.

———. *Whole Language Holidays.* (Books I and II). Beverly Hills, FL: Rhythm & Reading Resources, 1992.

Daniels, Harvey. *Literature Circles: Voice and Choice in the Student-Centered Classroom.* York, ME: Stenhouse Publishers, 1994.

Danielson, Kathy Everts, and Rogers, Sheri Everts. *Literature Connections Day-by-Day.* New York: Scholastic, 1994.

Davidson, Merrilyn et al. *Moving on with Big Books.* Auckland, New Zealand: Ashton Scholastic, 1989.

DeFord, Diane et al. *Bridges to Literacy.* Portsmouth, NH: Heinemann, 1991.

Dewey, John. *The Child and the Curriculum* and *The School and Society.* Chicago: Phoenix Books, combined edition, 1956.

Drutman, Ava Deutsch, and Huston, Diane L. *150 Surefire Ways to Keep Them Reading All Year.* New York: Scholastic, 1992.

Dudley-Marling, Curtis, and Searle, Dennis. *When Students Have Time to Talk.* Portsmouth, NH: Heinemann, 1991.

Eisele, Beverly. *Managing the Whole Language Classroom: A Complete Teaching Resource Guide for K-6 Teachers.* Cypress, CA: Creative Teaching Press, 199l.

Fairfax, Barbara, and Garcia, Adela. *Read! Write! Publish!* Cypress, CA: Creative Teaching Press, 1992.

Fiderer, Adele. *Teaching Writing: A Workshop Approach.* NY: Scholastic, 1993.

Fisher, Bobbi. *Joyful Learning: A Whole Language Kindergarten.* Portsmouth, NH: Heinemann, 1991.

Freeman, Yvonne, and Freeman, David. *Whole Language for Second Language Learners.* Portsmouth, NH: Heinemann, 1992.

Fulwiler, Toby, ed. *The Journal Book.* Portsmouth, NH: Heinemann, 1987.

———. *Programs That Work: Models and Methods for Writing Across the Curriculum.* Portsmouth, NH: Heinemann, 1990.

Goodman, Kenneth. *What's Whole in Whole Language?* New York: Scholastic, 1986.

Goodman, Kenneth, et al. *Language and Thinking in School: A Whole-Language Curriculum.* Katonah, NY: Richard C. Owen Publishers, 1987.

———. *Report Card on Basals.* New York: Richard C. Owen Publishers, 1988.

Goodman, Yetta. *How Children Construct Literacy.* Newark, DE: International Reading Association, 1990.

Goodman, Yetta M.; Hood, Wendy J.; and Goodman, Kenneth S. *Organizing for Whole Language.* Portsmouth, NH: Heinemann, 1991.

Graves, Donald. *Build a Literate Classroom.* Portsmouth, NH: Heinemann, 1991.

———. *Discover Your Own Literacy.* Portsmouth, NH: Heinemann, 1990.

———. *Experiment with Fiction.* Portsmouth, NH: Heinemann, 1990.

———. *Investigate Nonfiction.* Portsmouth, NH: Heinemann, 1989.

———. *Writing: Teachers and Children at Work.* Portsmouth, NH: Heinemann, 1983.

Graves, Donald, and Stuart, Virginia. *Write from the Start.* New York: New American Library, 1985.

Grindall, Karen. *Strategies and Activities for Building Literacy.* NY: Scholastic, 1993.

Haack, Pam, and Merrilees, Cynthia. *Ten Ways to Become a Better Reader.* Cleveland, OH: Modern Curriculum Press, 1991.

———. *Write on Target.* Peterborough, NH: The Society For Developmental Education, 1991.

Hall, Nigel, and Robertson, Anne. *Some Day You Will No All About Me: Young Children's Explorations in the World of Letters.* Portsmouth, NH: Heinemann, 1991.

Hansen, Jane. *When Writers Read.* Portsmouth, NH: Heinemann, 1987.

Hansen, Jane; Newkirk, Thomas; and Graves, Donald, eds. *Breaking Ground: Teachers Relate Reading and Writing in the Elementary School.* Portsmouth, NH: Heinemann, 1985.

Harste, Jerome, and Short, Kathy. *Creating Classrooms for Authors: The Reading-Writing Connection.* Portsmouth, NH: Heinemann, 1988.

Harste, Jerome; Woodward, Virginia; and Burke, Carolyn. *Language Stories and Literacy Lessons.* Portsmouth, NH: Heinemann, 1984.

Heard, Georgia. *For the Good of the Earth and Sun: Teaching Poetry.* Portsmouth, NH: Heinemann, 1989.

Holdaway, Don. *The Foundations of Literacy.* New York: Scholastic, 1979.

———. *Stability and Change in Literacy Learning.* Portsmouth, NH: Heinemann, 1984.

Hubbard, Ruth, and Power, Brenda. *The Art of Classroom Inquiry.* Portsmouth, NH: Heinemann, 1993.

Johnson, Paul. *A Book of One's Own.* Portsmouth, NH: Heinemann, 1992.

———. *Literacy Through the Book Arts.* Portsmouth, NH: Heinemann, 1993.

Karelitz, Ellen Blackburn. *The Author's Chair and Beyond.* Portsmouth, NH: Heinemann, 1993.

Kitagawa, Mary, and Kitagawa, Chisato. *Making Connections with Writing.* Portsmouth, NH: Heinemann, 1987.

Kovaks, Deborah, and Preller, James. *Meet the Authors and Illustrators: 60 Creators of Favorite Children's Books Talk about Their Work,* Vol. 1. New York: Scholastic, 1991.

———. *Meet the Authors and Illustrators: 60 Creators of Favorite Children's Books Talk about Their Work,* Vol. 2. New York: Scholastic, 1993.

Lynch, Priscilla. *Using Big Books and Predictable Books.* New York: Scholastic, 1987.

Mann, Jean. *Literacy Labels* (six book set). Columbus, OH: Essential Learning Products, 1994.

McCracken, Robert and Marlene. *Stories, Songs and Poetry to Teach Reading and Writing.* Chicago: American Library Association, 1986.

———.*Reading, Writing and Language: A Practical Guide for Primary Teachers.* Winnipeg, Man.: Peguis, 1995.

McVitty, Walter. *Children and Learning.* PETA (Heinemann), 1985.

———.*Getting It Together: Organizing the Reading-Writing Classroom.* Portsmouth, NH: Heinemann, 1986.

Moen, Christine Boardman. *Teaching With Caldecott Books.* NY: Scholastic, 1991.

———. *Teaching With Newberry Books.* NY: Scholastic, 1994.

Mooney, Margaret. *Developing Life-Long Readers.* Katonah, NY: Richard C. Owen Publishers, 1988.

Murray, Donald. *Learning by Teaching.* Portsmouth, NH: Boynton-Cook, 1982.

Olsen, Janet. *Envisioning Writing.* Portsmouth, NH: Heinemann, 1992.

Pavelka, Patricia. *Making the Connection: Learning Skills Through Literature.* Peterborough, NH: Crystal Springs Books, 1995.

Picciotto, Linda Pierce. *Managing an Integrated Language Arts Classroom.* Ontario: Scholastic, 1995.

Pigdon, Keith, and Woolley, Marilyn. *The Big Picture: Integrating Children's Learning.* Portsmouth, NH: Heinemann, 1993.

Raines, Shirley C., and Canady, Robert J. *Story Stretchers.* Mt. Ranier, MD: Gryphon House, 1989.

———.*More Story Stretchers.* Mt. Ranier, MD: Gryphon House, 1991.

———.*Story Stretchers for the Primary Grades.* Mt. Ranier, MD: Gryphon House, 1992.

Routman, Regie. *Transitions: From Literature to Literacy.* Portsmouth, NH: Heinemann, 1988.

———.*Invitations: Changing as Teachers and Learners K-12.* Portsmouth, NH: Heinemann, 1991.

Schlosser, Kristin G., and Phillips, Vicki L. *Building Literacy with Interactive Charts.* New York: Scholastic, 1991.

Strickland, Dorothy. *Emerging Literacy: Young Children Learn to Read and Write.* Newark, DE: International Reading Assoc., 1989.

Sunflower, Cherilyn. *75 Creative Ways to Publish Students' Writing.* New York: Scholastic, 1993.

Taylor, Denny. *Family Literacy.* Portsmouth, NH: Heinemann, 1983.

———.*Learning Denied.* Portsmouth, NH: Heinemann, 1990.

Taylor, Denny, and Dorsey-Gaines, Catherine. *Growing Up Literate.* Portsmouth, NH: Heinemann, 1990.

Vail, Priscilla. *Common Ground: Whole Language and Phonics Working Together.* Rosemont, NJ: Programs for Education, 1991.

Wells, Gordon. *The Meaning Makers.* Portsmouth, NH: Heinemann, 1986.

Wollman-Bonilla, Julie. *Response Journals.* New York: Scholastic, 1991.

Language Arts — Bilingual

Whitmore, Kathryn F., and Crowell, Caryl G. *Inventing a Classroom: Life in a Bilingual, Whole Language Learning Community.* York, ME: Stenhouse Publishers, 1994.

Language Arts — Spelling and Phonics

Bolton, Faye, and Snowball, Diane. *Ideas for Spelling.* Portsmouth, NH: Heinemann, 1993.

Booth, David. *Spelling Links.* Ontario: Pembroke Publishers, 1991.

Fry, Edward, Ph.D. *1000 Instant Words.* Laguna Beach, CA: Laguna Beach Educational Books, 1994.

———.*Phonics Patterns: Onset and Rhyme Word Lists.* Laguna Beach Educational Books, 1994.

Gentry, J. Richard. *My Kid Can't Spell.* Portsmouth, NH: Heinemann, 1996.

———. *Spel . . . Is a Four-Letter Word.* New York: Scholastic, 1987.

Gentry, J. Richard, and Gillet, Jean Wallace. *Teaching Kids to Spell.* Portsmouth, NH: Heinemann, 1993.

Trisler, Alana, and Cardiel, Patrice. *My Word Book.* Rosemont, NJ: Modern Learning Press, 1994.

———.*Words I Use When I Write.* Rosemont, NJ: Modern Learning Press, 1989.

———.*More Words I Use When I Write.* Rosemont, NJ: Modern Learning Press, 1990.

Wagstaff, Janiel. *Phonics That Work! New Strategies for the Reading/Writing Classroom.* New York: Scholastic, 1995.

Learning Centers

Cook, Carole. *Math Learning Centers for the Primary Grades.* West Nynack, NY: The Center for Applied Research, 1992.

Ingraham, Phoebe Bell. *Creating and Managing Learning Centers: A Thematic Approach.* Peterborough, NH: Crystal Springs Books, fall 1996.

Isbell, Rebecca. *The Complete Learning Center Book.* Beltsville, MD: Gryphon House, 1995.

Poppe, Carol A., and Van Matre, Nancy A. *Language Arts Learning Centers for the Primary Grades.* West Nynack, NY: The Center for Applied Research in Education, 1991.

———.*Science Learning Centers for the Primary Grades.* West Nyack, NY: The Center for Applied Research in Education, 1985.

Spann, Mary Beth. *Quick-and-Easy Learning Centers: Word Play.* NY: Scholastic, 1995. (Grades 1-3)

———. *Quick-and-Easy Learning Centers: Writing.* NY: Scholastic, 1995. (Grades 1-3)

Wait, Shirleen S. *Reading Learning Centers for the Primary Grades.* West Nynack, NY: The Center for Applied Research, 1992.

Waynant, Louise, and Wilson, Robert M. *Learning Centers, A Guide for Effective Use.* Paoli, PA: Instructo Corp., 1974.

Learning Styles / Multiple Intelligences

Armstrong, Thomas. *In Their Own Way: Discovering and Encouraging Your Child's Personal Learning Style.* NY: Putnam, 1987.

———.*Multiple Intelligences in the Classroom.* Alexandria, VA: Association for Supervision and Curriculum Development, 1994.

———. *Seven Kinds of Smart: Identifying and Developing Your Many Intelligences.* New York: A Plume Book, 1993.

Banks, Janet Caudill. *Creative Projects for Independent Learners.* CATS Publications, 1995.

Bloom, Benjamin S. *All Our Children Learning: A Primer for Teachers and Other Educators.* New York: McGraw-Hill, 1981.

———,ed. *Developing Talent in Young People.* New York: Ballantine, 1985.

Campbell, Bruce. *The Multiple Intelligences Handbook: Lesson Plans and More* . . . . Stanwood, WA: Campbell & Associates, 1994.

Campbell, Linda; Campbell, Bruce; and Dickinson, Dee. *Teaching and Learning Through Multiple Intelligences.* Needham Heights, MA: Allyn & Bacon, 1996.

Carbo, Marie. *Reading Styles Inventory Manual.* Roslyn Heights, New York: National Reading Styles Institute, 1991.

Carbo, Marie; Dunn, Rita; and Dunn, Kenneth. *Teaching Students to Read Through Their Individual Learning Styles.* Needham Heights, MA: Allyn & Bacon, 1991.

Gardner, Howard. *Frames of Mind: The Theory of Multiple Intelligences.* New York: Basic Books, 1985.

———.*Multiple Intelligences: The Theory in Practice.* New York: Basic Books, 1990.

———.*The Unschooled Mind: How Children Think and How Schools Should Teach.* New York: Basic Books, 1990.

Gilbert, Labritta. *Do Touch: Instant, Easy Hands-on Learning Experiences for Young Children.* Mt. Ranier, MD: Gryphon House, 1989.

Grant, Janet Millar. *Shake, Rattle and Learn: Classroom-Tested Ideas That Use Movement for Active Learning.* York, ME: Stenhouse Publishers, 1995.

Lazear, David. *Seven Pathways of Learning: Teaching Students and Parents About Multiple Intelligences.* Tucson, AZ: Zephyr Press, 1994.

———.*Seven Ways of Knowing: Teaching for Multiple Intelligences.* Palatine, IL: IRI/Skylight Publishing, Inc., 1991.

———.*Seven Ways of Teaching: The Artistry of Teaching With Multiple Intelligences.* Palatine, IL: IRI/Skylight Publishing, Inc. 1991.

Vail, Priscilla. *Gifted, Precocious, or Just Plain Smart.* Rosemont, NJ: Programs for Education, 1987.

———.*Learning Styles: Food for Thought and 130 Practical Tips for Teachers K-4.* Rosemont, NJ: Modern Learning Press, 1992.

Looping

Forsten, Char. *The Multiyear Lesson Plan Book.* Peterborough, NH: Crystal Springs Books, 1996.

Grant, Jim. *The Looping Classroom.* Peterborough, NH: Crystal Springs Books, 1996. (Video) Two versions: one for teachers and administrators and one for parents.

Grant, Jim; Johnson, Bob; and Richardson, Irv. *The Looping Handbook: Teachers and Students Progressing Together.* Peterborough, NH: Crystal Springs Books, 1996.

Hanson, Barbara. "Getting to Know You: Multiyear Teaching," *Educational Leadership,* November 1995.

Million, June. "To Loop or Not to Loop? This is a Question for Many Schools." *NAESP Communicator.* Vol. 18, Number 6, February 1996.

Multiage Education

American Association of School Administrators. *The Nongraded Primary: Making Schools Fit Children,* Arlington, VA, 1992.

Anderson, Robert H., and Pavan, Barbara Nelson. *Nongradedness: Helping It to Happen.* Lancaster, PA: Technomic Press, 1992.

Banks, Janet Caudill. *Creating the Multi-age Classroom.* Edmonds, WA: CATS Publications, 1995.

Bingham, Anne A.; Dorta, Peggy; McClasky, Molly; and O'Keefe, Justine. *Exploring the Multiage Classroom.* York, ME: Stenhouse Publishers, 1995.

Bridge, Connie A.; Reitsma, Beverly S.; and Winograd, Peter N. *Primary Thoughts: Implementing Kentucky's Primary Program.* Lexington, KY: Kentucky Department of Education, 1993.

Burruss, Bette, and Fairchild, Nawanna. *The Primary School: A Resource Guide for Parents.* Lexington, KY: The Prichard Committee for Academic Excellence and The Partnership for Kentucky School Reform, 1993. PO Box 1658, Lexington, KY 40592-1658, 800-928-2111.

Chase, Penelle, and Doan, Joan. *Full Circle: A New Look at Multiage Education.* Portsmouth, NH: Heinemann, 1994.

Davies, Anne; Politano, Colleen; and Gregory, Kathleen. *Together is Better.* Winnipeg, Canada: Peguis Publishers, 1993.

Crystal Springs Books. *Multiage Handbook: A Comprehensive Resource for Multiage Practices.* Peterborough, NH: CSB. Available in January, 1996.

Fogarty, Robin, ed. *The Multiage Classroom: A Collection.* Palantine, IL: Skylight Publishing, 1993.

Gaustad, Joan. "Making the Transition From Graded to Nongraded Primary Education." *Oregon School Study Council Bulletin,* 35(8), 1992.

———."Nongraded Education: Mixed-Age, Integrated and Developmentally Appropriate Education for Primary Children." *Oregon School Study Council Bulletin,* 35(7), 1992.

———."Nongraded Education: Overcoming Obstacles to Implementing the Multiage Classroom." 38(3,4) *Oregon School Study Council Bulletin,* 1994.

Gayfer, Margaret, ed. *The Multi-grade Classroom: Myth and Reality.* Toronto: Canadian Education Association, 1991.

Goodlad, John I., and Anderson, Robert H. *The Nongraded Elementary School.* New York: Teachers College Press, 1987.

Grant, Jim, and Johnson, Bob. *A Common Sense Guide to Multiage Practices.* Columbus, OH: Teachers' Publishing Group, 1995.

Grant, Jim; Johnson, Bob; and Richardson, Irv. *Multiage Q&A: 101 Practical Answers to Your Most Pressing Questions.* Peterborough, NH: Crystal Springs Books, 1995.

———. *Our Best Advice: The Multiage Problem Solving Handbook.* Peterborough, NH: Crystal Springs Books, 1996.

Grant, Jim and Richardson, Irv, compilers. *Multiage Handbook: A Comprehensive Resource for Multiage Practices.* Peterborough, NH: Crystal Springs Books, 1996.

Gutierrez, Roberto, and Slavin, Robert E. *Achievement Effects of the Nongraded Elementary School: A Retrospective Review.* Baltimore, MD: Center for Research on Effective Schooling for Disadvantaged Students, 1992.

Hunter, Madeline. *How to Change to a Nongraded School.* Alexandria, VA: Association for Supervision and Curriculum Development, 1992.

Kasten, Wendy, and Clarke, Barbara. *The Multi-age Classroom.* Katonah, NY: Richard Owen, 1993.

Katz, Lilian G.; Evangelou, Demetra; and Hartman, Jeanette Allison. *The Case for Mixed-Age Grouping in Early Education.* Washington, DC: National Association for the Education of Young Children, 1990.

Kentucky Department of Education. *Kentucky's Primary School: The Wonder Years.* Frankfort, KY.

———. *Multi-Age/Multi-Ability: A Guide to Implementation for Kentucky's Primary Program.* Frankfort, KY: Kentucky Department of Education, 1994.

Kentucky Education Association and Appalachia Educational Laboratory. *Ungraded Primary Programs: Steps Toward Developmentally Appropriate Instruction.* Frankfort, KY: KEA, 1990.

Maeda, Bev. *The Multi-Age Classroom.* Cypress, CA: Creative Teaching Press, 1994.

McAvinue, Maureen. *A Planbook for Meeting Individual Needs in Primary School.* Frankfort, KY: Kentucky Department of Education, 1994.

Miller, Bruce A. *Children at the Center: Implementing the Multiage Classroom.* Portland, OR: Northwest Regional Educational Laboratory; 1994.

———. *The Multigrade Classroom: A Resource Handbook for Small, Rural Schools.* Portland, OR: Northwest Regional Educational Laboratory, 1989.

———. *Training Guide for the Multigrade Classroom: A Resource for Small, Rural Schools.* Portland, OR: Northwest Regional Laboratory, 1990.

Nebraska Department of Education and Iowa Department of Education. *The Primary Program: Growing and Learning in the Heartland.* 2nd edition. Lincoln, NE, 1994.

Ostrow, Jill. *A Room With a Different View: First Through Third Graders Build Community and Create Curriculum.* York, ME: Stenhouse Publishers, 1995.

Politano, Colleen, and Davies, Anne. *Multi-Age and More.* Winnipeg, Canada: Peguis Publishers, 1994.

Rathbone, Charles; Bingham, Anne; Dorta, Peggy; McClaskey, Molly; and O'Keefe, Justine. *Multiage Portraits: Teaching and Learning in Mixed-age Classrooms.* Peterborough, NH: Crystal Springs Books, 1993.

Multiage Education — Audio/Video

Anderson, Robert, and Pavan, Barbara. *The Nongraded School.* Bloomington, IN: Phi Delta Kappa. An interview with the authors of *Nongradedness: Helping It to Happen.* Video, 30 minutes.

Association of Supervision and Curriculum Development. *Tracking: Road to Success or Dead End?* Alexandria, VA: audiocassette.

Cohen, Dorothy. *Status Treatments for the Classroom.* New York: Teachers College Press, 1994. Video.

Goodman, Gretchen. *Classroom Strategies for "Gray-Area" Children.* Peterborough, NH: Crystal Springs Books, 1995. Video.

Grant, Jim. *Accommodating Developmentally Different Children in the Multiage Classroom,* 1993. Keynote address at the NAESP Annual Convention. Audiocassette available from Chesapeake Audio/Video Communications, Inc. (6330 Howard Lane, Elkridge, MD 21227, product #180).

———. *Avoid the Pitfalls of Implementing Multiage Classrooms.* Peterborough, NH: Crystal Springs Books, 1995. Video.

Katz, Lilian. *Multiage Groupings: A Key to Elementary Reform.* Alexandria, VA: Association for Supervision and Curriculum Development, 1993. Audiocassette.

Lolli, Elizabeth J. *Developing a Framework for Nongraded Multiage Education.* Peterborough, NH: Crystal Springs, 1995. Video.

Oakes, Jeannie, and Lipton, Martin. *On Tracking and Ability Grouping.* Bloomington, IN: Phi Delta Kappa.

Thompson, Ellen. *The Nuts and Bolts of Multiage Classrooms.* Peterborough NH: Crystal Springs Books, 1994. Video, 1 hour.

———. *How to Teach in a Multiage Classroom.* Peterborough, NH: Crystal Springs Books, 1994. Video, 25 minutes.

Ulrey, Dave, and Ulrey, Jan. *Teaching in a Multiage Classroom.* Peterborough, NH: Crystal Springs Books, 1994. Video.

Parent Involvement / Resources for Parents

Baskwill, Jane. *Parents and Teachers: Partners in Learning.* Toronto, Ont.: Scholastic, 1990.

Bettelheim, Bruno. *A Good Enough Parent.* New York: Alfred A. Knopf, 1987.

Bluestein, Jane, and Collins, Lynn. *Parents in a Pressure Cooker.* Rosemont, NJ: Modern Learning Press, 1990.

Butler, Dorothy, and Clay, Marie. *Reading Begins at Home.* Portsmouth, NH: Heinemann, 1982.

Clay, Marie. *Writing Begins at Home.* Portsmouth, NH: Heinemann, 1988.

Coletta, Anthony. *Kindergarten Readiness Checklist for Parents.* Rosemont, NJ: Modern Learning Press, 1991.

Dinkmeyer, Don; Dinkmeyer, James; and McKay, Gary D. *Parenting Young Children* (for parents of children under six), Circle Pines, MN: American Guidance Service, 1989.

Elovson, Allanna. *The Kindergarten Survival Book.* Santa Monica, CA: Parent Ed Resources, 1991.

Frede, Ellen. *Getting Involved: Workshops for Parents.* Ypsilanti, MI: High/Scope Press, 1984.

Grant, Jim. *Developmental Education in the 1990's.* Rosemont, NJ: Modern Learning Press, 1991.

———. *"I Hate School!" Some Common Sense Answers for Parents Who Wonder Why.* Rosemont, NJ: Programs for Education, 1994.

———.*Jim Grant's Book of Parent Pages.* Rosemont, NJ: Programs for Education, 1988.

———.*Worth Repeating: Giving Children a Second Chance at School Success.* Rosemont, NJ: Modern Learning Press, 1989.

Grant, Jim, and Azen, Margot. *Every Parent's Owner's Manuals. (Three-, Four-, Five-, Six-, Seven-Year- Old).* Rosemont, NJ. Programs for Education. 16 pages each manual.

Henderson, Anne T.; Marburger, Carl L.; and Ooms, Theodora. *Beyond the Bake Sale: An Educator's Guide to Working with Parents.* Columbia, MD: National Committee for Citizens in Education, 1990.

Hill, Mary. *Home: Where Reading and Writing Begin.* Portsmouth, NH: 1995.

Karnofsky, Florence, and Weiss, Trudy. *How to Prepare Your Child for Kindergarten.* Carthage, IL: Fearon Teacher Aids, 1993.

Lazear, David. *Seven Pathways of Learning: Teaching Students and Parents About Multiple Intelligences.* Tucson, AZ: Zephyr Press, 1994.

LeShan, Eda. *When Your Child Drives You Crazy.* New York: St. Martin's Press, 1986.

Mooney, Margaret. *Reading to, With, and By Children.* Katonah, NY: Richard C. Owen Publishers, 1990.

Northeastern Local School District. *Every Child is a Promise: Early Childhood At-Home Learning Activities.* Springfield, OH, 1986.

———.*Every Child is a Promise: Positive Parenting.* Springfield, OH, 1986.

Rich, Dorothy. *Megaskills: In School and Life — The Best Gift You Can Give Your Child.* Boston: Houghton Mifflin, 1992.

Taylor, Denny, and Strickland, Dorothy. *Family Storybook Reading.* Portsmouth, NH: 1986.

Trelease, Jim. *Hey! Listen To This: Stories to Read Aloud.* New York: Penguin Books, 1992.

———.*The New Read-Aloud Handbook.* New York: Penguin Books, 1989.

Vopat, James. *The Parent Project: A Workshop Approach to Parent Involvement.* York, ME: Stenhouse Publishers, 1994.

Wlodkowski, Raymond, and Jaynes, Judith H. *Eager to Learn.* San Francisco: Jossey-Bass, 1990.

Themes

Atwood, Ron, ed. *Elementary Science Themes: Change Over Time: Patterns, Systems and Interactions, Models and Scales.* Lexington, KY: Institute on Education Reform, University of Kentucky, 1993. Set of four pamphlets, 50 pages each.

Bromley, Karen; Irwin-De Vitis, Linda; and Modlo, Marcia. *Graphic Organizers: Visual Strategies for Active Learning.* New York: Scholastic, 1995.

Davies, Anne; Politano, Colleen; and Cameron, Caren. *Making Themes Work.* Winnipeg, Canada: Peguis Publishers, 1993.

Haraway, Fran, and Geldersma, Barbara. *12 Totally Terrific Theme Units.* New York: Scholastic, 1993.

Herr, Judy, and Libby, Yvonne. *Creative Resources for the Early Childhood Classroom.* Albany, NY: Delmar, 1990.

Katz, Lilian G., and Chard, Sylvia C. *Engaging Children's Minds: The Project Approach.* Norwood, NJ: Ablex Press, 1989.

McCarthy, Tara. *150 Thematic Writing Activities.* New York: Scholastic, 1993.

SchifferDanoff, Valerie. *The Scholastic Integrated Language Arts Resource Book.* New York: Scholastic, 1995.

Schlosser, Kristin. *Thematic Units for Kindergarten.* New York: Scholastic, 1994.

trube, Penny. *Theme Studies, A Practical Guide: How to Develop Theme Studies to Fit Your Curriculum.* NY: Scholastic, 1993.

hompson, Gare. *Teaching Through Themes.* New York: Scholastic, 1991.

Tracking / Untracking

George, Paul. *How to Untrack Your School.* Alexandria, VA.: Association for Supervision and Curriculum Development, 1992.

Kohn, Alfie. *No Contest: The Case Against Competition.* Boston, MA: Houghton Mifflin, 1992.

Kozol, Jonathan. *Savage Inequalities: Children in America's Schools.* New York: Crown, 1991.

Oakes, Jeannie. *Keeping Track: How Schools Structure Equality.* New Haven: Yale University Press, 1985.

Tomlinson, Carol Ann. *How to Differentiate Instruction in Mixed-Ability Classrooms.* Alexandria, VA: Association for Supervision and Curriculum Development, 1995.

Wheelock, Anne. *Crossing the Tracks: How "Untracking" Can Save America's Schools.* New York: New Press, 1992.

Index

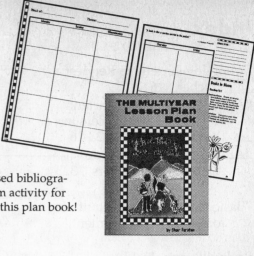